THE ROOTS
OF EGYPTIAN
CHRISTIANITY

STUDIES IN ANTIQUITY AND CHRISTIANITY

The Institute for Antiquity and Christianity
Claremont Graduate School
Claremont, California

STUDIES IN ANTIQUITY & CHRISTIANITY

THE ROOTS
OF EGYPTIAN
CHRISTIANITY

Birger A. Pearson &
James E. Goehring, editors

FORTRESS PRESS   **PHILADELPHIA**

Library of Congress Cataloging-in-Publication Data

Main entry under title:

The Roots of Egyptian Christianity.

(Studies in antiquity and Christianity)
Includes index.
1. Christianity—Egypt—Addresses, essays, lectures.
I. Pearson, Birger Albert. II. Goehring, James E.
III. Series.
BR1380.R66 1986   281'.7   85-47736
ISBN 0-8006-3100-5

1739H85   Printed in the United States of America   1-3100

Contents

v

Contributors

S. Kent Brown
  Professor and Chairman, Department of Ancient
    Scripture
  Brigham Young University

James E. Goehring
  Assistant Professor of Religion, Mary Washington College
  Fredericksburg, Virginia

Robert M. Grant
  Carl Darling Buck Professor of Humanities
  Professor of New Testament and Early Christian
    Literature
  University of Chicago Divinity School

Henry A. Green
  Director, Judaic Studies Program
  Associate Professor of Religion and Sociology, University
    of Miami

David W. Johnson, S.J.
  Professor of Coptic Language and Literature
  Department of Semitic and Egyptian Languages and
    Literatures
  The Catholic University of America, Washington D.C.

Charles Kannengiesser, S.J.
  Catherine F. Huisking Professor of Theology
  University of Notre Dame

A. F. J. Klijn
  Professor of New Testament, Rijksuniversiteit Groningen

Gary Lease
  Professor in the Program of the History of Human
    Consciousness
  Kresge College, University of California at Santa Cruz

Leslie S. B. MacCoull
  U.S. Representative of the Society for Coptic Archaeology
  Washington D.C.

Tito Orlandi
  Professor of Coptic Studies, University of Rome
  Director, Corpus dei Manoscritti Copti Letterari

Birger A. Pearson
  Professor of Religious Studies
  University of California at Santa Barbara

James M. Robinson
  Arthur Letts, Jr., Professor of Religion, Claremont
    Graduate School
  Director, Institute for Antiquity and Christianity

Khalil Samir, S.J.
  Professor of Christian Arabic Studies
  Pontifical Oriental Institute, Rome

Gedaliahu G. Stroumsa
  Lecturer, Department of Comparative Religions
  Hebrew University, Jerusalem

Janet Timbie
  Ph.D. Graduate of the Department of Religious Studies
  University of Pennsylvania

Roelof van den Broek
   Professor of Hellenistic Religions and Patristics
   Rijksuniversiteit Utrecht

Armand Veilleux
   Abbot of the Monastery of the Holy Spirit
   Conyers, Georgia

Preface

The Roots of Egyptian Christianity marks an auspicious beginning to a
new stage in the development of the Institute for Antiquity and
Christianity, for with it is inaugurated a series of volumes that is to
contain the bulk of the future productivity of the Institute. Containing
the papers presented at an organizational meeting of one of the newer
projects of the Institute, this volume also marks the transition from the
first generation of the Institute, and the six or seven projects with
which it began, to the second generation that is now under way. Most
of the original projects have been superseded by other projects, as the
completion of projects and the gradual replacement of the scholars
making up the community have come to be reflected in the Institute's
structure. Thus the Institute has come of age and moves forward into
an established future.

When the Institute for Antiquity and Christianity was being organized in the mid-1960s, the creation of a monograph series for the
Institute itself was proposed and seriously considered. After all, inspiration for the planning of a research center in Claremont was taken
from the statutes of the Göttingen Academy of Sciences, whose
Abhandlungen are an integral part of that august institution. But one of
the Institute's projects that antedated the founding of the Institute itself
by a generation, the International Greek New Testament Project,
directed by Ernest Cadman Colwell, had already made plans to publish
at Oxford University Press. And the other projects that came into
existence in conjunction with the founding of the Institute stood in
well-established scholarly traditions that already had appropriate

channels of publication. Since at its inception the Institute consisted primarily of these projects, an in-house series of volumes seemed at the time superfluous. The following is a list of such precursors to Studies in Antiquity and Christianity, a total of forty volumes, published by the Institute elsewhere:

1. The International Greek New Testament Project, directed by Ernest Cadman Colwell:
   The Gospel According to St. Luke. Edited by the American and British Committees of the International Greek New Testament Project. The New Testament in Greek 3. Oxford: Clarendon Press, 1984.

2. The Ugaritic and Hebrew Parallels Project, directed by Loren Fisher:
   The Claremont Ras Shamra Tablets. Edited by Loren Fisher. Analecta Orientalia 48. Rome: Pontifical Biblical Institute, 1971.
   Ras Shamra Parallels: The Texts from Ugarit and the Hebrew Bible. Volume 1. Edited by Loren Fisher. Analecta Orientalia 49. Rome: Pontifical Biblical Institute, 1972.
   Ras Shamra Parallels: The Texts from Ugarit and the Hebrew Bible. Volume 2. Edited by Loren Fisher. Analecta Orientalia 50. Rome: Pontifical Biblical Institute, 1975.
   Ras Shamra Parallels: The Texts from Ugarit and the Hebrew Bible. Volume 3. Edited by Stan Rummel. Analecta Orientalia 51. Rome: Pontifical Biblical Institute, 1981.

3. The Old Testament Form-Critical Project, directed by Rolf Knierim:
   Genesis: With an Introduction to Narrative Literature. By George W. Coats. The Forms of the Old Testament Literature 1. Grand Rapids: Wm. B. Eerdmans, 1981.
   1 Kings: With an Introduction to Historical Literature. By Burke O. Long. The Forms of the Old Testament Literature 9. Grand Rapids: Wm. B. Eerdmans, 1984.
   Wisdom Literature: Job, Proverbs, Ruth, Canticles, Ecclesiastes, and Esther. By Roland E. Murphy, O. Carm. The Forms of the Old Testament Literature 13. Grand Rapids: Wm. B. Eerdmans, 1981.
   Daniel: With an Introduction to Apocalyptic Literature. By John J. Collins. The Forms of the Old Testament Literature 20. Grand Rapids: Wm. B. Eerdmans, 1984.

4. The Dead Sea Scrolls Project, directed by William H. Brownlee:
   The Midrash Pesher of Habakkuk. Society of Biblical Literature Monograph Series 24. Missoula, Mont.: Scholars Press, 1979.
   Exegesis at Qumran: 4Q Florilegium in Its Jewish Context. By George J. Brooke. Journal for the Study of the Old Testament Supplement Series 29. Sheffield: JSOT, 1985.

5. The Corpus Hellenisticum Novi Testamenti Project, directed by Hans Dieter Betz:

    Plutarch's Theological Writings and Early Christian Literature. Edited by Hans Dieter Betz. Studia ad Corpus Hellenisticum Novi Testamenti 3. Leiden: E. J. Brill, 1975.

    Plutarch's Ethical Writings and Early Christian Literature. Edited by Hans Dieter Betz. Studia ad Corpus Hellenisticum Novi Testamenti 4. Leiden: E. J. Brill, 1978.

6. The Facsimile Edition of the Nag Hammadi Codices Project, directed by James M. Robinson:

    The Facsimile Edition of the Nag Hammadi Codices: Introduction. Leiden: E. J. Brill, 1984.

    The Facsimile Edition of the Nag Hammadi Codices: Codex I. Leiden: E. J. Brill, 1977.

    The Facsimile Edition of the Nag Hammadi Codices: Codex II. Leiden: E. J. Brill, 1974.

    The Facsimile Edition of the Nag Hammadi Codices: Codex III. Leiden: E. J. Brill, 1976.

    The Facsimile Edition of the Nag Hammadi Codices: Codex IV. Leiden: E. J. Brill, 1975.

    The Facsimile Edition of the Nag Hammadi Codices: Codex V. Leiden: E. J. Brill, 1974.

    The Facsimile Edition of the Nag Hammadi Codices: Codex VI. Leiden: E. J. Brill, 1972.

    The Facsimile Edition of the Nag Hammadi Codices: Codex VII. Leiden: E. J. Brill, 1972.

    The Facsimile Edition of the Nag Hammadi Codices: Codex VIII. Leiden: E. J. Brill, 1976.

    The Facsimile Edition of the Nag Hammadi Codices: Codex IX and X. Leiden: E. J. Brill, 1977.

    The Facsimile Edition of the Nag Hammadi Codices: Codex XI, XII, and XIII. Leiden: E. J. Brill, 1973.

    The Facsimile Edition of the Nag Hammadi Codices: Cartonnage. Leiden: E. J. Brill, 1979.

7. The Coptic Gnostic Library Project, directed by James M. Robinson:

    Nag Hammadi Codex I (The Jung Codex). Volume 1, *Introduction, Text and Translation.* Edited by Harold W. Attridge. Nag Hammadi Studies 22. Leiden: E. J. Brill, 1985.

    Nag Hammadi Codex I (The Jung Codex). Volume 2, *Notes.* Edited by Harold W. Attridge. Nag Hammadi Studies 23. Leiden: E. J. Brill, 1985.

    Nag Hammadi Codex II,2-7, Together with XIII,2*, Brit. Lib. Or. 4926(1) and P. Oxy 1, 654, 655. Volume 1, *Gospel According to Thomas, Gospel According to Philip, Hypostasis of the Archons, Indexes.* Edited by Bentley Layton. Nag Hammadi Studies 20. Leiden: E. J. Brill, in press.

    Nag Hammadi Codex II,2-7, Together with XIII,2*, Brit. Lib. Or. 4926(1) *and P. Oxy 1, 654, 655.* Volume 2, *On the Origin of the World, Expository Treatise on the Soul, Book of Thomas the Contender, Indexes.* Edited by Bentley Layton. Nag Hammadi Studies 21. Leiden: E. J. Brill, in press.

Nag Hammadi Codices III,2 and IV,2: The Gospel of the Egyptians (The Holy Book of the Great Invisible Spirit). Edited by Alexander Böhlig and Frederik Wisse in cooperation with Pahor Labib. Nag Hammadi Studies 4. Leiden: E. J. Brill, 1975.

Nag Hammadi Codices III,3–4 and V,1 with Papyrus Berolinensis 8502,3 and Oxyrhynchus Papyrus 1081: Eugnostos and the Sophia of Jesus Christ. Edited by Douglas M. Parrott. Nag Hammadi Studies 27. Leiden: E. J. Brill, in press.

Nag Hammadi Codices III,5: The Dialogue of the Savior. Edited by Stephen Emmel. Nag Hammadi Studies 26. Leiden: E. J. Brill, 1984.

Nag Hammadi Codices V,2–5 and VI with Papyrus Berolinensis 8502,1 and 4. Edited by Douglas M. Parrott. Nag Hammadi Studies 11. Leiden: E. J. Brill, 1979.

Nag Hammadi Codices IX and X. Edited by Birger A. Pearson. Nag Hammadi Studies 15. Leiden: E. J. Brill, 1981.

Nag Hammadi Codices XI, XII, and XIII. Edited by Charles W. Hedrick. Nag Hammadi Studies 28. Leiden: E. J. Brill, in press.

Nag Hammadi Codices: Greek and Coptic Papyri from the Cartonnage of the Covers. Edited by J. W. B. Barns†, G. M. Browne, and J. C. Shelton. Nag Hammadi Studies 16. Leiden: E. J. Brill, 1981.

The Nag Hammadi Library in English. San Francisco: Harper and Row; Leiden: E. J. Brill, 1977. Second [paperback] edition, San Francisco: Harper and Row, 1981; Leiden: E. J. Brill, 1984.

8. The Catenae of Patristic Biblical Interpretation Project, directed by Ekkehard Mühlenberg:

Psalmenkommentare aus der Katenenüberlieferung. Volume 1. By Ekkehard Mühlenberg. Patristische Texte und Studien 15. Edited by K. Aland and W. Schneemelcher. New York and Berlin: Walter de Gruyter, 1975.

Psalmenkommentare aus der Katenenüberlieferung. Volume 2. By Ekkehard Mühlenberg. Patristische Texte und Studien 16. Edited by K. Aland and W. Schneemelcher. New York and Berlin: Walter de Gruyter, 1977.

Psalmenkommentare aus der Katenenüberlieferung. Volume 3. By Ekkehard Mühlenberg. Patristische Texte und Studien 19. Edited by K. Aland and W. Schneemelcher. New York and Berlin: Walter de Gruyter, 1978.

As this list of publications indicates, the Institute for Antiquity and Christianity has matured into a productive center of scholarly activity. The time has come in its institutional development that its own series of volumes be published. Studies in Antiquity and Christianity will consist in part of a series of volumes emanating from the Institute's projects, either as their main publication objective, or as byproducts engendered along the way, as steppingstones toward the ultimate outcome. It will also occasionally include volumes from other Institute activities that have begun to emerge as the Institute has attained the critical mass to become itself a catalyst in scholarly activity. The Institute does not seek, however, to become a publisher of books not clearly related to the areas in which it has ongoing projects, since there are many other more appropriate organs for such general publications. While publication of some Institute projects through other commercial and academic houses will continue, Studies in Antiquity and Christianity will increasingly become the context in which the results of Institute research will appear.

The publication program of the Institute thus consists of (1) Studies in Antiquity and Christianity, for book-length treatments of basic research topics; (2) a series entitled IAC Reports, providing technical progress reports on the ongoing scholarly activity of the Institute during a given period (most recently IAC Report 1972–80, edited by Marvin W. Meyer, 1981); (3) Occasional Papers, article-length essays illuminating some aspects of the Institute's research; and (4) a small quarterly cast in a more popular vein, the *Bulletin* of the Institute for Antiquity and Christianity, designed to keep members and friends in a wider circle informed about the work of the Institute.

Current research projects of the Institute, and their directors, are the following:

Asceticism in Greco-Roman Antiquity, Ronald F. Hock and Vincent Wimbush
The Coptic Gnostic Library, James M. Robinson
Chreia in Greco-Roman Literature and Education, Edward O'Neil
The Nag Hammadi Archaeological Excavation, James M. Robinson
The Old Testament Form-Critical Project, Rolf Knierim
The Philo Project, Burton Mack
Q: A Lost Collection of Jesus' Sayings, James M. Robinson
The Roots of Egyptian Christianity, Birger A. Pearson

JAMES M. ROBINSON, Director
Institute for Antiquity and Christianity

Foreword

This book is the first of a series of projected volumes emanating from the Roots of Egyptian Christianity Project of the Institute for Antiquity and Christianity, in Claremont, California, with a second base in the Department of Religious Studies of the University of California, Santa Barbara. The project, of which Birger A. Pearson is Director, has as its long-term goal the publication of a comprehensive history of Christianity in Egypt from its beginnings until the Arab conquest in the seventh century C.E. The word "roots" in the project title thus connotes much more than "origins." While a plant has its origin in a seed, its roots spread out into the ground from which it sprouts and gains its nourishment. So too the Roots of Egyptian Christianity Project seeks to understand not only the inception of Christianity in Egypt but the various forces within Egypt that helped to shape Egyptian Christianity in the period prior to the Arab conquest. By studying the development of Egyptian Christianity as an expression of Egyptian culture, one is better able to understand what makes Egyptian Christianity Egyptian. The project will trace the history of the Christian religion in Egypt from its beginnings among Greek-speaking Jews in Alexandria to its spread among Greek-speaking Gentiles in Alexandria and other Greek population centers, from its earliest expansion among native Egyptian people to its flowering as the national religion of Egypt.

One of the first major undertakings of the new project was an international conference, funded largely by the National Endowment for the Humanities, whose purpose was to lay the foundation for future work by gathering a small group of scholars together to summarize the current state of scholarship in various areas of research pertaining to the background, rise, and development of Egyptian Christianity. The conference was held in Claremont on September 19–23, 1983, and included a day trip to the University of California, Santa Barbara, on September 21. Birger A. Pearson served as conference convener and James E. Goehring, at that time Assistant Director of the Institute for Antiquity and Christianity and Associate Director of the project, served as conference coordinator. Twenty-three papers were presented, and discussions took place that served to focus plans for further collaborative research. The seventeen chapters of this book have grown out of the Claremont conference and are based on the papers presented there, which in most cases have been substantially revised.

The sources of our knowledge of early Christianity in Egypt consist mainly of written texts. Fortunately the dry sands of Egypt have preserved much material, both of Egyptian and non-Egyptian provenience, which would have been irretrievably lost in most other climates. The first part of this volume deals with sources preserved in Greek, Coptic, and Arabic. James M. Robinson (chap. 1) provides some interesting background information on two of the most important manuscript discoveries of our century, the Nag Hammadi Coptic Codices and the Bodmer Papyri (Greek and Coptic), and stresses the importance of ascertaining the locations and circumstances of such finds. S. Kent Brown (chap. 2) summarizes what is known of Christian inscriptions in Egypt, Greek and Coptic. Christian inscriptions begin to appear in the fourth century and are mainly funerary in type. Leslie S. B. MacCoull (chap. 3) discusses the immense store of Coptic documentary papyri extant and their importance for providing knowledge of daily life among Christians in Egypt. Such documents date from the fifth century and later; the seventh- and eighth-century texts are the most numerous. There is no comparable study of Greek papyri in this volume, but the reader is referred to an excellent article on "Papyrus Documentation of Church and Community in Egypt to the Mid-Fourth Century," by E. A. Judge (who attended the Claremont conference) and S. R. Pickering (*JAC* 20 [1977] 47–71). Tito Orlandi (chap. 4) provides a particularly helpful overview of the history of Coptic literature, covering a thousand years, from the first rudimentary attempts to write Egyptian with Greek letters to the eclipse of Coptic literature by the Arabization of Egypt in the eleventh century. This important study is complemented by that of Khalil Samir (chap. 5), which treats the vast amount of material available in Arabic. Samir stresses the fact that much Egyptian Christian literature written originally in Greek or Coptic is now extant only in Arabic translations, and laments the lack of attention hitherto given to these resources.

No religion exists in a vacuum. A major concern of the Roots of Egyptian Christianity Project is to situate the development and early history of Christianity in Egypt firmly in its geographical, social, cultural, and religious setting. Two chapters of this volume deal with "The Environment of Early Christianity in Egypt" (part 2). Henry A. Green (chap. 6) applies a social-scientific approach to the setting of Egyptian Christianity, discussing the economic factors in Egyptian social stratification and the socio-economic background of the early Christianity of Egypt. Gary Lease (chap. 7) takes up for discussion one of the pagan religions of the Roman Empire, one that in many areas was an important rival to Christianity, namely, the religion of Mithra. The evidence for Mithraism in Egypt is surveyed, and Lease advances a hypothesis to account for the relatively weak presence of this religion in Egypt. Much more remains to be done along these lines, and future studies are projected that will deal with other religions in Greco-Roman Egypt, particularly as they impinge upon Judaism and Christianity, such as the "Egyptian" religions of Isis, Sarapis, and Hermes Trismegistus.

Part 3 deals with "The Emergence of Christianity in Egypt." Here the focus is on the early Jewish Christianity of Alexandria. Birger A. Pearson (chap. 8) analyzes the early Christian traditions relating to the beginnings of Christianity in Alexandria, situates the earliest Christians in the context of Alexandrian Judaism, and discusses some early Christian sites in Alexandria. A. F. J. Klijn (chap. 9) discusses the early Jewish Christian "Logos theology," which he sees as common to four otherwise different writings, and extrapolates from these texts some conclusions concerning the theological multiformity of early Christianity in Alexandria.

Part 4 is devoted to studies in theology. Robert M. Grant (chap. 10) discusses the development of theological education in Alexandria. Roelof van den Broek (chap. 11) analyzes a type of Jewish-Platonic speculation that is common to Philo, Valentinus, Origen, and one of the Nag Hammadi documents, *Eugnostos*. Charles Kannengiesser (chap. 12) examines the basic issues in the controversy between Arius and Athanasius and points up the importance of this debate for further developments in Alexandrian theology. David Johnson (chap. 13) explores the little-known anti-Chalcedonian literature preserved in Coptic in the "Monophysite" communities of Egypt.

The last part of the volume deals with various aspects of Egyptian monasticism. James E. Goehring (chap. 14) examines the literary and archaeological sources for the study of Pachomian monasticism and discusses the methodological difficulties involved in using these sources to reconstruct the history of the Pachomian movement at the various stages of its development. While Pachomius is a revered figure in the history of Christian monasticism in both East and West, the same cannot be said for Shenoute of Atripe (d. ca. 466), who is identified exclusively with Coptic monasticism and "non-Chalcedonian" Christianity. Janet Timbie (chap. 15) explores the current state of research on this important figure. Armand Veilleux (chap. 16) takes up for discussion the problem of the relationship between the Nag Hammadi Codices and Pachomian monasticism, and then explores the various literary and doctrinal contacts between monasticism and Gnosticism. Gedaliahu G. Stroumsa (chap. 17) argues that early Manichaeism in Egypt was essentially a monastic movement and that Manichees were in some instances able to infiltrate the churches and monasteries of Egypt, and even to influence in certain respects their anti-Manichaean opponents.

The Editors wish to take this opportunity to express their acknowledgment and thanks to those who have contributed in various ways to this publication: the individual authors whose contributions are published herein; Mr. Clayton N. Jefford, a doctoral student at Claremont Graduate School, who served as editorial assistant; Norman A. Hjelm, former Director of Fortress Press, and Dr. Harold Rast, the Director of Fortress Press, as well as the editorial staff of Fortress Press, for their encouragement and assistance; Prof. James M. Robinson and his colleagues on the Editorial Board of Studies in Antiquity and Christianity, for accepting the volume in this new series; the National Endowment for the Humanities, for major funding for the conference in Claremont in 1983; the Administration of the University of California, Santa Barbara, especially Chancellor Robert Huttenback, Associate Vice-Chancellor Marvin Marcus, and Provost David Sprecher, for additional funding assistance; and other patrons who helped with the expenses of the conference: Dr. J. Harold Ellens, the Holy Virgin Mary and St. Pshoy Coptic Orthodox Church of Los Angeles, Rev. James E. Furman, and Professors Edmund and Tova Meltzer.

We wish to dedicate this volume to the Copts of our day, both in Egypt and in the Diaspora, whose cultural and religious roots provide the occasion for both the book and the larger project.

Institute for Antiquity and Christianity   BIRGER A. PEARSON
Claremont, California   JAMES E. GOEHRING

Abbreviations

Aeg	*Aegyptus: Rivista italiana di egittologia e di papirologia*
AegT	Aegyptiaca Treverensia: Trierer Studien zum griechisch-römischen Ägypten
AEPHE.R	*Annuaire: Ecole pratique des hautes études, section des sciences religieuses*
AGJU	Arbeiten zur Geschichte des antiken Judentums und des Urchristentums
AJSL	*American Journal of Semitic Languages and Literature*
AKG	Arbeiten zur Kirchengeschichte
ALUB	Annales litteraires de l'Université de Besançon
AMG	Annales (Publications) du Musée Guimet
AMI	*Archäologische Mitteilungen aus Iran*
AnBoll	*Analecta Bollandiana*
AnCl	*Antiquité classique*
ANET	J. B. Pritchard, ed. *Ancient Near Eastern Texts*
ANRW	*Aufstieg und Niedergang der römischen Welt*
ANTT	*Arbeiten zur neutestamentlichen Textforschung*
Arch	*Archaeology: A Magazine Dealing with the Antiquity of the World*
ASAE	*Annales du service des antiquités de l'Egypte*
ASP	*American Studies in Papyrology*
AuC	Franz Joseph Dölger. *Antike und Christentum.* Münster in Westfalen: Aschendorff
Aug	*Augustinianum: Periodicum quadrimestre collegii internationale Augustiniani*
AUU	Acta Universitatis Upsaliensis

BA	*Biblical Archaeologist*
BASP	*Bulletin of the American Society of Papyrologists*
BBA	Berliner byzantinistische Arbeiten
BBI	*Bulletin of the Byzantine Institute*
BCNH	Bibliothèque Copte de Nag Hammadi
BEHE	*Bibliothèque de l'école des hautes études*
Bes	*Bulletin of the Egyptological Seminar, Columbia University*
Bess	*Bessarione: Pubblicazione periodica di studi orientali*
BGAPO	*Bulletin de géographie et d'archéologie de la Province d'Oran*
BGBE	Beiträge zur Geschichte der biblischen Exegese
BGU	*Aegyptische Urkunden aus den Koeniglichen Museen zu Berlin. Griechische Urkunden*
BHTh	Beiträge zur historischen Theologie
Bib	*Biblica*
BIFAO	*Bulletin de l'institut français d'archéologie orientale*
BKU	*Aegyptische Urkunden aus den Königlichen Museen zu Berlin. Koptische Urkunden*
BMus	Bibliothèque du Muséon
BRHE	Bibliothèque de la revue d'histoire ecclésiastique
BSAA	*Bulletin de la société archéologique d'Alexandrie*
BSAC	*Bulletin de la société d'archéologie copte*
BSFE	*Bulletin (trimestriel) de la société française d'égyptologie*
CAnt	Christianisme antique
CathEnc	*Catholic Encyclopedia.* New York: D. Appleton & Co., 1907–12
CCist	*Collectanea Cisterciensia*
CEg	*Chronique d'Egypte*
CF	*Collège de France: Annuaire*
CHS	Center for Hermeneutical Studies in Hellenistic and Modern Culture
CIL	*Corpus Inscriptionum Latinarum*
CIMRM	*Corpus Inscriptionum et Monumentorum Religionis Mithriacae*
CistS	*Cistercian Studies*
CistSS	Cistercian Study Series
CMC	*The Cologne Mani Codex*
CMCL	Corpus dei Manoscritti Copti Letterari
CO	Cahiers d'orientalisme
COS	Cambridge Oriental Series

CP	Corona Patrum Salesiana: Sanctorum Patrum Graecorum et Latinorum Opera Selecta
CPJ	*Corpus Papyrorum Judaicarum*
CPR	Corpus Papyrorum Raineri
CRAIBL	*Comptes rendus de l'Academie des inscriptions et belles-lettres*
CRI	Compendia Rerum Iudaicarum ad Novum Testamentum
CS	Coptic Studies
CSCO	Corpus Scriptorum Christianorum Orientalium. Louvain: Secrétariat du CSCO; Louvain: Durbecq
DACL	*Dictionnaire d'archéologie chrétienne et de liturgie.* Paris: Letouzey, 1907–39
DBS	*Dictionnaire de la bible: Supplément.* Paris: Letouzey, 1960
DGRG	W. Smith, ed. *A Dictionary of Greek and Roman Geography.* London: AMS, 1873 [1st ed.], 1966 [2d ed.]
DNGT	A. Calderini. *Dizionario dei nomi geografici e topografici dell'Egitto greco-romano.* Milan: Cisalpino-Goliardica, 1935
DPAC	Angelo Di Berardino, ed. *Dizionario Patristico e di Antichità Cristiane.* Rome: Marietti, 1983
DSp	*Dictionnaire de spiritualité, ascétique et mystique.* Paris: Beauchesne, 1952
DThC	*Dictionnaire de théologie catholique*
EcHR	*Economic History Review*
EEQ	*East European Quarterly*
EPRO	Etudes préliminaires aux religions orientales dans l'empire romain
EtAI.E	Etudes arabes et islamiques: Etudes et documents
ETH	Etudes de théologie historique
EvTh	*Evangelische Theologie*
FIFAO	Fouilles de l'institut français d'archéologie orientale (du Caire)
FVK	Forschungen zur Volkskunde
GCAL	*Geschichte der christlichen arabischen Literatur*
GCS	Griechische christliche Schriftsteller
GIF	*Giornale italiano di filologia*
Gn	*Gnomon: Kritische Zeitschrift für die gesamte klassische Altertumswissenschaft*
GNT	Grundrisse zum Neuen Testament
GOF	Göttinger Orientforschungen

GöMisz	Göttinger Miszellen: Beiträge zur ägyptologischen Diskussion
GRBS	Greek, Roman, and Byzantine Studies
GS	Gesammelte Schriften
HAW	Handbuch der Altertumswissenschaft
HDG	Handbuch der Dogmengeschichte
HNT	Handbuch zum Neuen Testament
HO	B. Spuler, ed. Handbuch der Orientalistik. Leiden: E. J. Brill, 1952 [1st ed.], 1970 [2d ed.]
HTR	Harvard Theological Review
HTS	Harvard Theological Studies
IKP	Actes du congrès international de papyrologie
JA	Journal asiatique
JAC	Jahrbuch für Antike und Christentum
JAOS	Journal of the American Oriental Society
JARCE	Journal of the American Research Center in Egypt
JEA	Journal of Egyptian Archaeology
JEBH	Journal of Economic and Business History
JEH	Journal of Ecclesiastical History
JEOL	Jaarbericht van het vooraziatisch-egyptisch genootschap 'Ex oriente lux'
JEtS	Journal of Ethiopian Studies
JJS	Journal of Jewish Studies
JNES	Journal of Near Eastern Studies
JRAS	Journal of the Royal Asiatic Society
JRS	Journal of Roman Studies
JSJ	Journal for the Study of Judaism in the Persian, Hellenistic, and Roman Period
JTS	Journal of Theological Studies
KlT	Kleine Texte für (theologische und philologische) Vorlesungen und Übungen
KRU	W. E. Crum and G. Steindorff. Koptische Rechtsurkunden des VIII. Jahrhunderts aus Djeme (Theben)
LÄ	Lexicon der Ägytologie. Wiesbaden: Harrassowitz, 1979
LCL	Loeb Classical Library
LPGL	G. W. H. Lampe. Patristic Greek Lexicon. Oxford: Clarendon Press, 1961
LSJ	H. G. Liddell, R. Scott, and H. S. Jones, eds. Greek-English Lexicon
LTP	Laval théologique et philosophique

MAH	*Mélanges d'archéologie et d'histoire*
MeyerK	H. A. W. Meyer. *Kritisch-exegetischer Kommentar über das Neue Testament*
MIFAO	Mémoires publiés par les membres de l'institut français d'archéologie orientale
MissCath	*Missions catholiques*
MSPER	Mitteilungen aus der Sammlung der Papyrus Erzherzog Rainer
MUSJ	*Mélanges de l'université Saint-Joseph*
NedThT	*Nederlands(ch)e theologisch tijdschrift*
NFAQJ	*Numismatic Fine Arts Quarterly Journal*
NHC	Nag Hammadi Codices
NHLE	James M. Robinson, ed. *The Nag Hammadi Library in English.* New York: Harper and Row; Leiden: E. J. Brill, 1977
NHS	Nag Hammadi Studies
NovT	*Novum Testamentum*
NovTSup	Novum Testamentum, Supplements
NTApo	E. Hennecke and W. Schneemelcher. *Neutestamentlich Apokryphen in Deutscher Übersetzung.* Tübingen: Mohr, 1959. (ET: *New Testament Apocrypha*, 2 vols., trans. R. McL. Wilson. Philadelphia: Westminster Press, 1963–65)
NThS	*Nieuwe Theologische Studien*
NTS	*New Testament Studies*
NumC	*Numismatic Chronicle and Journal of the Numismatic Society*
OCA	Orientalia Christiana Analecta
OLP	Orientalia Lovaniensia Periodica
OLZ	*Orientalische Literaturzeitung*
Or	*Orientalia* (Rome)
OrChr	*Oriens Christianus*
OrChrP	Orientalia Christiana Periodica
PapyBrux	Papyrologica Bruxellensia
Par	Paradosis
PatSor	Patristica Sorbonensia
PETSE	Papers of the Estonian Theological Society in Exile
PG	J. Migne. *Patrologia Graeca*
PL	J. Migne. *Patrologia Latina*
PO	Patrologia Orientalis
PSBA	*Proceedings of the Society of Biblical Archaeology*

PSFP.T   Publications de la société Fouad I de papyrologie: Textes
              et documents
PTA   Papyrologische Texte und Abhandlungen
PTS   Patristische Texte und Studien
PW   A. Pauly and G. Wissowa, eds. *Real-Encyclopädie der
              classischen Altertumswissenschaft*
RAEGR   A. Adriani. *Repertorio d'arte dell'Egitto greco-roman.* Series
              C, 2 vols. Palermo: Fondazione "Ignazio Mormino" del
              Banco di Sicilia, 1966
RAM   *Revue d'ascétique et de mystique*
RAPH   Recherches d'archéologie, de philologie, et d'histoire
RB   *Revue biblique*
RBén   *Revue bénédictine*
RDC   *Revue de droit canonique*
REA   *Revue des études anciennes*
RechSR   *Recherches de sciences religieuses*
REG   *Revue des études grecques*
REg   *Revue égyptologique*
RevQ   *Revue de Qumran*
RevThom   *Revue thomiste*
RHR   *Revue de l'histoire des religions*
ROC   *Revue de l'Orient chrétien*
RQ   *Römische Quartalschrift für christliche Altertumskunde und
              für Kirchengeschichte*
RSO   *Rivista degli studi orientali*
RThPh   *Revue de théologie et de philosophie*
RTPE   *Recueil de travaux relatifs à la philologie et à l'archéologie
              égyptiennes et assyriennes* (Paris)
SÄS   Schriften aus der ägyptischen Sammlung
SBLDS   Society of Biblical Literature Dissertation Series
SBLSCS   Society of Biblical Literature Septuagint and Cognate
              Studies
SBLTT   Society of Biblical Literature Texts and Translations
SC   Sources chrétiennes
SCent   *The Second Century*
SCH(L)   *Studies in Church History.* Ecclesiastical History Society
              (London)
ScrHie   Scripta Hierosolymitana
SDAW   Sitzungsberichte der deutschen Akademie der
              Wissenschaft zu Berlin

SE	*Sacris erudiri: Jaarboek voor godsdienstwetenschappen*
SGM	Sources gnostiques et manichéennes
SHG	Subsidia Hagiographica
SN.AM	Studies in Neoplatonism: Ancient and Modern
SÖAW	Sitzungsberichte der österreichischen Akademie der Wissenschaften in Wien
SOC	Studia Orientalia Christiana
SPP	*Studien zu Paleographie und Papyruskunde*
SROC	*Studi e ricerche sull'Oriente Cristiano*
SSH	*Soviet Studies in History*
StAns	Studia Anselmiana
StCath	*Studia Catholica*
StMon	*Studia Monastica*
StPatr	Studia Patristica
StT	Studi e Testi
SVTP	Studia in Veteris Testamenti Pseudepigrapha
TDSA	Testi et documenti per lo studio dell'antichità
TextS	Texts and Studies
ThLZ	*Theologische Literaturzeitung*
ThZ	*Theologische Zeitschrift*
TPL	Textus Patristici et Liturgici
TRE	*Theologische Realenzyklopädie*. New York and Berlin: Walter de Gruyter, 1978
TS	*Theological Studies*
TU	Texte und Untersuchungen
UCantP	University of Canterbury Publications
VC	*Vigiliae Christianae*
VetChr	*Vetera Christianorum*
WZKM	*Wiener Zeitschrift für die Kunde des Morgenlandes*
YCS	*Yale Classical Studies*
ZÄS	*Zeitschrift für ägyptische Sprache und Altertumskunde*
ZKG	*Zeitschrift für Kirchengeschichte*
ZKTh	*Zeitschrift für katholische Theologie*
ZNW	*Zeitschrift für die neutestamentliche Wissenschaft*
ZRGG	*Zeitschrift für Religions- und Geistesgeschichte*
ZSRG	*Zeitschrift der Savigny-Stiftung für Rechtsgeschichte*
ZSRG.K	*Zeitschrift der Savigny-Stiftung für Rechtsgeschichte: Kanonische Abteilung*
ZThK	*Zeitschrift für Theologie und Kirche*

PART ONE

GREEK, COPTIC, AND ARABIC SOURCES

JAMES M. ROBINSON

The Discovering and Marketing of Coptic Manuscripts: The Nag Hammadi Codices and the Bodmer Papyri*

Manuscripts buried in late antiquity in the dry sands of Egypt would ideally all be discovered under the controlled conditions of scientific archaeological excavation. For an artifact found in situ is scientifically much more valuable than it would be if its precise provenience were unknown. The stratum in which it lay provides not only a relative chronology but also a context of other artifacts, making it possible for bits of information from one artifact to aid in assessing another. Furthermore each artifact from a given locus helps to interpret that locus. For persons interested in the historical geography of Coptic Egypt, it is a tremendous loss that papyrologists are not able to pinpoint on a map what they can infer from a text about the place of discovery. One need only contrast Eric G. Turner's fascinating article on Oxyrhynchus,[1] based on the papyri discovered there in legitimate excavations, to the speculations he presented about Panopolis (Achmim) on the erroneous, and at my suggestion subsequently retracted, assumption that Panopolis is a provenience shared by the Bodmer Papyri, P. Beatty Panop., and the Chester Beatty Biblical Papyri[2]—the truth being that the only thing the papyri clearly have in common is that none comes from legitimate excavation.

---

*This paper has been published in an earlier draft in *Sundries in Honour of Torgny Säve-Söderbergh* (AUU; Boreas, Uppsala Studies in Ancient Mediterranean and Near Eastern Civilizations 13; Uppsala: Univ. of Uppsala Press, 1984) 97–114.

1. Eric G. Turner, "Roman Oxyrhynchus," *JEA* 38 (1952) 78–93.

2. E. G. Turner, *Greek Papyri: An Introduction* (Oxford: Clarendon Press, 1968) 52–53; and the "Supplementary Notes" of the paperback edition (Oxford: Clarendon Press, 1980) 201. In a letter of 13 October 1980 Turner requested that I publish his retraction on the basis of my identification of the provenience of the Bodmer Papyri with Abū

An even more painful reflection has to do with the loss involved in the chaotic procedure of clandestine digging and illegal marketing that is the fate of most manuscripts before they reach the safety of a museum or library, if they ever do, in whatever condition they may arrive. The more the academic community can learn about such procedures, the more it can seek to mitigate and even ultimately to eliminate them. The peasants tore Dead Sea Scrolls into pieces on the assumption that they could sell a plurality of fragments for a higher total amount than a single intact scroll. The detection of this practice made it possible to put an end to at least this vandalism, by setting up and making known the policy of paying by the square centimeter, thus eliminating any advantage to tearing one piece into several pieces. Manuscripts are not really safe even in the hands of such a highly intelligent and successful antiquities dealer as the Cypriot dealer in Cairo through whose hands most of the Nag Hammadi Codices and Bodmer Papyri passed. After the bitter experience of entrusting his Nag Hammadi Codices to the Department of Antiquities for safekeeping, only to have them nationalized, he said on acquiring the Bodmer Papyri, "If I get burnt I'll burn them." Too much is at stake for the academic community to stay aloof from this unthinkable world, upon which the future of Coptic studies depends much more than we would like to admit.

I propose then to scan the stories of two discoveries and their marketing, so as to compare them, and to begin to make generalizations about the way such things are done. By and large I shall not clutter the analysis with the names of individuals, but rather designate them by the typical trait of relevance to the discussion. This does not mean their identity and the other minutiae of the two stories are not known or cannot be divulged; quite the contrary, in the case of the Nag Hammadi story the listing and assessing of the details have been published,[3] and in the case of the Bodmer story they are to be

---

Manā. Colin H. Roberts (*Manuscript, Society, and Belief in Early Christian Egypt* [London: Oxford Univ. Press, 1979] 7) had followed Turner, though he did refer to Carl Schmidt ("Die neuesten Bibelfunde aus Ägypten," *ZNW* 30 [1931] 292–93; and "Die Evangelien-handschrift der Chester Beatty-Sammlung," *ZNW* 32 [1933] 225), who had reported from his trusted Egyptian contact person that the Chester Beatty Biblical Papyri came from Aphroditopolis and that they could not have come from Upper Egypt, in view of the group of dealers from which they came.

3. The story of the discovery and of the transmission of the Nag Hammadi Codices to the Coptic Museum has been reported in the late 1940s and 1950s primarily by Jean Doresse, whose information has been verified and supplemented by repeated interviews with Muḥammad 'Ali, his brother Abū al-Majd, his mother, and the middlemen

published. Meanwhile they are available upon request, but are here passed over so as not to clutter the presentation and thus distract attention from what may be typical.

Of course each clandestine discovery and its marketing is different from the next. And even two instances are too narrow a data base to be relevant statistically. At best, the details of two instances could begin a systematic data bank that, as it grew, could support progressively firmer generalizations. These two discoveries, separated only by some 12 km (at the Jabal al-Ṭārif and the Jabal Abū Manā, both behind—i.e., north of—the Dishnā Plain) and seven years (1945 and 1952), reflect at best practices in a relatively small part of Egypt during a relatively limited time. Nineteenth-century practices or practices in the Delta might provide considerably less by way of parallels than these two strikingly similar stories. For example, the stories of the discovery and marketing of the Toura Papyri near Cairo (1941)[4] and of the more familiar Dead Sea Scrolls (1945 or 1947)[5] do not present such close

who are still alive. One of them, Rāghib Andarāwus "al-Qiss" 'Abd al-Sayyid, and the principal of the Nag Hammadi Boys' Preparatory School, Abram Bibawi, who translated Muḥammadi 'Ali's reports, told their stories on 10 December 1976 at the second meeting of the International Committee for the Nag Hammadi Codices during the First International Congress of Coptology in Cairo. For fuller details, evidence, and documentation, see James M. Robinson, "From the Cliff to Cairo: The Story of the Discoverers and the Middlemen of the Nag Hammadi Codices," in *Colloque international sur les textes de Nag Hammadi (Québec, 22–25 août 1978)* (ed. B. Barc; Bibliothèque copte de Nag Hammadi, Section "Etudes" 1; Quebec: Presses de l'Université Laval, 1981) 21–58. For the same presentation except for the omission of the discussion of secondary literature, see J. M. Robinson, "The Discovery of the Nag Hammadi Codices," *BA* 42 (1979) 206–24. These detailed presentations and the present summary complete and where necessary modify the preliminary information presented in the first edition of *The Facsimile Edition of the Nag Hammadi Codices: Introduction* (Leiden: E. J. Brill, 1972), published as a brochure to accompany the publication of the first volume of the *Facsimile Edition* itself, supplemented in the opening paragraph of the preface to each successive volume of the *Facsimile Edition*, and in the second edition of the *Introduction*, published in 1984 as a separate and concluding volume to the series, esp. the preface (pp. 3–14).

4. Octave Guéraud, "Le papyrus de Toura: I. Sa découverte et son état de conservation," in *Origène sur la Pâque: Traité inédit publié d'après un papyrus de Toura* (ed. Octave Guéraud and Pierre Nautin; CAnt 2; Paris: Beauchesne, 1979) 15–23. See also his "Note préliminaire sur les papyrus d'Origène retrouvés à Toura," *RHR* 131 (1946) 85–108; Louis Doutreleau, "Que savons-nous aujourd'hui des papyrus de Toura?" *RechSR* 43 (1955) 161–76; and Ludwig Koenen and Louis Doutreleau, "Nouvel inventaire des papyrus de Toura," *RechSR* 55 (1967) 547–64. A news release by Thomas W. Mackay and C. Wilfred Griggs of Brigham Young University, Provo, Utah, reports the acquisition in 1983 by Brigham Young University, after a generation in a New England attic, of ten intact leaves from Didymos the Blind's Commentary on Psalms 26:10b–29:2, thus restoring a missing segment from the Toura codex, as well as an additional leaf sold by Sotheby's in April 1983. Like the publication of the rest of the codex, publication of these acquisitions will be in PTA.

5. William H. Brownlee ("Muhammad ed-Deeb's own Story of his Scroll Discovery,"

parallels. Of course a broader spectrum of manuscript discoveries in Egypt and of the marketing of the discovered manuscripts is also available in secondary literature devoted to this topic.[6]

Especially at the present premature stage even tentatively suggested generalizations must commend themselves by their ability to fit into the dynamics of village life in an intelligible way, in our case the local color of Upper Egypt since World War II. If one would like to get a very entertaining impression of that life style, one need only read Richard Critchfield's book *Shahhat: An Egyptian*,[7] a biography of a peasant with whom the author lived for two years a couple of decades later than and some 100 km upstream from the two discoveries that concern us here. Shahhat and the villagers I will be describing share the same struggle for existence, the same real poverty and blatant violence—with village life a law unto itself, yet with its own ground rules everyone knows and in their way abides by, and at times with a transcendence to which *we* could hardly rise under such severe and unconducive circumstances. Only when one has read such a book as this or has experienced the struggle for oneself, can one have some feel for the dynamics of peasant life in the village, on the basis of which any assessment of the traits shared by the two stories I will summarize, as to what might be typical and even predictable, may be ventured and evaluated.

The most obvious and perhaps the most important generalization to be drawn from the information I have collected is that such information is indeed available. For the common wisdom among Near East hands has been to the effect that the illegal nature of the clandestine excavations and their marketing necessarily means that the antiquities dealers either did not learn the details of the discoveries from the

---

JNES 16 [1957] 236–39) published an interview by Najib S. Khoury with the discoverer, which diverged from earlier reports, summarized, e.g., by Frank Moore Cross, Jr. (*The Ancient Library of Qumran and Modern Biblical Studies* [Garden City, N.Y.: Doubleday & Co., 1958] 1–36 [chap. 1, "Discovery of an Ancient Library"], esp. p. 3 [rev. ed. 1961, p. 6], where in a footnote Brownlee's new information is not preferred over the earlier reports). See also Brownlee, "Edh-dheeb's Story of his Scroll Discovery," *RevQ* 3 (1962) 483–94; "Some New Facts Concerning the Discovery of the Scrolls of IQ," *RevQ* 4 (1963) 417–20; and the rather controversial literature cited there on the subject.

6. Karl Preisendanz, *Papyrusfunde und Papyrusforschung* (Leipzig: Hiersemann, 1933); Turner, *Greek Papyri*, esp. chaps. 2–4; Oleg V. Volkoff, *A la recherche de manuscrits en Egypte* (RAPH 30; Cairo: Institut français d'archéologie orientale du Caire, 1970); and Bryan Fagan, *The Rape of the Nile: Tomb Robbers, Tourists, and Archaeologists in Egypt* (New York: Charles Scribner's Sons, 1977).

7. Richard Critchfield, *Shahhat: An Egyptian* (Syracuse, N.Y.: Syracuse Univ. Press, 1978).

middlemen from whom they acquired the artifacts or would not divulge them, for fear of incriminating themselves or cutting off their sources of supply. Furthermore the peasants, or *fellahin*, are notorious for lying and saying what they think the interrogator would like to hear. For such reasons there has been relatively little effort to track down the provenience of manuscripts, except insofar as it can be learnedly inferred from information in the manuscripts themselves. And this in turn points to another difficulty: the kind of philologically trained scholars who have to do with manuscripts are themselves usually not trained in or even disposed to get involved in "oral history," or detective work in the demimonde, the out-of-the-way hamlets beyond the control of governmental authority, with all the distastefulness, indeed the risks to life and limb, that are involved.[8]

All of this need not be so. Just as the widespread assumption that one could not get access to the Nag Hammadi Codices turned out to be itself the main obstacle to gaining access to them, since it discouraged anyone from trying, just so the widespread assumption that it would only be a waste of time to seek to track down the provenience of manuscript discoveries may be the main reason why we do not know more about their provenience. Thus the public dissemination of two stories of discoveries and their marketing until the time when they were safe in museums or libraries may dispel this unexamined presupposition and thus encourage the tracking down of comparable information about other discoveries.

Of course there are no doubt many instances when it was not in fact possible to get accurate information from antiquities dealers about the provenience of materials they had for sale. Perhaps the fact that the Nag Hammadi Codices and the Bodmer Papyri were discovered a generation ago and that the manuscripts have long since been sold has

8. Rodolphe Kasser and Martin Krause requested the inclusion of the following statement in the *Facsimile Edition: Introduction* to express such reserve regarding the Nag Hammadi story: "Rodolphe Kasser and Martin Krause wish to make it known here that they have serious reasons to put in doubt the objective value of a number of important points of the Introduction that follows. They contest especially the detailed history of the discovery of the Coptic Gnostic manuscripts of Nag Hammadi resulting from the investigation of James M. Robinson. Kasser and Krause and others who were involved do not consider as assured anything more than the core of the story (the general location and approximate date of the discovery), the rest not having for them more than the value of stories and fables that one can collect in popular Egyptian circles thirty years after an event whose exceptional significance the protagonists could not at the time understand." See the main points of a refutation of this itself undocumented rejection of my presentation, in the *Facsimile Edition: Introduction*, 3–4 n. 1.

made it easier to track the stories down. A sort of statute of limitations seems to have taken effect in that the authorities are hardly likely to intervene now in the lives of the individuals involved on the basis of information they have given in recent years (1975ff.). To be sure, there were instances of persons hesitant or even unwilling to admit their involvement, and some items were too compromising to be told in the presence of fellow villagers, lest village justice take effect. Names of persons who might still have materials were at times withheld and only ascertained through other channels. But by and large the information, in an unrefined and garbled form, is common village knowledge, which has long since reached the Egyptian Department of Antiquities, as we shall see. Thus by the time of my investigations there was no longer any real reason to hide the facts, a common-sense realization that may have facilitated the investigation. I also had the assistance of respected local Copts who were intelligent and honest as intermediaries and translators. In the process they both reproached villagers bringing far-fetched tales and at times reported to me that the informant was not reliable, thus providing an initial sifting. Of course at times I had to dredge up material being suppressed as irrelevant or gross or contradictory, important to me because of some fragment of relevant information it contained. The bloodcurdling narration by the discoverer of the Nag Hammadi Codices of the avenging of his father's murder was not translated by the devout Coptic translator, as unspeakable and irrelevant, until he was persuaded to translate it. But when the translation was finally elicited, it confirmed the validity of this identification of the discoverer, in that the main Cairo antiquities dealer had reported that the discoverer was a blood avenger.

The process of interviewing the same persons year after year on the same topics, redundant as it has seemed to the translators and villagers, and though producing minor variations with each retelling, does provide a check-and-balance system of cross-examination that has led to many clarifications, precisions, corrections, and confirmations. The very fact of getting from one villager the name and involvement of another, and then going to the other, even though he might live now at the other end of Egypt, to get his report, and then bringing this back to the first for a rebuttal, year after year, meant that in the process of time I came to know more about some details than the translators or even those I interviewed. A couple of anecdotes can illustrate this process: In the Nag Hammadi story the complex relationships among the intermarried priestly families is a part of the detail I was working out. At one point my main informant could not recall the name of a female ancestor, though he knew some twenty generations of the family's male priest genealogy by heart. I told him I would let him know the next day, which then, and especially the next day, provided a very useful levity to the process. By such incidents in a light vein I succeeded in establishing my authority with the villagers in such a way as to reduce the amount of invention they thought they could get away with.

The first time I interviewed the discoverer of the Bodmer Papyri, a man from the back of the crowd spoke up to the effect that he had had the books in his home and also should be interviewed. I asked him his name. In usual Arabic style he gave me his own name and as his second name that of his father. I immediately added his third name, that of his grandfather, much to the amazement of the room full of villagers. For the peasant's claim to have been involved was right—in fact he had taken over the books and done most of the dispersing of them. Already in the process of piecing the story together from the person who bought from him and sold with enough profit to move to Cairo, that is to say, long before I came to interview the discoverer in the village, I had recorded again and again the name of this middle-man, all his kith and kin, and the details of his involvement, so that I had his full name present in mind when I needed it for maximum effect. By showing that I knew the story already in this detail, the interview with the discoverer and this middleman had got off to a good start.

There is to be sure an untruthfulness factor, in that villagers observe that those involved in the story become the focus of attention and receive certain perquisites from their status as discoverers or middle-men, so that on the next visit various other persons surface with claims of having been involved. And narrators are tendentious, to put their action in a better light. In the story of the Bodmer Papyri the main middleman, resentful that his profit had been reduced by his agent's reporting truthfully to his partners what the books had brought (rather than a reduced figure, which would have reduced their shares), hired kidnappers to abduct the son of the agent so as to make up the shortfall in the form of ransom. (Actually in the dark they by mistake got a less valuable commodity, a daughter, who was freed after appeal to Nasser.) The middleman has explained that the persons he employed had had their own plans to kill the agent, who was their neighbor, so that the middleman's hiring the hit men only to kidnap the child comes, on his telling of it, almost to seem a rather kind and neighborly act.

Of course one should not be naive about villagers. But, if I may be permitted to say so, one should also not be naive about established scholars. The mutual public accusations of mendacity by prominent scholars involved in Nag Hammadi studies should have warned us to be on our guard. Indeed, here the danger of being naive may be even greater, since we are dealing with the familiar world in which we live, rather than the unfamiliar third world where culture shock prepares us for the unusual. Veracity, like virtue, does not automatically progress as one moves up the social, financial, cultural, and educational scale.

Nor is it necessarily the case that the academic procedure preserves facts more accurately than does memory in an oral culture. The *Comptes rendus* of the French Académie des Inscriptions et Belles-Lettres reported that two or three Nag Hammadi Codices had been seen by an anonymous academic in a Cairo antiquities shop, and the author of that vacillating report later clarified that actually it was three that had been seen. But this vacillation and then clarification turned out to be inaccurate, an error in detail first corrected by the two peasants from Upper Egypt who had put the books on consignment at the antiquities shop. They now live in different towns and were interviewed separately, yet both insisted that they had sold two books, not three, and divided the profit, as was no doubt impressed on their memory by the fact that on dividing the sale price each ended up with the amount they received per volume, LE 200, some $1,000. When the anonymous academic who had seen the codices in the shop was later identified, he confirmed that indeed he had seen only two codices. He had reported three traits, and these three traits, one about one book and two about another, had apparently been reified for the French Academy and the scholarly tradition into three books, each with one trait, a typically rational procedure of pedantic scholarship, from which the scholarly error resulted.[9] A somewhat similar instance would be the

9. Henri-Charles Puech and Jean Doresse ("Nouveaux écrits gnostiques découverts en Egypte," in *Comptes rendus des séances de l'année 1948*, of the Académie des Inscriptions et Belles-Lettres, 89, a report composed by Doresse) speak of "two or three." Doresse later spoke simply of "three"; see "Le roman d'une grande découverte," in *Les nouvelles littéraires* (25 July 1957) 1, and *Les livres secrets des gnostiques d'Egypte, I: Introduction aux écrits gnostiques coptes découverts à Khénoboskion* (Paris: Librairie Plon, 1958) 137 (ET: *The Secret Books of the Egyptian Gnostics: An Introduction to the Gnostic Coptic Manuscripts Discovered at Chenoboskion* [New York: Viking Press, 1960; London: Hollis and Carter, 1960] 119). The accuracy of the peasant report of only two codices was confirmed by Jacques Schwartz in a letter of 13 November 1972.

learned debunking by the secretary, soon to become the president, of the Section of Religious Sciences of the Ecole pratique des hautes Etudes, of the rumor that some of the Nag Hammadi material had been burned, a rumor he dismissed as just a standard cliché of papyrus discoveries. Repeated interviewing of the discoverer and his mother who had burned some of the material in their bread oven (not to cook tea, as had erroneously been reported), as well as of the villager who bought what was left after the burning, may leave details unanswered as to just what and how much was burned and why, but it establishes the fact that indeed some of the material was burned, the eminent scholar notwithstanding.[10]

Even garbled information that first seems to lead, then to mislead, may ultimately be seen to contain ingredients of relevance that in retrospect, once the story has been straightened out, can be separated out from the garbling in which they were imprisoned. One middleman sent a codex to Cairo for appraisal with a friend, whom he later suspected of having removed a few leaves before returning it. The version reported by the friend in Cairo does not contain all the same details, especially not the detail about the removal of a few leaves. Thus the middleman in Upper Egypt seemed unduly suspicious, and his accusation seemed hardly worth mentioning, until most of a fragmented leaf from this codex cropped up in the Beinecke Rare Book Library of Yale University. One must reconsider that the Cairo friend may have been for his part all too self-serving, for his report does confirm that he had indeed taken the codex to Cairo to ascertain its value, on behalf of a middleman who, unknown to him, had apparently counted the leaves before and after entrusting it to him. At least this seems to be the only explanation that has emerged for this material's having been separated off from the rest of the codex.

These stories are not legends, for they are not structured for the edification of and emulation by a devout community. They are purely secular. But they are not merely village gossip, for that preliminary and admittedly garbled version has long since been transcended. Rather these stories are the result of repeated critical interviewing of the

10. Puech and Doresse ("Nouveaux écrits gnostiques découverts en Egypte," 89) reported that "two had been burned," and Doresse ("A Gnostic Library from Upper Egypt," *Arch* 3 [1950] 69–70) reported "some were burned to heat tea." But Puech ("Les nouveaux écrits gnostiques découverts en Haute-Egypte [premier inventaire et essai d'identification]," *Coptic Studies in Honor of Walter Ewing Crum* [Boston: Byzantine Institute, 1950] 94) discounted the report, a view in which Doresse then concurred in "Le roman," 5.

discoverers and middlemen themselves, with but two instances of a principal's denying what a number of other witnesses report as their involvement. By and large the principals in the stories have given a consistent picture of what happened, even though they were often interviewed in widely separated places, where collusion in a contrived deception is utterly impossible.

Sometimes insignificant details, initially engendered as a diversion or smoke screen or gesture of interest and politeness in an interview, or at first thought to be relevant only in providing a grid of information in terms of which to test the reliability of a witness, may themselves come to have an importance not suspected by the person interviewed or the interpreter, or indeed even by the interviewer until in retrospect they fall into place in a larger context.

Let me then scan the stories of the discovery and marketing of the Nag Hammadi Codices and the Bodmer Papyri, not by narrating two distinct and specific stories, but by sifting from masses of relatively irrelevant details some shared traits that may turn out to be typical and hence significant. I shall usually give the Nag Hammadi instance first, then the Bodmer instance. The point is not to keep the two stories distinct but rather to appraise the relevance of the common traits itemized.

Peasants hunt for *sabakh* as fertilizer near the cliff beyond the limits of arable land. They tend to be young fellows, hardly out of their teens. Muḥammad 'Alī was 26, his brother Abū al-Majd, 15; Ḥasan of the Bodmer story appears to be of their generation. One really wonders why they are only looking for fertilizer and not for treasure. Put conversely, one may wonder whether the repeated claim that one is only looking for *sabakh* is not a cover for activities that are illegal in a way that *sabakh*-digging is not. The discoverers are Muslims, and illiterate, a situation that may change with the universal public education introduced by Nasser to replace the parochial schools of the Coptic church, and with rural electrification since the High Dam now reaching these outlying areas.

The discovery of old books is a letdown once the sealed jar has aroused hopes of buried treasure. There is a mythopoeic ingredient in the experiencing of the find, Muḥammad 'Alī thinking there might be a jinn in the jar, Ḥasan being told that the books are the books of giants, which may be expressing the feeling that they are from a culture alien to and hence horrendous to their own. A major mishandling of the books takes place at the site of the discovery by hands that up to this moment have been digging with a mattock, breaking clods of dirt and pulling camel's thorn from the ground. Their vandalism may also be the reflex of the letdown over the worthless nontreasure and may even express an apotropaic hostility toward the threatening eruption of the unknown. The site of the discovery would probably have yielded evidence in the form of abandoned or overlooked scraps, had it been reached promptly by a scientific expedition.

Ownership is only haltingly asserted over material that begins as nobody's possession, in that the dominant figure can propose a dismembering of the discovery into eight relatively equal lots to divide among the eight camel drivers involved, or in the Bodmer story books can be handed out to passers-by. Yet the material is after all clumsily bundled together somehow in the only container one has, the clothes one has on, and taken home. A lesser figure at the scene picks up a souvenir not officially part of the find, the lid of the jar or in the Bodmer case a stray board (variously interpreted as a mirror, a catalogue of the jar's contents, a book's cover), thereby not threatening the claim of the one who has asserted his right over the loot, for whatever it may be worth, but in a sense following the example of the dominant figure, in case anything should come of it.

One may note that at the time of the discovery there is no privacy, nor is a need for privacy sensed. The discovery begins as public knowledge among the villagers at the site. The discoveries are not in themselves, however, important events in village life. They do not function as pegs in terms of which other events are dated, but must themselves be dated in relation to other more significant events, such as the murder of Muḥammadi 'Ali's father or, in the case of the Bodmer papyri, the fall of King Farouk.

Once home, the books are not considered indoor material to be put in a house, but rather things of the outdoors, from where, after all, they came. Besides, no one ever saw a book inside anyone's house. They belong rather in the patio into which the gate of the family property opens, where the cattle are put overnight, their fodder stored, the oven located, and chickens kept. Since wood is so rare that firewood is almost nonexistent, chaff or reeds or straw strewn carelessly about the patio is for the cattle but also for burning. Here too major loss for the books can take place. The burning of some of the material is characteristic of this early handling, given the material's supposed worthlessness and its association with the tinder on the ground among which it lies. Burning is no doubt also out of playfulness and curiosity—in the

Bodmer story, to light a water pipe. One afterwards recalls and no doubt reconfirms the sweet odor of the burning papyrus and the long-burning parchment like a taper or oil lamp. After all, what else can one *do* with such things?

One of course seeks to get something for them, which is basically just part of the incessant haggling familiar in the Arab world. In this case it must also be a con job, to push off on fellow villagers a worthless commodity for some other nigh-worthless but somehow usable commodity such as bartered cigarettes or oranges or a few piasters. These efforts are basically unsuccessful, for the fellow villagers are as unable as are the discoverers to know what they would do with the books. A market emerges only with the intervention of persons from the larger villages along the river and the railroad, where contacts outside the region are possible. Word of the discovery soon reaches communication and trade centers with which the hamlet has an ongoing working relationship, as itself part and parcel of that relationship. Such a center plays its expected role of providing the know-how, energy, funding, and connections to do something with the material.

One needs to note, however, that the dispersal of the collection may begin very early, even before such a local market emerges, given the worthlessness of the material and the irrelevance of keeping it together, and continues throughout the marketing, even though some major metropolitan dealer may seek, after the fact, to reassemble from various middlemen and other antiquities dealers as much of the discovery as possible, knowing by then that large profits are in view. Hence the emergence of manuscripts at one dealer's shop would suggest that other manuscripts from the same discovery may be in the hands of other dealers. Thus the fact that materials reach scholarly attention through completely independent channels does not mean they may not come from the same discovery. One value of tracking down the provenience of individual manuscripts from a discovery is to restore them to the association with other manuscripts from the same discovery, as well as with the discovery site itself. Of course a shared provenience may remain a mere conjecture upon which nothing can be based; but it is also purely conjectural to multiply the number of discoveries until it equals the number of discrete lots.

As the books move from the discoverers to the local middlemen one shifts from Muslim to Coptic environment, perhaps because the script is recognized as Coptic, but also because the parochial school system elevated the Copts to the literate and white-collar, upper middle class, even to community leadership, especially in this part of Egypt, where the Coptic minority is unusually strong because of the monastic center of al-Qaṣr (Chenoboskia). The Coptic priest plays a significant role, both as an authority figure in the community who, especially in such a case, might be expected to know something relevant and as a haven of refuge less likely to be subject to police investigation, since the Muslim government seeks to avoid a confrontation between the two religions. Actually, the priest would not be capable of providing knowledgeable information about the books, though he may have aided in setting up the web of Coptic connections. Since in the Bodmer case the books were put in the priest's home to be safe from police search, and ultimately the priest was accorded the privileged position of an unindicted co-conspirator, one may in the Nag Hammadi case wonder whether it was pure coincidence that the priest gained access to the Nag Hammadi Codices at about the time that Muḥammad ʿAlī and his brothers were under police control for having avenged the murder of their father by themselves committing murder, at which time their home was repeatedly searched for weapons.

The church also provides ecclesiastical connections beyond the village. A teacher in the parochial school system, not a priest but a grandson of a priest and a brother-in-law of a priest, received Nag Hammadi Codex III from the latter priest, sent it to Cairo first in the hands of a fellow teacher at the parochial school of Dishnā, who showed it to the Coptic pope in Cairo, who had him show it to the curator of the Coptic Museum. The owner then sent it to Cairo a second time in the hands of the Bishop of Qinā and finally himself took it to Cairo, accompanied by a priest of Nag Hammadi, a relative, who took him first to a wealthy Coptic "Pasha," then to a Coptic physician and amateur Coptologist, who in turn alerted the Coptic Museum and the Department of Antiquities. In the Bodmer story the first in Dishnā to acquire a book showed it to a priest, to see if it were as valuable as the Nag Hammadi Codices, apparently knowing that the priest would be informed in this regard. For the priest was born in al-Qaṣr, the village of the Nag Hammadi discoverer, across the street from his blood relative the al-Qaṣr priest who had given Codex III to his brother-in-law, who had himself lived and taught at Dishnā. Through this channel the owner of the Bodmer Papyrus must have learned that the former owner of Nag Hammadi Codex III had sold his book to the Coptic Museum. For the owner of the Bodmer Papyrus had a son, a teacher at the same parochial school as was the former owner of Codex

III, and the son showed his father's Bodmer Papyrus to the Coptic Museum and only with the help of a powerful friend in Cairo avoided its confiscation and the intervention of the authorities. Thus the Coptic clergy and the lay leadership of the Coptic community were channels that came into play in both instances.

Another recurrent role is that of the goldsmith or jeweler. Since native jewelry is made out of precious metals in the villages themselves, these terms are merely two designations for the same profession. In the economic systems of the hamlets that are dependent on a given town, the downtown goldsmiths represent a source of available capital, much as would a bank in a more modern situation, with the peasant's gold jewelry being capital kept on his or her person for safekeeping, with liquidity achieved by using the goldsmith as a pawn shop. The value of gold jewelry is in its weight, not in its workmanship or aesthetic qualities. An old book might serve as collateral to acquire the modest funds needed for initial purchase. A grain merchant turned to a Nag Hammadi goldsmith to market Codex I in Cairo, with a division of profit suggesting that he turned to the goldsmith not merely because the latter would have known how to market things in Cairo but probably because the goldsmith was needed to put up some of the purchase price. The goldsmith in turn went not to an antiquities dealer in Cairo but to a fellow goldsmith, whose involvement may have been more than merely friendly. Or to give another instance, when the provincial antiquities dealer and his local contact man in the village took Nag Hammadi Codices II and VII to Cairo, they were accompanied by a jeweler of Qinā, who may have served in a similar capacity as financier. In the Bodmer story the discoverer's brother-in-law worked for a Dishnā jeweler who made the first cash purchase. The priest to whom this jeweler showed it to ascertain its value allied with himself three other goldsmiths. Although the principal one of these may have been cut in because he was already in through his own contacts, the inclusion of the other two, themselves partners, may have been to increase the capital base of the enterprise, especially since rumors about the Nag Hammadi Codices, of which the priest was aware, had created an inflated market in the region.

There is in the marketing of the books a rough correlation between the sequence of the sales and the rise of the market value. At the site of the discovery of the Nag Hammadi Codices the main discoverer offered the other camel drivers a share in the books, but the others declined, partly out of fear but no doubt also out of indifference. Efforts by the discoverer to sell for a few cigarettes or piasters, for an Egyptian pound, or perhaps the whole lot for as little as LE 3, were rebuffed. One codex became in effect a gift to the local priest and from him to his brother-in-law, a teacher of history and English in the Coptic parochial school system. The teacher then went to the discoverer's youngest brother and sought to acquire more. The lad gave him a second codex and declined payment on the grounds that they were neighbors. But the priest's brother-in-law, knowing the system, ascertained from the lad that he would like to get a *jallabiyah*, a peasant nightgownlike robe, and so gave him the piasters needed to get one.

Actual sales began as barter for sugar and tea at a local shop, then advanced to a sale of all that was left for forty oranges and a cash amount of LE 12, according to the seller, or a cash purchase of from LE 12 to LE 18, according to the buyer, which would mean a price per codex of some LE 2 or LE 3. Then, reflecting the impact of this middle-man's great success in Cairo, once he had been shown the way, the discoverer demanded back from the priest's brother-in-law the two codices he had been "given." The priest's brother-in-law could not return the codex the priest had given him, since it was in Cairo being evaluated. With threats, the discoverer reached a cash settlement of from LE 15 to LE 20 with the priest's brother-in-law who returned the second codex, the one the discoverer's youngest brother had given him. Then the priest's brother-in-law tried to sell the first book, once he had got it back from Cairo, at a price too high for a regional antiquities dealer in Qinā to pay. The priest's brother-in-law boasts that as a teacher of history he appreciates the value of ancient books. The discoverer sold locally the second codex he had succeeded in recu-perating, the Jung Codex, for a price the seller estimates at LE 11, the sons of the buyer at from LE 30 to LE 50. It was then sold in Cairo for some LE 200. This was the same price per codex that the provincial antiquities dealer and his local agent had obtained from another Cairo dealer, which suggests that the Cairo dealers kept rather well in touch with the market in setting their rates. The priest's brother-in-law was a few months later given LE 250 by the Department of Antiquities for Codex III.

The main antiquities dealer of Cairo, who brought together some ten Nag Hammadi Codices, perhaps with some financial involvement of a cultured Italian spinster of Cairo, reports having been offered some L 100,000, or L 10,000 per codex, by bibliophiles from Britain (presumably Sir Chester Beatty) and Switzerland (presumably Martin Bodmer), but was prevented since the Department of Antiquities had taken the books into safekeeping. He hence demanded that amount from the government, then came down to LE 65,000. The Minister of Public Education offered LE 40,000, but this offer was never accepted by the dealer or ratified by the government. The Italian lady brought legal proceedings against the government. A settlement of LE 5,000 was finally reached, about LE 500 (over $2,000) per codex. The Jung Codex was offered in America at about the rate the Egyptian government had tentatively offered, $20,000 plus ten percent commission, reduced in the haggling to $10,000 in gratitude for America's help to Belgium, the dealer's country, in World War I. The Jung Institute actually paid $8,009, contributed to the Institute for that purpose by George H. Page, an American expatriate living in Switzerland and a patron of the Institute.

In the case of the Bodmer Papyri there is a similar shift in market value from an initial nothing or sugar, before the Dishnā market emerged, to talk of hundreds and even thousands of pounds. Such a rapid and high escalation was no doubt facilitated by the Nag Hammadi story's having become common knowledge, with the astronomical figures that were bandied about but actually never paid being cited as what was in fact paid. The first sale, to a Dishnā goldsmith, was for LE 15, which is about what Nag Hammadi Codices were selling for locally at the end of their escalation. The goldsmith, after an unsuccessful trip to Cairo, sold to a Luxor dealer for LE 400. The main Dishnā middleman began buying in the hamlet for some LE 40, and paid LE 200 for all that was left in the home where the discoverer lived. The priest's neighbor is thought to have filched one of these books and to have sold it to a tailor in Dishnā for LE 30, who then sold it to the main Cairo dealer for LE 700. Thus again there is a sharp markup from the tens to the hundreds in selling to a dealer. The main middleman entrusted one manuscript to a provincial dealer to sell in Cairo, and when he was told that it had brought only LE 300 he demanded and obtained its return. The Luxor dealer who had acquired one for LE 400 acquired about ten more from this main middleman for LE 5,000 or LE 6,000, about double per book the price this main middleman had turned down. This Luxor dealer then sold to the main Cairo dealer for at least double what he had paid, in the presence of the main middleman from Dishnā. This middleman himself sold directly to the main Cairo dealer (and occasionally to an Alexandria dealer) for prices initially of LE 1,000 per manuscript, up to LE 7,000 for an unusually large book, LE 100 for small rolled letters the size of one's finger, and LE 200 for a final box of scraps. In some of these transactions he used a friend as an unpaid porter, since he himself was under virtual house arrest. When the porter in some of these transactions reduced the main middleman's profit by telling the latter's partners the actual sale price rather than a reduced sale price, thereby increasing their share, the main middleman considered his porter as owing him LE 2,000. At the time of the trial he paid bribes ranging from LE 300 to LE 500, then paid the judge LE 20 for each convict, a total of LE 160, for the privilege of appealing the case. These figures tend in general to confirm the range of the figures cited for the sale of the manuscripts themselves.

The actual amounts paid by the final repositories of the Bodmer Papyri are generally not known. For no information is available at the Bibliothèque Bodmer. But the Chester Beatty Library has made the registry of accessions available, from which a relevant instance can be cited: Accession 1389, the Beatty part of Papyrus Bodmer XXI, including the leather cover and most of the leaves of Joshua in Coptic, together with 1390, eight leaves containing a Greek school mathematical exercise and John 10:8—13:38 in Coptic, as well as two boxes of loose leaves, were acquired from the main Cairo dealer—early in 1956—for L 835, with 1390 and hence probably the whole lot identified as from the Dishnā discovery. This dealer reported that he was offered by British and Swiss bibliophiles L 10,000 each for Nag Hammadi Codices, upward of $50,000 per codex. This may have been his point of departure for these negotiations, but may not reflect what would have been the final price if the negotiations had led to an actual transaction. I was offered for almost that much a fourth century Bohairic papyrus codex containing the Minor Prophets on consignment at a Cairo antiquities shop almost a decade ago, a codex now in the Vatican Library. But this price would today be scorned on the international market as lacking a digit or so (for which inflated rate there have however been no takers). But I report this dramatic inflation as a sort of warning to Coptologists who perhaps all too smugly count on ongoing clandestine excavating and illicit marketing of Coptic manuscripts to be a dependable source of supply for texts to edit and interpret. The economic facts of life, if not lofty principle, may force us to get more seriously involved in trying to change the way the system operates.

One dimension of down-to-earth reality not unrelated to the price of the manuscripts is that their marketing often coincides with sudden improvement in the middleman's economic position. There is a small produce store in a Coptic quarter of Cairo named the Nag Hammadi Store. Its proprietor denies that he sold a Nag Hammadi codex, but villagers report he did, and relatives report his talking about having done so within the family circle. His move to the big time of Cairo took place at about the time the profit from a sale would have funded such a big step forward. Another instance has to do with the village contact man of the provincial antiquities dealer who sold most of the material after being shown the way to Cairo and the market there. With his enormous profit he bought a farm, bringing down upon himself the eternal enmity of the main discoverer, who felt the profit should have been shared. Or in still another instance, the avenging of the death of the discoverer's father about a month after the discovery made available the house of the murdered person, which was acquired by the local grain merchant who divided the profit with the jeweler for the sale of the Jung Codex in Cairo. In the Bodmer story, the main middle-man acquired a large duplex apartment building in Heliopolis near Cairo. The priest's brother-in-law who had sold Codex III to the Coptic Museum for hardly more than $1,000 constantly refers with real envy to the two "palaces" the Bodmer Papyri funded.

In both stories the discoverers have the most real fiscal complaint, and do complain bitterly that the books had left their possession before their value was realized, and that hence the discoverers, though most deserving (!), were the real losers. Indeed they are still living in the dirt-farmer life style of their youth. Part of the problem involved the ability to find one's way to Cairo. None of the discoverers actually got beyond their village with the books. Even those who got the books from them in the village for next to nothing usually had to find a trusted friend, such as a goldsmith, ecclesiastic, teacher, or regional dealer, who represented cosmopolitanism, as an agent to take the material to market on their behalf, or to accompany them in order to teach them the contacts.

In view of the initial poverty of the discoverers and first middlemen, their need to negotiate capital with goldsmiths, and the concrete use made of their profit, it does not seem very probable that manuscripts from such discoveries would be held back for long periods of time; nor would the antiquities market be likely to keep its money tied up in such stock for long, since the livelihood of the dealers too depends on a constant turnover. It took hardly more than a year for all the Nag Hammadi Codices to have arrived on the antiquities market in Cairo. In the case of the Bodmer Papyri, the virtual house arrest of the main middleman slowed down the trafficking, but he devised ingenious ways of selling all he had, in Cairo or Alexandria, within about three years.

Another typical fact of life in the Arab world is that of the son in the father's business. Teenage sons are often taken along with their fathers in their business, in an informal apprenticeship with male chauvinist overtones. Since the manuscripts passed from young illiterate discoverers to established middle-aged villagers, the tracking down of this second stage of the story a generation later runs into the problem that the primary figures have begun to die off. But their sons may well have been present at the decisive transactions and have eyewitness memories that their equivalents in a Western society, being raised at home by their mother or being in school, would not have. To be sure this information can be vague, compared to what another villager might still know. The village priest in whose home Codex III was stored has died, and his son, clerk of the court in Nag Hammadi, recalls the story, but in much less detail than does the priest's brother-in-law who acquired the codex from the priest. The local grain merchant who purchased the Jung Codex after the priest's brother-in-law was forced to return it to the discoverer has died, and his two sons recall only a few details about the codex, which they apparently never saw. But when the grain merchant sent the Nag Hammadi goldsmith to Cairo to sell the codex, the goldsmith took along his twenty-year-old son, who was a law student actually capable, according to his claim, of transcribing the pages. He recalls the purchase price, the name of the Cairo goldsmith to whom they went, the name of the antiquities dealer who bought the manuscript, both the buying and selling prices, and the way the money was divided. In fact this lawyer, now the goldsmith in his father's place, recalls with pride that it was he who put the codex into the hands of the purchaser. With regard to the deceased Cairo antiquities dealers, the daughter of the one who acquired most of the books from both discoveries, now living in the family home in Nicosia, is much less well informed than is the son of the one who acquired the Jung Codex, now living in Brussels. Similarly in the Bodmer story the main middleman's son, who now lives with his father in the duplex apartment building in Heliopolis, recalls having carried a jar containing the books into the house of the Dishnā priest. The son of this deceased priest recalls having broken the jar and thrown it down the Turkish toilet of the Dishnā church. Thus the fact that the more central principals in the story are in several crucial instances deceased does not mean that these segments of the stories are completely blank, thanks to the fact that their sons were apparently wide-eyed with amazement at scenes that are indelibly fixed in their memories.

A further relevant network consists of the antiquities dealers. It was an antiquities dealer in the provincial capital of Qinā who had, in addition to a little shop on the second floor of his home, a network of informants in the villages adjacent to antiquities sites to alert him when something turned up. His agent near Nag Hammadi was a notorious one-eyed badman, who notified him of the discovery. This local agent accompanied the provincial dealer to the main antiquities dealers of Cairo, first to Mansoor's shop at the old Shepheards Hotel, then to Tano, the main Cairo dealer in both stories, just off Opera Square. Once the provincial dealer had shown his village agent the way, the latter returned alone to Cairo with more codices, bypassing the provincial dealer, so as to keep for himself all the profit, much to the chagrin of the dealer. Tano, the Cairo dealer, then came to Nag Hammadi to negotiate for more of the material through his unnamed agent, who may have been this same contact man who had abandoned the provincial dealer for the big time.

Tano later heard of the Bodmer Papyri from people of Dishnā who came to Cairo to sell other antiquities. He then went to Luxor, where he set up a meeting with the goldsmith of Dishnā who was the main middleman, to whom he offered to go to Dishnā to get the papyri. The goldsmith was afraid to accept the offer, since he was already under police surveillance amounting to house arrest. A week later a different provincial antiquities dealer of Baliana, 74 km downstream from Dishnā, passed through Dishnā on his regular circuit, visited the goldsmith, and took a book on consignment to sell in Cairo. He was subsequently forced to return it to the goldsmith when, on his next visit to Dishnā, he reported he had sold it for a price the hard-nosed goldsmith was not willing to accept. Actually the first sale of a Bodmer manuscript on the antiquities market had been that of the first goldsmith to get a manuscript. The son of this goldsmith, after showing it to the Coptic Museum, sold to Zaki Ghali, an antiquities dealer in Luxor. Tano himself did not give up, in spite of his initial setback, but tracked down in Cairo a brother of the main goldsmith, whom he persuaded to take him to the goldsmith's home in Dishnā under cover of darkness. He worked out a clandestine system for the goldsmith to come to Tano's home in Cairo to sell bit by bit the bulk of the discovery. He even funded, through this powerful goldsmith as paymaster, a clandestine excavation of the site of the discovery of the Bodmer Papyri.

The authorities themselves constitute a network aware to some extent of what is taking place. After all, the head of the Department of Antiquities knew of two of the Nag Hammadi Codices the first summer after their discovery. One he seized for the Coptic Museum and the other he tied down, or thought he tied down, at the dealer's, by extricating a commitment not to export the codex (named the Jung Codex because it in fact did leave Egypt). In the case of the Bodmer Papyri the main middlemen were arrested hardly a month after the discovery, convicted, and then acquitted at the appellate court a couple of years later, except for two who had been caught red-handed and were convicted, one to be paroled and the other, the discoverer, to serve time. Thus there must be government records, if they could be located and access could be obtained, that would provide much information. Furthermore clandestine excavations were carried on at both sites after the discoveries in hopes of finding more, and in both cases the authorities intervened and forbade further digging at the sites. Yet the guard of the Department of Antiquities responsible for the site of the Nag Hammadi discovery had not been tracked down and interviewed, which again would seem an obvious thing to do, for these local representatives of the Department of Antiquities tend to be well informed, though ineffectual, with regard to such local matters regarding antiquities. The Department of Antiquities' infrastructure of university-trained inspectors and local peasant guards at antiquities sites throughout Egypt is being filled out, so that this form of information and ultimately control may well increase. Any efforts undertaken by non-Egyptians in Egypt to do something about the chaotic condition of the discovering and marketing of manuscripts would have to be carried out in cooperation with the Egyptian Antiquities Organization.

An instance of appeal to such public records is the locating in the Registry of Deaths kept at the Nag Hammadi Real Estate Taxation Office of the date of the death of the father of the main discoverer of the Nag Hammadi Codices, from which the approximate date of the discovery, as some six months later, could be established. Another instance of recourse to public records is the locating, in the Acquisitions Registry of the Coptic Museum, of the name of the priest's brother-in-law, the school teacher, as the seller of Codex III. Once he was tracked down in Upper Egypt, he ultimately unraveled the whole story of the discovery and marketing of the Nag Hammadi Codices. The neglect of such an obvious lead for a generation shows how unsystematic or nonexistent the efforts to track down the provenience of such a discovery have been.

The stories lead beyond Egypt. The diplomatic courier was used in both stories, not to speak of an abortive effort to export the Bodmer Menander's *The Girl from Samos* through the Tunisian embassy: it began complete, arrived in Geneva incomplete years later, after a rupture in diplomatic relations between the Arab Republic of Egypt and Tunisia had been healed. The Cairo dealers also traveled extensively outside Egypt. Nag Hammadi Codex I was shown to the Bollingen Foundation in New York by its owner, and it even turned up at the University of Michigan in Ann Arbor before entering a bank vault in Brussels. Tano regularly took material from Cairo to his family home in Cyprus and on at least one occasion from there to Geneva.

Much information is available from scholars outside Egypt, in addition to those who have advanced their reputations by associating themselves with a discovery and hence have often been assumed to be the persons on whom we are dependent for the information or lack of it concerning the discovery. Information from those who have not provided the "official" story may be all the more relevant. Such information regarding the Nag Hammadi Codices has been provided by François Daumas, Egyptologist if the University of Montpellier; Jacques Schwartz, papyrologist of the University of Strasbourg; Father Georges Anawati, director of the Cairo Institut dominicain des études orientales; Father B. Couroyer, Coptologist of the Ecole biblique et archéologique française in Jerusalem; Harriet C. Jameson, head of the Department of Rare Books and Special Collections of the Library of the University of Michigan; Mary C. Ritter, secretary of the Bollingen Foundation; C. A. Meier, director emeritus of the Jung Institute; George H. Page, patron of the Jung Institute; His Excellency Beat von Fischer-Reichenbacht, former ambassador of Switzerland to the United Arab Republic. Regarding the Bodmer Papyri, Father Louis Doutreleau, S.J., of the staff of Sources chrétiennes in Lyon, has provided crucial and voluminous information, and the Chester Beatty Library has made available valuable records. In spite of the number of leads that have been followed up, there is much that could still be done.

Of course tracking down such stories does involve a lot of travel, a dogged persistence, and considerable luck. In the Nag Hammadi case persons were interviewed at al-Qaṣr, Ḥamrah Dūm, Nag Hammadi,

Dishnā, Qinā, Cairo, Alexandria, Nicosia, Brussels, Paris, Strasbourg, Bilthoven, Zurich, Jerusalem, and Claremont, whereas in the Bodmer story persons were interviewed at Nag Hammadi, Dishnā, Abū Manā, Luxor, Cairo, Heliopolis, and Claremont. To illustrate the roles of persistence and luck the following anecdote may suffice: In March of 1966 I visited Nag Hammadi to see the site of the discovery. The police to whom I turned provided as interpreter a teacher at the local Boys' Preparatory School, who mentioned that his father had once been offered one of the books. When the subsequent ban on travel in that area was lifted on 1 November 1974 I returned to Nag Hammadi and went to the school to renew the contact, but was told by the vice-principal that the person had moved to Cairo. The vice-principal sent me to his brother the local pharmacist to get the Cairo address. But when the next summer I tracked down the Cairo address, no one there had ever heard of the person I sought. Since in Arabic, numbers, such as the street number, are written from left to right, even though the words are written from right to left, it occurred to me in my desperation that perhaps the pharmacist, in writing the address for me in English, had gotten the numbers backwards, reversing them just as he knew to reverse the direction of the words. So I reversed the street number and went to that address several miles away. At the new address I found not only my interpreter of 1966 but the vice-principal who had sent me to his brother the pharmacist for the garbled address in 1974. My 1966 lead had had a stroke and had lost his memory, which would seem to have ended that wild-goose chase, until the vice-principal volunteered the information that he had a colleague at the Nag Hammadi Boys' Preparatory School, the teacher of English, who was from the village of the discoverer. He thought this colleague could set up an interview with the discoverer, which in fact did take place a couple of weeks later. This of course broke the Nag Hammadi story wide open. Thus a bum steer derailed the investigation at a crucial point and a wild hunch brought it back right on target. Perhaps this was not just incredible luck, but the fruit of assuming that the local people, in this case the pharmacist who regularly receives shipments of medication from the Ciba Pharmaceutical Laboratory in Basel, Switzerland, which he dispenses without prescription on his own responsibility, are in their way intelligible, worth trying to understand.

It is to be hoped that such investigations into the discovery and marketing of two Coptic manuscript collections may serve not only to entertain but to inform concerning these two discoveries. It is also to be hoped that this reporting may create a different scholarly assumption regarding such matters, so that others will seek to carry through comparable investigations, thereby gradually augmenting the data base from which better generalizations may be drawn, as well as gaining the supplementary information about specific manuscripts and specific locations in Coptic Egypt that such investigations provide.

Coptic and Greek Inscriptions
from Christian Egypt:
A Brief Review

INTRODUCTION

In discussing inscriptional remains from Egypt's Christian past, one immediately observes a lack of organization. To be sure, this is true of most inscriptional evidence that comes to us from antiquity. At present, Greek inscriptions are receiving the type of attention that will eventually bring order from chaos. Thus the publication of the series *Inschriften griechischer Städte aus Kleinasien* in Bonn has been gathering all known documents according to region. Nothing of the sort, however, has or is being done for such texts produced by Egyptian Christians. One can note dozens of texts tucked away in field reports published scores of years ago. Since mention of Christian remains were often included only incidentally in such reports, an enormous effort will be required to pull these inscriptions together in organized fashion.

Although my survey does not pretend to be comprehensive, it may serve as an initial appeal that we do something to organize the inscriptional evidence from Christian Egypt. The organization of the Roots of Egyptian Christianity Project may offer the impetus to a more systematic study of the significance of these important documents. And they are important, as will become clear.

LIMITATIONS OF THE
DISCUSSION

At the outset, I need to detail the limitations of my discussion. The languages in which the majority of the texts appear were two, Greek and Coptic.[1] The inscriptional remains in Latin from Egypt are rather modest.[2] Those hieratic and hieroglyphic texts that date within the early Christian period are limited in both number and scope.[3] Demotic documents are confined largely to ostraca[4] and papyri[5] and thus will not come within our purview.

In the early decades of the common era, the preponderance of documents were naturally of other than Christian origin.[6] As time wore on, Christian texts appeared more frequently until the age of Constantine when we can probably assume with Jalabert and Mouterde that most if not all inscriptions were Christian.[7] Such an observation, of course, has allowed scholars to see how terminology and decorative motifs, drawn into a Christian milieu from their pagan moorings, were reshaped and redefined.

FUNERARY INSCRIPTIONS

By far, the most common type of inscription consisted of funerary memorials. Literally hundreds of these have been published, though not all with translations. Naturally, many stock formulas and abbreviations were employed, whether the text was Greek or Coptic or a mixture of the two. It is important to note that besides the inscribed death dates, calculated either according to the era of the martyrs or from the indiction cycle of years, one frequently finds a prayer for the

1. When writing of Christian inscriptions in Egypt, H. Leclercq could discuss the "two languages" of such monuments, i.e., Greek and Coptic; cf. his article "Egypte," in *DACL* 4/2:col. 2486. A few inscriptions in Coptic and Arabic have been noted; see, e.g., Urbain Bouriant, "Notes de voyage," *RTPE* 15 (1893) 176–80.

2. H. Leclercq, "Inscriptions latines chrétiennes," in *DACL* 7:cols. 694–850. See also *CIL* (ed. T. Mommsen, 1873) 3/2:967–68 (nos. 6023–26); *CIL* (ed. T. Mommsen, 1902) 3 suppl./1:1200-1214 (nos. 6576–6636) 1/2:702 (frag. 2267). Further mention of Egypt in the same series can be found, e.g., in *CIL* (ed. G. Henzen et al., 1893) 1/1:77, line 725; and in *CIL* (ed. A. Huebner, 1869) 2:264–66 (nos. 1970–71).

3. Cf. Sir Alan Gardiner, *Egyptian Grammar* (3d ed.; London: Oxford Univ. Press, 1957) 1:9–10; and W. F. Edgerton, *Medinet Habu Graffiti Facsimiles* (Chicago: Univ. of Chicago Press, 1937).

4. See M. Lichtheim, *Demotic Ostraca from Medinet Habu* (Chicago: Univ. of Chicago Press, 1957). Besides the collections of ostraca cited here on pp. vii and xi–xii, one should note a few unpublished pieces in the collections at Columbia University and the Coptic Museum in Old Cairo.

5. Bibliography is cited in Lichtheim, *Demotic ostraca*, xi–xii. See also Gardiner, *Egyptian Grammar*, 10.

6. For an example in Coptic, see H. Munier, "Remarques sur la Stèle copte 11799 du Musée d'Alexandrie," *BSAA* 22 (1926) 237–39.

7. L. Jalabert and R. Mouterde, "Inscriptions grecques chrétiennes," in *DACL* 7:cols. 623–94, esp. cols. 623–24. The larger questions, naturally, concern the extent and rapidity of the Christianizing of Egypt.

deceased as well as an admonition to the living not to grieve since "no one is immortal in this world."[8] An example of a prayer or, rather, an admonition to pray is "Everyone who comes to this place, pray for me, Abraham the servant of Jesus Christ. Amen."[9] This typical instance underscores the observation that, when such inscriptions were written, Egypt had become Christian—totally so. For in such inscriptions it is obviously assumed that the passer-by will offer the proper Christian prayer on behalf of the deceased.

Regarding funerary inscriptions, we should make two further brief observations. The first concerns the phraseology adopted in the more substantial texts whose length has invited a freer use of language to honor the dead. Maria Cramer has argued that such lengthy texts show clear influences from the Coptic liturgy celebrated at funerals, which consisted of a pastiche of biblical phrases drawn especially from the Psalms and the New Testament.[10] Moreover, she observed, these lengthy documents exhibit inspiration from Coptic legal testaments as well as from known dirges and hymnic pieces sung and recited among Copts.[11] Thus, for those deceased who had been honored by rather substantial grave markers—whether owing to economic or other factors—there were created elaborate memorials whose texts show links at least to the last rites administered by the church.

TOPOGRAPHY

While working with Greek inscriptions from Egypt eighty years ago, Gustave Lefebvre was the first to characterize inscriptions—particularly those on steles—by topographical region. In his study of some two hundred monuments, he was able to show regional peculiarities based on types of symbols, ornamentation, material, and written

---

8. G. Lefebvre ("Inscriptions chrétiennes du Musée du Caire," *BIFAO* 3 [1903] 80–81) has brought together illustrations of various parallel Greek formulas. In his corrections to W. E. Crum (*Coptic Monuments: Catalogue général des antiquités égyptiennes du Musée du Caire* [Cairo: L'Institute français d'archéologie orientale du Caire, 1902]), G. Daressy noted two more exemplars—one from Armant—in his "Renseignements sur la provenance des stèles coptes du Musée du Caire," *ASAE* 13 (1914) 266–71, esp. 268. Cf. an example of such a phrase in Coptic published by A. Pellegrini ("Stele funerarie copte del Museo Archeologico di Firenze," *Bess* 22 [1907] 20–43, esp. 37–38).

9. Published by L. Stern, "Koptische Inschriften an alten Denkmälern," *ZÄS* 23 (1885) 96–102; text appears on 97.

10. M. Cramer, *Die Totenklage bei den Kopten* (SÖAW 219; Vienna: Hoelder-Pichler-Tempsky, 1941) 41–47.

11. Cramer, *Totenklage*, 47–52.

formulas employed.[12] Let me briefly detail the results of Lefebvre's pivotal study.

For steles from the Fayyum the only material employed was limestone. Moreover, the formulas regularly used were four: (1) "He/she has fallen asleep in the Lord"; (2) "Lord, rest the soul of thy servant"; (3) "In remembrance of . . ."; (4) "Peace be to the one at rest in the Lord."[13] Of ornamentation, Lefebvre adduced three types. In the first, the top of the stele was either curved or shaped like a triangular pediment, with a cross—Greek or Latin—covering its whole front surface.[14] The funerary text itself was engraved either at the top of the piece or down along the two sides of the cross. More rarely it appeared at its base. The second type portrayed a portal of a church under which—between the two columns—appeared a cross or a rose window. The third type was more ornate than the other two. Here the stele also pictured a portal of a church under which was to be seen a person praying with upraised arms, the hands extended towards heaven. These figures were most often women wearing long white robes. But the figures of men thus clothed and those of women less fully clothed are also known. Generally the skill with which such memorials were executed was rather elementary, even childlike.

For monuments from Akhmim, there was almost no variation.[15] Always done in limestone, the steles consistently formed a rectangle topped by a triangular pediment. While occasionally the crowning triangular top was missing or was worked into an arch, there always appeared a small cross above the inscription and a small palm decoration within it. The length of the stone remained between twenty-five and thirty centimeters and the formulas were always the same, consistently saying, "Stele of . . . ," "He/she lived so many years," with a notation of the day of the month of death and the indiction number.[16]

In artistic quality, the decorations on steles from the neighborhood of Armant were the finest.[17] This site of ancient Hermonthis, lying

12. G. Lefebvre, *Recueil des inscriptions grecques-chrétiennes d'Egypte* (Cairo: L'Institut français d'archéologie orientale, 1907).

13. Lefebvre's observations (ibid., xxvi–xxviii) are repeated by H. Leclercq ("Egypte," in *DACL* 4/2:cols. 2486–2521, where he deals with epigraphy; on topography, see cols. 2492–94; the Greek formulas appear in col. 2493).

14. Such crosses were occasionally inscribed within a surrounding wreath of foliage; Leclercq, "Egypte," col. 2493.

15. Ibid.

16. These Greek formulas are reproduced in Leclercq (ibid., col. 2493).

17. Ibid., cols. 2493–94.

approximately eight miles southwest of Luxor on the west bank,[18] has yielded both the most numerous and the most artistically rich sculptured steles from the early Christian period. Here decoration almost totally overshadowed inscription. The monuments of Armant were all of a single type, with some modifications: a cross inscribed within a pavilion pictured under a triangular pediment, with an ornamented panel, and an inscription on the stele's architrave.[19] This basic style of ornamentation flourished in such a way that the creative work of the artisan came to dominate the funerary text. For its part, usually the name only, and occasionally the profession of the deceased, appeared on the architrave. In a few cases, one might also encounter one of three exclamations: (1) "God is one"; (2) "God the helper is one"; or (3) "Do not grieve, no one is immortal."[20]

Of the funerary monuments at Esna, the formula was always the same: "God the helper is one." Here the ornamentation of the steles derived their inspiration from the "school" of Armant, with the differences that the tops of the steles at Esna were almost always circular, the central cross was generally very ornate, and the material was always limestone, frequently cut smaller than the pieces from Armant.[21]

At this point, it is worthwhile evaluating briefly the decorations carved onto grave markers at Armant and Esna. In addition to what I have already noted, one observes that several motifs often appeared together, including specifically one or more crosses, an eagle representing the soul, a doorway or portal, and acanthus or grape leaves. But what is important is that the art became so preeminent in these two localities that the text was regularly reduced to little more than the name of the departed person. In these instances, the memorial message was conveyed entirely by the symbolism of the art. This is an observation made as early as 1926 by Munier.[22]

For the funerary pieces from Nubia, one need only focus on the recurring formulas, five in number, that are special to this locale: (1) "May thy soul rest with the saints," or "May thy soul rest in the tents of the righteous"; (2) "May thy soul rest in the bosoms of Abraham and

18. W. B. Donne, "Hermonthis," in DGRG (1966) 1:1058.
19. See, for instance, piece no. 8636 in W. E. Crum, Coptic Monuments, 133 and pl. 40.
20. Leclercq, "Egypte," col. 2494.
21. Ibid.
22. Munier, "Stèle copte 11799," 238. Cf. Pellegrini, "Stele funerarie copte," 38–39. For further examples from Armant and Esneh, cf. Crum, Coptic Monuments, nos. 8656, 8659, 8662, 8665, 8667 and 8671, described on pp. 136–39 and reproduced on pls. 44–46.

Isaac and Jacob"; (3) "God of the spirits and of all flesh"; (4) "There he/she has lain down"; and (5) "The blessed one," as the term for the dead. Consequently, as Lefebvre has pointed out, the funerary steles of Nubia can be rather quickly identified.[23]

LITURGICAL FORMULATIONS

We readily discover that Egyptian Christians were familiar both with those passages from the Old and New Testaments that lent themselves to worship and with other liturgical patterns. The familiarity with other liturgical patterns can be seen especially in reminiscences of, allusions to, and literal citations of fragments of prayers that were apparently the prototypes of formulas later codified in the church's liturgy.[24]

The borrowings from the Old Testament come from several books. One notable example is the formula employed in at least five exemplars: "God of the spirits and of all flesh," a phrase borrowed from the Septuagint version of Num. 16:22 and 27:16 where we read respectively of the "God of the spirits of all flesh," as well as of the "Lord, God of the spirits of all flesh." Virtually all the texts that have this borrowed phrase come from Nubia or Aswan and date between 993 and 1243 C.E.[25] Further, all the texts are in Greek and, although somewhat garbled, still reproduce this phrase in addition to others that allude to Ps. 45:6 and 70:8. What is more striking is the fact that the Nubians were undoubtedly unable to read the Greek of these inscriptions, as the fact that the text of each is unintelligible in places makes clear. From this we learn of the Nubians' religious conservatism. For even though they had lost the ability to translate into Coptic such complicated formulas, it was plainly their desire to respect the original text, realizing that it included extracts from Holy Scripture. Amazingly, these liturgical formulas continued to be preserved and recited even when not understood.

In a related vein, there exist some rather remarkable links between

23. Quoted by Leclercq, "Egypte," col. 2494.

24. This is Leclercq's argument (ibid., cols. 2494–95). The question can still be discussed whether the liturgical formulas inscribed on steles exhibit a stage prior to the final fixation of such elements in the church's liturgy or whether they in fact derive from already fixed ceremonials. Writing twenty years later, M. Cramer (*Totenklage*, 41–47) offered an explanation opposite that of Leclercq.

25. Leclercq, "Egypte," cols. 2495–98. In cols. 2495–96, he reproduced from Aswan an important stele of the presbyter Marianos, dated to 1157 C.E. Lines 19 and 20 of this document may carry an allusion to John 11:25 when, addressing God, the text's author says, "For Thou art [the] resurrection and the repose."

Egyptian inscriptions and the New Testament. The first I shall mention consists of an inscription written in black letters on the wall of the chapel—referred to as number 1—in a Coptic church built at the bottom of the mountain of Assiut. It was first published by Clédat in 1908 and republished by Lefebvre the following year.[26] The inscription reads as follows, in eleven lines:

> Luke was in fact a physician;
> He was a disciple of the apostles.
> Afterward he followed Paul.
> He lived eighty-four years.
> He wrote this gospel
> While living in Achaia: 28.
> Afterward he wrote the Acts: 24.
> The Gospel According to Matthew: 27;
> This is the first among the Gospels;
> It was written in Judaea.
> As for the Gospel of Mark itself, it was written in Italy.

A quick review of this inscription lets us know that we are dealing with a series of statements from tradition. So far, no one has been able to explain satisfactorily the presence of the numbers 28 after notice of the Gospel of Luke, 24 after Acts, and 27 after the Gospel of Matthew. But there is one striking detail that leads one to conclude that, although the writing of this text on the chapel's wall was likely done sometime during the sixth century or at the beginning of the seventh, the author depended on a source that reached back at least to the third century.

The proof of this comes from other sources that parallel almost exactly our chapel's inscription. By the early fourth century, as a matter of fact, Eusebius had drawn upon some such source for information specifically about Luke (*Ecclesiastical History* III.4.6). Further, one of the ten known manuscripts of the *Argumentum Evangelii secundum Lucam* records Luke's age at eighty-four. The other nine read either seventy-three or seventy-four. Interestingly, this single manuscript also claims that the Gospel was written in Achaia—as does our inscription—not elsewhere, as the other manuscripts affirm. Consequently, one can conclude that Eusebius must have drawn upon a source no older than the third century and followed a tradition about Luke of which one version is preserved both in a single manuscript of the *Argumentum* and in the inscription at Assiut.

26. J. Clédat, "Notes d'archéologie copte," *ASAE* 9 (1908) 216–23; G. Lefebvre, "Egypte chrétienne II," *ASAE* 10 (1909) 50–55; rediscussion by Leclercq, "Egypte," cols. 2498–2500.

A second interesting connection to the New Testament occurs on the walls of a chapel near the ancient site of Antinoe or Antinoopolis.[27] At the base of the cliff, one meets the remains of a chapel built inside a large rock quarry. On the inner walls of this small chapel appear two lines of text that run around the entire circumference of the room. Beginning on the south wall and circling clockwise we find the opening verses of each of four Gospels, starting with Luke 1:1–4. The first five verses of John were written next, beginning on the west wall. Part way along the north wall we find the first three verses of Matthew's Gospel. Likewise, on the east wall, one can read parts of the first two verses of Mark. Interspersed with these passages from the Gospels are the opening lines from Psalms 118, 127, 31, 40, and 111, each of which in its Greek version begins with the word *makarios*, "blessed." What is striking about this collection of texts is not only that they uniformly reproduce the opening lines of books in the biblical text but also that they go back to a manuscript prototype, or copy, of the Codex Alexandrinus. Almost uniformly, their readings agree with this text, with some incidental conformity to Codex Vaticanus. Thus, even though the chapel itself was likely built in the eighth century C.E., it is clear that the scribe who copied the text had access to a very early manuscript that bore links to Codex Alexandrinus.

In other epigraphic citations one will find phraseology borrowed from or reminiscent of the epistles of Paul, though infrequently.[28] What was more often repeated was language reminiscent of the major councils of the church, beginning with that at Nicea.[29] One finds such formulas as far south as Nubia and the island of Philae, whether on stone monuments or on manufactured articles such as lamps and panels carved from wood. One reads, for example, the Trisagion chant by the angels on the wall of a chapel at El Bagawât:[30]

Holy, holy, holy is the Lord of Sabaoth;
the heaven and the earth are full of his glory.

---

27. G. Lefebvre, "Egypte chrétienne III," *ASAE* 10 (1909) 260–69; repeated by Leclercq, "Egypte," cols. 2501–4. On the site's names, see W. B. Donne, "Antinoopolis, Antinoe," in *DGRG* (1873) 1:141.

28. Noted by Leclercq, "Egypte," cols. 2504–5.

29. Ibid., cols. 2505–6, where the findings of Lefebvre are summarized (*Recueil des inscriptions grecques-chrétiennes d'Egypte*).

30. Published by Lefebvre, *Recueil des inscriptions grecques-chrétiennes d'Egypte*, no. 777; and idem, "Egypte chrétienne I," *ASAE* 9 (1908) 180–81; then discussed by Gabriel Millet, "Note sur une inscription liturgique d'Egypte," *ASAE* 10 (1910) 24–25; cited by Leclercq, "Egypte," col. 2506.

This form of the recitation is attested as early as the Apostolic Constitutions (fourth century).[31] Interestingly, a variant version was found on a wooden seal at Deir el-Azam, near Assiut, which exhibits apparent influence from the Council of Chalcedon (451 C.E.).[32]

Among the most unusual pieces is an inscription on a stele from Sheikh Abadeh, the ancient necropolis of Antinoe. Discovered in 1910 and now on deposit at the Greco-Roman museum in Alexandria, this inscription offers an entirely unique note in Egyptian epigraphy when it mentions "the chorus of the angels."[33]

> The blessed Basileius has lain down, having been a trader in niter, on the twenty-sixth of (the month) Tybi, fifth indiction. May God cause his soul to rest among the chorus of the angels. Amen.

While this monument cannot be dated with precision, there is reason to believe that it was roughly contemporary with the Islamic invasion, the period when the Christian liturgy in its essential parts had already been fixed.[34] Leclercq has suggested that the phrase "chorus of the angels" may have been "inspired by a prayer of the church."[35] While that may be true, we must also recall that we have observed the influence of Scripture in such texts. One cannot forget references to heavenly choral anthems in such passages as Job 38:7, Isa. 6:3, and Luke 2:13–14. But, one must admit with Leclercq that "the word *choros* is employed equally to designate the assembly of the saints and that of the martyrs."[36] Whether one is meant to the exclusion of the other remains unknown.

Although more rarely in Greek inscriptions than in Coptic, one does encounter liturgical interests in litanies. As an example, one can turn to the same Coptic chapel at the mountain of Assiut that preserves the traditional materials about Luke and the other Gospel writers. On the partitioning wall to the right of the apse, and continuing on the pillars, there was written a litany of military martyrs. This text, after addressing the Father, Son, and Holy Spirit and listing the names of the martyrs, appealed to "our father Adam, our mother Zoe, our mother

---

31. Noted by Leclercq, "Egypte"; see his summarizing article "Constitutions apostoliques," in *DACL* 3/3:cols. 2732–48. See Eng. trans. in *The Ante-Nicene Fathers* (ed. A. Cleveland Coxe; trans. J. Donaldson; Grand Rapids: Wm. B. Eerdmans, 1979) 7:387–505.
32. Leclercq, "Egypte," col. 2506.
33. Lefebvre, "Egypte chrétienne III," 280–82; Leclercq, "Egypte," col. 2507.
34. So Leclercq argued (ibid., col. 2507).
35. Ibid.
36. Ibid.

Mary."[37] Mention of the virgin Mary in this spot illustrates that in this Coptic litany Mary did not occupy the first place after God. In fact, the cult of the Virgin seems not to have enjoyed great favor in Egypt.[38] Leclercq noted that we possess only three inscriptions that invoked the Mother of God. The following exemplar came from fourth- or fifth-century Nubia:

> Oh, our Lord and Mother of God (theotokos),
> give rest to the soul of the blessed Marinus,
> presbyter and nomikos.[39]

Occasionally liturgical reminiscences appeared in prayers.[40] An important example is a long inscription for a certain Zoneêne inscribed in 409 C.E. on a slab of limestone. The writing apparently disappeared after the inscription was published, although it was studied many times until seventy-five years ago.[41] On it appeared specific instructions to visitors to remember in prayer this Zoneêne and his exemplary life of piety.[42] In other instances, the invitation that a visitor offer a prayer was more formal: ". . . that the reader pray (for my soul/for me)."[43] In a final example noted by Leclercq, one observes that an inscription from El Bagawât mentioned God the Word, then the Holy Trinity, and finally alluded to the Lord's Prayer—if Lefebvre's restoration of nine letters is correct. This latter element varied from the version in Matthew's Gospel: "But deliver us from evil," reading kakou for Matthew's ponerou.[44]

37. Lefebvre, "Egypte chrétienne II," 56–58; compare the invocations addressed to St. Colluthus and to St. Thecla, in G. Lefebvre, "Egypte chrétienne I," ASAE 9 (1908) 175–77, nos. 811 and 812; cited in Leclercq, "Egypte," col. 2508.

38. "The holy Mary," appearing after "the holy Michael," is listed on a funerary inscription of unknown provenience published by Samuel Birch in "Varia," ZÄS 10 (1872) 121. Leclercq, "Egypte," col. 2508, could cite only three instances in which the Mother of God was noted in inscriptions. See further the chap. in J. N. D. Kelly, Early Christian Doctrines (London: Adam and Charles Black, 1977) 490–99.

39. Leclercq, "Egypte," cols. 2508–9.

40. Some prayers, as Leclercq has pointed out (ibid., col. 2509), may belong in the category of acclamations. See below.

41. Bibliography is cited by Leclercq (ibid., col. 2509 n. 2).

42. The Greek text is reproduced twice by Leclercq, first in his article "Alexandrie, Archéologie," in DACL 1/2:cols. 1152–53, and then in "Egypte," col. 2509. The inscription was found in an eastern necropolis of Alexandria in 1871. Zoneêne's death was 19 March 409 C.E. (23rd of the Coptic month Phamenoth).

43. Leclercq, "Egypte," cols. 2509–10. He also mentioned an inscription now held in the British Museum which reflected a widespread wish that God grant to the deceased a place of light and refreshment (col. 2510).

44. Published by Lefebvre, "Egypte chrétienne I," 182–83, no. 357. Lefebvre made corrections here of de Bock's earlier publication of this text; later cited by Leclercq, "Egypte," col. 2511.

With Leclercq we should also refer to a long inscription of eighteen lines first copied in 1906 from a wall at Deir Anba Shenoute. Dated perhaps to the twelfth century, the Greek prayers collected therein showed clear links to the Greek morning liturgy. The first seven lines were composed clearly by the aid of the Gloria in Excelsis, in its Greek form anterior to the Latin formulation. The last eleven lines of this prayer were drawn from diverse doxological hymns and exhibited ties to the Byzantine *horologion*.[45]

ACCLAMATIONS

Although acclamations were employed very frequently in inscriptions, especially in funerary texts, there was little variety. Leclercq brought together seventy-one acclamations that were to be addressed to the deceased, noting only four directed to the living. Of those addressed to the living, we might quickly mention the following exhortations:

Let the one who reads pray.
All those who read these written (words), let him pray for me.[46]

Among those written for the deceased, the following examples will serve to give a flavor of this type of inscription, which almost always employed an imperative verb form, expressed or implied:

Christ, give rest to the soul.
Lord, give rest to the soul.
Oh God of the soul's repose.
Take rest in the Lord God.
Have mercy upon the soul.
Lie down in the Lord.
Lie down in the name of the Lord.
Remember, O God, the one lying (here).
Remember (me), O Lord, when you come into your kingdom.
God alone is in heaven.
God is one.
God the Helper is one.

---

45. First published by Lefebvre, *Recueil des inscriptions grecques-chrétiennes d'Egypte*, 45, no. 237. It was later reproduced in his article "Deir-el-Abiad," in *DACL* 4/1:col. 485–86, fig. 3658, and then by Leclercq, "Egypte," cols. 2511–12, with discussion.
46. Leclercq, "Egypte," col. 2514.

Jesus Christ is victorious.
Jesus is God who conquers wickedness.[47]

Such acclamations, particularly spoken on behalf of the dead, illustrate an undergirding concept that words uttered vicariously for deceased ones were understood to be efficacious with God.

FORMS OF TITLES

Leclercq listed seven titular formulas employed in Egyptian inscriptions, some of which were also known from Attica and Asia Minor. Of the Egyptian exemplars, some exhibited clear regional affinities. For instance, the phrase "stele of (so and so) . . ." was used principally at Akhmim and, as he noted, "this formula seems special to the Christian epigraphy of Egypt."[48] A term found almost exclusively in Nubia was a verb which translates "he/she has completed. . . ." Another Nubian phrase is one that translates "he/she has been useful until the end of life."[49] Like moderns, Egypt's ancient Christians employed the phrase "in memoriam" as a title of a funerary text.[50]

EPITHETS FOR THE DECEASED

In discussing such, it is important to note only that the most widely employed epithet for the dead was "the blessed," *ho makarios*. Notably, it was used less frequently in places such as Nubia, Akhmim, Antinoe, and Thebes. It has been suggested that it may mean little more than if one were saying, "the late Mr. So-and-So." Other inscriptions have preserved such terms as "thrice-blessed" and "more blessed." In addition, one occasionally meets the epithet "the holy one" or "the servant of God" or "the brother," this last term appearing especially when the deceased enjoyed monastic affiliation.[51]

---

47. Ibid., cols. 2512–14; Leclercq's exemplars were collectively published earlier by Lefebvre, *Recueil des inscriptions grecques-chrétienne d'Egypte*.

48. Leclercq, "Egypte," col. 2514.

49. Ibid.

50. Ibid. This phrase—appearing in slightly variant forms—is known from a dozen examples and is not characteristic of any particular region.

51. Lefebvre, *Recueil*, published a large number; summarized by Leclercq, "Egypte," col. 2514.

SYMBOLS

ΑΩ : Our attention has been drawn to the fact that in Egypt the twin symbols of alpha and omega appear on about fifty inscriptions that date variously from the fourth century to the twelfth. Naturally, there were a number of ways that inscribers shaped the alpha and at least two ways in which the omega was written. What catches one's eye are three monuments on which these two letters were inverted, seemingly indicating, in Leclercq's opinion, a very ancient origin for these three pieces, perhaps reaching back to a period prior to the peace of the church.[52] The difficulty with such a conclusion, however, is that it cannot be positively demonstrated.[53]

Lefebvre noted the ornamental use of these two letters, principally on steles, in order to form different patterns. Occasionally they were placed together on either the right side or the left side of the monument. There are examples in which the alpha appeared on the left and the omega on the right of the decorated piece. In other instances, one letter appeared at the top and the other at the bottom of the stele. One configuration common to Egypt alone had alpha followed by the hieroglyphic ankh sign followed by omega, reading from left to right.[54]

ϥθ : The Coptic fai used with the Greek theta formed a sign that was employed even outside Egypt, particularly in Palestine and Syria. As a matter of fact, it constituted a numerical cryptogram for the word "amen" since the numerical value of the Greek spelling of the word as well as of this sign was ninety-nine. Consequently, one frequently found at the end of a funerary inscription a single "amen" followed by one or two abbreviations made up of fai and theta. Occasionally the "amen" was simply lacking and the fai-theta combination appeared in its place.[55]

---

52. Leclercq (ibid.) offered no reason why one should understand the inverted version to be earlier than the other.

53. Recent discussion on the alpha/omega symbol illustrates that the simple inversion of these two letters does not necessarily point to an early date; see G. H. R. Horsley, *New Documents Illustrating Early Christianity* (North Ryde, Australia: Macquarie Univ. Press, 1981–82) 1:66–67, no. 22; and 98–99, no. 59.

54. Lefebvre, *Recueil*, xxii–xxiii; quoted in Leclercq, "Egypte," cols. 2514–15. Horsley (*New Documents* 1:138–39, no. 88) noted on a fourth- or fifth-century epitaph the letters alpha and omega separated by a monogram of Christ (here the Greek letter rho which has been crossed by a single line drawn across its stem).

55. See bibliography and discussion in Leclercq, "Egypte," col. 2515. An example is recorded by Crum, *Coptic Monuments*, no. 8319. This combination may in fact have been inspired by the use of the obsolete Greek letter koppa with theta, a known combination, which also produced the sum 99; see Horsley, *New Documents* 2:179, no. 104.

xmᴦ : Interestingly, the three-letter symbol formed by the Greek letters chi, mu, and gamma has received much attention. These three letters have been variously construed as "Christ, Michael, Gabriel," or "Christ, Mary, Gabriel." The Greek phrase that translates "written by my hand" has also been suggested. It was B. P. Grenfell who suggested an attractive solution and Lefebvre who adduced substantial supporting evidence. On the basis of an inscription from the neighborhood of Aswan and a fragment of papyrus preserved in the Bodleian Library, they concluded that the symbol—in its Egyptian Christian manifestation—means "Mary gave birth to Christ."[56] Moreover, even if examples of this formula were to be found predating the Christian era, and one were obliged to conclude that it had a pagan, not Christian, origin, the view of Grenfell and Lefebvre would not be thereby affected.[57]

⳨ : The monogram for Christ, according to Leclercq's summary, exhibited five basic forms in Egyptian inscriptions. One of the most distinctive forms of the monogram, of course, was formed by the hieroglyphic sign ankh, which signified life and appeared at least twenty times in known inscriptions. The other forms were used rather abundantly, in some instances appearing at least fifty times. One version of this sign, which featured a rho with a single line crossing at right angles, was also written innumerable times on ostraca and papyri. Apparently, the earliest form of the monogram comprises a rho with a long tail, over which was superimposed the crossing lines of the Greek chi. This shape seems to have been used as early as the fourth century and is represented in eleven known examples.

TITLES AND PROFESSIONS

While inscriptions from Egypt do not bring to our attention unusual titles or professions of persons, we can observe a great variety preserved thereby. Concerning military officials, four texts mention that the dead men had held the office of tribune—all from Armant—and one the rank of centurion at Esna. In addition, one decurion, one legionnaire, and two soldiers had their professions inscribed on funerary steles. Among other types of occupations one finds mention of a potter, a gardener, a butcher, and a woodworker. Other professions

---

56. Leclercq, "Egypte," cols. 2415–16. An instance of this symbol can be seen in Crum, *Coptic Monuments*, no. 8414 and pl. 2.

57. The most recent summary of the difficulties associated with this symbol is that of Horsley, *New Documents* 2:177–80, no. 104.

included doctors, two architects, a sculptor, two scribes, and a public advocate. An inscription on white marble from Abukir even mentioned a muleteer.[58]

Perhaps more interesting and certainly more numerous are the hints furnished by inscriptions regarding the posts among the clergy, both within and without the monasteries. There are at least four known notations of anchorites or hermits who lived isolated existences. Interestingly, one inscription mentioned an Archimandrite who was a superior of a monastery. Many persons were known by the title "brother," but only two monks had ascribed to them the term "disciple." Several other common denominations were *monazôn* and *monachê*, as well as *monachos*.[59]

The titles Apa, Abba, Ama, and Amma did not bear the significance of an abbot or abbess of a monastery as they did in the West. Among inscriptions, only one archbishop has been mentioned, called in Greek *metropolitês*. Some ten bishops are also identified. Many priests or presbyters are known to us as well, in addition to one archdeacon, three archpriests, and two readers. We also know of deacons and *nomikoi* who had charge of a chapel. The majority of priests and deacons were married, something that has become clear from the inscriptions.[60]

SUMMARY

What can we conclude? It is evident from our review that the variety of inscriptions and the sheer amount of information available from them in Egypt are substantial. But much of what is contained, espe-

58. Leclercq mentioned most of these ("Egypte," cols. 2515–16). Examples can be found in Crum, *Coptic Monuments*: a tribune, no. 8469 (Crum mentioned no provenience for this Coptic-Greek stele); a potter, no. 8521 and pl. 21; a gardener or farmer, no. 8454 and pl. 10; a woodworker or carpenter, no. 8329; a scribe, no. 8521 and pl. 21; a public advocate (*ekdikos*), no. 8414 and pl. 2.

59. Leclercq ("Egypte," cols. 2517–18) produced the list. Again, see examples in Crum, *Coptic Monuments*: anchorites, nos. 8467 and 8514 as well as pls. 13 and 20; an Archimandrite, no. 8321; monazontes or (usually) celibate monks, nos. 8560 and 8672, reproduced on pls. 28 and 46; monachai or nuns, nos. 8341, 8353, 8417, the last pictured on pl. 3; monachoi or cenobitic monks, nos. 8413, 8441, 8449, the first on pl. 2 and the last on pl. 9.

60. Most were noted by Leclercq, "Egypte," cols. 2418–20. We note the following examples from Crum, *Coptic Monuments*: Apa, nos. 8442, 8492, and 8521, the latter two on pls. 16 and 21 respectively; Ama, no. 8589 and pl. 33; a bishop, no. 8322; priests, nos. 8335, 8347, 8364; an archdeacon, no. 8609 and pl. 36; archpriests, nos. 8321 and 8552, the latter reproduced on pl. 26; readers, nos. 8398 and 8416, the latter pictured on pl. 3; deacons, 8393, 8402, 8458, the last appearing on pl. 11.

cially on funerary steles, is of limited historical value, although inscriptions may prove to be of greater value for study of Coptic dialects than many have thought before now. There are features, of course, from Armant and Esna, that indicate that the art of sculpting funerary monuments reached a high peak of expression in late antiquity. In addition, there exist a few significant connections between Egyptian inscriptions and the textual tradition of the Bible. Further, we occasionally learn something more about an important personality or strategic locale from inscriptional evidence. But the importance of the inscriptions lies less with the historical than with the liturgical. For it is in this area that the greatest rewards will come from further study.

To be sure, the Christians were not isolated from their surroundings; in the early centuries they were influenced by the values of both their neighbors and Egyptian culture in general. Proofs of that show up in inscriptions. One piece of evidence consists of the pagan formula that appears in a variety of ways but always says basically, "Do not grieve, for no one is immortal in this world." One can note that this formula appeared widely in the Roman and Byzantine worlds. But what was once a distinctively pagan sentiment was in Egypt transformed by Christians from a totally materialistic consolation into an affirmation that the world that ultimately matters is found only when one passes through that change of environment called death. And, in the Christian view, it is only then that life, which appears to be mortal here, is shown to be immortal there.

Coptic Documentary Papyri as a Historical Source for Egyptian Christianity*

"To know what it was like to be human in Late Antiquity one must read papyri."[1] The Coptic documentary papyri give us a different and much fuller picture of Christianity as it was lived in time and space, from that presented by the historical, hagiographical, or homiletic texts. The process of extracting facts from these documents gives a result that is fresh and unmediated, meant for a restricted audience, and not bounded by the conveniences of a literary form or genre. Previous studies of these documents have been principally juristic or secular-historical in emphasis. The living details of these texts must now be considered by the researcher into the history of the Christianity of the See of St. Mark.

Collections of Coptic documents are fortunately numerous and have been published since late in the last century.[2] To these may be added several items both large and small. The present writer has published

*For research facilities, inspiration, support, encouragement, and love, I should like to thank, as always, Mirrit Boutros Ghali, President of the Society for Coptic Archaeology.

1. P. R. L. Brown, personal communication, April 1977.
2. It will be helpful to give here a historical, chronological outline of the extant publications:

1876	Revillout, *Apa Jeremias* and *Actes et contrats des musées égyptiens*. . . .
1893	Crum, *Coptic MSS. Brought from the Fayyum by W. M. Flinders Petrie*
1895	Krall, *CPR II, Koptische Texte*
1900–1914	Revillout, *Pesynthius*
1902	Crum, *Coptic Ostraca*
1902–4	Steindorff et al., *BKU* I-II
1905	Crum, *Catalogue of the Coptic MSS. in the British Museum*
	Hall, *Coptic and Greek Texts of the Christian Period*
1909	Crum, *Catalogue of the Coptic MSS. in the John Rylands Library*
1912	Crum/Steindorff, *Koptische Rechtsurkunden aus Djeme (Theben)*

individual items from the Freer, Walters, and Philadelphia collections; M. Green has worked on an eleventh-century family archive from near Ashmunein; G. M. Browne has published texts in Peoria. Editions are in progress or soon to appear: that of the Coptic portion of the eighth-century archive of Papas from Apollonos Ano, by this writer; of the Vatican Library Aphrodito Coptic documents, by L. Papini and this writer. An urgent desideratum is publication of the remaining documents in the Egyptian Museum and the Coptic Museum before any more are lost or destroyed. The Vienna collection still holds unpublished archives. Unknown collections remain. The International Association for Coptic Studies is sending questionnaires all over the world in search of unknown material, especially anything still in private hands. The results of this survey are eagerly awaited.

1913	Thompson, *Theban Ostraca*, part IV
1921	Crum, *Short Texts*
1922	Crum/Bell, *Wadi Sarga*
1926	Crum, *The Monastery of Epiphanius*
1927	Mallon, *Ostraca etmoulon*
1932	Schiller, *Coptic Legal Texts*
1937	Hopfner, *Papyrus Wessely Pragensis*
1938	Till, *Koptische Schutzbriefe*
1939	Crum, *Varia Coptica*
1941	Till, *Coptica der Wiener Papyrussammlung*
1942	Worrell, *Coptic Texts in the University of Michigan Collection*
1952	Stefanski/Lichtheim, *Coptic Ostraca from Medinet Habu*
1954	Kahle, *Bala'izah*
	Till, *Erbrechtliche Untersuchungen*
1956	Till, *Die koptischen Arbeitsverträge*
1958	Till, *CPR IV, Kopt. Rechtsurkunden Österr. Nationalbibliothek*
	Till, *Die koptischen Bürgschaftsurkunden*
1959	Schiller, *Coptic Papyri/Coptic Ostraca*
	Jernstedt, *Koptskije teksty . . . Ermitaga*
	Jernstedt, *Koptskije teksty . . . A. S. Pushkina*
1960	Till, *Kopt. Ostraka Österr. Nationalbibliothek*
1964	Till, *Kopt. Rechtsurkunden aus Theben übersetzt*
	Seider, *Universitäts-Papyrussammlung Heidelberg*
1966	Bartina, *Inventario de ostraca coptos . . . Barcelona*
	Williams, *The Giessen Coptic Texts*
1968	Satzinger, *BKU III*
	Schiller, *The Budge Papyrus*
1970	Uebel, *Die Jenaer Papyrussammlung*
1982	MacCoull, *Coptic Documentary Papyri in the Pierpont Morgan Library*
(in press)	MacCoull, *Coptic Documentary Papyri in the Beinecke Library, Yale University*
	MacCoull, *Coptic Documentary Papyri in the Alexandria Museum*

In addition, see A. Arthur Schiller, "A Checklist of Coptic Documents and Letters," *BASP* 13 (1976) 99–123. A second edition needs to be made. Note the statement on p. 103: "No recent description of the status of the Coptic collection [at Cairo] is known." This is unfortunately true; and six years' work by the author have yielded no results, owing to the near impossibility of obtaining permission to work with Coptic material.

It is to be regretted that the Coptic levels of most excavation sites in Egypt have been the first to be disregarded or even physically destroyed, without regard for the further documentation they might provide. As the late Sir Eric Turner wrote, "Naturally the strata reached first were those offering Arabic, Coptic, and Byzantine Greek papyri; collectors had little regard for products of so late a period, and many thousands, perhaps millions, of texts must have been destroyed" (*Greek Papyri: An Introduction* [Princeton: Princeton Univ. Press, 1968] 21). The whereabouts of so important a body of documents as the Coptic portion of the sixth-century Aphrodito archives remain largely unknown: the preface to *P. Cair. Masp.* III records boxes "ne contenant . . . que papyrus coptes." Since Maspero could not read Coptic, the boxes disappeared. The survival of this material is precarious indeed. We must use what we have to provide details of the Christian life of Egypt under the Byzantine and Umayyad empires in order to understand a society in which what one believed was the key to one's history and one's heart.

After the upheavals of the fourth century, the fifth marks a period of transition, still incompletely known,[3] from a Roman Egypt with its *strategoi*, its cities and their hinterland, to a different society, the world of the great estates,[4] the *pagi* with the *civitates*, the pageantry of patronage, and the growth at once of bureaucracy and of imperial grandeur.[5] Certainly by the reign of Anastasius we encounter in Byzantine Egypt a full-blown and flourishing Christian society. We can trace its evolution in documents ranging from private epistolography[6]

3. R. Remondon, "L'Egypte au 5e siècle de notre ère: les sources papyrologiques et leurs problèmes," in *Atti dell' XI congresso internazionale di papirologia, Milano 2–8 settembre 1965* (Milan: Istituto lombardo di scienze e lettere, 1966) 135–48. See also the statistical surveys by Roger S. Bagnall and Klaas A. Worp in *Bes* 1 (1979) 5–10, and *Miscellanea Papyrologica* (ed. Rosario Pintaudi; Florence: Gonnelli, 1980) 13–23. On the Christianization of Egyptian society, see Bagnall, "Religious Conversion and Onomastic Change in Early Byzantine Egypt," *BASP* 19 (1982) 105–24.

4. E. R. Hardy, *The Large Estates of Byzantine Egypt* (New York: Columbia Univ. Press, 1932); J. Gascou, *Les grands domaines, la cité et l'Etat en Egypte byzantine (5e, 6e et 7e s.); Travaux et mémoires* 9 (Paris, 1985) 1–90. One may disregard B. Bachrach, "Was There Feudalism in Byzantine Egypt?" *JARCE* 6 (1967) 163–66.

5. Germaine Rouillard, *L'administration civile de l'Egypte byzantine* (2d ed.; Paris: Geuthner, 1928) remains the standard guide to government. Much progress has been marked by the appearance of the work of Gascou (above, n. 4).

6. J. O'Callaghan (*Cartas cristianas griegas del siglo V* [Barcelona: Balmes, 1963]) gives an idea of forms in the transitional period, as does M. Naldini (*Il cristianesimo in Egitto. Lettere private nei papiri dei secoli II–IV* [Florence: Monnier, 1968]). We are now fortunate to have Anne Biedenkopf-Ziehner, *Untersuchungen zum koptischen Briefformular unter Berucksichtigung ägyptischer und griechischer Parallelen* (Würzburg: Zauzich, 1983), for epistolography (see also below, n. 22).

to the financial archives of that great family of two centuries and more, the Apions of Oxyrhynchus.[7] If "periods" are desirable constructs in this phase of the ancient world, Chalcedon (451) marks a convenient watershed, helping to locate and assess belief, identity, forms of legality, and even forms of landholding.[8] Our knowledge of the structure of daily life in post-Chalcedon Egypt derives largely from the bilingual world of the Greek and Coptic documentary papyri.[9]

Clearly the most prominent aspect of Christian life as we gather it from the Coptic documentary papyri is the whole cluster of matters dealing with the law of persons and of the family.[10] In Coptic legal documents we find in effect the bridge between theorizing decisions (or codifications) at the top and verbatim proceedings at the bottom. A document like the Budge papyrus[11] gives us both a legal analysis and a painfully suspenseful account of a family quarrel. (Coptic legal documents furnish us precious evidence for Coptic family structure and kinship terminology. Then as now, the national sport seemed to be

7. J. Gascou, "La famille des Apions," *Les grands domaines*, 61–75. A stemma of the Apion family is given in *Prosopography of the Later Roman Empire* II. Inquiries are being made into possible Apion material in the *Nachlass* of the late E. R. Hardy of Cambridge.
8. W. H. C. Frend, *The Rise of the Monophysite Movement* (Cambridge: Cambridge Univ. Press, 1972) 192–93, 274–76, surveying the rise of a parallel clergy; David D. Bundy, "Jacob Baradaeus: The State of Research, a Review of Sources, and a New Approach," *Muséon* 91 (1978) 45–86. Frend's paper in *SCH(L)* 18 (1982) 21–38 is unfortunately based on literary sources, not citing documentary papyri, and on an antiquated methodology. One must set out the documentary-evidential counterparts to the non-Chalcedonian texts treated in the present volume by David W. Johnson.
9. On the thoroughgoing bilingualism of this society see J. W. B. Barns and E. A. E. Reymond, *Four Martyrdoms From the Pierpont Morgan Coptic Codices* (Oxford: Clarendon Press, 1973) 18. Record-keeping was done in both languages, and often the survival of one or the other is a matter of accident (compare the testament of Bishop Abraham of Hermonthis [*P. Lond.* 1. 77]). This flexibility is even mirrored in the forms of handwriting studied by Coptic and Greek paleographers alike; Medea Norsa, "Analogie e coincidenze tra scritture greche e latine nei papiri," in *Miscellanea Giovanni Mercati* (Vatican: Biblioteca Vaticana, 1946) 6:110–14, is applicable to Coptic too. I have shown (*CEg* 56 [1981] 187) the identity of the Greek literary and Coptic documentary hand of Dioscorus of Aphrodito, in the sixth century. Coptic documents really come into their own in the century after the Arab conquest. Our valuable knowledge of life at Jeme (*KRU*) comes from documents thoroughly Coptic in content and character (see R. S. Bagnall and K. A. Worp, "Chronological Notes on Byzantine Documents, I," *BASP* 15 [1978] 244). An urgent desideratum in this field is the making of an album of dated Coptic documentary hands, as a dating tool. Bentley Layton's paleographical project is to include only literary hands.
10. Still the fundamental study from which all work begins is A. Steinwenter, *Das Recht der koptischen Urkunden* (HAW 10.4.2; Munich: Beck, 1955). To appear in the *Coptic Encyclopaedia* (Utah) is my short article, "Coptic Law."
11. A. A. Schiller, "The Budge Papyrus of Columbia University," *JARCE* 7 (1968) 79–118.

suing one's relatives.) Quotations from Schiller's translation should illustrate the atmosphere of this document.

Seek, then, for two men of our city and relate that which you ought to relate so that I may find them for their testimony and discover how to sue them. She waited, then, for some men worthy of being trusted; she related all of her affair to them. By reason of this, I am suing them regarding the house and that which is in it and rentals which they received since the day upon which I served the complaint upon them. (18–20) . . . And he came into the midst of the Great Men knowing full well that these scraps of written evidence—these which had neither beginning nor end—were not worth that a peasant of my sort introduce them, or that they be given to you as legal justification. And that the plea was of no use for any man to relate, particularly he, the deacon Iohannes, if he thinks that as I am a peasant and he is an urbanite and is a deacon, that any word is good enough to relate against me or to do to me. . . . But at all events he ought to know that, whenever the Lord places into your heart and you have heard our case, before God, these forgeries are not worthy of being brought before your illustrious lordships. . . . And even if I am a peasant and I do not know the matter, at all events I hear from those who know that a deed without signature upon it or witness or *completio* of a scribe is of no value to the man who brings it to court that it be there pleaded upon. (78–87) . . . since we know that the fear of God resides within you, and that you are not partial to (any) man, and that you observe justice unto us, so that the Lord, Jesus Christ, may preserve you and your children for a long peaceful time . . . (110–111). But I relied upon that which the Saviour relates in His mouth of truth through the law-giver Moses: through the mouth of two or three witnesses every word is established. (116–118) . . . We are astounded at Iohannes, the deacon, this one who says: they have entrusted me with the blood of Christ. Even more, Tsoker, this one who says: I go into the church of God, I pray and I hear the Holy Scriptures of the breath of God. (232–234)

Scripture is quoted at every turn; the stories of Judas Iscariot and of Daniel and Susanna are held up as examples; the tone is that familiar to speakers of English who were formed on the Authorized Version of the Bible and the Book of Common Prayer. Indeed all Coptic legal activity was strongly colored with Biblical language—and Justinianic phraseology as well.[12]

A Coptic document—a will, sale, lease, or text of similar type—followed a schema, all the elements of which can be seen to incorporate explicitly Christian wording. This schema includes the date, invocation, *intitulatio* ("I, X, from place Y . . ."), greeting, *soma* or body

12. Schiller's skeptical views in "The Courts Are No More," in *Studi in onore di Edoardo Volterra* (Milan: Giuffrè, 1969) 469–502, are to be taken with a grain of salt.

of the text, free will clause, oath, penalty clause, stipulation, *hypographe/stoichei*, subscriptions of the witnesses, *completio* by the notary. Each of these elements, when present, commonly includes Christian formulations and epithets, especially the oath and, of course, the invocation.[13] Thus the character of Egyptian society may be read in the wording of its sales, donations, labor contracts, leases, sureties, and especially wills and arbitrations.[14]

In post-Chalcedon Egypt the ascetic movement was an institution, an unshakable one that permeated every area of life. Document after document comes from a monastic milieu or witnesses to the activities of monks and clerics in every sort of endeavor.[15] Again from the jurist's point of view the brilliant studies of A. Steinwenter[16] on ecclesiastical property and the legal nature of ecclesiastical bodies have not been surpassed. The documents from the monasteries of, for example, Epiphanius, Phoebammon,[17] and Deir al Dik[18] show us how a community was run.[19] The multifarious life reflected in *Koptische Rechts-urkunden* and *Coptic Ostraca* also displays a constant interaction

---

13. R. S. Bagnall and K. A. Worp, "Christian Invocations in the Papyri," *CEg* 56 (1981) 112–33, 362–65.

14. Schiller's "Preface" in W. E. Crum and Georg Steindorff, *Koptische Rechtsurkunden des VIII. Jahrhunderts aus Djeme (Theben)* (rev. ed.; Leipzig: Zentralantiquariat den DDR, 1971).

15. Just one set of examples drawn from the papyri is set out in the excellent study of Ewa Wipszycka, *Les ressources et les activités économiques des églises en Egypte* (PapyBrux 10; Brussels: Fondation égyptologique reine Elisabeth, 1972). This deals only with churches; a parallel study needs to be done on the economic activities of monasteries.

16. A. Steinwenter, "Aus dem kirchlichen Vermögensrechte der Papyri," *ZSRG* 75 (1958) 1–34; idem, "Die Rechtsstellung der Kirchen und Klöster," *ZSRG* 50 (1930) 1–50; idem, "Byzantinische Mönchstestamente," *Aeg* 12 (1932) 55–64. To his study of child oblates ("Kinderschenkungen an koptische Klöster," *ZSRG.K* 42 [1921] 175–207) add my "Child Donations and Child Saints in Coptic Egypt," *EEQ* 13 (1979) 409–15; James E. Goehring, "Children of God: The Social Dislocation of Children in Early Egyptian Monasticism," paper presented at Pacific Coast Society of Biblical Literature, Fullerton, Calif., April 1983.

17. A. A. Schiller, "Checklist," 120–21; L. S. B. MacCoull and L. Koenen, "Papyrus Fragments from the Monastery of Phoebammon," in *Proceeding of the XVI International Congress of Papyrology* (Chico, Calif.: Scholars Press, 1981) 491–98.

18. Maurice Martin, *La laure de Deir al Dik à Antinoé* (Cairo: Institut français d'archéologie orientale du Caire, 1971). It is to be hoped that Père Martin will persist in his project of compiling a list of all monastic sites in Egypt, before any more destruction takes place.

19. Forms of dedicated life ran the gamut from that of the hermits of the desert of Esneh (Serge Sauneron et al., *Les ermitages chrétiens du desert d'Esna* [FIFAO 29; Cairo: Institut français d'archéologie orientale du Caire, 1972]) to that of the professional nurse-monks of the pilgrimage city of St. Menas (H. Wilsdorf, "Bemerkungen zu den mineralogischen Pharmazeutika der Kopten," in *Studia Coptica* [ed. Peter Nagel; BBA 45; Berlin: Akademie-Verlag, 1974] 79).

between monks and laity. Wadi Sarga gives us trade, and Bala'izah gives us economic involvement plus liturgical prayer. Requests for ordination are valuable evidence for the process by which society generated religious vocations.[20]

Above all, it is in Coptic private letters, probably the most numerous type of document, that we see the interplay between *politeia* and individual faith, the perennial divisiveness between peasant and landlord, countryside and city, beneficent manifestations of ascetic feeling and suspect irruptions of the demonic.[21] The development of terminology of address and farewell, the elaboration of language that parallels the elaboration of bureaucratic function in a world of high visibility,[22] lets us penetrate deeply into the operations of the network of social life at all levels. And since the introduction of the formal *invocatio* into the official formulary under Maurice,[23] we see public documents interwoven with the sort of openly pious phraseology that had become familiar from letter-writing. This state of affairs persisted in later, hostile circumstances. The eighth-century village scribe had learned his *en onomati* long before his *b'ism'illah*.

A few more quotations from the sources will be illustrative.

- *KRU* 13, sale of parts of two houses in Jeme, 30 November 733 C.E.

  In the name of the holy lifegiving Trinity, Father, Son, and Holy Ghost. Written on 4 Choiak, 2d indiction, under our lord Argama son of Ered, the most notable pagarch of the city of Hermonthis, in Kastron Memnonion Jeme, Chael son of Psme being dioicetes. I, Kyriakos son of Demetrios, the most God-beloved priest, *hegoumenos* and superior of the monastery of the gloriously victorious crown-bearing champion holy Apa Phoibammon of the mountain of Jeme, nome of the city of Hermonthis, give hereunder a subscription by a proxy signatory, that he signed for me, and trustworthy witnesses, that they have borne witness to this document of sale, in writing, not to be transgressed and

---

20. A. Steinwenter, "Die Ordinationsbitte koptischer Kleriker," *Aeg* 11 (1931) 29–34.

21. Coptic magic is of course a field all its own. Our fundamental collection and exposition is Angelicus Kropp, O.P., *Ausgewählte koptische Zaubertexte* (Brussels: Foundation égyptologique reine Elisabeth, 1930–1931); the number of texts published increases yearly (see under this heading in the *Enchoria* and *Orientalia* annual bibliographies).

22. Before the work of Biedenkopf-Ziehner (above, n. 6), there had been some attempt at classification of formulas in Jakob Krall, "Koptische Briefe," *MSPER* 5 (1889) 21–58. Work needs to be done along the lines pioneered by H. Zilliacus for Greek (e.g., his *Untersuchungen zu den abstrakten Anredeformen und Höflichkeitstiteln im Griechischen* [Helsinki: Societas Scientiarum Fennica, 1949]). We need a Coptic equivalent to O. Hornickel, *Ehren- und Rangprädikate in den Papyrusurkunden* (Giessen: Borna; Leipzig: R. Noske, 1930).

23. See above, n. 13; and cf. Bagnall and Worp in *BASP* 15 (1978) 240–44.

not to be legally overturned; and indeed it has been the more strengthened by my petitioning and my express wish. . . . These are the portions that the sons of the late Peshate son of Pestinos had given to the holy Apa Phoibammon of the mountain of Jeme as an offering for his poor soul; so that I may not be condemned at the judgment seat of our Lord Jesus Christ, and so that the holy martyr may not be angry with me, that I have well or ill used his *prosphora*, namely an offering on behalf of a soul. . . . If anyone should dare, be it now or at any time, to go to law against you, it shall not avail him anything, but above all he shall be a stranger to the holy oath of the Christians, which is observed, and the fate of Ananias and Sapphira shall befall him. . . . I have heard it (this document), I have written it in the Egyptian language, and I have given it from my hand.

- *KRU* 107, deed of donation of a piece of land, Jeme, 767–68 C.E.

  We are writing to the monastery of the holy Apa Phoibammon on the mountain of Kastron Jeme, represented by you, the most devout priest Apa Kyriakos, the *oikonomos* of the holy *topos*. Greeting. . . . We donate to you, Apa Phoibammon, one *nōh* of land, boundaries XYZ. . . . You shall be its possessor, you shall put it to use in the monastery for the holy lamp. . . . Whoever shall dare to go to law against the holy monastery before a lay or ecclesiastical tribunal, in court or out of court, or to bring a complaint against you before a high and honorable official, before all else it shall avail him nothing, but he shall be a stranger to the holy oath of the Christians by the Father, the Son, and the Holy Ghost. Then shall he see the kingdom of God open and not be able to enter in. . . .

- *KRU* 67, the testament of the monk Paham.

  I, Paham, have written this will with my own hand, while I am dwelling on the mountain of Jeme and am a monk. I have observed that a person does not know his own way [i.e., future], and I thought, lest an illness overtake me and I die suddenly, with no one at hand, that I ought to specify my wishes about the few small possessions that I have from my father and mother and from their home. I had three children. I went and became a monk. I left them, still alive. All three continued living in the world. The eldest son, Papnute, married against my wishes. I was very sad about this. His life never ran smoothly since he married her. When they began to have quarrels and upsets, they came south to me and told me the reason: her virginity had not been intact [at marriage]. I said that I wanted to have nothing to do with him, since he had not obeyed me. I put the matter in the hands of God, the just Judge, and the prayers of my holy father [i.e., the superior]. After he left, flattery blinded his mind. She stayed with him and he raised children with her, although he was troubled about it. He often used to come and tell me his troubles. He saddened me yet more, but I didn't want yet to turn him away completely; after all, he was my own flesh and blood *(splanchnon)*. I gave him a little place of his own, so he could stay in my house, together with his household goods, money, clothes, etc. But just after I had given him this, things turned out differently. For God took him home, like all people: he and his children died. He left no living heirs or successors. Now, as God had made him and his children strangers to this world, so I made [him and] his widow a stranger to my whole dwelling that had come to me from my parents. From the inherited property that I still have, no one representing him [or her] is to get anything. . . . And his widow is to swear an oath as to what property she had brought to the marriage, and is to take it back, fair shares. You, Jacob [the second son], are to treat her like the childless widows that live near you in your village, and let her go home decently, back to the village she came from. . . . (ET: MacCoull)

And finally, the case of the bishop and the chicken thieves (P. Ryl. 267; ET: Crum):

[T]he matter hath reached us, that they have entered the house of the mother of Sawep and have taken an artaba of corn and 6 quarts of flax and 2 chickens and a cock; now whether it be man or woman or stranger or native that hath taken them and doth not make them known, he shall be under the curse of the law and the prophets. And by the mouth of my humility He shall be wroth with them, even as He was wroth with Sodom and Gomorrah, and He shall bring upon them the curses of the Apocalypse and the plagues of the book of Job and the curses of the 108th Psalm. And these curses shall be as it were oil in their bones. "They have loved cursing: it shall be theirs. They desired not blessing: it shall depart far from them." I mean any one that shall have taken the corn and the flax and the chickens. . . . (from the bishop of Ashmunein)

It is hoped that the publication of still more collections of Coptic documents will call further scholarly attention to this rich fund of source material. Alongside the lives of saints and the homiletic literature, which are beginning to be recognized for their own worth and not just as hunting grounds for whatever "origins" or "survivals" they might contain, Coptic documentary papyri furnish our most direct approach to the creativity and originality of life in Egypt during a period when "Christian society" was neither a contradiction nor a dream but a living reality.

Coptic Literature

INTRODUCTION

A convenient handbook on Coptic literature does not exist. Among the sketches or preliminary essays for such a work,[1] four can be singled out as the most important. Two of these are sections of a book, and two are encyclopedia articles.

J. Leipoldt[2] has attempted to present a real history, setting the most important phenomena within Coptic literature in chronological succession. Much of his work is still valid. Many new documents have come to light since his work, however—e.g., the important manuscript discoveries at Edfu, Hamuli, Medinet Madi, and Nag Hammadi, and the Bodmer find. As a result, the outline of his work requires revision.

The present author,[3] still at the beginning of his work at the time of

---

1. Among other minor contributions, the following should be mentioned: Alla I. Elanskaja, "Koptskaja literature," in *Folklor i literatura narodow Afriki. Sbornik statej* (ed. D. A. Ol'derogge; Moscow: Akademiia nauk SSSR. Institut Afriki, 1970) 18–27; Antoine Guillaumont, "Copte (littérature spirituelle)," in *DSp* 1:2266–78; Henry Hyvernat, "Coptic Literature," in *CathEnc* 5:350–63, 16:27–31; Louis Theophile Lefort, "La littérature égyptienne aux derniers siècles avant l'invasion arabe," *CEg* 6 (1931) 315–23; Siegfried Morenz, "Die koptische Literatur," in *HO* I.1.2:239–50 (2d ed.), 207–19 (1st ed.); Martiniano P. Roncaglia, "La littérature copte et sa diffusion en Orient et en Occident (essai)," in *La signification du Bas Moyen Age dans l'histoire et la culture du monde musulman: actes du 8 congrès de l'union européenne des arabisants et islamisants (Aix-en-Provence, du 9 au 14 septembre 1976)* (Aix-en-Provence: Edisud, 1978) 219–42; Tito Orlandi, "Introduzione," in *Omelie copte* (CP; Torino: SEI, 1981); idem, "The Future of Studies in Coptic Biblical and Ecclesiastical Literature," in *The Future of Coptic Studies* (ed. R. McL. Wilson; CS 1; Leiden: E. J. Brill, 1978) 1–22.

2. Johannes Leipoldt, "Geschichte der koptischen Literatur," in *Geschichte der christlichen Literatur des Orients* (ed. C. Brockelmann et al.; 2d ed.; Leipzig: Amelangs, 1972) 131–82.

3. T. Orlandi, *Elementi di lingua e letteratura copta* (Milan: La Goliardica, 1970).

his contribution to the subject, chose as parameters for his work the authors and titles given in the manuscripts themselves and ordered the material chronologically according to those parameters. Therefore, while the documentation assembled is useful, it is limited by the fact that critical historical assessments remained to be done.[4]

O'Leary[5] and Krause,[6] in their articles, give useful lists of Coptic literary texts. Because of the nature of their articles, however, neither takes up the difficult chronological and historical problems in the texts. It is to be noted that Krause's article is the more current both in terms of documentation and interpretation.

In view of the current state of Coptic studies, one may question whether it is possible to present a true history of Coptic literature. It is clear that much material is still unknown and that much of what is known has not yet been properly evaluated. Many general problems must be solved before a critical history can be written.

Nonetheless, the present author has gathered some ideas about the development of Coptic literature that can serve as a basis for discussion. In what follows I shall describe the history of Coptic literature as I see it, calling the attention of my colleagues to the fact that the opinions set forth here must be taken cautiously, as a suggestion of problems rather than as a definitive statement.

THE BEGINNINGS

The "Old Coptic" Magical Texts

The initial stage of Coptic literature should tentatively be put in the period from the first century B.C.E. to the third century C.E. It is in this period that one finds the first extensive "experiments" in rendering the late Egyptian language in Greek transcription, followed by the first examples of literary Coptic texts.

The available documentation from this period begins with the so-called Old Coptic texts. This group of texts is often referred to as a unit, chiefly because, unlike the vast majority of Coptic texts, they do not

---

4. The present contribution should provide those assessments. In the notes I shall mention only the essential bibliography, while the reader is referred to the *Elementi* and to Krause ("Koptische Literatur," in *LÄ* 3:694–728) for more detail, esp. concerning the editions and translations of Coptic texts. Cf. also my *Coptic Bibliography* (CMCL; 3d ed.; Rome: CIM, 1984 [microfiche]).

5. Evans De Lacy O'Leary, "Littérature copte," in *DACL* 12/2:1599–635.

6. M. Krause, "Koptische Literatur," 3:694–728.

originate from the Christian church. It should also be noted that the texts in this group vary widely in both date and character.[7]

The oldest text appears to date to the first century C.E. The latest examples reach into the fourth or fifth centuries. Some use more "demotic" characters than normal Coptic, while others use exclusively Greek letters.

These texts testify to "the rise and development of attempts, other than the 'normal' Coptic ones, to produce graphic systems for texts where ancient linguistic forms are still preferred to the 'true' Coptic ones."[8]

The question remains whether or not these texts should be called literature in the true sense of the word. Given their character, mainly magical, this is doubtful. Nevertheless, the people who produced these texts may have had some influence on the beginnings of Coptic literature.

Translations of the Bible[9]

Three stages should be recognized in the activity of the Coptic translators of the Bible. During the first stage, which dates from the second to the early fourth century C.E., the translators worked more individually, in different dialects and with different methods. During the second stage, which dates to the fourth and fifth centuries, the canonization and standardization of the Sahidic translation occurred.

---

7. There is a survey of the relevant material in Paul E. Kahle, *Bala'izah* (London: Oxford Univ. Press, 1954) 252–56.

8. R. Kasser, "Les origines du Christianisme égyptien," *RThPh* 95 (1962) 11–28, esp. 17.

9. In general cf. Bernard Botte, "Versions coptes," in *DBS* 6:818–25; Willem Grossouw, "De koptische Bijbelvertalingen," *StCath* 9 (1933) 325–53; H. Hyvernat, "Etude sur les versions coptes de la Bible," *RB* 5 (1896) 427–33, 540–69, and 6 (1897) 48–74; R. Kasser, "Les dialectes coptes et les versions coptes bibliques," *Bib* 46 (1965) 287–310; Peter Weigandt, "Zur Geschichte der koptischen Bibelübersetzungen," *Bib* 50 (1969) 80–95. On the Old Testament cf. Frank Hudson Hallock, "The Coptic Old Testament," *AJSL* 49 (1932–1933) 325–35; Kurt Aland, "The Coptic New Testament," in *A Tribute to A. Vööbus* (ed. R. H. Fischer; Chicago: Lutheran School of Theology, 1977) 3–12; Caspar Rene Gregory, "Aegyptische Uebersetzungen," in his *Textkritik des neuen Testament* (Leipzig: Hinrichs, 1902) 528–53; R. Kasser, *L'Evangile selon saint Jean et les versions coptes de la Bible* (Neuchatel: Delachaux et Niestle, 1966); J. B. Lightfoot, "The Egyptian or Coptic Versions," in *A Plain Introduction to the Criticism of the New Testament* (ed. F. H. A. Scrivener; 4th ed.; New York: Bell, 1894) 365–407; Bruce M. Metzger, *The Early Versions of the New Testament: Their Origin, Transmission, and Limitations* (Oxford: Clarendon Press, 1977); Gerd Mink, "Die koptischen Versionen des neuen Testaments: Die sprachlichen Probleme bei ihrer Bewertung für die griechische Textgeschichte," in *Die Alten Uebersetzungen des Neuen Testaments . . .* (ed. K. Aland; ANTT 5; Berlin: Walter de Gruyter, 1972) 160–299; Arthur Vööbus, *Early Versions of the New Testament: Manuscript Studies* (PETSE 6; Stockholm: Estonian Theological Society in Exile, 1954).

The third stage represents the standardization of the Bohairic translation, which was probably completed by the ninth century.

Many interesting codices and fragments from the fourth and fifth centuries supply evidence for the first stage.[10] It must be noted at once, however, that as yet there does not exist a detailed and reliable study of the Coptic translations of the entire Bible, or even of the entire Old or New Testament separately. Older studies failed to distinguish the different stages of the translation work because they lacked the documentation; therefore, they tended to attribute the same characteristics to different texts. Recently scholars have chosen instead to study individual manuscripts.

The critical study of Coptic biblical translation has alternated between linguistic and philological investigation without achieving a comprehensive approach. Linguistic investigation approaches the problems in terms of the Coptic text alone. The philological approach deals with the relationship between the Coptic text, understood as a single uniform text, and the Greek text represented in the different textual families established by textual criticism.

The work required at present includes the separate consideration of each individual manuscript and the examination of it by means of a consistent set of criteria. Only then can comparisons be made and general conclusions drawn. Nobody can at present forecast those results, but we should stress the necessity to consider many different possibilities without taking anything for granted.

In fact, a translation may have been conceived and executed by a single translator or a small group of translators, sometimes even for individual use. On the other hand, it may have been produced on the basis of one or more preexistent texts, in the same or in different dialects. It may also have been revised through the use of a Greek text, which may or may not have been the same type as that used in the previous translations. Translations may also have been revised simply to improve the Coptic form, or to make it more correct in comparison with a Greek text that seemed better.

Of course, these problems are very difficult to solve because it is difficult to know precisely which particular Greek word or text lies behind any particular Coptic translation. Nonetheless, it is possible that a thorough investigation may in the future be successful.

All this makes it very difficult, though I think not impossible, to solve

10. A very good list for the New Testament mss. may be found in Metzger, *Early Versions*.

the greatest problems concerning the Coptic biblical translations. In terms of chronology these problems involve the date of the translations, the question of dialectical priority, and the relation between "official" and "private" translations. In terms of the relationships with the Greek manuscript tradition they include the reconstruction of the Greek model and the integration of the Coptic translations into the various Greek textual families.

Translations of "Gnosticizing" Texts

Without prejudging the general conclusions that can be drawn from the documents, it is possible to treat separately the group of texts found near Nag Hammadi, and the related documents in the previously known codices Askewianus, Brucianus, and Berolinensis Gnosticus.[11]

Though only a fraction (perhaps a small fraction) of the texts comprised in these manuscripts are of obvious gnostic character, their existence is proof of the activity of gnostic or gnosticizing circles in Egypt that used the Coptic language. Such groups probably produced their own translations independently of the activity of the "catholic church."

It is the opinion of this author that a history of Coptic literature should not be directly concerned with the theological, spiritual, or philosophical problems raised by the texts. The formal problems—e.g., literary genre and style—are also not relevant in this case since the texts are translations. It is the milieu in which the translations were produced that is most significant, for this information can help to shed light on the beginning of Coptic literature.

While much has been written on the subject, the recent important book by C. H. Roberts[12] indicates that the hypothesis that the Egyptian church was mainly gnostic in character during its first three centuries is untenable. Likewise, the idea that Coptic literature was in its beginnings the product of the Gnostics, who "anticipated the Catholics in their appeal to the native Egyptians" (p. 64), must be discarded. To the contrary, it now appears that there were diverse centers of production, with gnostic groups working concurrently with Catholic or "orthodox" centers (pp. 71–72).

---

11. Bibliographical information appears in Orlandi, *Bibliography*, and David M. Scholer, *Nag Hammadi Bibliography, 1948–1969* (Leiden: E. J. Brill, 1971), with annual supplements in "Bibliographica gnostica," *NovT*.

12. Colin H. Roberts, *Manuscript, Society, and Belief in Early Christian Egypt* (Oxford: British Academy, 1979).

It is to be noted, however, that the reconstruction of the long work of Shenoute, *Against the Origenists*, has shown that texts such as those from Nag Hammadi were widely read by the monks in Upper Egypt.[13]

It should also be noted that the more "orthodox" productions (the biblical codices, the Apocrypha, some homilies; see above and below) are very accurate with respect to language, orthography, and material construction. This is true for all dialects ranging from Sahidic to Bohairic, with few exceptions.[14] By contrast, the "gnostic" production is, on the whole, much less "professional," with frequent inconsistencies in orthography, personal notes of the scribes, inconsistent placement of titles, etc.

It is especially the translation technique, both the language itself and the syntactical and semantic ways of rendering the thought of the exemplar, that displays the greatest difference between the two categories, as every translator of the Nag Hammadi texts knows.

This can be explained in two ways: either the orthodox circles were the first creators of Coptic, and the Gnostics followed the path as best they could, without adhering to the numerous specialized rules that had been developed in order to translate clearly; or the Gnostics took the first steps, necessarily imperfect, and the "orthodox" consolidated and perfected the procedures.

Manichaean Translations

It is probable that the Manichaean translations were somewhat later than the other translations treated in this section. The codices, found in only one place (Medinet Madi in the Fayum, although they probably come from the region of Siout = Lycopolis), are attributed for paleographical reasons to the fourth or fifth centuries.[15] Therefore the translations may be dated to the early fourth century, thus allowing some time for the development of the manuscript tradition.

This date is supported by the fact that these texts reflect a rather peculiar milieu, probably influenced by the first experiments or produc-

13. T. Orlandi, "A Catechesis Against Apocryphal Texts by Shenute and the Gnostic Texts of Nag Hammadi," *HTR* 75 (1982) 85–95.

14. Two notable exceptions are R. Kasser, *Papyrus Bodmer III* (CSCO 177/178, 1958), and Hans Quecke, "Das saidische Jak-Fragment in Heidelberg und London (S25)," *Or* 47 (1978) 238–51.

15. Cf. the "contributions" of Hugo Ibscher in *Ein Mani-Fund in Aegypten* (ed. Carl Schmidt and Hans Jacob Polotsky; SDAW; Berlin: Walter de Gruyter,1933) 4–90; H. J. Polotsky, *Manichaeische Homilien* (Stuttgart: Kohlhammer, 1934); C. R. C. Allberry, *A Manichaean Psalm-Book* (Stuttgart: Kohlhammer, 1938).

tions of the Christian church. The group responsible for them could not carry on its work after the fourth century. As a result, these texts remained an isolated phenomenon in Coptic literature. Their features shed some light on the complicated situation in which the beginnings of Coptic literature took place.

It is especially interesting that the Manichaeans produced Coptic translations of their sacred books immediately after their expansion in Egypt. That expansion is dated around 350 C.E.; thus only a few decades passed before the production of Coptic translations.[16]

It is also to be noted that some of the texts appear to have been translated not from an (intermediate) Greek version, but directly from an Aramaic (Syriac) original.[17] Since Greek language and culture appear to form the basis for the "normal" production in Coptic during this period, the work of the Manichaeans is an important example of a center of production less interested in the Greek cultural influence, or perhaps even hostile to it. The only other center that displayed a similar attitude is the Pachomian center, though of course the nature of its production followed a very different pattern.

As in the case of the gnosticizing production, we are not interested in the theological and religio-historical problems. From a formal point of view, the dialect of these texts is interesting. The use of the Lycopolitan dialect confirms the possibility that the region of Siout was the main center of the Manichaeans, as well as of other heresies.[18] Various gnosticizing texts use the same dialect. It is also not to be forgotten that the Melitian schism originated in Siout-Lycopolis and had in part a nationalist-Egyptian character.[19]

The First Patristic Translations

It is clear from the date of some manuscripts that Coptic translations of certain patristic texts were produced at about the same time as the biblical translations.[20] It is also true that most of the others were

---

16. Cf. Josef Vergote, "Het Manichaeisme in Egypt," *JEOL* 9 (1944) 77–83 (German translation in *Der Manichaeismus* [ed. G. Widengren; Darmstadt: Wiss. Buchges., 1977] 385–99).

17. Peter Nagel, "Zographein und das 'Bild' des Mani in den koptische-manichaischen Texten," in *Eikon und Logos (Misc. Onasch)* (ed. H. Golz; Halle: Martin-Luther-Universität, 1981) 199–238.

18. Peter Nagel, "Die Bedeutung der Nag-Hammadi-Texte für die koptische Dialektgeschichte," in *Von Nag Hammadi bis Zypern* (Berlin: Akademie, 1972) 16–27.

19. F. H. Kettler, "Der melitianische Streit in Aegypten," *ZNW* 35 (1936) 155–93; L. W. Barnard, "Athanasius and the Meletian Schism in Egypt," *JEA* 59 (1973) 181–89.

20. The "Crosby Codex" is especially important; cf. William Willis, "The New Collec-

produced in the "classical" translation period. The distinction between the two is very important in establishing particular characteristics of the first translations; it is made difficult, however, by the obvious fact that late manuscripts can include early translations.

In my opinion it is possible to proceed by adding to the criterion of the relative antiquity of the manuscripts the following two observations. First, some of the texts found in early manuscripts are not found in the later tradition: this would point to a process of selection in the fifth and sixth centuries. Second, the texts found in the later manuscripts generally follow the "normal" patristic production patterns. Thus, their translation was probably executed as part of this "normal" production in the fourth and fifth centuries.

Apocrypha.[21] Two Old Testament Apocrypha (Apocalypsis Heliae; Visio Isaiae) are preserved in Coptic translation. They were originally written in a milieu characterized by the mixture of Jewish and Christian elements in the presence of some form of Egyptian nationalism. This is precisely the type of milieu where one can imagine that Coptic literature had its beginnings. On the other hand, the New Testament Apocrypha appear to be imported from Asia (Acta Pauli; Epistula Apostolorum; Acta Petri), thus indicating a connection with that environment. The connection is not between Asia and Alexandrian Christianity (cf. below) but between Asia and certain other centers in the Nile valley.

Homilies.[22] At least one homily among those transmitted to us was translated very early (second-third century): Melito of Sardis De Pascha.[23] But it is very probable that two others were translated in the same period, given their theological characteristics: Melito of Sardis De anima et corpore (later attributed to Athanasius);[24] and Pseudo-Basilius

---

tions of Papyri of the University of Mississippi," in Proceedings of the IXth International Congress of Papyrology (Oslo 1958) (Oslo: Norwegian Universities Press, 1958) 381–92; Allen Cabaniss, "The University of Mississippi Coptic Papyrus Manuscript: A Paschal Lectionary?" NTS 8 (1961–1962) 70–72.

21. Cf. T. Orlandi, "Gli Apocrifi copti," Aug 23 (1983) 57–72.

22. Details in T. Orlandi, "Le traduzioni dal greco e lo sviluppo della letteratura copta," in Graeco-Coptica: Griechen und Kopten im byzantinischen Ägypten (ed. P. Nagel; Halle: M. Luther Univ., 1984) 181–203.

23. Stuart George Hall, Melito of Sardis, on Pascha and Fragments (Oxford: Clarendon Press, 1979).

24. Ernest A. T. W. Budge, Coptic Homilies in the Dialect of Upper Egypt (London: British Museum, 1910) 115–32.

of Caesarea *De templo Salomonis*.[25] This third homily has the Asiatic cultural background in common with those of Melito.

It is somewhat surprising that the works of Melito, one of the greatest authorities of Asian theology, enjoyed such diffusion in Egypt, where the Alexandrian school never concealed its dislike for such a simple, naive, and in some respects dangerously materialistic exegetical school. In fact, we see once more a connection between the Asiatic culture and certain centers of the Nile valley, which do not share the Alexandrian reaction against that culture. They are probably monastic centers different from those of Nitria and Scetis, and also from the Pachomians. Some later documents produced by them may be the *Life of Aphou of Oxyrhynchus*, the *Life of Apollo (of Bawit)*, and the works of Paul of Tamma.[26]

General Observations

While the current state of affairs in Coptic studies does not permit one to draw positive conclusions from the evidence at our disposal, it is possible to present some general observations. The rise of Coptic literature was a very complicated process, the result of the work of many different centers whose interrelationships are still obscure.

One of these centers was in the catholic church of Egypt. It is possible that this center was located not in Alexandria but in another cultural center of the Nile valley (Siout, Shmun, . . .) that was in close contact with Alexandria. It is probably to this center that we owe the translation of the Bible.

Another center existed inside the catholic church that, in distinction from the former, opposed certain elements of Alexandrian theology. It was interested in receiving and Egyptianizing the texts of Asian Christianity, with their more simple exegesis of the Bible.[27]

Other centers were heretical in character, some gnosticizing and some Manichaean. Finally, some pagan centers also remained. These continued to produce Egyptian texts (mainly magical) in the Greek alphabet similar to those that represent the first example of Coptic language or writing.

The study of these centers is one of the major tasks confronting scholars in Coptic literature in the future.

---

25. Ibid., 105–14.
26. T. Orlandi, *Vite di Monaci Copti* (Rome: Città Nuova, 1984).
27. Manlio Simonetti, "Asiatica (cultura)," in *DPAC* 1:414–16.

THE FIRST ORIGINAL PRODUCTION

Hierakas

Hierakas must be mentioned here, because according to Epiphanius he wrote commentaries and treatises in "Egyptian" (i.e., Coptic).[28] He is generally assumed to have lived in the third century and may have been the first author to produce original Coptic literature. Epiphanius is, however, the only witness to his literary activity in Coptic. Although Epiphanius is rather well informed about Egypt, his report does not offer sufficient information for us to know whether and how Hierakas may have inaugurated Coptic literature. It is an open question whether the one text so far attributed to him is actually his work.[29] It must also be noted that the chronology of Hierakas's life remains uncertain. Thus he presents an open problem.

The Pachomian Literature

The case of Pachomius and his successors is very different. Though extensive sources from this group have survived, they must be used very carefully. Some of this material has long been known. It was published in a comprehensive manner by Lefort and derives from manuscripts of the ninth through eleventh centuries, with a few exceptions.[30]

Another portion however depends upon more recent discoveries. It contains both Greek and Coptic texts preserved in manuscripts that date to the fourth through sixth centuries, many of which were manufactured in a way unusual for the Coptic tradition (scrolls instead of codices).[31]

In the Pachomian literature one also finds a division between an earlier and a more recent manuscript tradition (cf. above). This fact, when used with caution, may permit one to solve certain literary problems.[32] Here too we cannot enter into details. It should be noted, however, that Jerome and Gennadius knew only a few works of

---

28. Cf. Giuseppe Rosso, *Ieraca* (Rome: CIM, 1983 [microfiche]); A. Guillaumont, "Christianisme et Gnoses dans l'Orient Preislamique," *CF* 81 (1980–81) 407–13.

29. Erik Peterson, "Ein Fragment des Hierakas?" *Muséon* 60 (1947) 257–60.

30. L. T. Lefort, *Oeuvres de s. Pachôme et de ses disciples* (CSCO 159/160, 1956).

31. Hans Quecke, *Die Briefe Pachoms: Griechischer Text der Handschrift W.145 der Chester Beatty Library ... Anhang: die koptischen Fragmente und zitate* (TPL 11; Regensburg: Pustet, 1975); T. Orlandi, "Due rotoli copti papiracei da Dublino (lettere di Horsiesi)," in *Proceedings of the Sixteenth International Congress of Papyrology, New York 24–31 July 1980* (ed. R. S. Bagnall; ASP 23; Chico, Calif.: Scholars Press, 1981).

32. There is detailed information in T. Orlandi et al., *Pachomiana Coptica* (in press).

Pachomius, Horsiesi, and Theodore. Furthermore, there is little evidence of the authentic Pachomian literature (as opposed to the hagiographic development of the *vitae*) in Greek and the other oriental languages. The discussion that follows will be limited to the works I consider genuine.

1. Pachomius. Rules: While discussion of the authenticity of the Rules is far from concluded, it is clear that they represent a very old example of original Coptic. Their character, however, is not literary. They had a practical function and as such they show little concern for a definite literary structure. Nagel has found traces of Roman army command style.[33]

Epistles: These also lack literary characteristics and structure. Most of them are composed of strings of biblical quotations. All are very difficult to understand, especially these that employ the *alphabeticum spiritale*.

2. Theodore. Epistles for the general assemblies of the Pachomians (one in Latin and one in Coptic): Both letters are very brief, difficult to understand, and similar in style to those of Pachomius.

3. Horsiesi. Liber:[34] The style of this work is similar to that of Pachomius's letters. It is replete with biblical quotations and occasionally employs the *alphabeticum spiritale*. The sentences are more developed, however, and above all the text, which is very long, has a certain internal structure.

Epistles: Here also the style recalls that of Pachomius, although longer personal interventions and some form of internal structure are visible.

Rules: These are in a more catechetical style than the rules of Pachomius. The title of "rules," however, has been supplied by the editor. As a catechetical work their form is far from the normal rhetorical style. As such they are representative of the little concern for literature in the Pachomian circles.

4. Apocalypse of Kjarur:[35] Little attention has been paid to this interesting text. Surely it belongs to a later period than those mentioned above. Nonetheless, it follows the patterns of the preceding Pachomian texts, although it is apocalyptic in character. Its meaning is very difficult to grasp so that its translation is far from certain.

33. Peter Nagel, "Diktion der römischen Kommandosprache in den Praecepta des Pachomius," *ZÄS* 101 (1974) 164–71.
34. Heinrich Bacht, *Das Vermächtnis des Ursprungs* (Würzburg: Echter, 1972).
35. Lefort, *Oeuvres*, 100–104.

The text is divided into two parts. The first part might be labeled *hermeneiai*, since it consists of brief sentences followed by an explanation. Unfortunately, both the sentences and the explanations are far from clear. The second part is in the form of an *erotapokrisis* on various themes between a certain Besarion (probably the same monk Besarion who lived during the time of Pachomius) and a certain Victor. The first part recalls the style of the epistles of Pachomius, while the second may be compared to the following text on Horsiesi.

5. The visit of Horsiesi in Alexandria:[36] This text is half historical and half moral in character. The historical part deals with the relations between the archbishop Theophilus and Horsiesi. Theophilus sends two deacons, Faustus and Timotheus, to Horsiesi with a letter summoning him to Alexandria. Horsiesi comes to Alexandria where he has a colloquium with Theophilus on moral questions. In a second section of the text, Faustus and Timotheus propose certain arguments to Horsiesi, who expresses his opinion on them. This text may have been written in Greek.

The General Character of Pachomian Literary Production

As we have seen, the works preserved in the early manuscripts are of a special literary character. In fact, it seems that literature as such, and also the literary forms presupposed by catechetical and pastoral activity, are beyond the scope of the first Pachomian generations.

This is not meant to suggest that the superiors of the Pachomian monasteries did not exert their authority through catechetical activity, though it is clear that they did so to a much lesser extent than the later tradition would like one to believe. The point is that the catechetical activity was not bound to a literary production, whether in Greek or in Coptic, comparable to that in use in the international centers of Asia and in Alexandria.

It is possible to note a cautious shift toward literature from Pachomius to Horsiesi (the later texts such as Kjarur and the Visit of Horsiesi have been mentioned at this point only for the sake of completeness). Thus the Liber of Horsiesi, probably his last work, is nearer than the others to the normal homiletical form. Likewise his letters are slightly more literary than those of his predecessors.

---

36. Walter E. Crum, *Der Papyruscodex Saec. VI–VII der Phillipps-Bibliothek in Cheltenham* (Strassburg: Trübner, 1915).

Nonetheless, if our suggestions are correct, one can affirm that the first manifestations of original Coptic literature involved a rejection of "literature" as such. It is to be understood as the simple use of external materials (paper, Scripture, and some original sentences), in opposition to literature as it was conceived in the circles representing Greek rhetorical culture.

The only real literary works that were admitted were the sacred books, the Bible. They were the basis and the horizon of the Pachomian culture. From this point of view, the problem of the eventual diffusion of the gnosticizing (Nag Hammadi) texts among the Pachomians should be reconsidered. It is possible that some of them were considered as sacred books. The diffusion of the others would require an explanation.

Certainly, such an attitude did not originate in a presumed cultural incapacity of Pachomius and his immediate successors. It is inconceivable that these great leaders did not use verbal exhortation in conjunction with their personal example. But it appears that exhortation aimed at the correction and edification of the monks, a practice that required personal interaction, was kept separate from the cultural patterns of the society at large. These necessarily carried within themselves the Greek and pagan ideas rejected by the monks. The early documents that survive were probably written for a practical, occasional purpose. They always presuppose an oral explanation of what is written.

Antony

The case of Antony is even more delicate. The seven letters attributed to him are known to us through a Georgian, an Arabic, and a humanistic Latin version made from the Greek. Some fragments of a Coptic version also survive.[37]

Provided that the letters are authentic, which seems probable, the question remains whether Antony actually wrote them himself or whether he used an amanuensis. Did he compose them in Coptic? Is the Coptic version that we have the Coptic original, or has it been (re)translated from the Greek?

---

37. Gerard Garitte, *Lettres de s. Antoine, version georgienne et fragments coptes* (CSCO 148/149, 1955); Wolf-Peter Funk, "Eine Doppelte Überliefertes Stück Spätägyptischer Weisheit," *ZÄS* 103 (1976) 8–21; Karl Heussi, *Der Ursprung des Mönchtums* (Tübingen: Mohr, 1936; Aalen: Scentia, 1981).

These problems have not yet been adequately debated. If the letters are genuine, Antony may have been the first real Coptic author. In such a case they would also link him to an advanced theological culture of Alexandrian provenience (Origenistic).

It may be that while Antony was an advanced theologian, he nonetheless dictated the letters, which were actually written in Greek by someone in his circle. We prefer to leave all this open for future research.

SHENOUTE AND BESA

Shenoute

History of Research[38]

It is known that no Greek source either historical or literary mentions Shenoute.[39] This remains one of the great mysteries of the Greek Christian tradition in Egypt. At present, it must simply be accepted as such.

Shenoute remained little more than a name from the time of the arrival in the West of the Bohairic translations of his Life written by Besa to the time of the first extensive publications of some of his works, done almost simultaneously by Leipoldt and Crum and by Amélineau.[40]

The peculiar status of the manuscript tradition of his works, however, has been an obstacle in the way of an accurate evaluation of his historical and literary personality. This tradition depends almost exclusively on the manuscripts of the White Monastery, manuscripts that have been dismembered and scattered throughout the libraries and museums of the world during the last century. The importance of Leipoldt's famous monograph, still the most reliable and comprehen-

38. For a bibliography on Shenoute other than my *Bibliography*, cf. P. J. Frandsen and E. Richter-Aeroe, "Shenoute: A Bibliography," in *Studies presented to H. J. Polotsky* (ed. D. W. Young; Beacon Hill, Mass.: Pirtle & Polson, 1981) 147–76.

39. Shenoute is mentioned in the "Coptic History of the Church" (cf. David W. Johnson, "Further Fragments of a Coptic History of the Church: Cambridge OR.1966 R," *Enchoria* 6 [1976] 7–17), perhaps translated from the Greek; but cf. my "Nuovi frammenti della Historia Ecclesiastica copta," in *Studi in onore di Edda Bresciani* (ed. S. Pernigotti; Pisa: Giardini, 1985) 363–83.

40. J. Leipoldt and W. E. Crum, *Sinuthii archimandritae vita et opera omnia* (CSCO 42, 73; Paris: e Typographeo reipublicae, 1908) vv. 3–4; Emile Clément Amélineau, *Oeuvres de Schenoudi* (2 vols. in 6 fasc.; Paris: Leroux, 1907–14).

sive study,[41] is vitiated today as a result of our improved understanding of the manuscript tradition.

Before Leipoldt, Amélineau and Ladeuze[42] had already written on Shenoute. Amélineau was not a sound historian, and his contributions are deservedly neglected. The case of Ladeuze is different, but his interests were too restricted.

It is important to keep in mind that the main interest of Leipoldt in writing his book was historical and not literary. Though he did some analysis of the literary activity of Shenoute, he used it only to help draw historical conclusions. Therefore his literary assessment reflects the prejudices of his historical treatment.

Those prejudices were liberalism and nationalism. (1) Liberalism. Leipoldt was too eager to bring forth the dogmatic and violent sides of the personality and behavior of Shenoute. He was also prone to emphasize Shenoute's redundant literary style, which was nevertheless a characteristic feature of his time. (2) Nationalism. Shenoute is seen by Leipoldt to represent the national Egyptian culture. Leipoldt, however, does not distinguish among an eventual plurality of Egyptian cultural currents and attitudes. The vital cultural struggle of this period, whether or not to accept Greek rhetorical norms and to produce original works according to them, was won by Shenoute, who supported the first option. All this is neglected by Leipoldt, both in his book and in the brief history of Coptic literature that he later wrote.[43]

The reevaluation of the work of Shenoute, both for the history of Coptic literature and for the history of Egyptian Christianity, is still to be completed, though some steps have been taken along these lines. One should especially mention the articles of Lefort and Weiss on the christological catechesis, that of Müller on the style of Shenoute (to be considered a first approach), and some considerations of Shisha-Halevy.[44]

41. J. Leipoldt, *Schenute von Atripe und die Entstehung des nationalägyptischen Christentums* (TU 25/1; Leipzig: Hinrichs, 1903).

42. Paulin Ladeuze, *Etude sur le cénobitisme pakhomien pendant le IV siècle et la première moitié du V* (Louvain: Linthout, 1898; Frankfurt: Minerva, 1961); Amélineau, *Les moines égyptiens: Vie de Schoudi* (AMG 1; Paris: Leroux, 1889).

43. Leipoldt, "Geschichte," 145–52.

44. L. T. Lefort, "Catéchèse christologique de Chenoute," *ZÄS* 80 (1955) 40–45; Hans-Friedrich Weiss, "Zur Christologie des Schenute von Atripe," *BSAC* 20 (1969–70) 177–210; Caspar Detlef G. Müller, "Koptische Redekunst und griechische Rhetorik," *Muséon* 69 (1956) 53–72; Ariel Shisha-Halevy, "Unpublished Shenoutiana in the British Library," *Enchoria* 5 (1975) 53–108; idem, "Commentary on Unpublished Shenoutiana in the British Library," *Enchoria* 6 (1976) 29–61; and idem, "Two New Shenoute-Texts from the British Library," *Or* 44 (1975) 149–85.

The Major Works of Shenoute

The works of Shenoute were conserved almost exclusively in the library of the monastery founded by him, today known as the White Monastery. For this reason they became known only through the fragments of the codices of this library that reached Europe between about 1750 and about 1900. The work of editing was undertaken relatively quickly, first as part of the publication of catalogues (Zoega, Mingarelli), and then in more comprehensive editions.

The Borgian collection was studied by Amélineau between 1907 and 1914 and the Paris collection by Leipoldt and Crum between 1908 and 1913. Neither collection was completely published. Wessely's transcription of the Vienna fragments dating from about 1905 should also be mentioned here. Other minor publications (Guerin, Lefort) also occurred. The recent work of D. Young should also be noted.[45]

There still exist some codices, complete or semicomplete, that may shed light on the transmission of Shenoute's works. The first to be recognized is conserved at the Louvre. Unfortunately, Guerin's edition is so difficult to obtain that it remains almost unknown.[46] At a later date, two codices arrived at the Institut français d'archéologie orientale in Cairo largely intact. While the first has been published in transcription by Chassinat, the second remains unpublished.[47]

The work that remains to be done on the Shenoute codices depends on the general problem of the reconstruction of the White Monastery codices. The present author has begun this task. To date, the project has emphasized the recognition of the most important sermons and catecheses. Much work remains to be done.

Beyond the usual methodology employed in the reconstruction of the White Monastery codices, two elements that aid one in dealing with the codices of Shenoute should be noted. Both must be treated with care. The first element is the existence of "indexes," one of which we possess in part in a fragment from Vienna.[48] The second element is

45. Henri Guerin, "Sermons inedits de Senouti," *REg* 10 (1902) 148–64, and 11 (1905) 15–34; Dwight W. Young, "A Monastic Invective Against Egyptian Hieroglyphs," in *Studies Presented to H. J. Polotsky* (ed. Young) 348–60; idem, "Unpublished Shenoutiana in the University of Michigan Library," in *Egyptological Studies* (ed. S. I. Groll; ScrHie 28; Atlantic Highlands, N.J.: Humanities Press, 1983) 251–67.

46. Guerin, "Sermons," 1.148–64.

47. Emile Chassinat, *La quatrième livre des entretiens et epîtres de Schenouti* (MIFAO 23; Cairo: IFAO, 1911).

48. Vienna, Nationalbibl., Papyrussamml. K9634 (*Griechische und Koptische Texte*

the notes and general titles added by the scribes at the beginning or end of some codices.

Both of these elements testify to the existence of something like an authoritative edition of the works of Shenoute existing in the White Monastery from which our codices ultimately derive. One must take into account, however, the fact that the scribes of the ninth through the eleventh centuries did not understand well the system of that edition, and thus could attribute titles and notes to the wrong part of the material. As a result some sermons might have been copied as part of a book of letters, etc.

What is given below represents a first attempt at evaluating the literary work of Shenoute. A more thorough study must be undertaken before satisfactory evaluation can be reached. Some idea of the content of the most extensive works of Shenoute will also be supplied.

It seems expedient to distinguish the major sermons of Shenoute by categories, according to their content. The first category, probably the richest, is that of the moral sermons.

(W40?).[49] Everybody must be worthy of his position. Judas is a good example of the contrast, and also Adam and Eve. If the clerics sin, what will lay people do? The wrath of God is noted. There are some who are esteemed on earth but cursed in heaven.

De disoboedientia ad clericos (W44?).[50] We clerics are sinners even in the sanctuary of God. Biblical examples are given of sinners who are punished. We must be faithful and especially obedient. The personification of obedience is invoked. A section against sodomites and heretics is included.

De castitate et Nativitate.[51] This sermon discusses free will, and then the place of chastity in the monastic life, with citations from Athanasius. Some teachings come from God, even if they are spoken by a man, John the Baptist. A discussion of Christmas and the glorification of Christ occurs.

Another category of sermons is directed against the pagans. This subject is certainly important in Shenoute, but it has been largely overvalued.

Theologischen Inhalts [ed. Carl Wessely; Leipzig: Avenarius, 1917] v. 9. no. 50). The reference W00 is to the original numbers of this index. Otherwise we refer to the final index of the Cairo Codex (Chassinat, *Le quatrième livre*). It is impossible to give detailed lists of fragments. We shall refer to those editions listed above in nn. 40, 45, and 47, even if some fragment is to be added after our research.

49. Amélineau, *Oeuvres* 2:2, mistakenly printed as 17.
50. Ibid. 1:6.
51. Guerin, "Sermons" 1.159–64; 2.15–16.

(Chassinat 1).[52] The pagans are worse than the demons because the latter have at least once recognized Christ. The pagans fight against the Christians as once the Hebrews fought against the prophets. A section against the heretics occurs. Christians rightly destroy the pagan idols. If Christians do sin, they should come back to the right way. The resurrection of the dead and the final punishments are discussed. Christians should not be afraid of pagans and heretics.

Adversus Saturnum (Chassinat 5).[53] This sermon is aimed against a pagan, perhaps a magistrate, who importuned the monks.

Contra idolatras, de spatio vitae (W69).[54] The idolaters say that the life of each person is fixed by fate. To the contrary, nothing happens without the will of God. God is like a king who sends his representatives to distant provinces to make his orders known. If life-spaces were fixed in advance, then homicide would not be a crime.

Another category of sermons is directed against the heretics.

Contra Origenistas et gnosticos.[55] This is a very long work in the form of a homily. It was probably conceived to be read rather than heard. Its aim is to oppose heretics (especially Origenists but also Arians, Meletians, and Nestorians, and the Gnostics in general) and the apocryphal books they used and circulated. The subjects touched upon are the plurality of the worlds, the position and work of the Savior, the meaning of Pascha, the relations between Father and Son, the origin of souls, Christ's conception, the Eucharist, the resurrection of the body, and the four elements.

Contra Melitianos (W58.59).[56] The Meletians participate in the Eucharist many times a day, especially in the cemeteries, likening it to the carnal meals. They also maintain that one should communicate on Sunday.

De Vetere Testamento contra Manichaeos (W81).[57] The value of the Old Testament, alongside the New, is affirmed against the opinion of the Manichaeans. (Exegesis of Matt. 11:13 and Luke 17:16.)

De praeexistentia Christi.[58] Exegesis of biblical passages related to the Christ is presented in order to demonstrate that he existed even before his birth from Mary. (Also against Nestorius.)

52. Amélineau, *Oeuvres* 1:11; Leipoldt and Crum, *Sinuthii*, no. 25.
53. Chassinat, *Le quatrième livre*, no. 5; Leipoldt and Crum, *Sinuthii*, no. 24.
54. Leipoldt and Crum, *Sinuthii*, no. 17.
55. Orlandi, *Shenute Contro gli Origenisti* (Rome: CIM, 1985).
56. Guerin, "Sermons" 2.17–18.
57. Amélineau, *Oeuvres* 1:5.
58. Lefort, "Catéchèse christologique," 40–45.

An interesting group of sermons is based on Shenoute's interviews with the magistrates who visited him because of his fame and his great authority. The Chassinat codex contains a group of four such works. The magistrates in question are Chosroe, Flavianus, and Heraklammon.[59] Shenoute touches the following arguments: the license for him to correct even generals in spiritual matters, the dimensions of the sky and of the earth (!), the devil and free will, the punishment of sinners, the duties of judges, the duties of important personages, e.g., bishops, the wealthy, and generals.

The Character of Shenoute's Literary Activity

Taking into consideration the works listed above, two aspects of the literary activity of Shenoute that have been neglected to date stand out.

First, one must note the great variety of subjects that Shenoute addressed, many of which Shenoute had previously been thought to treat only in minor allusions. This fact suggests a different assessment of his theological personality, his spirituality, and his moral and political behavior.

Second, his position in relation to the development of Coptic literature must be reexamined. Shenoute has sometimes been seen as rejecting Greek culture and being personally unacquainted with Greek rhetoric. Two elements in his works suggest, in fact, that the contrary is true. First, in the development of Coptic literature, he took the step of accepting literary activity into the religious field, following the example of the international Greek Christianity of the great church fathers but contrary to the Coptic attitude. This development counters the apparent position of the Pachomians. Second, his style, which has no Coptic precedent, is clearly based on a careful study of the scholastic rhetoric of his times, i.e., the Greek rhetoric of the "second sophistic." On other aspects of Shenoute's style, already well known, it is not necessary to dwell here.

Besa

Besa will be dealt with at this point because of his close connection with Shenoute. It should be noted, however, that he belongs to the period of post-Chalcedonian literature, the general characteristics of which will be described in a later section.

The work of Besa is known much better than that of his predecessor

---

59. Chassinat, *Le quatrième livre*, nos. 6–10.

Shenoute, because of the excellent edition by Kuhn.[60] Kuhn has also examined Besa's works in a series of articles, though in terms of their spirituality and history rather than their style and place in the development of Coptic literature.[61]

The literary character of Besa's work still needs to be examined. We can only say now that he followed also in this respect the way prepared by Shenoute, whose acceptance of the Greek rhetorical rules, both in form and in content, he fully inherited. Thus he also wrote catecheses, mainly of moral character, and letters, for the monks for whom he had responsibility. While the latter are written with less rhetoric, they nonetheless reveal the same mastery of the Coptic language. The stormy times in which he lived did not leave their mark in the style of his work.

THE TRANSLATIONS OF THE
"CLASSICAL" PERIOD[62]

If the idea is accepted that the work of Shenoute represents a juncture in the development of Coptic literature in that he accepts the Greek literary traditions already in use in the Christian literature of the great international centers (Antioch, Caesarea, Alexandria, etc.), then the hypothesis proposed by Leipoldt that most of the translations from Greek into Coptic were produced in the White Monastery under his supervision also becomes more acceptable.[63] In this case we may have some guidelines for evaluating the characteristics of those translations.

But before speaking of the true translations (viz., those of the texts of patristic literature), we have to mention the work done to produce a standardized text of the Bible. It is the result of this effort that is most often represented in the manuscript tradition of the eighth through twelfth centuries in Sahidic.

This standard text was produced from one or more previous translations. This is evident because certain very old manuscripts (third- or fourth-century) preserve the same redaction found in the later standardized text. While the standardized text may be so different at places

60. K. Heinz Kuhn, *Letters and Sermons of Besa* (CSCO 157/158, 1956).
61. K. Heinz Kuhn, "A Fifth-Century Egyptian Abbot: I. Besa and His Background. II. Monastic Life in Besa's Day. III. Besa's Christianity," *JTS* 5 (1954) 36–48, 174–87, and 6 (1955) 35–48.
62. Orlandi, "Le traduzioni"; for the editions of the texts cf. n. 4.
63. Leipoldt, "Geschichte," 154-55.

that one must postulate the existence of different redactions, it none-theless preserves parts of the text so close to that of the older models that it must have been based upon them.

As for the patristic translations, one of the main problems here is the false attributions that we find in the late manuscript tradition. Not only do we find the name of some great father of the church attached to works originally written in Coptic in the seventh or eighth century, but often we find an incorrect attribution of texts actually translated from Greek originals of the fourth or fifth century.[64]

Some of our previous contributions on Coptic literature are mainly concerned with the distinction between real translations and late forgeries.[65] It is presumed here that one should exclude those seemingly late texts from the study of Coptic translations. For many of the others the Greek text is known. Thus one can leave aside the remaining problematic texts (possible translations, but without a known Greek model), without prejudice for the characterization of the translation work in general.

The characteristics of the Coptic translations can be summarized as follows:

1. For the homiletical genre, one finds almost exclusively single texts translated for liturgical use and not systematic translations of the corpora of the most important authors (like Basil, Gregory of Nazianzus, even Athanasius). The most relevant exceptions are a corpus of a few homilies of Basil, a corpus with extracts from the homilies of John Chrysostom on the epistles of Paul, and perhaps the remains of a corpus of Severus of Antioch, dispersed in several manuscripts.

2. The fundamental theological works of the fathers were generally not translated. Similarly, homilies aimed at specific theological questions were not taken into consideration. The only exception is a small corpus of works of Gregory of Nyssa.[66] Not even the Alexandrian bishops (Athanasius, Theophilus, Cyril) received different treatment.

3. The choice of the texts appears to be dictated by an adherence to

---

64. E.g., Athanasius-Basilius (cf. Orlandi, "Basilio di Cesarea nella letteratura copta," *RSO* 49 [1975] 52–53); Eusebius-John Chrysostom (cf. Giovanni Mercati, "A Supposed Homily of Eusebius of Caesarea," *JTS* 8 [1906–7] 114).

65. T. Orlandi, "Patristica copta e patristica greca," *VetChr* 10 (1973) 327–42; idem, "Basilio," 49–59; idem, "Cirillo di Gerusalemme nella letteratura copta," *VetChr* 9 (1972) 93–100; idem, "Demetrio di Antiochia e Giovanni Crisostomo," *Acme* 23 (1970) 175–78 = *Misc. De Marco*; "Teodosio di Alessandria nella letteratura copta," *GIF* 2 (1971) 175–85.

66. T. Orlandi, "Gregorio di Nissa nella letteratura copta," *VetChr* 18 (1981) 333–39.

the necessities of moral catechesis and monastic spirituality. We cannot say for certain whether the translations were intended for reading during public services or for individual meditation. Later, at least, the public use prevailed in the manuscript transmission. In either case, the need of the audience or the readers was of the character stated above.

4. The texts entered Coptic culture with little concern for their actual author or provenience. Content was the only significant factor. The texts appear to derive from a "minor" Greek manuscript tradition that gathered into anthologies works directed to a special public that had moral and practical rather than intellectual interests.[67]

5. This "minor" tradition is at the origin of the widespread phenomenon of pseudepigraphical authorship, which both in Greek and in Coptic is due to two factors, only apparently contradictory: the convenience of attributing to famous authors the works of less-known authors that one wished to circulate, and indifference to the authorship of the works in comparison with the content.

As to the hagiographic translations, we find on one hand the same shift from the translation of Greek texts to the later production of similar texts in Coptic, which claimed to come from the same sources. On the other hand, the cultural interaction between the two languages is even greater since the later Coptic creations followed the same patterns and aims as some Greek texts produced in Egypt in earlier times.

Therefore, to have a clear view of the literary evolution of this genre, it is necessary to investigate both the Greek and the Egyptian hagiographic tradition. Only then can one hope to separate the texts according to their Greek or Coptic origin and illustrate the peculiar characteristics of each. Here also the work is only just beginning, and we must limit ourselves to a few observations.

It is possible, in this author's opinion, to bring together the conclusions of the two fundamental works by Delehaye (on the Egyptian origin of the "epic genre") and Baumeister (on the development of the "koptischer-Konsens—genre").[68] By this means a path can be charted

---

67. Jean Gribomont, "Les succès litteraires des pères grecs et les problèmes d'histoire des textes," SE 22 (1974–75) 23–49.

68. Hippolyte Delehaye, "Les martyrs d'Egypte," AnBoll 40 (1922) 5–154; Theofried Baumeister, Martyr Invictus: Der Martyrer als Sinnbild der Erlösung in der Legende und im Kult der frühen koptischen Kirche (FVK 46; Münster: Regensberg, 1972). Cf. also T. Orlandi, "I Santi della Chiesa copta," in XXVIII Corso di cultura sull' arte ravennate e bizantina (Ravenna: Girasole, 1981) 21–30.

that leads from the genuine historical martyrdoms that derive from official acts to the epic genre and finally to the "koptischer Konsens." In the first two stages the Coptic texts are probably translations from the Greek, whereas the Coptic texts belonging to the last stage are probably original. They will be treated in a later section of this article.

We have only two texts of the first type: the *Passio Colluthi* and the *Passio Psotae*. It is possible to add the *Passio Petri Alexandrini*, which, though not deriving directly from official acts, may be attributed to the same period and school.

In the period of the epic genre one can note a tendency toward the creation of cycles, which will become the main feature of the later, original Coptic school. One of the cycles is constructed around the prefect Arianus. Another is that of the Julian martyrs, which must be dated after 362 and is further connected with the rise of the legends of the birth of Constantine and of the discovery of the cross *(Passio Iudae Cyriaci, Passio Eusignii, Excerptum de Mercurio)*.

We have also individual passions of the epic genre built around saints of various proveniences, each with his own peculiarities. These include Epimachus, Menas, James the Persian, Leontius of Tripolis, Mercurius, Pantoleon, Eustathius, Cyrus and John, Philotheos, and the forty Martyrs of Sebaste. Other passions in this same genre have typically Egyptian features of a strictly internal nature and are preserved only in Coptic, but very probably are translated from a Greek original: *Passio Coore, Passio Herai, Passio Dios*.

The Passions of the martyr-monks deserve special consideration because of the union of the hagiographic school with the monastic environment: *Passio Paphnuthii, Pamin, Pamun et Sarmatae, Panine et Paneu*.

THE HISTORICAL-POLEMICAL LITERATURE
AFTER CHALCEDON

If up to this point the development of Coptic literature was marked by spiritual and cultural events, after the Council of Chalcedon historical and political events become determinative. Therefore the period between Chalcedon and the Arab invasion may be divided into two stages: (1) Before Justinian each of the two ecclesiastical parties hoped to prevail both in Egypt and elsewhere. As a result, the literary production was chiefly apologetic, and remained in the frame of the "international" culture (probably, *Historia ecclesiastica*,[69] *Vita Iohannis de Lykopoli*,[70] *Vita Longini*,[71] *Plerophoriae*,[72] *Memoriae Dioscori*.[73] (2) Between Justinian and the bishop Damianus, the Coptic church was overcome by the "catholic" party, sustained by the imperial power. Therefore literary works, when they could be produced, were directed mainly to an internal and monastic audience (probably, *Vitae Apollinis, Abraham, Moses, Zenobii*).[74]

It was at this time, so it seems, that Greek began to be seen as the language of a foreign and oppressive people. Nonetheless, the formal question of language must not have come immediately to the fore. The evidence suggests rather a natural historical process in which the will to produce works different from the Byzantine culture led to dissociation, first, from the new Byzantine production, and then, from the language itself. This process involved only literary production in the two languages. Administrative and ecclesiastical affairs, including relations with other non-Chalcedonian churches, were still carried on in Greek.

Thus one can see for some time after Chalcedon the concurrent production in the Coptic church of works in both Greek and Coptic. The choice in this period probably was more dependent on geographical than on cultural factors. The works conceived near Alexandria and in the communities gravitating around it were probably written in Greek. In the South, where Sahidic was probably already in common use for literature, as is attested by Shenoute, new works continued to be composed in it.

All these reasons make it difficult to know for certain the original language of the works mentioned in this chapter unless a Greek original survives. In any case, it appears that the choice of language was on the whole of secondary importance and that Coptic translations were in most cases immediately executed.

---

69. T. Orlandi, *Storia della Chiesa di Alessandria* (TDSA 17.31; Milan: Cisalpino, 1970); "La bibliografia più recente," in idem, "Nuovi frammenti."

70. Paul Devos, "Feuillets coptes nouveaux et anciens concernant s. Jean de Siout," *AnBoll* 88 (1970) 153–87, and other articles.

71. T. Orlandi and A. Campagnano, *Vite dei monaci Phif e Longino* (TDSA 51; Milan: Cisalpino, 1975).

72. T. Orlandi, "Un frammento delle Pleroforie in copto," *SROC* 2 (1979) 3–12.

73. D. Johnson, *A Panegyric on Macarius Bishop of Tkow, Attributed to Dioscorus of Alexandria* (CSCO 415/416, 1980).

74. Cf. A. Campagnano, "Monaci egiziani fra V et VI secolo," *VetChr* 15 (1978) 223–46.

The Period of Damianus and the Arab Conquest

It was G. Garitte who first drew attention to a sentence in the *History of the Patriarchs* by Severus of Ashmunein, in a chapter on Damianus that points to the celebration of a particular period in the history of the Coptic church:[75]

> Et il y eut de son temps des évêques qui le remplissaient d'admiration pour leur pureté et leur mérite, et parmi eux Jean de Burlus, et Jean son disciple, et Constantin l'évêque, et Jean le bienheureux reclus, et beaucoup d'autres.

Severus is probably alluding only to the ecclesiastical achievements of such bishops, although Garitte pointed out that each of them also has a place in the history of Coptic literature.

Thus it is possible to see a special connection at this time between the life of the Coptic church and its literature. Indeed the Coptic church was emerging from a very difficult period, dating from the time of Justinian, when not only the political power of Byzantium had successfully suffocated much of its activity, but also the tritheistic and other polemics had damaged its relations with the Syrian anti-Chalcedonian community.

Bishop Damianus had succeeded in giving order and life to the church, even though the problems both with the court and with the Syrians remained unresolved. This new life of the Coptic church also led to renewed literary activity. The new literary production differed from the polemical literature of the previous age. It returned to the efforts of Shenoute and his successor Besa to meet the needs of the daily liturgical activity of the church. This time, however, the effort was not limited to the monasteries.

It is almost natural in this framework that nationalism pervades almost all the texts. It is a particular kind of nationalism whose aim is to put Egypt in the foreground, in terms of both its good and its bad achievements. This is undoubtedly a sign of the proud isolation in which the Coptic church was enclosing itself. Moreover, one notices an effort to identify the old leading personalities, especially Athanasius, as the founders of the Coptic church, which is now identified as the Egyptian church as a whole.

---

75. G. Garitte, "Constantin évêque d'Assiout," in *Coptic Studies in Honor of Walter Ewing Crum* (Boston: Byzantine Institute, 1950) 298; reprinted in *BBI* 2.

Another important feature is a defense of the right to produce new works in Coptic rather than simply to translate or to rely upon the sermons of the older fathers available in Greek. From some passages in the sermons that we have, it is possible to surmise that in the literary circles of the church this was a subject of extensive debate.[76]

The style of all of these writers is rather similar and recalls the typical canons of the "second sophistic," the Greek literary movement of the second through the fourth centuries, which had served as the accepted style of the great preachers of the golden age of patristic literary production.

One does note the ability of the authors of this period to express various concepts in Coptic with great precision. This development represents the natural progress in the language and its growing independence from Greek. It is a relatively new development in this period. Neither the translations of the Bible nor those of the homilies and martyrdoms are written in a language like this, which has at last become independent of the Greek model and self-sufficient in its syntactical and stylistic elements. Only Shenoute approached this level of diction (and Besa after him). He is to be understood as a precursor of the Coptic style of this period.

Among the authors of this period, Damianus himself has left us two of his works, certainly written in Greek, but immediately translated into Coptic. One is a synodical letter sent to the Syrian church after his consecration. It is known also in Syriac. The other is a homily on the Nativity, of which we have only some fragments.

The other writers surely produced works originally in Coptic. The first to be mentioned is Constantine of Siout, whose personality seems to be the most remarkable. From him we have two *Encomia* of Athanasius, two of the martyr Claudius, and some other minor homilies, portions of which survive only in Arabic.

Rufus of Shotep wrote commentaries on the Gospels. We have fragments of one on Matthew and one on Luke. The texts have not yet been published, so an evaluation is difficult. But it seems that they are a good, late witness to the "Alexandrian" exegetical school. The exegesis is in fact an allegorical one, though it does not rule out philological attention to the literal text.

The main characteristic of John of Shmun seems to have been his

---

76. T. Orlandi, *Constantini episcopi urbis Siout Encomia in Athanasium duo, Versio* (CSCO 350, 1974) ix–x.

nationalism. The two major works of his that survive are panegyrics on two figures that represent the most important phases of Egyptian Christianity as he saw it: Mark, the Evangelist and founder of the Egyptian Church; and Anthony, the founder of anchorite monasticism. Egypt is foremost in his thoughts when he writes. He defends his own position and that of his fellow men of letters who produced works in Coptic even when ancient Greek models were available.

Another John, Bishop of Paralos in the Delta, wrote an important treatise against the apocryphal and heretical books that still survived in the Egyptian church of his day. Like the work of Shenoute mentioned above, this is an important witness to the role and survival in the Coptic church of works similar to those found at Nag Hammadi.

The group of authors active in the period of Damianus lived in the age just before the Arab invasion. They probably witnessed the Persian invasion, and some may also have experienced the Arab conquest. In any event, they established a tradition of writing extensive works in Coptic for the everyday life of the Coptic church, a tradition that continued in the first century after the Arab conquest.

It seems that the attitude of the Arabs to Coptic culture, as to all the cultures of the Christian Orient, was at first respectful.[77] Thus the most important personalities in the Egyptian church were still able to produce their works more or less freely. Later, as we shall see, the situation changed radically.

From this period we have a long homily of Benjamin of Alexandria on the wedding of Cana, which is important not only for its theological remarks but also for its autobiographical content. Benjamin also wrote a panegyric on Shenoute of which only a short passage is extant.

There also exists a homily by Benjamin's successor, the Patriarch Agathon, who narrated episodes related to the consecration of a church in honor of Macarius at Scetis by Benjamin. The same Agathon is probably the author of a panegyric on Benjamin, of which only some fragments remain.

Another patriarch, John III, wrote a panegyric on St. Menas, whose sanctuary in Mareotis attracted numerous pilgrims (and still does today). He also composed a theological treatise in the form of *erotapokriseis*, which was finally redacted by one of his presbyters.

77. C. D. G. Müller, *Geschichte der orientalischen Nationalkirchen (Die Kirche in ihrer Geschichte,* 1/2; Göttingen: Vandenhoeck & Ruprecht, 1981) 269–367, here 332–33; Friedhelm Winkelmann, *Die Östlichen Kirchen in der Epoche der Christologischen Auseinandersetzungen (5. bis 7. Jahrhundert)* (Bielefeld: Luther-Verlag, 1980) 118–21.

In this same period, Menas, Bishop of Pshati (Nikius), wrote the life of the patriarch Isaac, an important historical document, and a panegyric on the martyr Macrobius of Pshati. And Zacharias, Bishop of Shkow, wrote two homilies of exegetical content and possibly the life of John Colobos.

THE CYCLES

The present author has already expressed his opinion concerning the credit to be given to the titles in the Coptic manuscripts of the ninth through twelfth centuries. In this section it will be argued that many of the texts recognized as pseudonymous with respect to the titles that they bear in the manuscripts themselves come from a single late period and were produced by a homogeneous literary school.[78]

Briefly, the reasons for this are as follows: (1) These texts can be reassembled in different groups by paying attention to certain episodes and certain personages that go together and appear in about the same form in each group of texts. (2) The content and form of these texts presuppose a cultural sedimentation and literary style that are typical of Damianus's period. It is difficult to imagine any reason during Damianus's era, however, for someone to produce falsely attributed texts. Therefore it seems reasonable to place such texts somewhat later than Damianus's era, when there were reasons to create them (see below).

A typical example of the cycles is represented by the texts that gravitate around the figure of Athanasius. These might be works attributed to him or works that tell of his life. For example, there exists an anonymous *Vita*, a panegyric attributed to Cyril of Alexandria, and several homilies attributed to Athanasius himself, in which he relates the same unhistorical episodes we find in the *Vita* and the *Panegyric*.

Another good example of a cycle is the one that has as its subject the life of John Chrysostom.[79] An acephalous homily, which was probably one of his encomia, tells of an exile of John on the island of Thrace, where he converted the people to Christianity. Another homily,

78. Cf. Orlandi, "Gregorio di Nissa," 333–39. A bibliography appears in Orlandi, "Patristica."

79. Cf. T. Orlandi, "La tradizione copta sulla vita di Giovanni Crisostomo," in *Quattro omelie copte: vita di Giovanni Crisostomo, Encomi dei 24 vegliardi (ps.Proclo e Anonimo), Encomio di Michele arcangelo di Eustazio di Tracia* (ed. A. Campagnano, A. Maresca, and T. Orlandi; TDSA 60; Milan: Cisalpino, 1977).

attributed to a certain Eustathius, Bishop of Thrace, besides recounting a typical, late romance-story, also reports the conversion of this people through the work of Chrysostom. A third homily, attributed to Proclus of Cyzicus, tells of the Christianizing of a certain city of Ariphorus, in Thrace, also through the work of Chrysostom.

Coptic literature recognizes a strange tradition concerning the consecration of Chrysostom as a priest at Antioch by a bishop of Antioch named Demetrius.[80] Demetrius is a purely fictitious figure. This tradition is adopted in an encomium on the martyr Victor, attributed to the same Chrysostom, where he speaks autobiographically. To this Demetrius, then, are devoted no less than three homilies, in whose inscription it is expressly stated that it was he who consecrated Chrysostom as priest.

Another typical production of this genre is the cycle of Theophilus,[81] whose homilies allude to the construction of churches upon the ruins of pagan temples and to the exploiting of riches found in the pagan temples closed by Constantine and Theodosius. The source of the legend seems to be a passage of the Coptic History of the Church:

> Theophilus appropriated many riches because the emperor had commanded that he be given the keys to the temples; and he had assembled great riches.

The following texts belong to this cycle: a homily on the construction of the Church of the Holy Family on Mount Coscam; a homily on the Three Saints of Babylon in which Theophilus tells of having sent the monk John Colobos to Babylon in order to take and bring back to Alexandria the relics of the Three Saints; and finally, a homily in honor of the archangel Raphael, in which Theophilus celebrates in front of Theodosius II the construction of a church on the island of Patres. Theodosius I is reported to have collaborated in the initial construction.

A last example (among others which could be mentioned) is the cycle of Cyril of Jerusalem,[82] to whom various homilies were attributed that form an appendix to the collection of his authentic *Catecheses*. There is a homily on the Passion and the resurrection, which contains a commentary on the appropriate passages of the Gospels; a homily on

---

80. Orlandi, "Demetrio," 175–78.

81. Orlandi, "Theophilus of Alexandria in the Coptic Literature," in *StPatr* XVI (ed. E. Livingstone; Berlin: Akademie, in press).

82. A. Campagnano, ed., *Ps. Cirillo di Gerusalemme, Omelie copte sulla Passione, sulla Croce e sulla Vergine* (TDSA 65; Milan: Cisalpino, 1980).

the cross, which contains, among other things, the legend of the rediscovery of the cross; and a homily on the Virgin, which tells the life and dormition of Mary, and includes some apocryphal citations.

Finally, it must be remembered that it was in this period, with its characteristic use of cycles, that the last Coptic hagiographers produced their works. The study of T. Baumeister carefully describes the "clichés" on which they were based.[83] The cycles produced were that of the family of Basilides the General and that of Julius of Kbehs, the witness to the martyrdoms.

With the cyclic texts it is possible to penetrate the Coptic culture of the late period. The authors worked from general ecclesiastical and political motives. One can perceive in these authors, whose names will forever remain unknown, the desire to form a Coptic ecclesiastical society with definite, limited horizons. This new society was clearly independent and self-sufficient with respect to what had been until then the dominant Greek cultural society.

The texts were compiled for various purposes. An important aim, that of propaganda, existed on various levels. For those within the church, the purpose was to strengthen the people's faith in the tradition of the Coptic church, to reinforce and elevate the moral sentiments and customs. For those outside the church, the purpose was to affirm the antiquity and orthodoxy of the doctrine of the Coptic church in comparison with that of those separated from it.

THE SYNAXARIAL SYSTEMATIZATION

After the anonymous and even clandestine flourishing of the production of the cycles, the final decline of Coptic literature begins during the ninth through eleventh centuries. In this period the only literary activity to be noticed involves the reassembling and rearranging of older material that still had useful purposes. Almost no original production can be detected.

The Arabic language was slowly but surely submerging Coptic, both as a vehicle of Christian culture and as the administrative and everyday language. The political troubles and the ever difficult relations between the two communities led to the use of a common language to avoid an isolation that could only damage the conquered community.

In the Egyptian Middle Ages, Christian life was essentially centered

---

83. Baumeister, *Martyr.*

on the monasteries. They arranged all extant and still valid texts according to their specific use within the community.

The texts were read during the synaxeis. Therefore they were copied on books specifically designed for that purpose, with clear titles for their identification and the identification of the proper occasions on which they were to be read. These were the so-called *synaxaria* (according to the title used by the Eastern church) or homiliaries. It was in these works that various kinds of old texts were given similar form, namely, that of a homily, or of the life of a saint. Texts that originally differed from this genre were simply and often naively rearranged in order to fit the general pattern. A new title and a few lines of introduction were enough to achieve that aim.

We should bear in mind that this kind of systematization is the principal cause for the very low esteem the texts of Coptic literature have usually been accorded. They appear at first glance as something boringly uniform, without those differentiations of character and age that can form the guidelines for the historical appreciation of a literature.

Arabic Sources for Early
Egyptian Christianity*

INTRODUCTION

The subject assigned to me is "Arabic sources for early Egyptian Christianity." A real problem appears immediately, however, in the title itself: How can we speak of "sources" or "roots," when we are dealing with texts from the tenth century or even later?

The only solution I can find to solve this problem is to limit my field

---

*This paper presents only a third of the original lecture given at the conference. The outline distributed during the conference is presented here:
1. Introduction
    1. Arabization of the Copts
    2. Difficulties of the Argument
    3. Delimitation of the Topic
2. Arabic Biblical Versions
    1. The Pentateuch
    2. The Book of Judges
    3. The Scientific Version of Ibn al-ʿAssāl
3. Pseudepigraphical Literature
    1. Adam's Cycle
        1. Cave of Treasures
        2. Adam's Combat
    2. History of Joseph the Carpenter
    3. Homilies on the Assumption of Mary
4. Patristical Literature
    1. The Pachomian Cycle
    2. Macarius/Symeon
    3. Evagrius Ponticus
    4. Later Authors (Benjamin, Severus)
    5. Non-Coptic Authors (Andrew of Crete, James of Sarug)
5. Hagiographical Patristic Studies
    1. Constantine of Assiut
    2. Theodore of Edessa
    3. Claudius of Antioch
6. Canonical Literature
    1. Apostolic Canons

to the *early* Arabic *translations* of the Coptic tradition, excluding the original works written by Copts in Arabic during that period. I shall also limit myself to the period extending from the ninth to the beginning of the fourteenth century. But first, some points need to be clarified.

ARABIZATION OF THE COPTS

In 640–641 Egypt was conquered by the Arabs, and very early the process of its Arabization was initiated. In the beginning the Muslim administration was always bilingual, either Greek and Arabic, or Coptic and Arabic. But Arabic soon became the main language of the administration. In 780 C.E. it became the only recognized language.

From that moment, any Egyptian wanting to make a career in administration had to know Arabic perfectly. By the ninth century most educated Copts spoke and wrote in Arabic. Coptic was progressively disappearing, at least in the cities.

An author of the tenth century, Sawīrus (Severus) Ibn al-Muqaffa', bishop of al-Ashmūnayn in Middle Egypt, confirms this situation. He complains that nobody understands Coptic any more and that Islamic thinking is invading the Christian community. This is the reason he decided to write all his books in Arabic. We have a list of twenty-six historical and theological volumes written by him.

A confirmation of this Arabization of the Copts is given by the fact that we have no original Coptic production after the ninth century. We possess only a few translations into Coptic. By this time Cairo and the Delta had replaced Thebes as the center of the Coptic community for obvious social reasons. This explains the virtual disappearance of the Sahidic dialect and the development of Bohairic.

Parallel to the gradual regression of Coptic, Arabic texts become numerous in the Coptic community from the tenth century, and reach their peak in the thirteenth century, the golden age of Coptic-Arabic literature.

2. Didascalia
3. Others
7. Varia
   1. Magical Literature (Cyprian's Prayer, the Psalms)
   2. Esoteric Literature (The Mystery of Greek Letters)
   3. Histories of Churches and Monasteries (Abū Ṣāliḥ, Abū al-Makārim)
8. Conclusion
   1. Interest of This Literature
   2. Concrete Propositions

SOME PROBLEMS

A Large and Unknown Literature

The corpus of Coptic-Arabic literature is very large. In the 1940s, Mgr. Georg Graf offered a survey of Arabic Christian literature in his famous *Geschichte der christlichen arabischen Literatur.*[1] The five volumes contain approximately 2400 compact German pages. The first volume is dedicated to the old anonymous *translations* into Arabic and covers about 700 pages. This volume is not in fact a history but simply a checklist. For each Greek, Coptic, or Syriac work, Graf gives a list of the manuscripts of the Arabic translation. The Arabic titles are not supplied, and there is an average of two or three references per line. This gives some idea of the extent of this literature.

At least half of this literature is attributable to the Copts. In fact, during the Middle Ages the Copts alone produced as much as all the other churches together—Nestorians, Melkites, Syrians, and Maronites. One reason for this is that Copts wrote only in Arabic, while the other communities composed also in Syriac or Greek. It is also true that their numbers were more or less equal to that of the other oriental Christians of the Arab world combined.

Finally, Graf's first volume on the anonymous translations was published in 1944, over forty years ago. Many catalogues available today had not yet appeared by 1944, and many of those that were available were of rather poor quality. Graf was the first to attempt such a tremendous undertaking. The difficulties inherent in such an effort account for the many mistakes in this first volume and its lack of precise information. It is, nonetheless, the best tool available today.

What Is Coptic-Arabic Literature?

It is impossible in most cases when one deals with translations to distinguish between Coptic-Arabic literature and other Christian Arabic literatures. This distinction is relatively easy to make in the case of original works, since we usually know whether or not a particular author is Egyptian. But how can one determine if a particular translation of Cyril of Alexandria, for instance, belongs to the Coptic church, when, as is almost always the case, the translator is unknown? We do not even know in which church this text was produced. For this reason Graf did not try to distinguish among the communities in the first

1. Georg Graf, *GCAL* (StT 118, 133, 146–47, 172; Vatican City: Biblioteca Apostolica Vaticana, 1944–53).

volume (that of the translations) as he did in the other volumes (those of the original works).

I have decided that any Arabic translation circulating in the Coptic church will be taken into consideration and considered as a Coptic-Arabic text, even if the translation was made outside the Coptic church. It seems to me that the use of a text is more important than its origin.

According to this principle, if a text of John Chrysostom is copied by a Copt or circulating within the Coptic church, I will consider it as part of the legacy of the Coptic church in that period. This principle is naturally more valid when a text is preserved in many manuscripts from Egypt. It is then clear that it was read and used widely in the Coptic community (monasteries, churches, etc.).

This principle is fundamental. It means that the Coptic-Arabic tradition is not limited to the ancient Coptic tradition but includes all the other oriental traditions, especially Greek and Syriac. During the Middle Ages, the Copts assimilated a great deal of the Greek and Syriac literature, thanks to their common Arabic language.

In fact, this is not something unknown or new in the Coptic church. It seems that it was always the case. If we take, for example, Coptic hagiography, which is indeed a very important part of Coptic literature, we notice that many of these "Coptic" saints are not of Egyptian origin. Some of the most popular saints of Egypt (like Saint George or Saint Theodore, Tadros) have nothing to do with Egypt.

The same can be said for the official liturgies of the Coptic church. The daily liturgy of Saint Basil and the festive liturgy of Saint Gregory were not originally Coptic, although they are the normal liturgies of the Coptic church. Even the liturgy of Saint Cyril, which is the only Alexandrian liturgy and which is used now during Lent in the Coptic church, has been changed under Syriac influence in the last decade so that its whole structure is similar to the Basilian liturgy!

How Can the Egyptian Character or Provenience of a Translation Be Established?

It is indeed difficult to determine if a particular Arabic translation was circulating in the Coptic church. Certainly the first approach is to examine the manuscript itself for a colophon indicating its Coptic origin, foliation in Coptic cursive numerals, handwriting typical of the Egyptian script, and so on. One cannot, however, examine personally the tens of thousands of Christian Arabic manuscripts. We are, therefore, sent back to the catalogues of manuscripts.

Unfortunately, no manuscript catalogue gives us this information. A few of them give some very incomplete information about the origin of the manuscripts. Only the new catalogue of the Christian Arabic manuscripts of Paris written by Gerard Troupeau, however, supplies complete information on this point.[2]

On the other hand, according to our definition of what is Coptic, all the manuscripts that are now preserved in the Coptic Church of Egypt (in the Coptic Patriarchate, the Coptic Museum of Cairo, the Coptic monasteries and the Coptic churches) must be considered as belonging to the Coptic heritage.

As a result, my research is based chiefly on Troupeau's catalogue of the Christian Arabic manuscripts of Paris and the various catalogues of the Christian Arabic manuscripts of Egypt (excluding the Sinai, which is not a Coptic community).[3] To these sources I have added a few manuscripts I have seen previously and can certify were written by a Copt.

DELIMITATION OF THE TOPIC

The Coptic-Arabic translations cover virtually all fields: biblical and patristic literature; a well developed apocryphal and hagiographical literature; canonical, liturgical, monastic, and spiritual materials; and some historical, mystical, and magical documents.

Obviously, it is impossible for me to present all of these texts or even to make a survey of this literature. I shall limit myself to some examples, paying special attention to biblical, patristic, and hagiographic literature.[4]

ARABIC BIBLICAL VERSIONS

From the biblical versions, I shall give only three examples, taken from the Pentateuch, the Book of Judges, and the Gospels.

The Pentateuch

We know at least four different Arabic versions of the Pentateuch used in the Coptic church. They derive from Hebrew, Greek, Syriac, and Latin texts.

---

2. Gerard Troupeau, *Catalogue des manuscrits arabes*, vol. 7: *Manuscrits chrétiens* (Paris: Bibliothèque Nationale, 1972, 1974).
3. For the first reference, see ibid.
4. Cf. asterisked note above.

The Version from Hebrew

The Arabic version normally used in the Coptic church during the Middle Ages was the one produced by the Egyptian Jewish exegete Saʿid Ibn Yūsuf al-Fayyūmī, known in Jewish circles as Saadia Gaon. He was born in Egypt about 892 and died in Iraq in 942 C.E. His Arabic translation (based on the Hebrew text with a slight paraphrase) was widely adopted by the Coptic church. This is clear from the numerous manuscripts copied by Copts, which date back to the thirteenth century, and which are spread today around the world.[5]

Of these manuscripts, three belong to the thirteenth century,[6] three to the fourteenth century,[7] one to the fifteenth century.[8] Two were written in Cairo in 1584–85 by the Muslim ʿAbd Rabbih Ibn Muḥammad al-Anṣārī[9] and used for the Paris Polyglot Edition of the Bible.[10]

The Versions from Greek, Syriac, and Latin

In the Middle Ages the Coptic church also used Arabic translations made from Coptic, Greek, and Syriac. The translation made in the tenth century by al-Ḥārith b. Sinān b. Sunbāṭ and based on the Syro-Hexapla was widely used in the Coptic church. The same thing happened with an old Arabic translation from the ninth century that was based on the Greek text of the Septuagint and that spread in the Coptic church. In the eighteenth century one even finds translations based on the Latin Vulgate.

This fact illustrates well the situation of the Coptic church in the Middle Ages. At that time, Copts did not limit themselves to the original Coptic tradition but assimilated everything that was oriental. This point is very important for the medieval Arabic tradition, and I shall insist on it during my exposition.

5. Cf. Graf, GCAL 1:101–3. To my knowledge, we do not have any Christian Arabic manuscript from Egypt before the thirteenth century. So when I say that a ms. belongs to the thirteenth century, that means that it is an old, or one of the oldest known, mss. The reason is that old mss. were destroyed and replaced by new ones.

6. Leiden Warn. 377 (= Orient. 2365), written in 1239–40; Florence Laurentiana Orient. 112, written in 1245–46; and Paris Arabic 4, not dated but written in the thirteenth century.

7. Cairo, Coptic Patriarchate Bible 22 (= Graf 234; Simaika 2); London Christ. Arab. 1; and Vatican Borgia Arabic 129. They are not dated but written in the fourteenth century.

8. Vatican Arabic 2.

9. Cairo, Coptic Patriarchate Bible 32 (= Graf 235; Simaika 23); and Paris Arabic 1. On the fact that they were both written by the same scribe, cf. Khalil Samir, "Trois versions arabes du Livre des Juges: Réflexions critiques sur un livre récent," OrChr 65 (1981) 87–101, esp. 99–101.

10. Cf. Graf, GCAL 1:93–96, esp. 94, para. 1.

The Book of Judges

Another biblical example is the Book of Judges. Recently, Bengt Knutsson has published a detailed study of three Syriac-Arabic versions.[11] Two of these three versions are to be found only in the Coptic church. The third version is common to all Arabic-speaking communities. These three Arabic versions are based on the Syriac text of the Peshitta.

The Critical Version of the Gospels of Ibn al-ʿAssāl

The role played by the Awlād al-ʿAssāl in the cultural and religious revival of the Coptic church in the second third of the thirteenth century is well known.[12] Abū al-Faraǧ al-Asʿad b. al-ʿAssāl decided to make a critical translation of the Gospels. He gathered manuscripts belonging to the Greek, the Syriac, and the Coptic traditions. Here is his description of the different manuscripts used:

> For *Greek* I had two complete codices, one of them in two columns, Greek and Arabic, derived from the translation (F.384a) of Theophilus b. Tufail, the Muʿallim the Damascene, bishop of Miṣr. He had a good knowledge of Arabic and I think that Ibn al-Faḍl imitated him in his exposition. He has put the Arabic on the margin of his translation, which is dated A. H. 438. The other codex is Arabic only, the translation of the same and is dated 591.
>
> For *Syriac*, of the Gospel of Matthew I had an ancient Arabic codex, the translation and commentary of Bišr b. al-Sirrī. It has no date but his commentary indicates his excellence. I also had another Arabic codex, the translation (F.384b) and commentary of Abū al-Faraǧ b. al-Ṭayyib, the priest.
>
> Of the Gospel of Mark I had a single Arabic codex whose translator I do not know.
>
> Of Luke I had a codex of the translation and commentary of the afore-mentioned Ibn al-Sirrī. It agrees closely with the Greek and there is a note in it in a hand other than that of its scribe that it was collated in Raǧab A. H. 433. [I also had a copy from] the codex whose translator I do not know.

11. Cf. Bengt Knutsson, *Studies in the Text and Languages of Three Syriac-Arabic Versions of the Book of Judicum with Special Reference to the Middle Arabic Elements* (Leiden: E. J. Brill, 1974). Also see Samir, "Trois versions arabes," 87–101.

12. Cf. Alexis Mallon, "Ibn-ʿAssāl. Les trois écrivains de ce nom," *JA* 6 (1905) 509–29; idem, "Une école de savants égyptiens au moyen âge," *MUSJ* 1 (1906) 109–31, and *MUSJ* 2 (1907) 213–64; and G. Graf, "Die koptische Gelehrtenfamilie der Aulād al-ʿAssāl und ihr Schrifttum," *Or* n.s. 1 (1932) 34–56, 129–48, 193–204.

Of the Gospel of John I had a codex of the translation and commentary of Ibn al-Ṭayyib and the codex whose translator I do not know. Whenever then I say "some Syriac," I mean one of these codices only.

For *Coptic*, I had a complete codex (F.385a) in the hand of Stephen b. Ibrāhīm, the pupil of Abū al-Faraǧ, the monk of Damanhūr. Its date is A. Martyr. 921 and there has been collated with it an ancient codex which is in Jerusalem. On this codex I relied.

And of Luke especially, besides the codex of Ambā Stephen, I had, except for a little at the beginning, another codex in the hand of Macarius, the monk.

And of John especially, besides the codex of Stephen, I had another codex in the hand of Ambā Gabriel, the priest. Whenever, then, I say "some Coptic," I mean one of these codices only.[13]

Al-Asʿad assigned an abbreviation to each manuscript, as we do nowadays, and he gives us the table of sigla. He established his critical edition of the Gospels and indicated in the margin the various readings in red, exactly as we do. This appears to be an old Coptic tradition. Origen had done it in the beginning of the third century. This work is also typical of this period of openness and scientific revival.

PATRISTIC LITERATURE

I shall limit myself here to two examples belonging to the Coptic tradition: Stephen the Theban and Evagrius Ponticus. For reasons of space I cannot treat here such other material as the Pachomian literature, Shenoute, Macarius/Symeon, Benjamin the 38th Patriarch, Severus bishop of Ashmūnayn, or such non-Coptic authors as Andrew of Crete and James of Sarūg.[14]

Stephen the Theban[15]

All that we know about Stephen the Theban is that he was a monk. His teaching has been transmitted to us in Greek, Arabic, and Georgian, but not in Coptic. The Greek tradition attributes three works to him: a *Logos Asketikos*, *Entolai*, and a *Diataxis*. Only the *Ascetic Sermon*, edited in 1969 by Fr. E. des Places on the basis of *Paris Greek*

13. Cf. Duncan B. MacDonald, "Ibn al-ʿAssāl's Arabic Version of the Gospels," in *Homenaje á D. Francisco Codera en su jubilación del profesorado* (ed. D. E. Saavedra; Saragossa: Escar, 1904) 375–92, here 385–86. I have modified slightly the transcription of Arabic proper names.

14. Cf. asterisked note above.

15. This page on Stephen the Theban is a summary of the study I have written for the *Coptic Encyclopaedia*, which will be published in 1987 by Macmillan Co., New York.

1066 from the eleventh/twelfth century,[16] can, however, rightly be attributed to him. The Georgian text was published in 1970 by Gérard Garitte on the basis of *Sinai Georgian 248* from the tenth century.[17]

The Arabic text is attested in five manuscripts, the oldest one written in the Monastery of St. Saba in 885 C.E. The oldest Coptic Arabic manuscript was copied in Egypt in the fourteenth century. The collection of sentences is divided into 109 sections, edited in 1964 by J. M. Sauget.[18]

Around 1230, the Copt al-Ṣafī b. al-ʿAssāl summarized the *Ascetic Sermon* into an epitome *(mukhtasar)*, which is not yet edited. It is attested in two fifteenth-century manuscripts. Both were written in Egypt, although one is written in Syriac characters *(garshuni)*. This text offers, in a decidedly more literary style, a very abbreviated and summarized version of the "normal" recension.[19]

Evagrius Ponticus

Evagrius was obviously not a Copt but he had strong ties with Coptic monasticism, to which he belonged spiritually. It seems clear that a *damnatio memoriae* has played an important role against him in the Coptic church. All that we have from him in Coptic is the small fragment called *Expositio in Orationem dominicam*, published by de Lagarde,[20] and some small fragments collected by J. Muyldermans.[21]

Yet the medieval and present-day Coptic church knows Evagrius quite well. We possess an Arabic corpus of Evagrius's work attested in four Coptic Arabic manuscripts from the fourteenth century. Two of them are preserved today in the Coptic Patriarchate at Cairo, one in the National Library in Paris, and one in the Vatican Library.[22]

This corpus contains the following titles:

16. Etienne des Places, "Le 'Discours ascétique' d'Etienne de Thèbes: Texte grec inédit et traduction," *Muséon* 82 (1963) 35–59.

17. Gérard Garitte, "Le 'Discours ascétique' d'Etienne le Thébain," *Muséon* 83 (1970) 73–93.

18. Joseph-Marie Sauget, "Une version arabe du sermon ascétique d'Etienne le Thebain," *Muséon* 77 (1964) 367–406.

19. Graf, *GCAL* 1:413, para. 1, attributes to Stephen the Theban texts that actually belong to another Stephen.

20. Paul de Lagarde, *Catenae in Evangelia Aegyptiacae quae supersunt* (Göttingen: Hoyer, 1886) 13–14.

21. J. Muyldermans, "Evagriana Coptica," *Muséon* 76 (1973) 271–76.

22. The information given here is not to be found elsewhere. It is the synthesis of a study entitled *Evagre le Pontique dans la tradition arabe*, which I prepared for the Third International Congress of Coptic Studies, held in Warsaw in August 1984.

1. Lucius's letter to Evagrius
2. Treatise addressed to Elogius the Monk
3. Treatise on the vices opposed to the virtues
4. On prayer
5. "Practical" treatise
6. *Antirrheticus*
7. Treatise on the eight spirits of evil
8. On Evil Thoughts
9. Extract in the manner of the Ecclesiasticus
10. Extract in the manner of the Canticle of Canticles
11. On the Proverbs of Solomon
12. Sentences to monks
13. On the way of life of Egyptian and Syrian monks
14. Letter to Evagrius, Bishop of Antioch, on patience
15. Commentary on the Our Father (cf. bohairic text)
16. Letter to Anatolius
17. Anonymous Life of Saint Evagrius
18. Another anonymous Life of Saint Evagrius
19. Fragment from the spiritual fathers

Beside these works, we find four others attributed to Evagrius in the Arabic manuscripts of the Copts, which are not in the corpus:

20. Homily on the Master and the disciple
21. Scholia on Genesis
22. Sentences
23. *Kephalaia Gnostica* in a manuscript written in 1275.

With the exception of a few pages, this very rich corpus is unknown and unedited. This medieval Egyptian tradition is still alive. In a homily pronounced during Lent of 1980, Pope Shenudah III quoted a text from the *Antirrheticus* according to a manuscript preserved in the monastery of Dayr al-Suryān. It is interesting to note that Evagrius, after a banishment of many centuries, entered again into the Coptic church and the spiritual Coptic tradition through the medieval Arabic versions.

HAGIOGRAPHIC LITERATURE

Coptic-Arabic literature is particularly rich in hagiographical material. Graf has given a checklist of the Arabic manuscripts that deal with the Coptic saints.[23] The importance of this material is due to the fact that many of these documents are lost in Coptic but preserved in Arabic. Hagiography is a very popular genre in the Coptic church.

As examples of this rich literature, I shall discuss material on Constantine of Assiut and Victor the General, son of Romanos (martyred in the Diocletian persecution).[24]

Constantine of Assiut

Almost all our information on Constantine, Bishop of Assiut, comes from Arabic documents, the majority of which have been listed by Garitte[25] and completed by Coquin.[26] These include the first Arabic encomium of Saint John of Heraclea, the "History of the Patriarchs" of Severus of Ashmūnayn, the "Synaxarion of Upper Egypt" (20th Khoiak), and the ms. *Paris Arabic 4895* dating from the fifteenth-sixteenth century.

The Coptic-Arabic tradition provides us with seven works attributed to Constantine. Four of these are unknown in any other language.

1. The first Panegyric of Saint Claude the Martyr. The Arabic text is unpublished, though it has been translated into French by Amélineau.[27] From Arabic it was translated into Geʿez in the fourteenth century by Abba Salāmā and edited with a Latin translation by F. M. Esteives Pereira.[28] The Arabic text corresponds to the Coptic edition published by Godron.[29]

2. The second Panegyric of Saint Claude is unpublished and corresponds to the Coptic text published by Godron.[30] We know of two Arabic manuscripts that contain it.

3. Panegyric of Saint George. The beginning of this text is found in

---

23. Graf, *GCAL* 1:531–40.

24. I am summarizing here material from articles I wrote for the *Coptic Encyclopaedia* (see n. 15).

25. G. Garitte, "Constantin évêque d'Assiout," in *Coptic Studies in Honor of Walter Ewing Crum* (Boston: Byzantine Institute, 1950) 287–304; reprinted in *BBI* 2, and in Garitte, *Scripta disiecta 1941–1977* (Louvain-la-Neuve: Université Catholique de Louvain, Institut Orientaliste, 1980) 1:119–36.

26. René-Georges Coquin, "Saint Constantin, évêque d'Asyut," *Collectanea* (SOC 16; Cairo: Centro francescano di studi orientali cristiani, 1981) 151–70.

27. Emile Amélineau, *Contes et romans de l'Egypte chrétienne* (Paris: Leroux, 1888) 2:1–54.

28. F. M. Esteives Pereira, *Acta Martyrum* (CSCO 37, 1907) 1:195–216; Latin translation in CSCO 38 (1907) 175–94. This Ethiopian version is incomplete and corresponds to pp. 1–42 of Amélineau's translation.

29. Gérard Godron, *Textes coptes relatifs à saint Claude d'Antioche* (PO 166; Turnhout: Brepols, 1970) 86–169.

30. Ibid., 170–247.

Sahidic and was published by Garitte with a Latin translation.[31] The complete Arabic text is known from a single manuscript of the Coptic Museum at Cairo.

4. The first Panegyric of the Martyr John of Heraclea has survived only in Arabic and is preserved in six manuscripts varying considerably from one another. It is intended for the 4th of Paoni.

5. The second Discourse in Honor of the Martyr John of Heraclea has survived in a single Arabic manuscript from the Coptic Museum at Cairo (History 475). The text is entitled "On the Finding of His Body and the Dedication of His Church on 4 Khoiak." The Coptic text is unknown.

6. The Homily on the Fallen Soul and Its Exit from This World has survived in a single Arabic manuscript from the Coptic Patriarchate at Cairo (Theology 245). No Coptic text is known.

7. The Panegyric of Saint Isidore of Antioch (or of Chios) is preserved in a single Arabic manuscript from the monastery of Saint Antony (History 123). It is intended for 19 Pakhon. The Coptic text is unknown.

In relation to the Coptic, the Arabic tradition is lacking the two panegyrics of Saint Athanasius. It provides, however, the complete text of the panegyric of Saint George, two panegyrics of the martyr John of Heraclea, the panegyric of Saint Isidore, and a homily on the fallen soul. This shows the richness and the importance of this tradition. However, *none* of these Arabic texts has been published to date!

Victor the General

The Coptic-Arabic tradition concerning Saint Victor the General, son of Romanos, is particularly rich. Unfortunately, none of it has as yet been edited. Graf[32] collected a considerable portion of the material; his classification of the manuscripts has resulted in more confusion, however, than clarification. What is more, he confused this material with that concerning Saint Victor of Shu. The various pieces must be distinguished according to their incipits. I have collected five different accounts of the martyrdom of Saint Victor for his feast on 27th Pharmouthi and two different accounts of miracles for the anniversary of the dedication of his church on 27th Athor.

31. G. Garitte, "Le panégyrique de S. Georges attribué à Constantin d'Assiout," *Muséon* 67 (1954) 271–77.
32. Graf, *GCAL* 1:540, para. 2.

1. The panegyric by Cyriac of al-Bahnasā is the most frequently encountered in the manuscripts (at least six). In four nineteenth-century manuscripts it is attributed to Demetrius, Patriarch of Antioch. The text covers more than 200 pages. It appears to be unknown in Coptic.

2. The panegyric by Demetrius of Antioch (unknown) is found in two complete manuscripts preserved in Paris and Cairo. The text is even longer than the foregoing. It is unknown in Coptic.

3. The panegyric by Celestine of Rome is found in one complete manuscript *(Paris Arabic 4782)* and one incomplete manuscript from Cairo. The text is shorter than the two foregoing ones. It may be the translation of the Sahidic text published by E. A. Wallis Budge.[33]

4. The fourth panegyric is attributed to Theopemptos of Antioch. This name was not identified until recently, and Graf writes simply, "von (?), Erzb. von Antiochien."[34] I identified it through comparison with the ms. *Pierpont Morgan 591.*[35] The Arabic text is preserved in a single manuscript from the Coptic Patriarchate at Cairo *(History 27)* written in 1723 C.E. The length of the panegyric corresponds to eighty percent of that attributed to Cyriac of Bahnasā (Nr 1).

5. One finds in the second half of the Coptic-Arabic Synaxarion of Michael of Athrib and Malīǧ a brief note covering three pages, for the feast of Saint Victor on 27th Pharmouthi.

6. Four manuscripts give us a homily of Saint Demetrius, Patriarch of Antioch, on the building of the Church of Saint Victor, son of the Vizier Romanos, and on his miracles. We have thus two pieces joined together: a homily on the building of the church, and the account of the miracles that accompanied this event. There are usually fourteen miracles, although one sometimes finds a fifteenth. This text poses some problems we cannot discuss here.

7. Finally, the anonymous author of the first part of the Synaxarion recounts on 27th Athor the building of two churches in honor of Saint Victor, as reported by mother Martha. The first was in Antioch under the Patriarch Theodore, and the second in Upper Egypt where the saint spent a whole year before his martyrdom.

---

33. E. A. Wallis Budge, *Coptic Martyrdoms Etc. in the Dialect of Upper Egypt, Edited With English Translation* (London: British Museum, 1914); the second text is entitled "The Encomium of Celestinus, Archbishop of Rome, on Victor the General."

34. Graf, *GCAL* 1:540.

35. Henri Hyvernat, ed., *Bybliothecae Pierpont Morgan Codices coptici photographicae expressi* (Rome, 1922) vol. 28.

Four other manuscripts dealing with Victor the General remain unidentified because of the excessively vague information given by the catalogues. It is finally interesting to note that nine churches designated by the name of this Saint Victor are mentioned by Abū Ṣāliḥ (ca. 1210). They were located in Arḍ al-Habaš near Cairo, opposite to it, at Ǧīzah, at Ǧalfah (district of Banī Mazār), at al-Qalandamūn near Antinoe, at Sāqiyat Mūsā south of al-Ashmūnayn, at al-Khuṣūṣ east of Assiut, at Qifṭ, and at Qamūlah (district of Qūṣ).[36]

Once again I would like to underline the abundance of this Arabic material and the absence of editions in any form for most of it.

CONCLUDING REMARKS

Interest of the Coptic-Arabic Literature

To begin with, Coptic-Arabic literature is a very rich and large tradition. There are different explanations for this fact.

One is that the Copts were very interested in religious questions, and they tried to translate into Arabic every religious text they could find (if it was not directly opposed to their faith). They assimilated the tradition of the non-Coptic Christians, sometimes by "copticizing" them. So the Coptic-Arabic literature reflects not only the old Coptic literature but also the Syriac and the Byzantine literatures, not to speak of the earlier patristic literature.

Another explanation is the time span covered by this literature. The translation of texts into Arabic started in the ninth century and continues today. Last year while I was teaching in the Coptic Catholic Seminary of Maadi, near Cairo, two seminarians asked to borrow a rare book that I had so that they might copy it during the night since I was leaving the next day. As opposed to Coptic, Arabic is not a dead language but a living one.

As a consequence, many Coptic texts lost in the original can be found in Arabic, saved by the Copts of the Middle Ages. Very often Coptic texts are fragmentary, and it happens more than once that we find these fragments not only in one complete Arabic version but in two or even three. As a result, Arabic is very important for saving or reconstructing the Coptic tradition. Even when we possess the Coptic text, Arabic often helps us to understand it or better to reconstruct it.

36. Abû Ṣâlih, *The Churches and Monasteries of Egypt and Some Neighboring Countries: Attributed to Abû Ṣâlih, the Armenian* (trans. B. T. A. Evetts; 2d ed.; London: Butler & Tanner, 1969) fol. 41b, 42a, 74a, 90a, 92a, 103a, 104a.

Coptic-Arabic literature has another interest usually neglected by the Coptologists: it helps us to understand a still living culture. Coptic tradition did not end in the ninth century. For over a thousand years Coptic-Arabic tradition has developed the possibilities that were present in the first millennium of Coptic thought.

Let us take an example. One can hardly imagine an Islamicist working on early Islam who would ignore the later tradition. Even if he is interested only in the primitive Islamic tradition, he will understand it much better through the interpretation of modern Muslims. Why not the same for the Coptic tradition? I firmly believe that something must change in our attitude toward medieval and modern Coptic thinking. Coptic literature must not be considered only a museum piece!

Two Concrete Proposals

I would like to conclude with two suggestions. First, most of these Coptic-Arabic texts (let us say at least eighty percent of them) are still unpublished and not translated. The first priority is thus a systematic editing and translating of this material. This will make the material available to those who know only Greek or Coptic. For different reasons (cultural, economic, political), this work cannot be done in Egypt, but must be undertaken in the West.

There are three fields where Coptic-Arabic literature is especially useful because of its richness: pseudepigraphical, hagiographical, and monastic literatures. I would argue that systematic work in these three fields should have priority. It should consist first of an inventory of the manuscripts accompanied by their incipits in order to make their classification possible, and then the production of *critical* editions, translations, and lexica.

In these three fields small, limited projects could be initiated. The projects could focus on particular streams of tradition, such as Adam's cycle, the homilies on the assumption of Mary, the dossier of Constantine of Assiut, the homilies in honor of Saint George or of Saint Claudius, the lives of Pachomius, or the works of Shenoute. As we have seen, the list is large.

My second suggestion is that a specialist in Coptic-Arabic literature should be employed wherever Coptic is being taught. As it is now, there are hardly any specialists in this field anywhere in the world. Furthermore, it is unfair to suggest that someone specialize in Coptic-Arabic literature if there are no positions available for that person at the end of his or her training. The current situation is, I think, very deleterious for Coptic studies in general. Ideally, each center for Coptic studies should have an Arabist *specialized in* and dedicated to Coptic-Arabic studies.

My aim in this paper has been to show the importance of Coptic-Arabic literature in itself, as well as its importance for Coptic studies in general. It is certainly not a primary source for our knowledge of early Egyptian Christianity; but though a secondary source, it is often more important than the Coptic literature because of its richness. It is my hope that some might see it as an indispensable complement to Coptic studies. If so, I shall be repaid for my effort!

PART TWO

THE ENVIRONMENT OF
EARLY CHRISTIANITY IN EGYPT

The Socio-Economic Background
of Christianity
in Egypt*

Every age has its own conceptual models and presuppositions for understanding the rise of religious movements. Within this century, for example, phenomenology, history of religions, form criticism, psychology, and more recently, sociology have all contributed to the understanding of the origins of Christianity. The solutions proposed vary with the questions asked in spite of the fact that they may share formal or substantive, systematic or normative frameworks.

The use of social scientific paradigms to understand the origins of Christianity over the last decade has brought with it a series of models and generalizations, many of which lack specificity. In part the reasons lie in the paucity of data, unreliable crosscultural adjustments and technical terminology. Efforts have concentrated primarily on obtaining information about sociological contexts from the New Testament itself. Studies by Theissen, Malherbe, and Gager, among others, provide interesting and helpful hypotheses about the relationship between the beliefs of early Christians and their social milieu but also are notable for the absence of complementary socio-economic data.[1]

*My thanks to Bob Sider and Birger Pearson, who have commented on earlier drafts. The research for this paper was funded by the Social Sciences and Humanities Research Council of Canada.
    1. Gerd Theissen has written extensively on the sociology of early Christianity; see *Sociology of Early Palestinian Christianity* (trans. J. Bowden; Philadelphia: Fortress Press, 1978) and *The Social Setting of Pauline Christianity: Essays on Corinth* (ed. and trans. J. Schütz; Philadelphia: Fortress Press, 1982). For a survey of Theissen's publications, see John Schütz, "Steps Toward a Sociology of Primitive Christianity: A Critique of the Work of Gerd Theissen," paper presented at the annual meeting of the Society of Biblical Literature, American Academy of Religion, San Francisco, 1977. See also Abraham Malherbe, *Social Aspects of Early Christianity* (2d enl. ed.; Philadelphia:

Judge and Meeks have contributed significantly to redressing this difficulty but have not focused on Egypt.[2]

The roots of Egyptian Christianity can be viewed from a variety of different perspectives within sociology. One approach would be to understand it as a sectarian movement within Judaism that appealed to the socially unintegrated and provided normative values and behavioral patterns that competed for dominance in the Roman world. Another might be to approach it as a response to fluctuations in a political economy in which social groups have lost status and are seeking holistic experiences to compensate for their anomie. In each case, the task for those employing sociological paradigms is to explain or point out the critical juncture points where meanings are institutionalized and where economy and the development of ideology intersect. If indeed there is a "new consensus" emerging that situates early Christians at a social level noticeably higher than did Deissmann,[3] can it be documented socially and economically? Can social class be related to the quest for a salvation religion? The purpose of this paper is to pursue such an approach by examining some of the socioeconomic data surrounding Octavian's defeat of Cleopatra in the first century C.E. and to set the stage for the entrance of Christianity into Egypt.

The defeat of the Ptolemies, the descendents of Alexander the Great's general, forced the Romans to face the identical problem that had confronted the Ptolemies: how to control socially a foreign race and culture whose language and social formation (mode of production) were incongruent with their own. Neither the Greeks nor the Romans wished to be assimilated into the culture they had conquered, nor did they advocate opening their ranks and providing mobility for the native Egyptians. But political and economic situations frequently erupt that evoke a repositioning of normative values (e.g., wars, droughts, trade). Early Greek behavioral patterns that advocated ethnic segrega-

Fortress Press, 1983), and John Gager, *Kingdom and Community: The Social World of Early Christianity* (Englewood Cliffs, N.J.: Prentice-Hall, 1975).

2. See E. A. Judge, *The Social Pattern of Christian Groups in the First Century: Some Prolegomena to the Study of the New Testament on Social Organization* (London: Tyndale Press, 1960); idem, *Rank and Status in the World of the Caesars and St. Paul* (UCantP 29; Christchurch: Univ. of Canterbury Press, 1982); and Wayne Meeks, *The First Urban Christians: The Social World of the Apostle Paul* (New Haven: Yale Univ. Press, 1982).

3. See Malherbe, *Social Aspects*, 31.

tion, closed kinship systems, and legal prescriptions for social interaction dissolved over time. By the end of the Ptolemaic epoch a
number of native Egyptians had been incorporated into the army and
received veteran (cleruch) land, had married Greek citizens, and were
able to enter the gymnasium. These native Egyptians represented the
more upwardly mobile of their class. Their numbers, however, never
amounted to a significant proportion of the non-Greek elite.[4]

When Augustus Caesar began his tenure, Egypt was an economically
and administratively broken country. Productivity had fallen considerably and systems of taxation no longer guaranteed the state ready
capital.

The Ptolemies had followed the ancient Pharaonic system whereby
the state had been personified in and identified with the king. Egypt's
territory was his private property, and the exploitation and distribution
of the country's resources were for him to decide.

This policy grew out of the unique geographical and climatic
conditions of Egypt. Egypt is a desert with a ribbon of inhabited land
bordering the Nile. Irrigation farming is necessary to nourish the dry
soil and to encourage the collection of silt. The productivity of the state
is dependent on the proper maintenance of the irrigation system. And
the proper maintenance of the irrigation system is dependent on the
dominant class being able to control the means of production.

Rostovtzeff long ago pointed out that it was ironic that the Ptolemies
"almost entirely ignored the essence of the Greek economic system:
private property recognized and protected by the state as the basis of
society, and the free play of economic forces and economic initiative.
. . ."[5] Only in the last hundred years of Ptolemaic domination is there
evidence that possession of land had begun to undergo a transition and
slowly acquire the character of private property.[6] Nevertheless, the
overwhelming majority of the producers were responsible to the state
and were compelled to buy their agricultural and industrial goods from

---

4. See M. Avi-Yonah, *Hellenism and the East: Contacts and Interrelations from
Alexander to the Roman Empire* (Ann Arbor, Mich.: University Microfilms, 1978), and H.
A. Green, "The Economic and Social Origins of Gnosticism" (Ph.D. diss., St. Andrews
University, 1982) 114.
5. M. Rostovtzeff, *The Social and Economic History of the Hellenistic World* (3 vols.; 2d
ed.; Oxford: Clarendon Press, 1959) 1:273.
6. Ibid. 2:733 and 3:1499 n. 151. See also R. Taubenschlag, *The Law of Graeco-Roman
Egypt in the Light of the Papyri 332 B.C.E.–640 C.E.* (2d ed.; Warsaw: Państwowe
Wydawnictwo Naukowe, 1955) 235.

TABLE 1

Mode of Production*

Ptolemaic period	Roman period
absence of private property	private property
public irrigation	private and public irrigation
state control of the means of production	private and state control of the means of production
state control of distribution	private and state control of distribution
fertile period of technological development	technology almost stagnant
state management of the economy, salaried bureaucracy	some decentralization of state management of the economy, salaried and unsalaried bureaucracy
city as industrial producer and consumer	city as industrial producer and consumer
status stratification (Greeks, epigoni, other, Egyptians)	status stratification (Romans, Greek citizens, other, Egyptians, slaves)

*SOURCE: H. A. Green, "The Economic and Social Origins of Gnosticism" (Ph.D. diss., St. Andrews University, 1982) 120.

state monopolies and to sell their surpluses to the state at predetermined prices.[7]

Roman conquest of Egypt significantly altered the Ptolemaic mode of production. Private ownership was emancipated from external constraints, several state monopolies were devolved, the bureaucracy was restructured and private accountability was increased. (For a comparison between the modes of production during the Ptolemaic and Roman periods, see table 1.)

Surprisingly, slavery remained a negligible factor in Egypt despite

7. See Avi-Yonah, *Hellenism*, 194–218; Taubenschlag, *Law*, 658–84; Rostovtzeff, *Hellenistic World* 1:255–422; and C. Préaux, *L'Economie royale des Lagides* (Brussels: La Fondation égyptologique reine Elisabeth, 1939).

the fact that the Italian economy was based on the slave mode of production. Nearly a century ago Max Weber wrote that "production based upon slavery . . . played no role whatever . . . ,"[8] and this position continues to be reaffirmed by scholars today: "il est absolument certain que l'économie agraire de l'Egypte n'est pas fondée sur le travail servile. . . ."[9] At best, agrarian slavery remained "a residual phenomenon that existed on the edges of the main rural work force."[10] Land was cultivated by free peasants as tenants of the state, the temples, or private landholders.

The introduction of private property in Egypt coincided with the development of the concept of absolute property in Roman law. In Godelier's assessment, this transition occurred alongside the expansion of the Roman Empire.[11] War, tribute, and slaves led to new relations of production, and "economic relationships progressed constantly [thereafter] in the direction of the reinforcement of rights of private property. . . ."[12] The combination of introducing private ownership and at the same time maintaining control of key sectors in the economy was politically astute. It allowed Roman notables immediate domination of social class and simultaneously reaffirmed the state as an equal partner in Egypt's destiny.

Octavian's policies of privatization included selling off some crown land, defining *cleruch* land as private, offering Roman veterans land grants, confiscating temple land and redistributing it to private owners, and extending to imperial favorites imperial grants.

By the early first century C.E., taking land out of the public sector (i.e., crown land) was a common practice:

> To Gaius Seppius Rufus, from Polemon son of Tryphon and Archelaus . . .
> we wish to purchase in the Oxyrhynchite nome of the crown land
> returned as unproductive. . . .[13]

8. Max Weber, *The Agrarian Sociology of Ancient Civilizations* (trans. R. I. Frank; London: NLB, 1976) 247.

9. See Modrzejewski's comments in response to D. Bonneau's paper, "Esclavage et irrigation d'après la documentation papyrologique," in *Actes du Colloque 1973 sur l'Esclavage* (ALUB 182; Paris: Belles Lettres, 1976) 327. More recently, see N. Lewis, *Life in Egypt Under Roman Rule* (London: Oxford Univ. Press, 1983) 57.

10. P. Anderson, *Passages from Antiquity to Feudalism* (New York: Humanities Press, 1974) 21.

11. M. Godelier, "The Concept of the 'Asiatic Mode of Production' and Marxist Models of Social Evolution," in *Relations of Production: Marxist Approaches to Economic Anthropology* (ed. D. Seddon; London: Cass, 1978) 244.

12. A. I. Pavlovskaia, "On the Discussion of the Asiatic Mode of Production in *La Pensée* and *Eirene*," *SSH* 4 (1965) 43.

13. P. Oxy. 721. See H. MacLennan, *Oxyrhynchus: An Economic and Social Study*

Similarly, the confiscation of temple land and its redistribution on the open market, especially in Lower Egypt, commenced soon after Octavian's tenure.[14] In both these reclassifications of land, the goal was to encourage Egyptians, Semites or Greeks, to purchase unproductive land and personally to bear the responsibility of increasing its productivity.

The distribution of land to imperial favorites had a different goal. Its aim was to reward the socially and politically elected economically. This policy significantly affected the political economy of Egypt as numerous individuals received large land grants but remained absentee landlords. These included Livia (Augustus's wife),[15] Messalina (Claudius's wife),[16] Petronius,[17] Seneca[18] and Dorphorus,[19] among others, in the first century C.E. Some well-placed aristocratic Alexandrians may also have been recipients of imperial land grants.[20] Called *ousiae*, these land grants have been traditionally viewed as tied to the emperor. Parassoglou's recent evidence, however, that *ousiae* also can be applied to private estates with no imperial connections has radically changed perceptions regarding the extent of private holdings in the first century C.E.[21] (See table 2 for private [nonimperial] *ousiae* in the Arsinoite nome in the first century C.E.) This implies that large tracts of fertile land were placed in the open market and offered to Roman, Greek, and Semitic elites. According to Parassoglou, Livia and Seneca are among the more well known who bought land on the open market.[22] The consequences of this policy were twofold. First, urban wealth lay in rural holdings that acted as a hinterland to support city needs. Second, it solidified the socio-economic domination of Romans in spite of the fact that they were absentee landlords.

(Amsterdam: A. M. Hakkert, 1968) 16; and G. M. Parassoglou, *Imperial Estates in Roman Egypt* (ASP 18; Amsterdam: A. M. Hakkert, 1978) 8 and n. 20.

14. For example, see P. Tebt. 302, the temple of Soknebtunis, and J. A. S. Evans, "A Social and Economic History of an Egyptian Temple in the Graeco-Roman Period," *YCS* 17 (1961): 149–283.

15. See, e.g., SB 9150; P. Lond. 445 (II, p. 166); P. Mich. 560; PSI 1028; P. Ryl. 126; and P. Mil. 6.

16. See, e.g., P. Ryl. 87, 684; WChr. 367; and P. Flor. 40.

17. See, e.g., P. Ryl. 127 and BGU 650.

18. See, e.g., P. Ryl. 99, 207; P. Hamb. 3; P. Lips. 115; BGU 104, 172, 202; P. Bour. 42; P. Chic. 5, 16, 18, 26, 53, 62, 65, 67, 71; P. Mich. 223–25; PSI 448; and P. Oxy. 2873, 3051.

19. See, e.g., P. Ryl. 99, 171; SB 9205, 10512; P. Oslo. 21; P. Chic. 52; P. Bour. 42; P. Mich. 223–24; and P. Stras. 210.

20. M. Rostovtzeff, *The Social and Economic History of the Roman Empire* (2d ed.; Oxford: Clarendon Press, 1957) 1:293–94 and 2:672 n. 45.

21. Parassoglou, *Imperial Estates*, 7 and 10.

22. Ibid.

TABLE 2

Private (Nonimperial) Ousiae in the Arsinoite
Nome in the First Century C.E.

Date (C.E.)	Place	Ousia - Reference
29	Karanis	P. Osl. 33
ca. 30	Theogonis	SB 10535
34		P. Mich. 312
26	Euhemeria	P. Ryl. 166
ca. 30		P. Ryl. 128
31		P. Ryl. 131
32–33		P. Ryl. 132, 133
34		P. Ryl. 135
39		P. Ryl. 167
39		P. Ryl. 146
42		P. Ryl. 152
34–35	Philadelphia	P. Sorbonne inv. 2367
65–66	Hermoupolis	P. Lond. 1213; 1214; 1215 (III, p. 121)
36	Arsinoite nome	P. Mich. 232
38		P. Ryl. 145

*SOURCES: G. M. Parassoglou, *Imperial Estates in Roman Egypt* (ASP 18; Amsterdam: Hakkert, 1978) appendix 1; D. Crawford, "Imperial Estates," in *Studies in Roman Property* (ed. M. Finley; Cambridge: Cambridge Univ. Press, 1976) 59; M. Rostovtzeff, *The Social and Economic History of the Roman Empire* (2d ed.; Oxford: Clarendon Press, 1957) 2:669 n. 45.

The devolution of state monopolies is similarly indicative of Octavian's policy of private ownership of production and consumption. Although the state continued to control the more important industries (e.g., mining,[23] the production of linen and wool and the fulling of cloth,[24] and banking[25]), others such as the brewing of beer[26]

23. A. C. Johnson, *An Economic Survey of Ancient Rome: Roman Egypt to the Reign of Diocletian*, in *An Economic Survey of Ancient Rome* (ed. Tenny Frank; 2d ed.; Paterson, N.J.: Pageant Books, 1959) 2:241.
24. Ibid., 326.
25. Taubenschlag, *Law*, 677.
26. Ibid., 669; and S. Wallace, *Taxation in Egypt from Augustus to Diocletian* (Oxford: Oxford Univ. Press, 1938) 187.

and the manufacture and sale of perfumes,[27] oil,[28] and paper[29] entered the private market for the first time.

By the end of Octavian's reign, Egypt had been restored to economic health.[30] His reclamation of large tracts of land, his restoration of the irrigation system, and his policy of increased productivity by privatizing property and industry all acted as stimulants. The increase in economic prosperity, however, may be as much a reflection of the degeneration of Ptolemaic economic life and state management as of Roman creativity. In real terms technology barely advanced in Egypt in the first century C.E.[31] Tools for agricultural production remained relatively constant[32] and industries (with the exception of the silk and glass industries[33]) made little technological progress. At best, without major technological developments or changes in the relations of production, agricultural productivity could have appreciated only modestly from the peak periods under the Ptolemies. Success, in the final analysis, depended more on weather than on planting techniques or even labor.[34] Consequently, the relative increase in economic prosperity in the first century C.E. in Roman Egypt may be due more to Octavian's restoration of the irrigation system, coinciding with a century of good floods. In the words of Forbes, "the lack of stimulants to industrialize [i.e., to create a new means of production] left ancient technology practically stagnant during the Roman Empire."[35] With the exception of religion, the Roman world was uncreative.

The economic effects of Roman sovereignty on the Egyptian inhabitants were mixed. In one sense, little changed. The nature of life in antiquity counteracted such developments as the growth of an urban movement or the increased importance of industry and commerce over

27. Taubenschlag, *Law*, 670; and Johnson, *Roman Egypt*, 340.

28. Johnson, *Roman Egypt*, 328; and Evans, "Egyptian Temple," 226.

29. Strabo *Geography* 17.1.15. See also N. Lewis, *Papyrus in Classical Antiquity* (Oxford: Clarendon Press, 1974).

30. See Johnson, *Roman Egypt*, 12; Wallace, *Taxation*, 136; and Rostovtzeff, "Roman Exploitation of Egypt in the First Century A.D.," *JEBH* 1 (1929) 337–64.

31. See Claude Mosse, *The Ancient World at Work* (trans. J. Lloyd; London: Chatto & Windus, 1969) 31; and M. I. Finley, "Technical Innovation and Economic Progress in the Ancient World," *EcHR* 18 (1965) 29–45.

32. See the comments of K. D. White, *Roman Farming* (London: Thames & Hudson, 1970) 156.

33. On silk, see Strabo *Geography* 2.5.12 and 17.1.13. See also Johnson, *Roman Egypt*, 339. On glass blowing, see D. B. Harden, "Glass and Glazes," in *A History of Technology* (ed. C. Singer et al.; Oxford: Clarendon Press, 1956) 2:337.

34. For a similar argument concerning the third century C.E., see C. R. Whittaker, "Agri Deserti," in *Studies in Roman Property* (ed. M. I. Finley; Cambridge: Cambridge Univ. Press, 1976) 137–65.

35. R. J. Forbes, *Studies in Ancient Technology* (Leiden: E. J. Brill, 1964) 2:99.

agriculture.[36] Eighty percent of the labor force in antiquity remained deployed in agriculture. "The bulk of the labour force in the Roman Empire was primarily peasants who produced most of what they themselves consumed and consumed most of what they produced."[37] And everyone was involved in agriculture, including soldiers and the innumerable petty officials.[38]

The native Egyptian peasants continued to perform the same economic tasks they had performed under the Ptolemies, and received the same social benefits. Crown land continued to be leased to them. Leases were for short terms and indicated category of production, projected agricultural yield, and also biographical data. Similarly, imperial and private *ousiae* developed rental conditions for the Egyptian peasant that were standardized to those of crown land. If the average rental for crown and private land between 26 and 100 C.E. was less than seven and three-quarters *artabae* of wheat per *arura*, and the average income of the ordinary peasant was 210 *drachmae* a year, the peasant's ability to purchase private property was minimal.[39] The sale value of private property between 27 and 99 C.E. averaged 185 *drachmae* per *arura*.[40] Consequently, the transition from public to private property had little meaning for the peasants. Economically deprived, their vocation socially stigmatized them. Added to this humiliation, the land they farmed was differentiated by sectors of the population. The Egyptian peasants farmed corn land; others farmed orchard land.[41] Moreover, it was these same Egyptian peasants who were obligated by the corvée to work for five days a year on the public irrigation system[42] and to maintain the embankments of the irrigation system of the private landholder.[43]

The Egyptian and Semitic elite that had become upwardly mobile during the final stages of the Ptolemaic epoch took advantage of the distribution of land on the open marketplace.[44] They were not bound by leases and shared in the Roman exploitation of the Egyptian

36. For an opposing view, see Rostovtzeff, *Roman Empire* 1:273; and Wallace, *Taxation*, 339.

37. K. Hopkins, "Taxes and Trade in the Roman Empire," *JRS* 70 (1980) 104.

38. M. I. Finley, *The Ancient Economy* (Berkeley and Los Angeles: Univ. of California Press, 1973) 97; and Lewis, *Life in Egypt*.

39. See Johnson, *Roman Egypt*, 81, 304, and 504. All figures are approximations.

40. Ibid., 147.

41. See D. Crawford, "Imperial Estates," in *Studies in Roman Property* (ed. Finley) 45.

42. Johnson, *Roman Egypt*, 13. See also Suetonius *Life of the Caesars* 2.18.2.

43. Johnson, *Roman Egypt*, 13.

44. See Avi-Yonah, *Hellenism*, and Green, "Origins of Gnosticism."

peasants. But changes in Roman fiscal policy and administration that accompanied the economic transformation altered the economic and social possibilities of the non-Roman elite. With privatization came the loss of revenues. In part, to compensate for this loss new taxes in the industrial and agricultural sectors were introduced.[45] The civil service was reformed. Under the Ptolemies government bureaucrats were employed to collect taxes after the tax farmer had insured the royal treasury against loss. Under the Romans, the new policy compelled the tax farmer to collect the taxes himself. Consequently, he had to adopt the role of civil servant without receiving any remuneration and simultaneously had to risk a capital loss on his investment. This policy would later contribute significantly to the collapse of Roman Egypt and the rise of a new social formation (i.e., feudalism).

The most socially damaging fiscal reform was the introduction of the *laographia* (poll tax) in 24 B.C.E. Only those possessing Greek or Roman citizenship were exempted. For the Egyptian peasant it meant a further tax burden. For the Semite, in particular the Jew, and the upwardly mobile Egyptian, it was both an embarrassment and an impediment. For thirty years both social groupings were able to deflate the issue. But in 5 C.E. the Romans actively developed criteria to establish who was a Greek. Those who had claimed exemption on the basis of their social status were compelled thereafter to forfeit their civic privileges and be identified as non-Greek, Egyptian. High social status is not identical to high social class. As Gager says, "it is precisely this distinction between class and status that makes it possible to explain why some persons of relatively high social status but few of high social class, were attracted to Christianity."[46] The immediate consequences for the socially stigmatized were many: occupational mobility was curtailed, jobs in the civil service were closed, Greek education through the gymnasium was restricted, and the tax burden was increased. Stripped of material benefits and legal rewards, they saw their status and social position in the stratification system deteriorate rapidly. Differences in social status both affect a person's experience of social structure and delimit the person's means of expressing it. The polarization of the population into Romans/Greeks and Egyptians lay at the root of social and psychic dislocation in the first century C.E. for educated minority groups

---

45. See Wallace, *Taxation*.

46. J. Gager, "Social Description and Sociological Explanation in the Study of Early Christianity: A Review Essay," in *The Bible and Liberation: Politics and Social Hermeneutics* (ed. N. Gottwald; Maryknoll, N.Y.: Orbis Books, 1983) 439.

previously sharing high status. The social degradation carried by this fiscal reform contributed significantly to the development of salvation religions, such as Gnosticism and Christianity.

This brief synopsis of the socio-economic situation in Roman Egypt in the first century C.E. sets the stage for the arrival of early Christian missionaries. Who they were or when they arrived remains a mystery. There are no hard data for the beginning of Christianity in Egypt. Eusebius's remark that Mark was the founder and first bishop of the church in Alexandria is evidence solely of ecclesiastical tradition, not fact.[47] Similarly, his list of bishops who succeeded Mark is unreliable until Demetrius's appearance in 189 C.E. With the exception of Apollos, an Alexandrian Jew[48] who was an associate of Paul's and active in the Corinthian[49] and Ephesian churches,[50] Alexandrian Christians are unknown in the first century.

The rise of religious movements is an expression of both social and psychic experiences. It points to social conflict and the search for social integration, to psychic revolt and the quest for meaning. In Alexandria, in the wake of numerous Greek-Jewish clashes, a segment of the population was experiencing acute social and psychic dislocation. Anomic, they also possessed a social cause. A salvation religion has the best chance of being permanent when a privileged class loses its political power to a bureaucratic, militaristic state.[51] Both Christianity and Gnosticism were new salvation religions. Their development intersected Roman socio-economic development in Egypt.

The Jewish community in Egypt was large and prominent enough to attract "teachers" of many kinds. In the first century C.E. ten to fifteen percent of the Egyptian population was Jewish.[52] Alexandria, in Mommsen's words, was "almost as much a city of the Jews as of the Greeks."[53] Jewish proselytism was encouraged. Matthew,[54] Juvenal,[55] Dio,[56] Philo,[57] and Seneca[58] all mention it.

47. Eusebius H. E. 2.16.1.
48. Acts 18:24.
49. 1 Cor. 3:16.
50. 1 Cor. 16:12.
51. M. Weber, The Sociology of Religion (trans,. E. Fischoff; Boston: Beacon Press, 1964) 121.
52. See Green, "Origins of Gnosticism," 171–87.
53. T. Mommsen, The Provinces of the Roman Empire from Caesar to Diocletian (trans. W. F. Dickson; New York: Charles Scribner's Sons, 1899) 2:177.
54. Matt. 23:15.
55. Juvenal Saturae 3.10–18 and 14.96–106.
56. Dio Cassius Hist. Rom. 57.5.
57. Philo Spec. 1.51–52, and Flacc. 46.
58. Seneca De Superstitione in Augustine De Civ. Dei 6.11, and Epis. Mor. 108.22.

The large demographic presence and high profile of the Jews in Alexandria are well documented.[59] The particular consequences of the *laographia*—social stigmatization and legal disenfranchisement—and the resulting status dissonance to a subgroup of the educated within the Jewish mosaic, however, signify a critical juncture in the history of Alexandrian Judaism. According to Weber, the distinctive character of the disenfranchised is that they tend "to work in the direction . . . of seeking salvation through mystical channels."[60] The quest for transcendence implies a search for authority outside the institutionalized offices of normative society. It exposes in its formative stages "the mind-set of a minority group."[61]

If Christian missionaries were active in Egypt, this disenfranchised Jewish minority group would have been extremely receptive. The magnetism of Christianity for these secularized and assimilated Jews was compensation for their anomie and lowered social status. In seeking salvation, they remained wedded to monotheism. If Paul's attempt at social organization of early Christians is typical, then an appeal by Christians would have been made in the synagogues and in the homes of anomic Jews in Alexandria.[62] Responsive Jews in turn would have acted as catalysts for other educated and disenfranchised minority groups—native Egyptians, other Semites, and Greeks—who shared their social and personal dislocation. These downwardly mobile elites would have had increased motivation to turn to Christianity after 70 C.E., the year Jerusalem was destroyed and the Flavians confiscated *ousiae*.[63] Romans no longer considered language and cultural assimilation as sufficient grounds for social and legal integration.

The socio-economic background of Christianity in Egypt has been examined in this paper as a means of pinpointing a particular social group with rank and status. Greek in thinking and monotheistically inclined, these outsiders would have achieved social and psychic integration through belief in Jesus Christ. It would have enabled them to attain spiritual solace and collectively unite as members of a new community.

59. V. Tcherikover, A. Fuks, and M. Stern, *CPJ* (3 vols.; Cambridge: Harvard Univ. Press, 1957–64).
60. Weber, *Sociology of Religion,* xliii.
61. Malherbe, *Social Aspects,* 38.
62. See Malherbe's informative discussion of house churches in *Social Aspects,* 66. See also Meeks, *First Urban Christians.*
63. Parassoglou, *Imperial Estates,* 29; Crawford, "Imperial Estates," 53.

The development of Christianity after the first century C.E. is beyond the scope of this paper. A few comments, however, will indicate the contours of future research.

One approach would be to investigate the ideological and structural influences on Christianity in Roman Egypt by exploiting the models and typologies developed by those studying sectarian movements.[64] The distinctiveness of Christian exclusivism led to organizational forms in which doctrine and structure became centralized, hierarchized, and formalized. Such an undertaking would necessitate specifying the juncture points where meanings are institutionalized. Another approach would be to map the relationship between social class and the development of Christianity against the background of economic development in Egypt. Do the disenchanted and disenfranchised minority elites continue to act as the vanguard for Christian salvation?

By the end of the first century the government's inability to find tax farmers was endemic.[65] The reorganization of the civil service was in actual fact compulsory public service to ensure the treasury a constant source of capital. The refusal of tax collectors to volunteer was due to their personal liability for the payment of arrears, and ultimately the loss of their private property as compensation. Even profiteering to make up losses was not always a fail-safe proposition. The desertion of land by the peasant is a recurring phenomenon and too unpredictable to guarantee the potential tax farmer profits. These two developments, the lack of tax farmers and the desertion of the land, combined to produce a large rural native Egyptian population severed from its history and the government. In addition, the increasing discrimination between landowners and peasants, inflation, and the collapse of the irrigation system further disrupted the delicate balance between social contribution and marginality. By the third century C.E., civil war and runaway inflation led to large tracts of land being incorporated into privately owned estates, an early sign of feudalism.

The socio-economic development of Roman Egypt from the second to the fourth centuries, therefore, can be presumed to have directly influenced the growth and speed of the development of Christianity. Normative values were transformed with the changing political and economic situation. Roman behaviorial patterns promoting ethnic segregation, closed kinship systems, and legal prescriptions for social

64. See especially the works of Bryan Wilson.
65. See, e.g., P. Oxy. 44 and MacLennan's discussion in *Oxyrhynchus*, 19.

interaction dissolved. Similar to the Ptolemies, the Romans accommodated the native Egyptian.

The initial gravitation by urban Jews, Greeks, and Egyptians to Christianity was a product of their anomic situation. In contrast, by the late second century, Christianity in Egypt progressively appealed to urban educated Greeks and non-Egyptians. It would require nearly another century, however, before significant numbers of rural Egyptian peasants became Christians. The spread of Christianity from social class to social class and from urban areas to rural environments is tied also to the socio-economic development of Roman Egypt. The fragmentation of Roman ideology and economy in Egypt and the institutionalization of Christian belief systems and social organizations are highly correlated.

The use of sociological models to map the interaction between social classes and the intersection of economy and Christian ideology has the potential of bringing forth a wealth of data to the analysis of orthodoxy and heresy, Catholic, Coptic and gnostic Christianity in Roman Egypt. By locating Christianity in its wider social context the social anxieties felt by particular social groupings can be identified. Their social position in the stratification system may help us to understand more specifically how early Egyptian Christianity adjusted to the commanding ethos of its contemporary world.

Mithra in Egypt

THE PROBLEM

Extensive and widespread material remains of Mithraism have been located throughout Northern Africa from Algeria to Libya. Over fifty years ago, however, it was recognized that this presence of Mithraic worship in Northern Africa was due primarily to the influence of Roman military operations.[1] On the other hand, at the other end of the Mediterranean Basin, in Syria and Palestine, where a large number of Roman military operations were carried out over a period stretching from the second century B.C.E. through the end of the fourth century C.E., an active Mithraic presence is surprisingly absent.[2] Sandwiched between these two areas is Egypt. As a center of Roman activity from the very beginning of the imperial period to the final success of Christianity as the religion of the land, and as a hotbed of indigenous and exotic foreign religious activity, the land of the Nile might well be expected to be an area in which Mithraism was well represented. If Mithraism flourished here, it would have constituted a vital element of the world in which Christianity grew and developed into its unique

1. Cf. P. Rancillac, "L'insuccès du Mithriacisme en Afrique," *BGAPO* 52 (1931) 221–28, esp. 228. This was confirmed twenty-five years later by Marcel Leglay (*Les Religions orientales dans l'Afrique ancienne* [Algiers: Gouvernement général de l'Algérie, 1956] 29).
2. For Syria, cf. the scraps of evidence compiled by Lewis Hopfe ("Mithraism in Syria," an as yet unpublished study soon to appear in *ANRW*). Hopfe's conclusions: Mithraism was limited in Syria, its appearances being rare and poor. In Palestine, together with Syria one of the most excavated portions of the globe, there has emerged in all the archaeological probes over the decades only one Mithraeum! Cf. Lewis Hopfe and Gary Lease, "The Caesarea Mithraeum: A Preliminary Announcement," *BA* 38 (1975) 2–10.

Egyptian form. But was Mithra, in fact, ever a major factor in the Egyptian religious world of late antiquity?

Adolf von Harnack, one of the most perceptive and acute observers of late antiquity in this or any other century, commented as early as 1902 that for all intents and purposes Mithra was unknown in Egypt outside Alexandria.[3] Indeed Harnack claimed that the key areas of Hellenistic culture throughout the Near East were closed to the worship of Mithra. The meager collection of Mithraic materials assembled by Vermaseren for Egypt certainly seems to support Harnack's contention: not more than fifteen items, most of them fragments, constitute the section on Egypt![4] But material remains are not the only testimony to the presence of religious activity. Though it does not appear that Mithraism had a noticeable impact on the development of Christianity elsewhere in the Mediterranean Basin,[5] a thorough survey of all possible evidence concerning the presence of Mithraism in Egypt might well be important in detailing the history of nascent Christianity in that religiously turbulent land.

THE MATERIAL REMAINS

In the Greco-Roman room of the Egyptian Museum in Cairo, one can still see today a group of three reliefs apparently of Mithra. One of them, executed in marble, deserves more than a glance. While the right arm and head are missing, the figure kneeling on top of a bull, left hand grasping the nostrils, cloak spread out behind, and accompanied by a snake underneath the bull, is clearly Mithra. On either side figures stand with torches, the one on the left held down, and both heads carry Phrygian caps. Outside the central niche of the relief are radiate heads representing the sun and the moon. Just inside the upper edge of the niche is a bust of Saturn. All in all, this is a classic presentation of the Mithraic tauroctone, and solid evidence of Mithra's presence in

3. Cf. the first edition of his *Die Mission und Ausbreitung des Christentums in den Ersten Drei Jahrhunderten* (Leipzig: Hinrichs, 1902) 534–35. Harnack reconfirmed and emphasized this conclusion in the fourth edition of the same work, *Mission und Ausbreitung*, 938–39.

4. Cf. M. J. Vermaseren, *CIMRM* (The Hague: Martinus Nijhoff, 1956–60) 1:81–84. In one of the latest collections of Mithraic materials and studies, the expansion of Mithraism in the Roman Empire is treated by region: the Danube, Roman Gaul, Roman Germany, and Rome together with Italy. The province of Egypt is not even worth a separate entry! Cf. Julien Ries, *Le culte de Mithra en Orient et en Occident* (Louvain: Centre d'histoire des religions, 1979).

5. Cf. G. Lease, "Mithraism and Christianity: Borrowings and Transformations," in *ANRW* 2:23 and 1306–32, esp. 1329.

Egypt.[6] In order to interpret this relief adequately, however, one must know the location of its discovery as well as the nature of the site where it was first brought to light. Unfortunately, only confusion greets our effort to establish this piece's heritage.

The explanatory sign accompanying the relief in the Cairo Museum states unequivocally that it, along with the two additional reliefs also on display, was recovered by Eugene Grebaut (1846–1915) during excavations at Mit-rahine (= Memphis) in 1901. This information is repeated in Gaston Maspero's Museum Guide of 1911.[7] Yet already in 1904 Strzygowski had related that the group of pieces containing the two smaller reliefs of Mithra had been found in a Mithraeum just east of Mit-rahine in 1885. Unfortunately the discoverers neglected to make any notes concerning the site or its location.[8] Strzygowski was not alone in his assertion. Franz Cumont, the pioneer historian of Mithraism, had already sent the same story abroad, adding only that the site was approximately one kilometer east-northeast of the village of Mit-rahine along the road from Sakkara to the cultivated fields.[9] Yet long before Cumont, Strzygowski, and Maspero had published their accounts, the Austrian consul general in Cairo, Anton Ritter von Laurin, had reported to one of the first meetings of the newly founded Viennese Academy of Sciences that as early as 1838 he had received evidence of a Mithraeum at Memphis![10] Did von Laurin see the marble

6. The exhibit number for all three reliefs is 990; the Cairo catalogue no. for the larger, marble piece is 85747. While Vermaseren (*CIMRM*, 1:81) lists this particular piece (his no. 91), his referenced plate (no. 34) is in fact of his no. 92, one of the two smaller reliefs. For a partial correction, cf. his *CIMRM*, 2:17. Guenter Grimm and D. Johannes have published the best photo of this relief in *Kunst der Ptolemaer- und Roemerzeit im Aegyptischen Museum Kairo* (Mainz: Von Zabern, 1975) pl. 73, their text no. 38. Grimm claims that this relief of Mithra is qualitatively the best so far found in Egypt (p. 11).

7. Cf. G. Maspero's fifth edition, published in German translation as *Fuehrer durch das Aegyptische Museum zu Kairo* (Cairo: Diemer, 1912), which gives the state of the museum's displays as of the summer of 1911. The pieces in question are described as being from a temple of the "Persian god Mithra, whose cult also reached as far as Memphis during the Roman period. Found by Grebaut" (p. 64).

8. Josef Strzygowski, *Catalogue général des antiquités égyptiennes du Musée du Caire* (Vienna: Holzhausen, 1904) 12 (Koptische Kunst, 9–15).

9. Cf. F. Cumont, *Textes et monuments figures relatifs aux mystères de Mithra* (Brussels: Lamertin, 1896) 2:520–22.

10. Cf. von Laurin's letter to Arneth, dated Cairo, 24 January 1849, and presented by Arneth to the meeting of the Academy of Sciences in Vienna on 14 March 1849, in *Sitzungsberichte der Philosophisch-Historischen Classe der Kaiserlichen Akademie der Wissenschaften zu Wien* (Vienna: Braumueller, 1849) 2:248–54. Von Laurin relates how some eleven years before he had received a number of items from the ruins of Mit-rahine, among them a broken piece of an "Apis," or bull, together with the "accessories" one would expect in company with Mithra—for example, a dagger in the hand of a youth, who uses it to wound the animal in its neck. Von Laurin speculates that "prob-

relief that sits today in the Egyptian Museum in Cairo? Guenter Grimm thinks not, and opts instead for an origin further up the Nile, at present-day Ashmunein, earlier Hermopolis magna.[11] What is to be made of such confusion?

Clearly the two smaller reliefs still present in the display in the Egyptian Museum of Cairo were the ones seen by Cumont, Strzygowski, and Maspero. Their descriptions as well as their illustrations leave no doubt that at the time of their compilations, the larger relief was not yet in the possession of the Museum.[12] At some point after 1915 (Maspero's last catalogue), the Museum came into possession of another Mithraic relief, and promptly placed it on display together with the previous two reliefs thought to have come from Memphis. Vermaseren inherited this confusion and assumed that the Museum's identification was correct. All the pieces on display presumably stemmed from the Memphis find.[13]

This tiring unraveling of decades of errors and mistaken identifications serves to demonstrate how much in the dark we still are in regard to the very few Mithraic material remains that have so far surfaced in Egypt. For all intents and purposes the only Mithraeum reported found in Egypt is irretrievably lost to us without adequate recording, indeed, without any recording at all! Because we lack more certain knowledge concerning the location and context of the discovery, these few

---

ably the Persian king Cambyses, who is supposed to have destroyed this temple [the Apis temple], rededicated the spot to the Persian Mithra, thus also giving the name to the village nearby." According to von Laurin, "Metrahene" means either "the house of Mithra" or "here is Mithra." The correct etymology for "Mit-rahine" traces the name to the Egyptian *mi't rhnt*, "street of the rams/ram-headed sphinxes (of Amun)." A. Wiedemann ("Die Mithrasdenkmaeler von Memphis," *WZKM* 31 [1924] 310–12) is the only commentator to mention von Laurin's account of a Memphis Mithraeum.

11. G. Grimm, *Ptolemaer- und Roemerzeit*, 11. Unfortunately Grimm gives no reason for his statement, while dating the relief to the second or third century C.E.

12. While Maspero does not describe the individual pieces, the following correlations can be made between the three other reporters: Vermaseren, *CIMRM*, 92 (31) = Cumont, *Textes et monuments*, 285b (520) = Strzygowski, *Catalogue général* 7259 (9); Vermaseren, *CIMRM*, 93 (81–82) = Cumont, *Textes et monuments*, 285c (520–521) = Strzygowski, *Catalogue général*, 7260 (10).

13. In a letter to the late dean of contemporary Egyptologists, J. Yoyotte of the Mission française des fouilles de Tanis mentions that the written entry in the Cairo Museum's catalogue journal for the marble relief of Mithra in a niche is dated 1942! Cf. Yoyotte-Labib Habachi, 7 July 1980. A place of origin is not mentioned, though it is possible that Grimm gained a hint of where the piece was found from this entry. In addition, Vermaseren was not even able to link his descriptions with his illustrations (see n. 6 above). Since Grimm has not seen fit to inform us of his grounds for identifying Hermopolis magna as the site of discovery for the later relief, it remains useless for evaluating Mithraism's Egyptian course.

remains from that Mithraeum can tell us very little about Mithraism's presence and history in Egypt.

Besides the three so-called Memphitic reliefs of Mithra slaying the bull, Vermaseren also reports a variety of small statues and fragments of statues, presumably from the same site at Memphis.[14] Torches, Phrygian caps, and lion heads are the motifs that allow him to list these items as presumably Mithraic in origin. Even today one can still find in the souvenir shops in Cairo small terra-cotta heads bearing Phrygian caps and listed as originating in the Fayyum.[15]

More intriguing, however, are two representations of a monstrous figure often linked with Mithra, a winged human body crowned with the head of a lion and encircled by a twisting snake.[16] Most commentators are now agreed that this depiction was a frequently used representation in Mithraic cult activities.[17] Though it has been argued that this figure takes its origins from aspects of ancient Persian religion, Pettazzoni has made it clear that its appearance in Mithraic service was an obvious act of late ancient syncretism.[18] In fact, he makes the persuasive case that the depiction of Time as used in Mithraism is dependent mainly upon Alexandrian feasts for Aion and Kronos. These

14. Vermaseren, *CIMRM*, 82–83 (his nos. 94–101).

15. One such head is now in my possession. Measuring 8 cm high and 6 cm wide, it is broken off at the neck. The face looks straight ahead and is likely from a representation of Cautes or Cautophates rather than of Mithra himself. Whether the head in fact came from the Fayyum is, of course, uncertain. On the other hand, it is entirely possible. A papyrus from the Fayyum dated from the third century B.C.E., contains an inventory of cattle belonging to several temple properties, among which is one for Mithra. This may well have been a cult center introduced by the Persian occupation but certainly will not have been the later mystery cult of late antiquity; cf. below the discussion of the history of Mithraism in Egypt. For the papyrus cf. J. G. Smyly, *Greek Papyri from Gurob* [Cunningham Memoirs] (Dublin: Hodges, Figgis and Co., 1921) 12, 36ff., no. xxii. line 10.

16. The first one (i.e., Vermaseren's no. 102) was reported by Wiedemann in 1924. He maintained that he had acquired it in 1882 from a man "who had just come from Kus, the ancient Apollinopolis," and thus that it provided evidence for the presence of Mithraism in Upper Egypt. See Wiedemann, "Mithrasdenkmaeler," 311–12. The other (i.e., Vermaseren's no. 103) was found in Oxyrhynchos and currently reposes in the Museum of Greek and Roman Antiquities in Alexandria. It was first published by E. Breccia ("Un 'Cronos Mitriaco' ad Oxyrhynchos," in *Orient Grec, Romain, et Byzantin*, vol. 2 of *Mélanges Maspero* [Cairo: IFAO, 1934–37] 257–64). Other discussions of this particular piece, as well as of the entire spectrum of such figures, can be found in Doro Levi, "Aion," *Hesperia* 13 (1944) 269–314; and Raffaele Pettazzoni, "La Figura mostruosa del Tempo nella Religione Mitriaca," *AnCl* 18 (1949) 265–77 ("The Monstrous Figure of Time in Mithraism," in *Essays in the History of Religion* [ed. H. J. Rose; Leiden: E. J. Brill, 1967] 180–92).

17. For the latest summary, cf. M. J. Vermaseren, *Mithras: Geschichte eines Kultes* (Stuttgart: Kohlhammer, 1965) 94–104.

18. Cf. R. Pettazzoni, "Aion-(Kronos) Chronos in Egypt," in *Essays on the History of Religion* (ed. Rose) 171–79.

celebrations, certainly as old as the Ptolemaic period, are linked to even more ancient forms of worship directed to the Egyptian divinity Re, a deity who ruled time as the sun.[19]

While admitting that Mithraism retained some traces of its Persian origins—for example, the name Mithra—Pettazzoni also argues that Mithraism was able to be successful only to the degree that it divested itself of its oriental elements and adapted to the culture of the western Mediterranean.[20] It retained, however, together with the name Mithra, the figure of Time, which devours all.[21] The figure of Time is not present in the classical world of Hellenism. Thus it would seem that this "monstrous" figure of Time as found in a number of Mithraea is a product of a syncretistic combination of Egyptian practices and Persian concepts. It is not surprising that the Alexandrian feasts of Aion and Kronos were appropriated. A similar statue uncovered in Rome also makes use of Sarapian iconography, thus completing the act of syncretism that issued in the bizarre figure of Time found in Mithraic representations.[22]

19. Cf. Pettazzoni, "Aion-(Kronos)," 176. In fact, the two late ancient celebrations of Aion (6 January) and Kronos (25 December) are *not* connected with two different Hellenistic deities imported into Egypt but rather are two different Hellenistic interpretations of the same event, originally Egyptian in origin (p. 175). R. L. Gordon, however, as well as A. D. H. Bivar, has rejected the role of Egyptian influence in the formation of this lion-headed iconography, even though, as Bivar admits, a similar figure is to be found on Egyptian magical amulets. Both maintain that the general syncretism of the time is sufficient explanation for the emergence of such a figure, the former in "Cumont and the Doctrines of Mithraism," in *Mithraic Studies* (ed. J. Hinnell; Manchester: Manchester Univ. Press, 1975) 1:223; and the latter in "Mithra and Mesopotamia," in *Mithraic Studies* 2:282.

20. Pettazzoni, "La figura Mostruosa," 266–67.

21. Pettazzoni, "La figura Mostruosa"; a human body with the head of a lion entwined by a snake, reminiscent of the Persian Zervan.

22. For example, the Mithraeum at Sassoferrato has such a Time figure in its annex: Levi, "Aion," 287–88. The lion-headed human body found by Otto Brendel at Castello Gandolfo has a number of interesting variations, among them a figure of "Cerberus" with the three heads—wolf (= past); lion (= present); dog (= future)—of the Sarapic symbol of time as reported from the Alexandrian Sarapaeum. Cf. Breccia, "'Cronos Mitriaco,'" 263–64; Pettazzoni, "La figura Mostruosa," 272–76. In fact, Pettazzoni even suggests that the inclusion of Mithra in this iconography is the result of an Egyptian effort to forge an all-inclusive divinity—Bes pantheos—capable of incorporating all the various divinities coursing through Egypt in late antiquity and is not the end product of a choice by Mithraism of Egyptian elements (pp. 274–77). Similarly Vermaseren has recently argued that the lion-headed god figure found associated with Mithraism does not represent the Persian divinity Ahriman but rather symbolizes Eternity, or all-devouring Time. He agrees that Egypt was one of the main influences in conceptualizing this figure of Eternal Time in late antiquity, but emphasizes even more the syncretistic process. Neither Iran nor Egypt alone formed the cult of the lion-headed god in Mithraism, but rather the Hellenistic age in general; cf. "A Magical Time God," in *Mithraic Studies* 2:453–56.

The result of our survey of Mithraic material remains in Egypt can hardly be a surprise. With only one Mithraeum actually recovered, and that one entirely unrecorded, one can hardly speak with any assurance of the "Mithraic presence in Egypt." From the other remains we can only conclude that apparently Mithraism, like all religious constructions of late antiquity, made liberal use of concepts and iconography available to it in its newly experienced Western world. On the other hand, competing cults—in this case primarily Alexandrian in origin— also borrowed the figure of Mithra for their use. It is clear that plastic depictions of these combinations likely stood under Egyptian influence.[23] What might be less clear is why so few such figures have surfaced in Egypt itself. Of the two so far actually recovered there, only one has a certainly known location, namely Oxyrhynchos. Such sparse evidence hardly allows any safe or solid conclusions, but the very paucity of the evidence does lead one to doubt the strength and vibrancy of Mithraism in Egypt. But if the material remains reveal little to us regarding Mithraism in Egypt, perhaps the textual evidence will be more fruitful.

THE TEXTS

In 1903 Albrecht Dieterich surprised the scholarly world with the publication of what he deemed to be the only surviving Mithraic liturgy.[24] The text Dieterich produced was part of the Great Paris magical Codex, containing a veritable hodgepodge of incantations, magical descriptions, and religiously oriented texts covering a wide spectrum of Egyptian culture up to the early fourth century C.E. Though his arguments were long and involved, Dieterich's reasons for assigning this text to Mithraic origins were basically two: Mithra is actually mentioned, and the basic themes of the document can be comfortably assigned to Mithraic practices and beliefs. His conclusion was strong. Through this text we at last not only had firm evidence that Mithraism was a major factor in Egypt but we could discern its very nature.[25]

Dieterich's first point is hardly persuasive. The name Mithra occurs

23. Cf. Vermaseren, *Mithras*, 103.

24. Albrecht Dieterich, *Eine Mithrasliturgie* (Leipzig: Teubner, 1903); Otto Weinreich edited a posthumous third edition in 1923.

25. Dieterich, *Eine Mithrasliturgie*, 92. Indeed it may be the only liturgy—outside Christianity—to have survived antiquity. Since it thus represents "a solid liturgical form of profound ritual of a powerful and high-standing cult," it can also reveal much to us concerning other mystery religions throughout the Mediterranean.

once in the document, and then only at the very beginning in conjunction with the further name Helios. Given the frequent occurrence of Mithra's name in combination with the names of other divinities this hardly constitutes strong evidence that the document is exclusively the witness to a Mithraic community.[26] Even less persuasive is the claim that the themes represented in the document establish its Mithraic tenor. The divinity's function as guard of the ascent to heaven through the heavens is hardly restricted to Mithraism, and the other themes such as those of humanity in divinity and divinity in humanity, and of union of the human and divine in love, rebirth, etc., sound like a catalog of what was to be found in most of late antiquity's mystery cults.[27]

The defenders of this document as a Mithraic liturgy have been few, whereas those who have rejected this claim are among the most knowledgeable historians of the period. Harnack was unconvinced that the text in question was a Mithraic document, and he quoted a letter from Cumont, who agreed, saying that the so-called "Mithraic liturgy was neither a liturgy nor was it Mithraic."[28] Reitzenstein, and following him, A. D. Nock, viewed the text as a statement of liturgical piety prescribing a procedure whereby an individual might mount through the heavens and obtain immortality. In their view it most certainly is not a statement describing the liturgical actions of a community, much less a Mithraic community.[29] More recently the "liturgy" has been described as an Egyptian magical text with some Mithraic elements in it, having been heavily Egyptianized. In this view the text does not even qualify as a liturgy![30] However one may finally judge the

26. For the occurrence, cf. Dieterich, *Eine Mithrasliturgie*, 2. As one example of a syncretistic combination using Mithra's name, and this from Egypt, cf. Nonnus of Panopolis (ca. 400 C.E.) in his *Dionysiaca* 40.400–401: Mithra = Kronos = Egyptian Zeus (= Sarapis) = Babylonian Sun = Delphic Apollo. In Rome, in the Baths of Caracalla, one finds "One Zeus, Mithra, Helios," in Vermaseren, *CIMRM*, 463. A delightful menagerie can be also found in Martianus Capella, who names the "unknown father" as Phoebus, Sarapis, Osiris, Ammon, Attis, and Mithra, in *De Nupt.* 2.185.

27. For the first, see Dieterich, *Eine Mithrasliturgie*, 89–91; for the latter, the long discussion, ibid., 92–212. Dieterich himself admits at the very end that these concerns were, in fact, common to all the great mystery religions, as well as to Christianity and Manichaeism, since the age was one of extensive syncretism!

28. Cf. Harnack, *Mission und Ausbreitung*, 2:941 n. 1. Cumont's letter to Harnack is from 11 February 1906.

29. See the account in A. D. Nock, "Greek Magical Papyri," now to be found in his *Essays on Religion and the Ancient World* (Cambridge: Harvard Univ. Press, 1972) 1:176–94; the discussion here is on 192–93.

30. Cf. Martin Schwartz, "Cautes and Cautophates, the Mithraic Torchbearers," in *Mithraic Studies* 2:406–23, here 414 n. 31.

argument between Dieterich and his opponents regarding the pedigree of the so-called Mithraic liturgy, it is clear that scarcely sufficient certainty exists about the text to allow a firm interpretation of either its contents or its origins. For our purposes it is of little use in attempting to determine the nature and development of Mithraism in Egypt.

The "liturgy" is, however, not the only mention of Mithra in Egypt. As we saw earlier, a "temple of Mithra" is recorded for the Fayyum as early as the third century B.C.E.[31] Who that Mithra might have been, and what the temple and its services might have been like, is unavailable to us. Firmer, or at least more recognizable, ground is recovered with the mention by Statius, a Roman poet of the late first century C.E., that the sun can be Osiris, or as the Persians term it, "in a cave under rocks, Mithra of the twisted horns."[32] This subtle linking of an Egyptian divinity with Mithra hardly carries us further, however, since it does not refer directly to an Egyptian practice, but only to a cosmopolitan Roman's observations.[33] Once again sparse and unclear references leave us without any firm hold in our attempt to specify more clearly Mithraism's role in the religious developments of the Egypt of late antiquity. Perhaps a survey of the history of that period will afford us the grasp we need.

THE HISTORY

That early forms of Persian religion contained a divinity with the name of Mithra is universally accepted. Much more difficult, however, is the establishment of a consensus regarding the relationship between such a Persian divinity and the late ancient mystery cult also centered on Mithra. Some have argued for direct lineage, but most observers today consider the mystery religion of the first through the fifth centuries C.E. to be a separate formation, at most making use of various Persian elements.[34]

31. Cf. Smyly, *Greek Papyri*, 36.
32. Statius *Thebais* 1:717–720.
33. This becomes even more clear when we study the commentary on Statius written by Lactantius Plaidas (sixth century C.E.). In explaining the "twisted horns" of Mithra, he says that they refer to a figure of bulls' horns, and that it signifies the moon from which light is received. The national nomenclature is explained simply as the fact that the sun is termed "Mithra" by the Persians, while the Egyptians call it "Osiris"! These rather simplistic comments say nothing of Egypt in particular. In Lactantius, "Commentary on the 'Thebais' of Statius," on lines 718 and 720; to be found in Theodor Hopfner, *Fontes Historiae Religionis Aegypticae* (Bonn: Marcus and Weber, 1922–1925) 4:693–94.
34. Cf. Ries, *Le culte de Mithra*, 112–14, for a summary of current conclusions

If the connection between the Persian god Mithra and the late mystery cult whose god had the same appellation is tenuous, then Mithraic beginnings in Egypt are vague in the extreme. Darius I and Darius II, during the Persian conquest of Egypt beginning in the late sixth century B.C.E., were called god by the Egyptians, and it is reported that they built temples along the Nile. Darius III is reported to have been given the title "Sharer of the Throne with Mithras."[35] At the same time the traditions of Plato's trip to Egypt also contain his desires to converse with the Persian Magi. Regardless of the accuracy of the tradition as far as Plato is concerned, this shows at least that accounts from the third century B.C.E. assume that knowledge of the Persian religions was not to be had in Egypt.[36] What little evidence there is leads one to accept Cumont's earlier judgment that the history of Mithra in Egypt really only begins under the Romans.[37]

While one would assume that Alexandria, crossroads of the Mediterranean Basin during late antiquity, would have had a place for Mithraic worship in its panoply of gods, the city was primarily known for its cults of Sarapis and Isis. And certainly there is no lack of linkage between these two divinities and Mithra.[38] Yet the links demonstrate

---

concerning Mithra's Indo-Iranian background and history. For the origins of the mystery religion, cf. Carsten Colpe's fine study "Mithra-Verehrung, Mithras-Kult, und die Existenz iranischer Mysterien," in *Mithraic Studies* 2:378–405. Michael Speidel (*Mithras-Orion* [Leiden: E. J. Brill, 1980] 2–3) has also argued that the mystery cult's origins are no earlier than the first century C.E. And C. M. Daniels ("The Roman Army and the Spread of Mithraism," in *Mithraic Studies* 2:249–74) agrees that the spread of Mithraism was dependent entirely upon the journeys of the Roman army.

35. Cf. Carl Clemen, *Fontes Historiae Religionies Persicae* (Bonn: Marcus and Weber, 1920) 28.15–16; 71.5. In view of the fact that Mithra may indeed have been a "house god" for the Achemenids, these reports are not surprising. This may even explain the earlier cited report of a Mithra temple in the Fayyum during the third century B.C.E.; cf. A. Shapur Shahbazi, "From *Parsa* to *Taxt-E Jamsid*," *AMINF* 10 (1977) 206–7, where he shows that the mount to the east of Persepolis was dedicated to Mithra and thus indicates the connection between that site and the location of Darius's royal citadel.

36. Cf. E. D. Francis, in F. Cumont, "The Dura Mithraeum," in *Mithraic Studies* 1:156 n. 29.

37. Cf. Cumont, *Textes et monuments* 1:242, where he emphasizes that the reported Mithraeum at Memphis is the exception that proves the rule. Though this location probably was occupied by an important Persian garrison and though Persian soldiers are noted as being in Arsinoe as early as the third century B.C.E., all the statuary seen by Cumont must be dated to a much later age. Campbell Bonner, a sober judge of such evidence (*Studies in Magical Amulets Chiefly Graeco-Egyptian* [Ann Arbor, Mich.: Univ. of Michigan Press, 1950] 33), felt sure that "some scholars have exaggerated the influence exerted by Persian religious concepts, modified by transmission through Babylon, upon the mystery religions of the Hellenistic and Roman periods."

38. Sarapis heads are found in several Mithraea, stretching from one end of the Mediterranean to the other: In Spain (Vermaseren, *CIMRM*, 783); England (*CIMRM*, 818); Italy (*CIMRM*, 479, 693); Mesopotamia (*CIMRM*, 40). In Italy a Mithraeum was dedicated by the same person who also dedicated a sanctuary to Isis and Sarapis

not a common worship but rather a strong compatibility.[39] There are also, for example, some traces of Mithraic motifs on a number of Egyptian magical amulets, but this demonstrates less a substantial link than only a commingling so typical of the age.[40] All in all, while we can be sure that there was a Mithraic presence in Alexandria, there is no evidence that it ever achieved a major position there as a rival to Sarapis and Isis. And if that is the case for Alexandria, how much more will it be true for the rest of Egypt!

The most famous account touching upon Mithraism in Egypt is, of course, the story of George of Cappadocia's downfall as patriarch of Alexandria. As an Arian, George gained the patriarchal throne after Athanasius had been deposed by Constantius. He promptly instituted a reign of terror and crime against the populace, which culminated in his building a Christian church on the ruins of an abandoned Mithraeum. George's career came to an abrupt end at the death of Constantius and the accession of Julian in 361 C.E. On the eve of the feast of Natalis Invicti, 24 December 361, an enraged mob of Alexandrians stormed the jail where he was being held, dragged him forth, and killed him, later tossing his body into the sea.[41] As a result, Julian addressed a letter to the citizens of Alexandria, remonstrating with them on account of their violent behavior. Yet in this letter he mentions neither a Mithraeum nor a Christian profanation of such, leading one to assume that the effects of this episode on the Mithraic

---

(*CIMRM*, 648). The Baths of Caracalla feature an inscription linking Zeus and Mithra; but it had been Sarapis originally, before someone obliterated that name and substituted Mithra (*CIMRM* 2:463). Vermaseren points out that the title "sol invictus" was given both to Sarapis and to Mithra (*CIMRM* 1:251).

39. Cf. R. E. Witt, "Some Thoughts on Isis in Relation to Mithras," in *Mithraic Studies* 2:479–93, here 493.

40. Cf. Bonner, *Magical Amulets*, 264–65, where he is able to list only four gems showing the Mithraic tauroctone. Certainly, he comments, Mithraism was affected by the general syncretism of the time, and certainly the Mithraicists would have been as prone as anyone else to add items found in their religious environment to their own system. On the other hand, Egyptian magical papyri and amulets also borrow the name of Mithra for their incantations, just as they borrowed other divine names (e.g., Iao). "Yet among the published amulets I find no convincing evidence that the mysteries of Mithra were penetrated by Egyptian religion" (pp. 38–39).

41. A number of accounts exist of this sorry chapter in the history of the Alexandrian patriarchate: Ammianus Marcellinus 22.11; Gregory Nazianzen *Or.* 21.16; Socrates *H.E.* 3.2; Athansius *h.Ar.* 73; Epiphanius *Haer.* 76. Not only did George order a church built on top of the Mithraeum, but in the process of clearing the ruin's debris the workers chanced upon bones and skulls, presumably from a cemetery connected with the site. These bones were then paraded by the Christians through the streets of Alexandria, outraging the non-Christian populace. For commentary, cf. E. Gibbon's account, *The History of the Decline and Fall of the Roman Empire* (ed. J. B. Bury; London: Methuen & Co., 1909) 2:496–98.

community were not long-lasting. Indeed the fact that the Mithraeum was *abandoned* implies that there had been a marked shrinkage in that community for some time.[42]

We next hear of a Mithraeum in Alexandria during the course of the infamous destruction of the Sarapaeum under the patriarch Theophilus in 391 C.E. As part of his general program to cleanse the city of its non-Christian centers of worship, Theophilus first cleared a Mithraeum before advancing on the Sarapaeum.[43] Whether there were any other Mithraea in the vicinity that suffered a like fate at this time is not clear. There certainly is no mention of any, and what little history can be recounted of Mithraism in Egypt fades into silence at the end of the fourth century.[44]

CONCLUSIONS

It would seem that the expectation of a "near vacuum in Egypt" of Mithraism has been fulfilled.[45] Traces of influences are for all practical purposes nonexistent, though there are scattered references to the presence of "Persian" religionists as late as the fourth century C.E.[46] And there were, of course, Mithraic-sounding elements in the Manichaean message that reached Egypt during the first part of the fourth century. In the course of that century the Manichaean missionaries did finally

42. Cf. Robert Turcan (*Mithras Platonicus* [Leiden: E. J. Brill, 1976] 116), who also argues that during the fourth century Mithraism became more of a Platonic mysticism than anything else (p. 105). Julian also demanded a strict accounting of the patriarch's library and its shipment to him; see Julian's letters, nos. 9, 60.

43. Socrates *H.E.* 4.16. Jacques Schwartz ("La Fin du Serapeum d'Alexandrie," *ASP* 1 [1966] 109) argues that this account smacks of a doublet, borrowed initially from the account of George of Cappadocia, some thirty years before. The Emperor Theodosius gave the order that the non-Christians in Alexandria were not to be punished for the deaths of any Christians that had occurred in the preceding riots but that they must surrender their places of worship to the Christians. This effectively sealed the fate of those temples (16 June 391, *Cod.* 16.10.11).

44. There seems, for example, to be no solid evidence for a Mithraeum at Menuthis (nor at Abukir, some 12 miles from Alexandria, and a suburb of Canopis, where Pachomian monks were settled), though there was certainly an Isaeum located there. The Isis cult was carried on in secret for almost a century until its betrayal and destruction in the 480s; cf. Sozomen *H.E.* 7.15; and Rudolf Herzog, "Der Kampf um den Kult von Menuthis," in *PISCICULI: Doelger Festschrift* (ed. T. Klauser; Muenster: Aschendorff, 1939) 122.

45. Daniels, "The Roman Army," 249–74, here 251.

46. For example, see Peter of Alexandria's letter to the bishop of Siut, Apollonius, mentioning his meeting with Basilios the Persian in Egypt. Basilios's creed is "in the sun, and the moon, the water and fire, which also illuminates the whole oikumene," in ms. copte, Bibl. Nat., 131, 1, f. 1, as cited in Cumont, *Textes et monuments*, 20–21 n. 7. This hardly constitutes a "Mithraic" reference!

identify Christ with the sun, but this development is adequately explained by directions within Mani's message, without demanding recourse to a possible Mithraic influence.[47]

More promising at first glance is the figure of the mounted saint, found so frequently in Coptic Christian art. We do know that Mithra was often shown mounted, and frequently at the hunt.[48] While Coptic art also made use of the mounted hunter, the figure would seem to be an assimilation of Parthian examples to the Egyptian figure of Horus.[49] The famous monastery of Apa Apollo at Bawit, southwest of modern-day Ashmunein, has several such hunting scenes, some showing Phrygian costume. While some Persian, or more likely Parthian, influence is granted, the usual interpretation establishes the origin for the composition in a Horus myth.[50] In sum, the Coptic horseman "appears to constitute an iconographical type peculiar to the Nile Valley. If the image is to be related to alien traditions, these may be identified more accurately as Late Roman or Byzantine for the early types dating from the late fourth to the middle of the seventh century, with the clear understanding that the iconography itself is distinctively Egyptian and provincial."[51]

47. Cf. Franz Doelger, "Konstantin der Grosse und der Manichaeismus: Sonne und Christus im Manichaeismus," in *AuC* 2 (1930): 301–14. The earliest Manichaean missionaries to Egypt did not speak of the sun as divine but only as the way to god (pp. 310–11); by 348 (Cyril of Jerusalem) the identification is complete, however, though Arius remains unclear (p. 312).

48. The most famous example comes from the Mithraeum at Dura-Europos, but there are many such scenes in Germany's Mithraea, too. The British Museum (BM 124091) has a striking silver plate from the fourth century C.E. showing the Persian Sasanian king Shapur I. astride a large stag. He is grasping the right antler with his left hand, while with his right he is plunging a sword into its neck right at its juncture with the back. Blood is spurting from the wound, but the stag continues at full gallop. Underneath another stag now dead, blood still pouring from a wound in its neck but also from its nostrils. To be found in Providence O. Harper, *The Royal Hunter: The Art of the Sasanian Empire* (New York: Asia House Gallery, 1978) 34–35. Harper comments that Shapur "was perhaps deliberately likened to Mithra, who is shown as a hunter, pursuing stags and other animals, in the third century wall paintings of the Mithraeum at Dura-Europos" (p. 34).

49. See Pierre du Bourguet (*The Art of the Copts* [New York: Crown Pubs., 1971] 36–91), who places the location for such an assimilation in Alexandria. Later, this cyclic theme of the mounted hunter is assumed by Christianity. Examples appear not only in the fourth century but continue as late as the ninth, when a relief of Christ as a Parthian horseman can be found in the monastery of Sohag (p. 176).

50. Cf. Jean Cledat, *Le monastère et la nécropole de Baouit* (MIFAO; Cairo: IFAO, 1916) 1:62 (pl. 27), 80 (pls. 53, 54); and 2:39 (pl. 17).

51. Suzanne Lewis, "The Iconography of the Coptic Horseman in Byzantine Egypt," *JARCE* 10 (1973) 32–33. Of interest is the St. George figure found in Ethiopian iconography. While the initial introduction likely came from Egypt, a wide variety of introduced materials has been established, with the earliest appearances not before the eleventh century. See S. Chojnacki, "The Iconography of St. George in Ethiopia," *JEtS*

If there is little trace of Mithraism in Egypt, and even less evidence of its influence there, one must still confront the question of why this is so. One might expect that the worship of Mithra, a sun god, would have an affinity in Egypt with the sun worship in that country's indigenous religious traditions. Certainly what traces of Mithra's use have turned up show this connection.[52] On the other hand, Mithra's cult might have had a difficult time gaining entry to Egypt precisely because of the strength of the Egyptian sun deities. Mithra's role in Egypt may well have been a subordinate one, mainly as an additional figure supportive of the native sun cults, just as in the magical amulets.[53]

More obvious, however, is the fact that Mithraism was so intimately connected with the presence of the Roman army.[54] Where the legions were, Mithra followed. The absence of Mithraic remains in Syria and

11 (1973) 91. Chojnacki ("Note on the Early Iconography of St. George and Related Equestrian Saints in Ethiopia," *JEtS* 13 [1975] 41 n. 5) also notes that the common representation in Egypt of Horus on horseback spearing a crocodile is well known and remarks that this is an assimilation of the Egyptian Horus to the image of a Parthian horseman or Roman soldier.

52. For example, the "great god, Helios Mithra" of the so-called Liturgy of Mithra; cf. Dieterich, *Eine Mithrasliturgie*, 2.

53. As analyzed by Bonner, who speaks, in fact, of "a syncretistic solar religion" in Egypt (*Magical Amulets*, 132–33). Cf. also Lease ("Mithraism and Christianity," 1329 n. 173), who concedes that Christian use of a Mithraic motif may be present in the monastery of Apa Apollo at Bawit (sixth century), but who says that if so, it is present in a strongly subordinate manner; in fact, the borrowing is better explained by recourse to much older native Egyptian representations than to Mithraic iconography. For example, the "mysteries" of the sun god (= Re) were celebrated in Chmunu (= late ancient Hermopolis magna, modern Ashmunein, just north of Bawit) as early as Ramses III (1198–1167 B.C.E.), a good thousand years before the advent of western Mithraism! These "mysteries" consisted of "dramatic" presentations of the birth of the sun (= first appearance of the sun from out of the primeval chaos), the sun's triumph over its enemies, and the sun's journey to the island of flames. The celebrations took place on New Year's Day within the great temple park at Chmunu. Cf. Guenther Roeder, ed., *Hermopolis 1929–1939: Ausgrabungen der Deutschen-Hermopolis-Expedition* (Hildesheim: Gerstenberg, 1959) 36, 169, 196–97. Though no historical link can obviously be established, it is astonishing to see the same major events celebrated in the Egyptian sun "mysteries" and in the Mithraic mythology: birth, struggle and triumph, and final journey of completion. Perhaps Mithraism had little appeal for the native Egyptians because it was simply redundant! Equally suggestive is the limestone stele on display in the State Collection of Egyptian Art in Munich which shows the sacred bull Mnevis. Dating from the nineteenth dynasty (250 B.C.E.), this statue shows the bull that was often termed the speaker or representative of the sun. With a sun disk between its horns, Mnevis was the earthly appearance of the sun god Re and was kept in the Re temple in the sacred city of Heliopolis (Aes 1399, 1400). Cf. also Dietrich Wildung, *Ni-User-Re: Sonnenkoenig-Sonnengott* (SAS 1; Munich: Staatliche Sammlung Aegyptischer Kunst, 1984).

54. Cf. Speidel, *Mithras-Orion*, 38; Daniels, "Roman Army," 251; Vermaseren, *Mithras*, 23ff. And of course, Harnack's usually trenchant remarks, *Mission und Ausbreitung*, 939–41.

Palestine can be attributed to the fact that the legions there had their long-term residences in a very few places. It is not an accident that the only Mithraeum so far uncovered in Palestine was in Caesarea, the main station for Roman troops in that unhappy province.[55] Roman troops in Egypt had their main posts in and around Alexandria in the delta. For example, the Fifth Legion "Macedonia" was stationed there during the first century before being posted to Palestine for service in the First Jewish Revolt. Afterwards it was sent to the Danube where Mithraea confirm the legion's religious proclivities. It is highly unlikely, however, that its brief garrison duties in Alexandria provided the troops with their Mithraic inspiration.[56] From the second century on, figures show that a vast number of recruits for the army in Egypt came from the local populace and not from outside Egypt. The army in Egypt from the second century onwards was primarily one of garrison duty and not a field army. Roman soldiers stationed there tended in the main to worship the local divinities and did not import their cults from elsewhere.[57] During the early second century at the time of the great Jewish Revolt in Egypt (115–17 C.E.), Trajan dispatched the Second Legion "Traiana" and the Twenty-Third Legion "Deiotariana" from the Parthian front to aid in the struggle. They were sent up-country to aid the local militia, which had been overwhelmed. As soon, however, as the revolt had been put down, the legions departed. Presumably it was the Twenty-Third Legion "Deiotariana" that was annihilated in Palestine during the Second Jewish Revolt a few years later (132–35 C.E.).[58] Such a short presence in Upper Egypt, at towns such as Hermopolis and Lycopolis, was surely far too brief to allow the establishment of Mithraic communities that had the strength and numbers to survive.

Later developments point in the same direction. The lack of troops in Upper Egypt led to constant incursions out of the deserts to the south and west. Civil authority after Constantine fell to a large extent into the hands of the bishops.[59] At the same time it appears that the local Egyptian cults came through the periods of Hellenization and Christianization stronger than has been generally accepted. Particularly

55. Cf. Hopfe and Lease, "Caesarea Mithraeum," 9–10.

56. Cf. Daniels, "Roman Army," 251.

57. J. Grafton Milne, *A History of Egypt Under Roman Rule* (3d ed.; London: Methuen & Co., 1924) 174–75.

58. F. Mary Smallwood, *The Jews Under Roman Rule* (Leiden: E. J. Brill, 1981) 402, 446–47.

59. Cf. Milne, *History of Egypt*, 76, 85.

among the poor and illiterate their usage was widespread for a long time (into the fifth and sixth centuries).[60] As late as the mid-fifth century the temple of Isis on the island of Elephantine (Philae) was part of a treaty with the Blemyes (raiders from the south). The temple was kept open and maintained for the Blemyes' use (451 C.E.).[61]

The only conclusion to this survey of Mithraism in Egypt is that its presence there was an extremely limited one. Few testimonies of its life and history there remain to tell us how it came to be in Egypt, or where it flourished and how and when it ceased to be a vital part of that country's variegated religious scene. The inherent strength of Egypt's local cults and worship proved to be too dense for Mithraism to penetrate, while the lack of Roman soldiery stationed widely and for long periods of time in the province robbed Mithraism of its most important base of support. Under such conditions gaining a foothold, much less broad expansion, was next to impossible. For the study of Christianity's rise and development in Egypt it is important to recognize that in stark contrast to the situation in other areas of the Mediterranean Basin, here Mithraism proved to be neither a major competitor nor an influence of note. Christianity's struggle to gain the adherence of the Egyptian populace had very different rivals to fear.

---

60. Cf. ibid., 192: "There must throughout the Graeco-Roman period have been a steady adherence to the traditional faiths of the country among the peasantry, which found little record on the monuments or in written documents but gradually asserted itself again when the official importance of the artificial Alexandrian system of theology declined."

61. Ibid., 100.

THE EMERGENCE OF CHRISTIANITY IN EGYPT

8

Earliest Christianity in Egypt: Some Observations

INTRODUCTORY REMARKS

The obscurity that veils the early history of the Church in Egypt and that does not lift until the beginning of the third century constitutes a conspicuous challenge to the historian of primitive Christianity.

With these words, Colin H. Roberts, one of the most prominent papyrologists of our time, opens a ground-breaking study of early Christianity in Egypt: *Manuscript, Society, and Belief in Early Christian Egypt.*[1] Acknowledging that the extant documentary papyri provide no useful evidence for the earliest period, i.e., before the third century,[2] Roberts turns his attention to the evidence provided by the earliest Christian literary papyri. The importance of the results he obtains is considerable, not least because the theory of Walter Bauer that the earliest type of Christianity in Egypt was "heretical," specifically "gnostic,"[3] a view widely held,[4] is cogently called into question, if not definitively overturned.

1. The Schweich Lectures of the British Academy for 1977 (London: Oxford Univ. Press, 1979).
2. Ibid., 1 and n. 2. For a valuable new study of the documentary evidence see now E. A. Judge and S. R. Pickering, "Papyrus Documentation of Church and Community in Egypt to the Mid-fourth Century," *JAC* 20 (1977) 47–71. The evidence treated includes personal correspondence, letters involving churches, official inquiries, petitions, public records, wills, other contracts, etc. The earliest evidence is dated to the early third century.
3. See W. Bauer, *Orthodoxy and Heresy in Earliest Christianity* (trans. and ed. R. A. Kraft et al.; Philadelphia: Fortress Press, 1977) 44–53.
4. See, e.g., Helmut Koester, "*GNŌMAI DIAPHORAI*: The Origin and Nature of Diversification in the History of Early Christianity," in James M. Robinson and Helmut Koester, *Trajectories Through Early Christianity* (Philadelphia: Fortress Press, 1971) 114, according to which Bauer is "essentially right." In his recent treatment of Christian

A survey of the extant Christian manuscripts (or fragments thereof) dating to the second century and preserved in Egypt is very illuminating: ten biblical manuscripts (seven Old Testament, three New Testament: Gospel of John, Matthew, Titus) and four nonbiblical (Egerton gospel, *Shepherd of Hermas*, P. Oxy. 1 = *Gospel of Thomas* 26–28, and Irenaeus *Adversus haereses*).[5] The only possible evidence for "Gnosticism" that can be extrapolated from this list is not unambiguous: the *Gospel of Thomas*, which not everyone agrees is "gnostic."[6] To be sure, this is evidence from the second century, not the first. Unfortunately, we have no manuscript evidence at all from the first century.

Probably the most important feature of Roberts's book is his discussion of *nomina sacra* in early Christian manuscripts and his conclusions concerning the nature and origin of earliest Christianity in Egypt based on the evidence provided by the *nomina sacra*. These *nomina sacra* consist of certain proper names and religious terms that are given special treatment in writing, usually by means of abbreviation with superlineation. The four basic ones are *Iēsous, Christos, kyrios,* and *theos,* but there are fifteen in all.[7] Roberts argues that the use of *nomina sacra* is a Christian, not a Jewish, invention, though it is obviously influenced by the Jewish reverence for the name of God.[8] The *nomina sacra* occur in the earliest Christian manuscripts, and Roberts argues persuasively that this scribal practice arose already in the first century in the church in Jerusalem, where a "theology of the name" was especially prominent.[9] The starting point for the development of the *nomina sacra* is the name *Iēsous*. Early forms of the *nomen sacrum* are *IĒ* (a suspended form) and *IĒS* and *IS* (contracted forms, the latter eventually becoming standard). The form *IĒ* occurs in the

---

origins in Egypt, Koester still credits Bauer's thesis, though he also talks of "several competing Christian groups" in Alexandria, an important modification. See H. Koester, *Introduction to the New Testament* (2 vols.; Philadelphia: Fortress Press, 1982) 2:219–39, esp. 219 and 220. See also the literature cited in Klijn's contribution to this book.

5. Roberts, *Manuscript*, 12–14. Of course, the term "biblical" used of NT mss. from this period is anachronistic.

6. See, e.g., Stevan L. Davies, *The Gospel of Thomas and Christian Wisdom* (New York: Seabury Press, 1983).

7. The others are *pneuma, anthrōpos, stauros, patēr, huios, sotēr, mētēr, ouranos, Israēl, Daveid, Ierousalēm.* See Roberts, *Manuscript*, 27. Of course, the common names in this list occur as *nomina sacra* only in certain theologically loaded contexts.

8. Jewish mss. accord special status to the Tetragrammaton, but the *nomina sacra* are only found in Christian mss. Some scholars have argued for a Jewish origin for the *nomina sacra*; see Roberts, *Manuscript*, 26–34.

9. The early chapters of Acts tend to bear this out: see Acts 3:6; 4:7, 10, 12, 17, 18; 5:28, 40. Cf. Roberts, *Manuscript*, 41.

Egerton gospel fragment and other early papyri and is probably presupposed in the *Epistle of Barnabas* 9.8.[10]

Roberts's study has shed important new light on Christian origins in Egypt. He concludes that the preponderance of the evidence points to Jerusalem as the earliest source of Egyptian Christianity, that the earliest Christianity in Egypt was Jewish, and that, furthermore, the earliest Christians in Egypt would naturally have been regarded as Jews and indistinguishable as a separate religious group. It is, of course, obvious that Alexandria, the home of the largest Jewish community of the Diaspora, would have been the first place to which the earliest Christian missionaries to Egypt came.[11]

To be sure, all of this is based on conjecture and circumstantial evidence. The fact remains that the history of Christianity in Egypt before the time of Hadrian is exceedingly obscure, but Roberts is surely correct in reminding us that our knowledge of Gnosticism in Egypt before the time of Hadrian (when Basilides and Valentinus were flourishing) is even more obscure than for non-gnostic Christianity.[12]

It has already been noted that the documentary evidence for Christianity in Egypt does not begin until the early third century. But, as Roberts points out,[13] the earliest Christian documents would generally have been indistinguishable from Jewish ones. One important document bearing upon Judaism in first-century Alexandria, not discussed by Roberts, has sometimes been thought to contain a veiled reference to Christians. I refer to the famous letter of the Emperor Claudius to the Alexandrians, dated 10 November 41 C.E.[14] The relevant passage reads as follows:

> Nor are they [the Jews] to bring in or invite Jews coming from Syria or Egypt, or I shall be forced to conceive greater suspicion. If they disobey, I shall proceed against them in every way as fomenting a common plague for the whole world.[15]

The possibility has been entertained that "Jews coming from Syria"

---

10. Ibid., 35–36. *Barnabas* is probably to be placed in Alexandria; see below.

11. See Roberts, *Manuscript*, 49–73 (chap. 3: "The Character and Development of the Church").

12. Ibid., 52. He points out, for example, that there are no specifically gnostic *nomina sacra* (p. 43); and we have already noted above that the second-century manuscript evidence provides only the barest suggestion of a gnostic presence.

13. Ibid., 57–58. For the Jewish documents see V. A. Tcherikover, A. Fuks, and M. Stern, *CPJ* (3 vols.; Cambridge: Harvard Univ. Press, 1957–64).

14. *CPJ*, no. 153 (= P. Lond. 1912); cf. Tcherikover, Fuks, and Stern, *CPJ* 2:36–55.

15. Ibid., lines 96–100 (Greek text, p. 41; ET, p. 43).

could include Jewish Christian missionaries from Palestine, but obviously no certainty can be achieved on this question.[16]

In any case, whatever the meaning of Claudius's letter, it is clear that the earliest Christian missionaries to Alexandria would have been "Jews coming from Syria," i.e., from Palestine,[17] specifically Jerusalem.

In what follows I want to take another look at the early Christian traditions pertaining to the Christian presence in Alexandria, explore the Jewish community of Alexandria as the locus of earliest Christianity in Egypt, and discuss some specific loci associated with early Alexandrian Christianity.

MISCELLANEOUS EARLY CHRISTIAN TRADITIONS

The New Testament provides only the barest hints of a Christian mission to Egypt. The Pentecost account in Acts numbers among the devout Jews in Jerusalem in attendance at Peter's sermon persons from "Egypt and the parts of Libya belonging to Cyrene" (Acts 2:10). The disputants in the controversy with the "Hellenist" protomartyr Stephen included Jews from Cyrene and Alexandria (Acts 6:9). The original homes of Stephen and five of his co-workers are not given, but all of them were Jews with Greek names (Acts 6:5), and some of them could have come from Alexandria.[18] (Nicolaus is singled out as a convert to Judaism, a "proselyte," and is said to have come from Antioch.) In any case, the traffic between Jerusalem and Alexandria was extensive in both directions, and one might easily suppose that some Alexandrian Jews who were converted to Christianity in Palestine would have returned home to spread their faith. Such persons could have been included among the (Hellenist) Christians hounded out of Jerusalem (Acts 8:1). Unfortunately, our evidence is very scanty, not least because the author of Acts happens to tilt his geographic focus toward Asia Minor, Greece, and Rome, rather than toward Egypt and Alexandria (or, for that matter, eastward into the interior of Syria).

---

16. See Tcherikover's note to this passage, CPJ 2:53–54. Tcherikover rejects the hypothesis that the passage refers to Christians. G. M. Lee finds the hypothesis "attractive." See Lee, "Eusebius on St. Mark and the Beginnings of Christianity in Egypt," in StPatr XII (TU 115; Berlin: Akademie-Verlag, 1975) 422–31, esp. 431.

17. On the name Syria as applied to Palestine see Tcherikover, Fuks, and Stern, CPJ 1:5 and n. 13.

18. The names Philip and Nicanor occur among the Jews of Egypt. See ibid. 3: appendix 2 ("Prosopography of the Jews in Egypt").

A hint of the existence of a Christian community in Egypt in the forties of our era is provided by the story in Acts of Apollos, one of Paul's co-workers in Ephesus and Corinth. He is said to have been "a Jew . . . a native of Alexandria . . . an eloquent man, powerfully trained in the scriptures" (18:24). A variant reading at Acts 18:25 asserts that this Apollos "had been instructed in the word in his home country."[19] This reading, if historically accurate, would presuppose the existence of a Jewish Christian community in Alexandria by the late 40s or early 50s C.E.,[20] i.e., during the reign of the Emperor Claudius (41–54). But the New Testament is totally silent on the question of who the earliest organizers of the Alexandrian church might have been.

Here is where extra-canonical Christian tradition and legend attempt to fill the gap. One interesting account is provided by the pseudo-Clementine literature, specifically *Homily* 1: The young Clement, in a first-person narrative, tells of his journey from Rome to Judea to find out about the Son of God, concerning whom he had heard some reports. His ship is blown off course and comes to Alexandria, where he falls in with a Hebrew from Judea named Barnabas. This Barnabas instructs Clement in the Christian faith and then sets out for Judea to observe "the festival." Clement soon follows Barnabas to Judea and comes to Caesarea, where Barnabas introduces him to the apostle Peter (*Hom.* 1.8.3–15.9). In this account Barnabas is the only Christian identified by name in Alexandria, but "Clement" reports that he had been told by certain Alexandrian "philosophers" that they had heard about the Judean reported to be Son of God "from many who had come from there" (8.4).

Whether this reference to Barnabas's activity in Egypt was invented by the author of the Clementine romance or was based on an independent tradition is hard to say. It is not found in Eusebius nor in any other document datable before the fourth century. It is to be noted that the companion document, the *Recognitions*, places Clement's encounter with Barnabas in Rome rather than Alexandria.[21] It is possible that the story of Barnabas's preaching in Alexandria is

---

19. Codex Bezae (my translation), representing the "Western Text." The same ms. also calls this man *Apollōnios* in v. 24. *Apollōs* is a short form of *Apollōnios*; cf. Silas/Silvanus (Acts 15:22, etc.; 1 Thess. 1:1, etc.).

20. The activity of Apollos in Ephesus predates the Pauline mission there (Acts 19), 52–55 C.E. For these dates see Koester, *Introduction* 2:104.

21. Ps.-Clem. *Recogn.* 1.6–12. Cf. R. A. Lipsius, *Die Apokryphen Apostelgeschichten und Apostellegenden* (2 vols.; Braunschweig: Schwetschke und Sohn, 1883–90; repr., Amsterdam: Philo, 1976) 2/2:271–73.

somehow to be traced to the diffusion of the *Epistle of Barnabas*, widely held to be of Alexandrian origin.[22] In any case, that the earliest Christian missionaries came to Alexandria from Judea, as this report says, is inherently probable, even if there is reason to doubt that Barnabas was one of them.

THE MARK LEGEND

The standard tradition of the Egyptian church as to its origins is that Saint Mark the Evangelist was the founder and first bishop of the church in Alexandria.[23] It is noteworthy that the New Testament provides not the slightest hint of this tradition, though Mark is mentioned in a number of contexts. According to the Book of Acts, the church in Jerusalem met in the home of Mary, mother of John Mark (Acts 12:12; the events there narrated are placed during the reign of Herod Agrippa, i.e., 41–44 C.E.). This Mark is said to have accompanied Barnabas and Paul from Jerusalem to Antioch (12:25). From there he went with them on their missionary journey to Cyprus and Asia Minor, leaving them in Perga to return to Jerusalem (13:5, 13). Later Paul refused to take Mark along on another journey, and chose Silas (Silvanus) instead (15:37–40). Mark then went with Barnabas back to Cyprus (15:39), and we hear no more of him after that in Acts. Mark turns up with Paul, as a "fellow worker," during one of Paul's imprisonments (Phlm. 24), probably in Ephesus ca. 54–55 C.E.[24] The deutero-Pauline Epistle to the Colossians identifies Mark as the cousin of Barnabas (Col. 4:10); the Colossians are counseled to receive him if he comes to them. Mark is remembered in 2 Tim. 4:11 as one who had been "useful" to Paul. He may also have been at some time useful to the apostle Peter as well, for the author of 1 Peter places Mark in Rome with Peter, and has Peter refer to him as his "son," sending greetings to the recipients of the letter in Asia Minor (1 Pet. 5:13).[25] Thus the New

22. R. Trevijano, "The Early Christian Church of Alexandria," in *StPatr XII*, 471–77, esp. 471. See also below, on the *Epistle of Barnabas*.

23. For a good summary of the standard Coptic tradition see A. S. Atiya, *History of Eastern Christianity* (Notre Dame, Ind.: Univ. of Notre Dame Press, 1967) 25–28.

24. Koester, *Introduction* 2:104, 131.

25. "Babylon" is clearly a symbolic name for Rome, and the addressees of the letter are located in northern Asia Minor (1:1). Cf. Koester, *Introduction* 2:292–95. H.-M. Schenke and K. M. Fischer argue that 1 Peter has nothing to do with the historical Peter. According to them the letter was originally ascribed to Paul; the name Peter in 1:1 is a secondary substitution for Paul; see *Einleitung in die Schriften des Neuen Testaments* (Berlin: Evangelische Verlagsanstalt, 1978) 1:199–216 (vol. 1: *Die Brief des Paulus und Schriften des Paulinismus*).

Testament materials connect Mark solidly with Jerusalem, Antioch, Cyprus, Asia Minor, and (less solidly) Rome,[26] but nothing is said of his connection with Egypt. It is all the more surprising, therefore, that such a connection should occur in later Christian tradition.

Eusebius is usually thought to be our earliest source for the tradition placing Mark in Egypt. But we now have a fragmentary letter of Clement of Alexandria, published by Morton Smith,[27] according to which Mark wrote his Gospel during Peter's sojourn in Rome, and after Peter's martyrdom came to Alexandria. There he expanded his earlier Gospel, with his own and Peter's notes, and produced a "more spiritual gospel" for use in the Alexandrian church, a gospel the Carpocratian heretics subsequently falsified and misused.[28] This fragment says nothing of Mark's role as founder of the Alexandrian church. To the contrary, it implies that the church there was already in existence when Mark arrived from Rome after Peter's death. Nothing is said of any earlier sojourn of Mark in Alexandria, though this is not necessarily excluded by the wording of the fragment.

Eusebius's account of Mark's activity in Alexandria follows immediately upon that of the activity of Mark and Peter in Rome, and reads as follows:

> They say that this Mark was the first to be sent to preach in Egypt the Gospel which he had also put into writing, and was the first to establish churches in Alexandria itself. The number of men and women who were there converted at the first attempt was so great, and their asceticism was so extraordinarily philosophic, that Philo thought it right to describe their conduct and assemblies and meals and all the rest of their manner of life.[29]

---

26. The earliest extra-canonical testimony to Mark's activity in Rome as a follower (and "interpreter") of Peter is provided by Papias, who may have extrapolated this from 1 Pet. 5:13. Papias adds information on the writing of the Gospel of Mark in this connection. See Eusebius *H. E.* 2.15.1–2; 3.39.15. Cf. also Schenke and Fischer, *Einleitung* 1:200.

27. *Clement of Alexandria and a Secret Gospel of Mark* (Cambridge: Harvard Univ. Press, 1973).

28. I am here summarizing the relevant portion of the text of the letter (text, p. 448; ET, p. 446). I accept the authenticity of the Clement fragment, but I do not accept Morton Smith's theories pertaining to the "Secret Gospel of Mark." Incidentally, this new fragment of Clement is of special interest in connection with John Chrysostom's testimony *(hom. 1 in Matt.)* that Mark wrote his Gospel in Egypt. See Lipsius, *Apostelgeschichten* 2/2:322.

29. *H. E.* 2.16; Kirsopp Lake's translation in the LCL edition, here and elsewhere. Eusebius goes on to summarize Philo's account of the Therapeutae (cf. Philo *Vit. Cont.*) in the belief that these Jewish ascetics were Christians. This belief was solidly established in the church down to modern times.

This information is supplemented by Eusebius in his *Chronicle*, according to which Mark arrived in Alexandria in the third year of Claudius, i.e., in 43 C.E.[30]

Though Eusebius says nothing here of Mark's role as a bishop, he later reports the accession of Annianus in 62 C.E. in the following terms:

> In the eighth year of the reign of Nero Annianus was the first after Mark the Evangelist to receive charge of the diocese of Alexandria.[31]

Some observations regarding these statements are in order. Regarding the first, the words, "they say," imply that Eusebius is passing along a previously existing tradition.[32] One could also infer from the immediately preceding context that it was Peter who sent Mark to Egypt, an inference actually made in later accounts of the tradition.[33] The Gospel of Mark is closely associated with this tradition, but the presence in Alexandria of the Gospel of Mark as early as the third year of Claudius, when the *Chronicle* reports that Mark arrived in Alexandria, is clearly problematical. The notice in the *Chronicle*, however, could be taken to imply that Eusebius allowed for more than one visit of Mark to Alexandria, such as the later accounts, in fact, explicitly relate.[34]

As to the statement concerning the accession of Annianus, this is

---

30. According to the Latin reworking of Eusebius by Jerome. See Rudolf Helm, ed., *Die Chronik des Hieronymus*, in *Eusebius Werke* (GCS 47; rev. ed.; Berlin: Akademie-Verlag, 1956) 7:7: third year of the 205th Olympiad. According to the Armenian version of Eusebius, Mark arrived in Alexandria in the first year of the 205th Olympiad, i.e., 41 C.E. See Alfred Schoene, ed., *Eusebi Chronicorum canonum quae supersunt* (2 volumes; Dublin and Zurich: Weidmann, 1967) 2:152. This is the date noted by Lipsius (*Apostelgeschichten* 2/2:322). On the *Chronicle* of Eusebius (which was written before his *Ecclesiastical History*), see Alden A. Mosshammer, *The Chronicle of Eusebius and Greek Chronographic Tradition* (Lewisburg, Pa.: Bucknell Univ. Press, 1979); cf. Robert M. Grant, *Eusebius as Church Historian* (Oxford: Clarendon Press, 1980) esp. 3–10. The *Paschal Chronicle* places the arrival of Mark in Alexandria two years before the accession of Claudius, i.e., in 39 C.E.; see PG 92.560A. Severus (Sawirus 'ibn al-Muqaffa), bishop of al-Ashmunein, states that Peter sent Mark to Alexandria "in the fifteenth year after the Ascension of Christ." See B. Evetts, ed., *History of the Patriarchs of the Coptic Church of Alexandria* (PO 1/2; Paris: Firmin-Didot, 1948) 140. Cf. n. 47 below. Severus's rival, Eutychius of Alexandria (also of the tenth century), specifies the ninth year of Claudius (49–50 C.E.). See his *Annales*, as rendered into Latin from Arabic, PG 111.982A.

31. *H. E.* 2.24. In the very next section Eusebius reports on the Neronian persecution in Rome and the deaths of Peter and Paul.

32. G. M. Lee marshals a great deal of evidence from Greek literature to show that *phasi*, "they say," can be taken to mean that Eusebius was drawing on written records for this information. See "Eusebius on St. Mark," 425–27.

33. E.g., Epiphanius *Haer.* 51.6; Severus of al-Ashmunein (n. 30 above); and the Byzantine church historian Nicephorus Callistus, PG 145.792C.

34. E.g., The *Acts of Mark*, on which see below. Does the phrase "at the first attempt," *ek prōtēs epibolēs* (*H. E.* 2.16.2), hint at this?

clearly derived from a bishop list of the church of Alexandria.[35] It is noteworthy that Eusebius does not report the death of Mark in connection with the accession of Annianus.[36] He obviously knows nothing of the martyrdom of Mark.

This brings us to the *Acts of Mark* (*Passio,* April 25). The basic document exists in two Greek recensions and was rendered into several other languages. It also underwent various expansions and additions.[37] The story can be summarized as follows:[38]

When the apostles were sent out, Mark received as his lot the country of Egypt and its surrounding territories (1). He came first to Cyrene,[39] where he did many marvelous works and converted many to the faith. While there he received a vision that he should go to Pharos in Alexandria, and the brethren sent him off on a ship with their blessings (2). Mark arrived in Alexandria the next day and came to a place called Mendion.[40] As he was entering the gate of the city, the strap of his sandal broke, and he went to a cobbler to have it fixed. The cobbler, working on the sandal, injured his left hand and cried out, "God is One [εἷς θεός]." Mark healed the hand in the name of Jesus Christ, and was invited to the home of the cobbler (3). There Mark

35. Such a list is posited for the second-century Alexandrian church by Lipsius, *Apostelgeschichten* 2/2:323., Eusebius is usually thought to be relying on Julius Africanus's *Chronographies.* See Grant, *Eusebius,* 52.

36. Jerome reports that Mark died in the eighth year of Nero and was buried in Alexandria, Annianus succeeding him. This is probably read out of Eusebius's account. See *Vir. Ill.* 8.

37. The two recensions, represented by mss. in Paris and the Vatican, are printed respectively in *PG* 115, cols. 164–69, and in the *Acta Sanctorum* (rev. ed.; Paris: Palmé, 1863–1940) 12: April, 3, XXXVIII–XL. They differ basically only in the opening and concluding passages. The *Acts* underwent several expansions in Greek, one of which has recently been published (F. Halkin, "Actes inédits de saint Marc," *AnBoll* 87 [1969] 343–71), a fabulous piece of hagiography utterly devoid of historical value. Lipsius (*Apostelgeschichten* 2/2:329) mentions Latin, Arabic, and Ethiopic versions, but there also exist scattered fragments of a Coptic version. See, e.g., T. Lefort, "Fragment copte-sahidique du Martyre de St.-Marc," in *Mélanges d'histoire offerts à Charles Moeller* (Louvain: Bureaux du Recueil; Paris: Picard et fils, 1914) 1:226–31; and O. von Lemm, "Zur Topographie Alexandriens," *Kleine Koptische Studien XLI* (repr. ed.; Leipzig: Zentralantiquariat der DDR, 1972) 253–57. See also *Bibliotheca Hagiographica Graeca* (3d ed.; Brussels: Societé des Bollandistes, 1957) 2:77–79, nos. 1035–38; *Bibliotheca Hagiographica Latina* (Brussels: Societé des Bollandistes, 1900–1901) 783–84, nos. 5272–92; *Bibliotheca Hagiographica Orientalis* (Brussels: Societé des Bollandistes, 1910) 134–35, nos. 596–604. A very important Ethiopic version has recently been published, which is closely related to the basic Greek version and manifestly translated directly from Greek. See Getatchew Haile, "A New Ethiopic Version of the Acts of St. Mark," *AnBoll* 99 (1981) 117–34.

38. This summary, with chapter divisions, is based on the *PG* version (Paris ms.).

39. The other version adds that he was a native of Cyrene; the new Ethiopic version has the same variant.

40. The other version and the Ethiopic have "Bennidion." On this place see below.

began to preach the gospel of Jesus Christ, son of God, son of Abraham, telling the man of the prophecies related to Christ. The man said that he did not know of these writings, though he was familiar with the *Iliad* and the *Odyssey* and other things that Egyptians learned from childhood. But the man was eventually converted, and he and his whole household were baptized, and many others besides. The man's name was Ananias (4).[41]

Eventually the pagan people of the city, hearing that a Galilean had come to do away with idolatry, sought to kill him. Mark ordained for the church Ananias (Annianus) as bishop, three presbyters (Milaius, Sabinus, and Cerdo),[42] seven deacons, and eleven other persons for special service, and returned to Pentapolis. When he came back to Alexandria after two years he found the community flourishing, a church having been built in a place called Boukolou, near the seashore (5). The pagans, meanwhile, were very angry at Mark for all of his mighty works (6). On the occasion of a paschal celebration, which occurred on the same day as a Sarapis festival, Pharmouthi 29 (= April 24),[43] the pagans seized Mark at the service, put a rope around his neck, and said, "Let us drag the *boubalos* in Boukolou."[44] They dragged him thus, the holy Mark giving thanks to Christ all the while, and that evening they threw his bloodied body into a prison (7). During the night Mark was visited first by an angel and then by Christ himself, receiving words of encouragement (8).

The next morning the pagan crowds dragged him again, and Mark expired. The mobs built a fire in the place called Angeloi[45] and put the body of Mark on it, but a great storm arose, and the pagan crowds fled in terror (9). The faithful rescued the body and brought it to where the services were going on. They prepared the body according to custom, and placed it in a stone tomb, located to the east of the city. Mark the evangelist and protomartyr of the Alexandrian church died on Phar-

41. The other version and the Ethiopic have Anianus. See below for discussion of the name.
42. The other versions (Vat. and new Ethiopic) have Milius, Sabinus, and Cerdo. Milius = Abilius, second bishop after Annianus (Eusebius, *H. E.* 3.14); Cerdo is the successor to Abilius (*H. E.* 3.21). Sabinus may be a corruption of the name of Primus, successor to Cerdo (*H. E.* 4.1). Cf. Lipsius, *Apostelgeschichten* 2/2:333 n. 3. According to the *Apostolic Constitutions* 7.46, Mark ordained Annianus as the first bishop of Alexandria, and Luke the evangelist ordained Abilius as the second.
43. The Paris ms. wrongly reads Pharmouthi 26; the Vatican ms. leaves out the date, but it is correct in the new Ethiopic version.
44. *boubalos* = "buffalo"; *ta boukolou* can mean "cow pastures." See below on *boukolou*.
45. On this name see below.

mouthi 30 (= April 25), when Gaius Tiberius Caesar was emperor (10).[46]

The *Acts of Mark* constitutes one of the basic sources of Severus's *History of the Patriarchs*,[47] and is also utilized by the author of the Arabic *Synaxary* of the Coptic church (thirteenth century).[48] The question arises as to whether or not any of this late material can be credited with historical value. At least one western scholar thinks so. F. Pericoli-Ridolfini has made an attempt to reconstruct the outline of Mark's life, using mainly the *Synaxary*, Eusebius, and the New Testament.[49] His conclusions cannot be discussed in detail here, but the main points are of interest to us. He posits several visits on the part of Mark to Alexandria, beginning in 43 C.E.,[50] and connects the martyrdom of Mark with the pogrom against the Jews conducted by the Roman prefect of Alexandria, Tiberius Alexander, in 66 C.E.[51] One valuable feature of Pericoli-Ridolfini's work is that he places Mark's activities, and earliest Alexandrian Christianity in general, firmly in the context of Alexandrian Judaism.

There are, nevertheless, some basic obstacles in the way of treating these late accounts, including the *Acts of Mark*, as straight history. In

46. The Latin version of Surianus has, more plausibly, Claudius Nero Caesar (Nero Claudius Caesar, 54–68 C.E.); see *PG* 115.170. The other Greek version adds a description of Mark's physical appearance; this is absent from the new Ethiopic version.

47. Cf. n. 30. Severus's biography of Mark is based on three sources: Eusebius (= Evetts, 140), the *Acts of Mark* (=Evetts, 141–48), and another source, otherwise unknown, telling of Mark's early life in Cyrene (cf. n. 39), his move to Palestine, and his activities there as one of the "seventy disciples" (= Evetts, 135–40). Cf. T. Orlandi, "Le fonti copte della *Storia dei Patriarchi di Alessandria*," in his *Studi Copti* (TDSA 22; Milan: Istituto editoriale cisalpino, 1968) 51–86, esp. 75; but Orlandi overlooks the short paragraph based on Eusebius, *H. E.* 2.16. On Severus's methods of research, see F. R. Farag, "The Technique of Research of a Tenth Century Christian Arab Writer: Severus ibn al-Muqaffa'," *Muséon* 86 (1973) 37–66. On the various lists of the "seventy disciples" and Mark's place in them (Ps.-Dorotheus et al.) see D. Theodor Schermann, *Prophetenund Apostellegenden nebst Jüngerkatalogen des Dorotheus und verwandter Texte* (TU 31/3: Leipzig: Hinrichs, 1907) 133–353, esp. 285–87.

48. See René Basset, *Le synaxaire arabe jacobite (rédaction copte)* (PO 16/2; Paris: Firmin-Didot, 1922) 4:344–47 (Barmoudah 30, Arabic and French); I. Forget, *Synaxarium Alexandrinum* (CSCO 90, Scriptores Arabici 13, 1926) 2:96–97 (Barmūdah 30, Latin). On this synaxary see O. H. E. Burmester, "On the Date and Authorship of the Arabic Synaxarium of the Coptic Church," *JTS* 39 (1938) 249–53.

49. F. Pericoli-Ridolfini, "Le origini della Chiesa d'Alessandria d'Egitto," *Accademia Nazionale dei Lincei, Rendiconti* (Classe di scienze mor., 1962) 17:317–43.

50. Based on Eusebius's *Chronicle* (cf. n. 30). Pericoli-Ridolfini's reconstruction is rather complicated, made all the more so by his placing Colossians and Philemon in Rome, and by his acceptance of the authenticity of the pastoral epistles, which forces him to send Mark back to Rome and Asia Minor after the ordination of Annianus in 62. See pp. 319–20, 324–28.

51. Ibid., 327–28. See Josephus *Bell.* 2.487–98; and cf. n. 70.

his discussion of the dating of the *Acts*, which he places at the end of the fourth, or the beginning of the fifth, century, Lipsius summarizes the matter as follows:

> Vermutlich schon längere Zeit vor ihrer Abfassung zeigte man in Alexandrien das Grabmal der Evangelisten *en topois Boukolou* und erzählte sich von seinem Märtyrertod. Die nähere Ausführung der Legende haben dann wol erst die *Acten* gebracht.[52]

But it is precisely the martyrdom of Mark that is most problematical, in view of the lateness of its attestation. Apart from the *Acts* itself, the earliest testimonies are accounts relating to the *martyrium* of Saint Mark: In the *Lausiac History* of Palladius (early fifth century), there is a story of a presbyter from Galatia by the name of Philoromus who visited Alexandria and prayed in the *Martyrion* of Mark.[53] And in the *Passio S. Petri*,[54] the story of the martyrdom of Peter, Archbishop of Alexandria (d. 25 November 311), it is reported that the wall of the prison in which Peter was being held was breached and the soldiers then took him to Boukolou, where he prayed at the tomb of Saint Mark the evangelist and protomartyr, after which he was beheaded. Lipsius entertained the possibility that the *Passio* of Peter is a fourth-century witness to the *Acts of Mark*,[55] but subsequent scholarship has shown that the story of Peter's praying at the tomb of Mark (together with other features of the text) is a later addition to the original fourth-century account of the death of Peter.[56]

That the added material in the *Passio S. Petri* pertaining to Saint Mark the protomartyr is closely related to the *Acts of Mark* cannot be denied. But how is this relationship to be explained? I would suggest that the developing legend surrounding the death of Bishop Peter, the "Last Martyr" of Egypt,[57] led to the development of a story according to

---

52. Lipsius, *Apostelgeschichten* 2/2:346.
53. *H. Laus.* 45.
54. BHG 1502 = J. Viteau, ed., *Passions des saints Ecaterine et Pierre d'Alexandrie, Barbara, et Anysia* (Paris: Bouillon, 1897) 69–85, esp. 77.
55. Lipsius, *Apostelgeschichten* 2/2:338–39.
56. See esp. William Telfer, "St. Peter of Alexandria and Arius," *AnBoll* 67 (1949) 117–30.
57. *Passio*, Viteau, ed., *Passions des saints*, 77. This very common term for Peter is even attributed to the martyr himself in a Coptic letter-fragment attributed to him! In that document, Peter reports a divine voice commanding him to return to Alexandria and addressing him as "Peter, the last martyr" *(Petros phae martyros)*. See Carl Schmidt, *Fragmente einer Schrift des Märtyrbischofs Petrus von Alexandrien* (TU 20; Leipzig: Hinrichs, 1901) 4 (Coptic text) and 5 (ET). Schmidt (too optimistically!) accepts the authenticity of this fragment.

which Mark, the first bishop of Alexandria, also suffered a martyr's death, thus becoming the first of the martyrs of Egypt.[58] The mode of Mark's death could have been suggested by an actual event involving another bishop of Alexandria during the time of Julian the Apostate. George, an Arian bishop, was dragged through the streets of Alexandria by an enraged pagan mob and put to death.[59] The account of Mark's martyrdom would, in that case, have emerged as an addition to an earlier tradition that Mark died and was buried in Alexandria. The account of Mark's activity and his burial in the area of the city called Boukolou is probably a reminiscence of an old local tradition.[60]

Before leaving the *Acts of Mark* some additional comments are in order. It is to be noted that there is no reference to Jews or Judaism in it, though later expansions of the story of the martyrdom specify that Jews were involved in Mark's death.[61] I would explain this feature of the *Acts* as a reminiscence of the fact that the earliest Christians in Alexandria were Jews. Other pointers in the same direction include the name of Mark's first convert, Ananias (= Hananiah),[62] and the account of Mark's appeal to the Old Testament in his preaching of Christ.[63]

To sum up: The tradition of the association of St. Mark with earliest Christianity in Egypt is traceable to the second century and may originate even earlier. The historicity of this tradition, though unprovable, should not be ruled out.[64] Indeed the tradition of the preaching of

58. The close association of Peter with Mark may even apply to the relics of Saint Mark. There is a possibility that the head of Saint Mark in the Cathedral of Saint Mark in Alexandria is actually that of Peter! See Otto Meinardus, *Christian Egypt Ancient and Modern* (2d ed.; Cairo: American Univ. in Cairo Press, 1977) 37–38.

59. Ammianus Marcellinus 20.11.8–10; cf. Socrates *H. E.* 3.2; Sozomen *H. E.* 5.7. On Arius's connection with the church in Boukolou, see below. This treatment of people seems to have been all too common in Alexandria. Josephus mentions that three fleeing Jews were "dragged off to be burnt alive" during the pogrom of 66 C.E. (*Bell* 2.492; cf. n. 51), but it can hardly be argued that one or more of these was a Christian, much less Mark himself. Cf. also Philo *Leg. Gai.*, for similar attacks on Jews during the time of Caligula.

60. See below on Boukolou.

61. See, e.g., Halkin, "Actes inédits" (cf. n. 37) 366–70. The hostility of Jews against Christians is a stock feature in many martyrdoms, e.g., *Mart. Pol.* 12.2; 17.2.

62. This variant of the name Annianus may be original. There are three occurrences of "Ananias" in the Prosopography of the Jews in Egypt (Tcherikover, Fuks, and Stern, *CPJ* 3:169). "Annianus" is an alternative Hellenization of the Hebrew name; see Pericoli-Ridolfini, "Le origini," 324.

63. The detail that Ananias was ignorant of the Scriptures, only acquainted with the *Iliad* and the *Odyssey* (*Acts* 4), is a fanciful addition to an earlier form of the story.

64. See, e.g., L. W. Barnard, "St. Mark and Alexandria," *HTR* 57 (1964) 145–50; and Lee, "Eusebius." Walter Bauer propounds a completely different opinion, viz., that it was the Roman church, the defender of "orthodoxy," that "placed at the disposal of ortho-

Mark in Alexandria may antedate the acceptance of the canonical Gospel of Mark in the Alexandrian church.[65] And even if we acknowledge, as we must, that Eusebius was wrong in connecting the Jewish community of the Therapeutae with Mark's first converts,[66] we should nevertheless acknowledge that he was correct in stressing that the "apostolic men" of the days of Philo and Mark were "of Hebrew origin and thus still preserved most of the ancient customs in a strictly Jewish manner."[67] It was probably not until the early second century that Christians emerged as a group, or groups, distinct from the Jewish community.

THE LOCUS: ALEXANDRIAN JUDAISM

We are relatively well informed about the Jewish community of Alexandria in the Hellenistic-Roman period, the largest and most important of the Greek-speaking Diaspora. For the first century Philo and Josephus are our main literary sources, and this evidence is supplemented by documentary material.[68] The Jews were constituted as a *politeuma*, with their own political and legal structures, and they were encouraged by official Roman policy to live according to their own ancestral customs.[69] The Jewish population in Alexandria numbered in the hundreds of thousands.[70] According to Strabo,[71] a great part of the

---

dox Alexandria the figure of Mark as founder of the church and apostolic initiator of the traditional succession of bishops," presumably in the time of Demetrius (189–231), the first orthodox bishop according to Bauer. See *Orthodoxy and Heresy*, 53–58 and 60.

65. Roberts (*Manuscript*, 59, 61) calls attention to the paucity of evidence in Egypt for the Gospel of Mark before the fourth century. He has revised his earlier views to the effect that the tradition of the founding of the Alexandrian church by Mark is bound up with the arrival in Alexandria of the Gospel of Mark. See *Manuscript*, 59 n. 5.

66. See above, and n. 29.

67. *H. E.* 2.17.2.

68. The available material has been admirably sifted by Tcherikover in his Prolegomena to *CPJ* 1:1–111. The Jewish inscriptions from Egypt are also included as an appendix in *CPJ* 3:138–66 (Alexandria: 138–41). See also E. Mary Smallwood, *The Jews under Roman Rule: From Pompey to Diocletian* (Leiden: E. J. Brill, 1976), esp. 220–55, 364–68, 389–412, and 516–19; articles by M. Stern, S. Safrai, and S. Appelbaum, in *The Jewish People in the First Century: Historical Geography, Political History, Social, Cultural, and Religious Life and Institutions* (CRINT 1/1; Philadelphia: Fortress Press; Assen: Van Gorcum, 1974); John J. Collins, *Between Athens and Jerusalem: Jewish Identity in the Hellenistic Diaspora* (New York: Crossroad, 1983) esp. 102–34; and Henry Green's contribution to this volume.

69. See, e.g., the aforementioned letter of Claudius (n. 14), lines 82–88.

70. Philo (*Flacc.* 43) claims that in his time there were at least a million Jews in Egypt. How many lived in Alexandria is not known, but the number was doubtless high. Cf. Tcherikover's cautious remarks, *CPJ* 1:4. Josephus reports that 50,000 Jews were killed during the massacre of 66 C.E. perpetrated by Philo's apostate nephew, Tiberius

city of Alexandria had been allocated to the Jews. Philo reports that the city was divided into five quarters named after the first letters of the alphabet, and "two of these are called Jewish because most of the inhabitants are Jews, though in the rest also there are not a few Jews scattered about."[72] During a vicious pogrom in 37–38 C.E. the Jews of Alexandria were ejected from four of the "letters" and crowded into a small part of one. "The Jews were so numerous that they poured out over beaches, dunghills and tombs, robbed of their belongings."[73]

Philo does not tell us which "letters" were predominantly Jewish. Josephus, in the context of his discussion of the pogrom of 66 C.E. in his *Jewish War*, reports that the Jews had been assigned a quarter of their own (τόπον ἴδιον) by the successors of Alexander the Great. Josephus goes on to describe how the Roman troops let loose by Tiberius Alexander "rushed to the quarter of the city called 'Delta,' where the Jews were concentrated," and massacred them in large numbers.[74] In his treatise *Against Apion* Josephus quotes Apion to the effect that the Jews came from Syria and settled "by a sea without a harbour, close beside the spot where the waves break on the beach." Josephus claims that this is Alexandria's "finest residential quarter," located "near the palaces."[75] The area specified can easily be identified as the north-eastern section of the city, east of Cape Lochias (modern Silsileh). It is usually assumed that the area described here is the same as that referred to in the *Jewish War* as Delta.[76] But this identification is rendered highly doubtful by the evidence of a papyrus document of 13 B.C.E. that refers to the Kibotos harbor located "in Delta."[77] The Kibotos

---

Alexander, prefect of Egypt and governor of Alexandria (*Bell.* 2.497). As noted above, Pericoli-Ridolfini places the death of Mark in this context.

71. Quoted in Josephus *Ant.* 14.117 from an otherwise lost portion of Strabo's *Geography*. In his famous description of the city of Alexandria in Bk. 17 Strabo does not refer to the Jewish quarters.

72. *Flacc.* 55, Colson's translation in the LCL edition, here and elsewhere. Other writers (e.g., Ps.-Callisthenes 1.32) mention the five "letters." On this and other aspects of Alexandrian topography see the invaluable work by A. Calderini ("Alexandreia," in *DNGT* 1/1); and now equally indispensable, the work of A. Adriani (*RAEGR*). On an interesting inventory of buildings in the five quarters embedded in the *Chronicle* of Michael bar Elias (twelfth century), see P. M. Fraser, "A Syriac *Notitia Urbis Alexandrinae*," *JEA* 37 (1951) 103–78.

73. *Flacc.* 56; cf. *Leg. Gai.* 124–27.

74. *Bell.* 2.488, 495.

75. *Ap.* 2.33–36.

76. So even P. M. Fraser in his monumental work *Ptolemaic Alexandria* (3 vols.; Oxford: Clarendon Press, 1972) 1:55. He does take note of the problem posed by the papyrus; see 2:109 n. 270.

77. *BGU* 1151, lines 40–41: ἐν τῷ Δ . . . πρὸς τῇ κειβωτῷ.

was a small harbor within the larger western harbor called Eunostos.[78] Accordingly, the Delta quarter must have been located in the northwestern part of the city and was presumably one of the two Jewish quarters referred to by Philo.[79] One can reconcile the apparently contradictory evidence by supposing that during the pogroms of 38 and 66, described by Philo and Josephus respectively, the Jews were driven into the northeastern section during the first one and the northwestern section (Delta) during the second one.[80] The northeastern section, described by Josephus, was probably the oldest and most prominent Jewish quarter. We do not know what letter was assigned to it.[81] In any case, the location of the two Jewish areas at opposite ends of the city, northeast and northwest, accords well with such archaeological evidence as we have, i.e., the discovery locations of the two extant synagogue inscriptions from Alexandria.[82]

The religious life of the Jews of Alexandria was centered in the synagogues. Philo reports that there were many synagogues *(proseuchai)* in the city, located in all the districts. Of these, one is singled out as "the largest and most notable." During the pogrom in the time of Gaius Caligula all the synagogues had been desecrated with images, and the chief synagogue had a bronze statue placed in it, mounted on a four-horse chariot that had been hastily requisitioned from the Gymnasium.[83] It is this synagogue that is doubtless referred to in a famous description preserved in rabbinic sources. This synagogue, "the glory of Israel," is described as a double-colonnade basilica so large that the *ḥazan* had to wave a scarf to signal the people at the other end of the building when to say amen during the prayers. According to the same account this synagogue was destroyed by the emperor Trajan,

---

78. Strabo 17.1.10.

79. So *RAEGR* 1:239.

80. See *Flacc.* 55–56 and *Bell.* 2.495, discussed above. Josephus would presumably have known that there were two Jewish quarters in Alexandria, though he does not specifically mention this fact. Josephus had visited Alexandria himself in ca. 70 C.E. (*Vita* 415).

81. The only quarters expressly mentioned in the eight documents from Alexandria of the early Roman period published in *CPJ* (nos. 142–49) are Delta and Beta. See A. Fuks's discussion in *CPJ* 2:1–2. But Beta seems to have been located in the central part of the city. See Adriani, *Repertorio* 1:239.

82. No. 1432 (first century B.C.E.) was found in Gabbary in the western part of the city, and no. 1433 (second century B.C.E.) in Hadra in the eastern part of town. See Tcherikover, Fuks, and Stern, *CPJ* 3:139. Both Gabbary and Hadra were necropolis areas in antiquity.

83. *Leg. Gai.* 132–35; cf. *Flacc.* 41.

presumably during the revolt of 115–117 C.E.[84] This synagogue was probably located in the main Jewish area in the northeastern section of the city, though no trace of it has ever been found.[85] The one synagogue from the Diaspora uncovered by archaeologists that is most comparable to the Alexandrian synagogue described in the rabbinic sources is the one at Sardis in Asia Minor.[86]

It is to be expected that, in such a large and well-established Jewish population as existed in first-century Alexandria, a considerable degree of religious and cultural diversity would be found. For example, Philo and the author of 3 Maccabees represent opposite points of view regarding the issue of acculturation and participation in the larger Greek community.[87] From the various writings of Philo alone we can obtain a good picture of the range of attitudes toward the law found among the Jews of Alexandria, from a strict literalist interpretation to an espousal of the kind of allegorical interpretation represented by Philo himself, from a total rejection of the Scriptures and their "myths" to a spiritual reading of the Scriptures leading to a rational abandonment of the observances of ritual law.[88] Apocalyptic and gnostic groups were also probably present in the Alexandrian Jewish community.[89] Many Jews also chose the path of total cultural assimilation and apostasy.[90] Philo's own nephew, Tiberius Alexander, is the most famous case of this. On the other hand, a number of Gentiles affiliated with the Jewish religious community as proselytes.[91]

---

84. *t. Sukk.* 4.6; *y. Sukk.* 5.1; *b. Sukk.* 51b. The tradition is attributed to R. Judah b. Illai. The passage is quoted and commented on in E. R. Goodenough, *Jewish Symbols in the Greco-Roman Period* (New York: Pantheon Books, 1953) 2:85–86.

85. Philo's discussion of the desecration of the chief synagogue (*Leg. Gai.* 135) suggests that it was located not far from the Gymnasium that was situated on the main east-west street, Via Canopica (modern Horriya Street), probably not far from the main Jewish quarter. See Strabo *Geography* 17.1.10, and my map (p. 159).

86. See now esp. Andrew R. Seager and A. Thomas Kraabel, "The Synagogue and the Jewish Community," in *Sardis from Prehistoric to Roman Times: Results of the Archaeological Exploration of Sardis 1958–1975* (ed. George M. A. Hanfmann; Cambridge: Harvard Univ. Press, 1983) 168–90, and literature cited there. Kraabel offers a specific comparison between the Sardis synagogue and that of Alexandria (p. 188).

87. See Tcherikover's discussion of this issue in *CPJ* 1:67–75.

88. See, e.g., *Conf.* 2–14; *Mig.* 89–93.

89. For Gnosticism see my article, "Friedländer Revisited: Alexandrian Judaism and Gnostic Origins," *Studia Philonica* 2 (1973) 23–39; see Koester, *Introduction* 1:225–29, for a brief discussion of pre-Christian Gnosticism in Egypt. For apocalypticism see now esp. Martin Hengel, "Messianische Hoffnung und politischer 'Radikalismus' in der jüdisch-hellenistischen Diaspora," in *Apocalypticism in the Mediterranean World and the Near East* (ed. David Hellhom; Proceedings of the International Colloquium on Apocalypticism, Uppsala, 12–17 August 1979; Tübingen: Mohr [Siebeck], 1983) 655–86.

90. See, e.g., Philo *Virt.* 182; *Mos.* 1.30–31; *Spec.* 3.29.

91. *Virt.* 182; *Q. Ex.* 2.2.

The earliest Christians of Alexandria are to be placed in this variegated Jewish context. We should surmise that a variety of beliefs and practices were represented in Alexandrian Christianity almost from the beginning. If Walter Bauer and others can extrapolate backwards in time from such early second-century gnostic teachers as Basilides, Carpocrates, and Valentinus,[92] it is equally valid to extrapolate into the first century other varieties of Christianity, including more "orthodox" ones, such as are represented in other early second-century literature.[93] One can plausibly trace a trajectory backwards from Clement of Alexandria and such second-century texts as the *Teachings of Silvanus* (NHC VII,4) to a first-century religious Platonism represented on the Jewish side by Philo and on the Christian side by Apollos.[94] Of course it is also highly likely that less intellectually sophisticated varieties of Christianity existed in first-century Alexandria, such as can be found in the Christian "halachic" traditions reflected in the *Epistle of Barnabas*, especially the "Two Ways" tradition,[95] and the various gospel traditions preserved in second-century texts and fragments.[96]

As has already been pointed out, the canonical Gospels of Matthew and John are represented in second-century papyri found in Egypt. An array of noncanonical gospels also circulated there early on,[97] of which

92. Bauer, *Orthodoxy and Heresy*, esp. 48. Note that these three early teachers represent three quite different types of Christian gnosis!

93. Manfred Hornschuh rightly criticizes Bauer for his one-sidedness and points to a number of non-gnostic texts in this connection. See his *Studien zur Epistula Apostolorum* (PTS 5; Berlin: Walter de Gruyter, 1965) esp. 114. But I do not agree with his views on the Alexandrian provenience of *Ep. Apost.* (accepted, however, by A. F. J. Klijn in his contribution to this volume). In my view *Ep. Apost.* was written in Asia Minor. For the various arguments on this question see Hornschuh's discussion, *Studien*, 99–115. The attestation of this document in Upper Egypt (Coptic version) and Ethiopia (Ethiopic version) is no argument in favor of a composition in Egypt. Asian Christian literature (e.g. Melito of Sardis) was early favored in Upper Egypt. See T. Orlandi's contribution to this volume.

94. See my article "Philo, Gnosis, and the New Testament," in *The New Testament and Gnosis: Essays in Honour of Robert McL. Wilson* (ed. A. H. B. Logan and A. J. M. Wedderburn; Edinburgh: T. and T. Clark, 1983) 73–89. See also R. van den Broek's contribution to the present volume.

95. *Barn.* 18–20; cf. *Did.* 1–5. See esp. Robert A. Kraft, *The Didache and Barnabas*, vol. 3 of *The Apostolic Fathers* (New York: Thomas Nelson & Sons, 1965). L. W. Barnard uses *Barnabas* as an important source for reconstructing "Judaism in Egypt A.D. 70–135," in his *Studies in the Apostolic Fathers and Their Background* (New York: Schocken Books, 1966) 41–55.

96. On the early Jewish-Christian "Logos Christology" in Alexandria see Klijn's contribution to this volume. On the early Christian "theology of the Name" see discussion of Roberts's book, above.

97. Mentioned above were the Egerton fragment and P. Oxy. 1 (*Gospel of Thomas*). For these and other fragments see Edgar Hennecke and Wilhelm Schneemelcher,

at least two were probably compiled in Alexandria: the *Gospel of the Hebrews*[98] and the *Gospel of the Egyptians*.[99] The Jewish Christian character of the former is obvious, and is also reflected in the latter, even if its dominant tendency is in the direction of asceticism, a phenomenon certainly not unknown in Alexandrian Judaism.[100] Neither of these gospels is gnostic in any recognizable sense, and the application of such labels as "unorthodox" or "heretical" to such early Christian texts is clearly anachronistic.[101] I would suggest that the *Gospel of the Hebrews* was compiled for the Jewish Christians of Alexandria, and the *Gospel of the Egyptians* for the "Egyptians" who were predominant in the Rhakotis district of Alexandria. The latter seems to be a reflex of early missionary activity on the part of Jewish Christians among their Gentile neighbors.[102]

The earliest Christians in Alexandria doubtless lived in the same areas of the city as the other Jews there, and can be presumed to have participated in the life of the synagogues. They would also have worshiped in house churches, such as are known elsewhere from New Testament sources.[103] The final split between church and synagogue in Alexandria was late in coming, and was probably not complete until the time of the Jewish revolt under Trajan (115–17 C.E.), as a result of which the Jewish community, probably even including some Christians, was virtually exterminated.[104] It is around this time that the

---

NTApo (trans. R. McL. Wilson; Philadelphia: Westminster Press, 1963) 1:91–116. Cf. also the "Secret Gospel of Mark," discussed above. Use of the terms "canonical" and "non-canonical" for literature of this period is, of course, anachronistic.

98. See Hennecke and Schneemelcher, *NTApo* 1:158–65; cf. Koester, *Introduction* 1:223–24.

99. See Hennecke and Schneemelcher, *NTApo* 1:166–78; cf. Koester, *Introduction* 1:229–30. Koester notes the relationship among the *Gospel of the Hebrews*, the *Gospel of the Egyptians*, and the *Gospel of Thomas*, and argues that *Thomas* is a source used by the other two (pp. 224, 230), a view I find somewhat difficult to accept. It could be argued that the three gospels share common Jewish Christian traditions; but this is a problem that deserves further study.

100. Including Philo himself. See esp. his description of the Therapeutae in *Cont.*

101. *Pace* Bauer, *Orthodoxy and Heresy*, 50–53.

102. This represents a modification of Bauer's hypothesis (*Orthodoxy and Heresy*, 50–53). Cf. also Carl Andresen, "'Siegreiche Kirche' in Aufstieg des Christentums: Untersuchungen zu Eusebius von Caesarea und Dionysios von Alexandrien," in *ANRW* (Berlin: Walter de Gruyter, 1979) 2/23/1:387–495, esp. 440.

103. Acts 2:46; 5:42; 20:20; Rom. 16:5; 1 Cor. 16:19; Col. 4:15; Phlm. 2. For a social description of the house churches in the Pauline mission see Wayne A. Meeks, *The First Urban Christians: The Social World of the Apostle Paul* (New Haven: Yale Univ. Press, 1983) 75–81. Much of what Meeks discusses would apply also to Alexandrian Christianity.

104. See Tcherikover's discussion in *CPJ* 1:85–93. That Alexandrian Jewish apocalypticism was involved in this revolt has been forcefully argued by Hengel ("Messianische

Epistle of Barnabas is to be dated, a document that is almost certainly of Alexandrian origin. It contains a plethora of Jewish halachic and haggadic traditions but now edited with a distinctly anti-Judaic bias, reflecting the final split between church and synagogue.[105]

EARLY CHRISTIAN LOCI IN ALEXANDRIA

The evidence for the existence of church buildings in Alexandria[106] before the fourth century is very slim.[107] That such church buildings existed in Egypt before the fourth century is indicated in reports of the massive destruction of churches during the Diocletianic persecutions,[108] and there is some documentary evidence for the existence of church buildings (with the use of the term *ekklēsia* for such buildings) in Egypt as early as the late third century.[109] So it is not unreasonable to suppose that there were church buildings in Alexandria as early as the third century, though it is not easy to determine where they were.

In an important article on third-century Alexandrian Christianity Carl Andresen has made a very interesting case for locating both the catechetical school and the center of ecclesiastical Christianity in general in the main Greek area of the city, in the area then called Bruchium *(Pyroucheion)*.[110] It may nevertheless be interesting to note

---

Hoffnung"). On Jewish-Christian relations in the empire, esp. in Alexandria, see Robert L. Wilken, *Judaism and the Early Christian Mind: A Study of Cyril of Alexandria's Exegesis and Theology* (New Haven: Yale Univ. Press, 1971) 9–68.

105. See esp. Barnard, "Judaism in Egypt." Bauer's desperate attempt to connect *Barnabas* with "Gnosticism" must be categorically rejected. Indeed it could be argued that the use of the term *gnosis* in *Barnabas* is anti-gnostic, centered as it is on the "way of righteousness" (*Barn.* 5.4) and involving a christological interpretation of the Old Testament as well as an emphasis on right conduct. For an interesting theory placing the Epistle of Jude in Alexandria between 120 and 131, see now J. J. Gunther, "The Alexandrian Epistle of Jude," *NTS* 30 (1984) 549–62.

106. For discussion of the various churches in ancient Alexandria and their attestation see esp. *DNGT* 1/1:165–78; and *RAEGR* 1:216–17.

107. There is scattered archaeological evidence from the fourth century and later. Barbara Tkaczow reported on "Archeological Sources for the Earliest Churches in Alexandria" at the Third International Conference of Coptic Studies in Warsaw (August 1984) and is preparing a volume on this topic to appear in a future issue of *Etudes et Travaux*, published by the Centre d'archéologie méditerranéene de l'Académie polonaise des sciences. Epiphanius lists the Alexandrian churches known to him (*Haer.* 69.2; *PG* 42.204–5): "Caesarea" (a church built on the site of the Caesareum); "of Dionysios"; "of Theonas" (see below); "of Pierios"; "of Serapion"; "of Persaea"; "of Dizya"; "of Mendidion" (Bendidion, see below); "of Annianus"; "of Baukalis" (see below); "and others."

108. Eusebius *H. E.* 8.2

109. See Judge and Pickering, "Papyrus Documentation," 59–61, 69.

110. See Andresen, "'Siegreiche Kirche,'" 428–52.

that the earliest documentable church, that of Saint Theonas (bishop 282–300),[111] lay in the northwestern part of the city, in the area we have identified as Delta, one of the "Jewish" quarters in the first century. This may imply a Jewish Christian presence in that area of the city before the time of the building of that church, and that presence could have extended back to the first century. As has already been indicated, the earliest Christians would have lived side by side with other Jews, sharing the life of the synagogues and worshiping in house churches.[112]

A look at the places mentioned in the *Acts of Mark* bears out this assumption, namely, that the earliest Christians lived in close proximity to centers of Jewish life. (It must be admitted, of course, that the authenticity of the geographical references in that writing is no guarantee of its historicity.) The first Alexandrian place mentioned is Pharos (chap. 2), an island separated from the mainland by a seven-stade causeway (the Heptastadion), where the famous lighthouse was located.[113] It should not be forgotten that this island was the traditional site of the translation of the Hebrew Scriptures into Greek and the site of an annual Jewish festival commemorating that achievement.[114]

The next place mentioned is Mendion (or Bennidion),[115] where Mark is said to have met the cobbler Ananias (chap. 3). The place in question is named after a temple, usually referred to as the Bendideion, but probably devoted to the Egyptian god Mendes rather than the Thracian goddess Bendis.[116] The site in question became the location of a church, first referred to as Mendidiou,[117] and subsequently named for Saint Athanasius. Calderini suggests that this site was located in the eastern part of the city, but Adriani is probably correct in placing it in the northwest, not far from the Heptastadion and the western agora.[118] It

---

111. See esp. *DNGT* 1/1:169–70; and *RAEGR* 1:217.

112. See discussion above.

113. For ancient references see *DNGT* 1/1:156–64; *RAEGR* 1:234–35.

114. See esp. *Ep. Arist.* 301–9; Philo *Mos.* 2.35–42.

115. Cf. n. 40. Another form of the name is Mendesion, which occurs, e.g., in Halkin, "Actes inédits," instead of Mendion or Bennidion (chap. 16, p. 358). Cf. also Ps.-Callisthenes 1.31 and variant readings in the mss., on which see Leif Bergson, *Der griechische Alexanderroman: Rezension β* (Stockholm: Almqvist & Wiksell, 1965) 46.

116. On "Bendideion," see *DNGT* 1/1:101, 166; *RAEGR* 1.210, 216. Von Lemm argues for "Mendes" rather than "Bendis" on the strength of a Coptic fragment of the *Acts of Mark*; see "Topographie," 253–55. Cf. also the Coptic fragment published by Helmut Satzinger, *BKU* 323. Cf. n. 116 below.

117. Cf. Epiphanius *Haer.* 69.2.

118. *DNGT* 1/1:101, 166; and *RAEGR* 1:210, 216. It is possibly of interest to note here than an unpublished Coptic text in the Pierpont Morgan Library (M 606, p. 39 of the ms.) puts Mark's meeting of the cobbler Anianus in the agora. This text is cited by H. Satzinger in his publication of BKU 323. The text is an encomium on Peter and Paul attributed to Severianus of Gabala.

would thus have been located in one of the two "Jewish" quarters (Delta, as suggested above).

The most important of the early Christian holy places in Alexandria was undoubtedly Boukolou, where, according to the *Acts of Mark*, the earliest Christians had their place of worship (chap. 4) and where the saint met his death and was buried (chaps. 7, 10).[119] Here was erected the *martyrium* of Saint Mark, attested from the late fourth century on.[120] Here was the church in which Arius served as a presbyter in the early fourth century. Epiphanius refers to it as "the church of *Baukalis*,"[121] which I take to be a corruption, or variant, of Boukolos.

The word *boukolos* means "cowherd." Thus "the places of the *boukolos*" could mean something like "cow pastures," *boukolia*.[122] Now there is no doubt that the memorial to Saint Mark was located in the northeastern part of town ("in the eastern district," "beside the sea, beneath the cliffs"),[123] probably near the site of the present College of St. Mark run by the Christian Brothers. By the fourth century, when our documentation begins, the area in question was outside the city, a place for "cow pastures." But in the first century this area was the main Jewish neighborhood, described in glowing terms by Josephus.[124] This Jewish quarter was presumably destroyed during the time of the rebellion under Trajan (115–17), and in the fourth century the area in question probably lay well outside the main part of the city. Exactly what the condition of the city wall was at that time, or even where it

119. On *Boukolou topoi* - *Boukolia*, see *DNGT* 1/1:105; *RAEGR* 1:210.
120. See discussion above and nn. 53–60.
121. *Haer.* 69.1 (*PG* 42.201) and 69.2 (*PG* 42.204–5). A *baukalis* is a vessel used for cooling water or wine. See *LSJ* 311b.
122. The word *boukolos* has secondary meanings associated with the worship of Dionysos (in his bull manifestation): "worshiper of Dionysos." In Orphic-Dionysiac cult associations the *boukolos* seems to function as a leading officer, as indicated, e.g., in two Orphic hymns (1.10; 31.7); see A. Athanassakis, *The Orphic Hymns: Text, Translation, and Notes* (SBLTT 12; Missoula, Mont.: Scholars Press, 1977) ix, 6–7, 44–45, 113. We might therefore see in the place name Boukolou an indication that a Dionysiac shrine was located in the area. In fact some Dionysiac artifacts have been found here (see below, n. 129). Alternatively, an indication of Sarapis worship might be implied, for a *boukolos tou Osarapi* is a "devotee of Sarapis" (see *LSJ* 324b, and references cited) and we recall the explicit mention of a Sarapis festival coincident with the death of Mark (*Acts* 7). Yet another explanation of the place name Boukolou is possible: the name *Boukoloi* was given to a group of bandits living in the Delta area outside Alexandria. Dio Cassius (72.4.2) reports an assault of *Boukoloi* on Alexandria in 172 or 173 C.E. For references see Sethe, "*Boukoloi*," in PW 3/1:1013.
123. *Acts of Mark* 10 and 5. See *DNGT* 1/1:105; *RAEGR* 1:210. For the later history of this and other churches dedicated to Saint Mark, see M. Chaine, "L'Eglise de saint-Marc a Alexandrie construite par le patriarche Jean de Samanoud," *ROC* 24 (1924) 372–86.
124. See discussion above and n. 75.

was, is not clear.[125] The Arab wall built in the ninth century, traces of which still remain, enclosed a much smaller area of the city than had been the case in the first century. The area of the first-century Jewish quarter lies well outside its perimeter.

One other place name mentioned in the *Acts of Mark* (chap. 9) calls for comment: Angeloi, where Mark's body was to be burned. The name Angelion is an alternate name for a church built in the sixth century in honor of Saint John the Baptist at the site of the great Serapeum. The Serapeum, a magnificent structure whose ruined foundations still remain, was destroyed by Bishop Theophilus in 391 C.E. It was located in the Rhakotis district of Alexandria, the Egyptian quarter. If there was a place called Angeloi, it would have been located near Boukolou, as the context in the *Acts of Mark* demands.[126] But it is possible that our extant versions are corrupt at that point,[127] and the name Angeloi may have crept into the text under the impact of the name of the church at the site of the Serapeum, perhaps under the influence of the references in the text to the festival of the god Sarapis. Traditions related to the mission and death of Saint Mark are, in any case, closely associated geographically with that area of Alexandria which, in the first century, was the main Jewish quarter. Christian activity in that area at that time would have been carried out under the shadow of the great synagogue, the "glory of Israel."[128]

CONCLUDING REMARKS

In the preceding discussion I have attempted to add to the growing scholarly consensus regarding the Jewish character of earliest Christianity in Egypt, first of all by sifting the earliest Christian traditions regarding the establishment of Christianity there, specifically in

125. Dio Cassius reports (22.16.15) that the walls of Alexandria were destroyed as a result of the disturbances in the time of Aurelian (272 C.E.). On the city walls see *DNGT* 1/1:152–54; *RAEGR* 1:227–28. E. Breccia claims that the wall was rebuilt in the second century by the emperors Hadrian and Antoninus (*Alexandrea ad Aegyptum* [Bergamo: Istituto Italiano d'Arti Grafiche, 1922] 71), i.e., after the destructions during the revolt of 115–17; and a map of third- and fourth-century Alexandria produced in 1893 by Sieglin (repr. in *RAEGR* 2, tavola 2) shows the eastern wall extending in a straight line down from Lochias, coinciding at one stretch with the eastern part of the Arab wall. I do not know the basis for these judgments, though it is well known that Hadrian sponsored a considerable amount of construction during his reign. On this see, e.g., *RAEGR* 1:27–28.

126. See *DNGT* 1/1:88, 116; *RAEGR* 1:206, 216.

127. The Bollandist editors of the *Acts* suggest that the original reading was *eis ton aigialon*, "to the sea-shore." See *Acta Sanctorum*, 12.352. Cf. the phrase *eis aigialous* in Philo *Flacc.* 56 (cf. n. 73).

128. See discussion above and n. 84.

Alexandria. I have tried to show that Alexandrian Judaism itself was a variegated phenomenon in the first century, and that early Christianity there also would have displayed a degree of religious and theological variety, leading to the varieties of Christianity that appear more clearly in our second-century sources. I have stressed that the history of Christianity in Egypt, at least until the time of the Jewish revolt against Trajan (115–17), is intimately entwined with the history of the Jewish community there. Accordingly, I have attempted also to provide a sketch of what can be known regarding the main centers of Jewish life in Alexandria and the areas of the city where Jews were concentrated. We have also seen that the earliest identifiable Christian sites and holy places in the city are associated topographically with centers of Jewish life in the first-century city.

Much remains to be done, even if the possibilities are necessarily limited. More can be done in the analysis of our literary sources, and perhaps more can be done, too, in the realm of archaeology. Archaeological research is virtually excluded in the western part of the city, which has been continuously inhabited over the centuries and is now densely populated. As to the area of Alexandria where the main first-century Jewish quarter was located, no systematic archaeological excavations have been done there, apart from some limited probes that have turned up nothing identifiably Jewish or Christian.[129] Areas for potential archaeological excavation include the Shallalat Gardens, especially north of Horriya Street (ancient Via Canopica), or the vicinity of the modern non-Muslim cemeteries, especially north of the Latin cemetery, where the famous Alabaster Tomb was found.[130] Underwater excavations might be feasible offshore, east of ancient Lochias (modern Silsileh), where Ptolemaic-period foundations can be seen just beneath the surface of the sea. (Alexandria has subsided some four meters over the last two millennia.)

129. During the course of the demolition of the ninth-century Arab walls in 1902, G. Botti found in what is now the Shallalat Gardens the base of a statue with a dedicatory inscription to Ptolemy V Epiphanes (*Inscriptiones Graecae Aegypti*, no. 31). Nearby, in 1905, E. Breccia found fragments of a statue group, with Dionysos and a faun, now in the Graeco-Roman Museum (cat. 10694–95), and in another location in the vicinity a fragment of an obelisk. For a summary of the finds, with locations, see A. Adriani, "Saggio di una pianta archeologica di Alessandria," in *Annuario del Museo Greco-Romano* 1 (1932–33) 55–96, esp. 86–87.

130. This tomb, of the Ptolemaic period, has been variously identified, e.g., as the Nemesion destroyed by the Jews in 117 C.E. (Breccia) and as the *Soma*, or Tomb of Alexander the Great (Adriani). It is probably just a private tomb. See Fraser, *Ptolemaic Alexandria* 2:108 n. 263 for references; and cf. *RAEGR* 1:242–45.

But the limitations upon future expansion of our knowledge of Judaism and Christianity in first-century Alexandria must finally be acknowledged. Perhaps we shall never be able finally to lift that "obscurity that veils the early history of the Church in Egypt."[131]

131. Roberts, *Manuscript*, 1.

APPENDIX:
ANCIENT ALEXANDRIA (MAP)

The map presented here is essentially that published by A. Adriani as tavola A in *RAEGR* 1:269. It, in turn, is largely based on the "Carte de l'Antique Alexandrie et de ses fauborgs," published by Mahmoud-Bey in 1866 (reproduced by Adriani as tavola 3 in *RAEGR*, vol. 2). It should be stressed at the outset that many reconstructions of the topography of Alexandria have been attempted, and many maps have been published, often with strikingly different interpretations. Adriani has published some of the most important maps in his *RAEGR* 2:tav. 3–5). Since then others have been published, of which the most useful (which has heavily influenced my own reconstruction) is that of Andresen, published as a foldout in his article, "'Siegreiche Kirche'" (between pp. 440 and 441).

The longitudinal and latitudinal streets shown here, as well as the placement of the city walls, are the reconstruction of Mahmoud-Bey, but his work has often been challenged. Especially problematical is his placement of the eastern wall, which also, of course, affects our understanding of the extent of the ancient Jewish quarter. The alternative placement shown here midway between the Arab wall and Mahmoud-Bey's is that of E. Breccia. (His map is reproduced as fig. 12, tav. 5, in *RAEGR*, vol. 2.) The best discussion of the topography of Ptolemaic Alexandria, absolutely indispensable, is that of P. M. Fraser (*Ptolemaic Alexandria* 1:7–37, with voluminous documentation in the notes in vol. 2). His map (foldout, facing p. 8 in vol. 1) is also very useful. Fraser maintains a very healthy skepticism regarding earlier attempts to reconstruct the topography of Alexandria, especially that of Mahmoud-Bey.

I might add that my own understanding of the topography of ancient Alexandria has been aided by a visit to Alexandria in the spring of 1982 and by conversations with the director of the Polish excavations of Alexandria, Dr. Mieczyslaw Rodziewicz.

I present here only those sites that are of immediate relevance to the various items discussed in my essay.

Key:
1. Pharos Lighthouse
2. *Martyrium* of St. Mark in Boukolou
3. Caesarium
4. Kibotos Harbor
5. Western Agora
6. Bendideion, St. Athanasius Church
7. Alabaster Tomb
8. St. Theonas Church
9. Gymnasium
10. Arab Wall
11. Serapeum

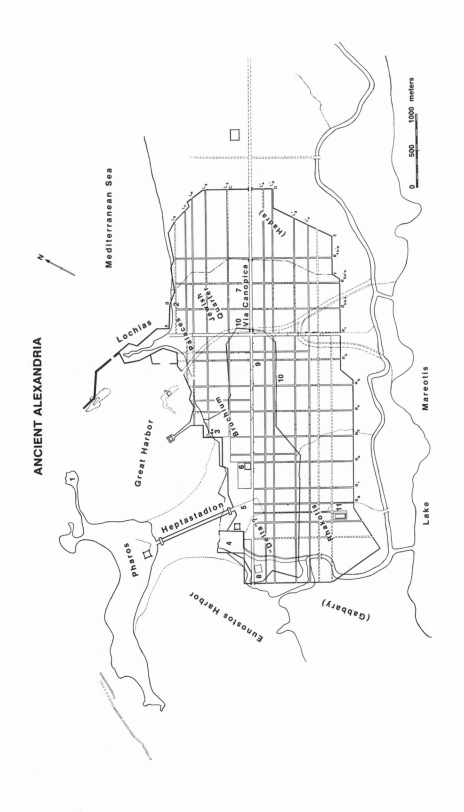

ANCIENT ALEXANDRIA

N

Mediterranean Sea

Pharos

Great Harbor

Lochias

Heptastadion

Eunostos Harbor

(Gabbary)

Rhakotis

Jewish Quarter

Bruchium

Via Canopica

(Hadra)

Lake Mareotis

0   500   1000 meters

9

A. F. J. KLIJN

Jewish Christianity
in Egypt

The study of early Christianity in Egypt shows a gradual development. The beginning of it can be characterized by a remark once made by A. von Harnack: "Die empfindlichste Lücke in unserem Wissen von der ältesten Kirchengeschichte ist unsere fast vollständige Unkenntnis der Geschichte des Christentums in Alexandrien und Ägypten...."[1] The second stage is represented by W. Bauer, who in 1934 repeated that we do not know much about early Christianity in Egypt. He explained this lack of knowledge on the assumption of its heterodox ideas. According to Bauer, both Jewish and Gentile Christians based themselves "auf synkretistisch-gnostischer Grundlage."[2] The third stage

1. A. von Harnack, *Die Mission und Ausbreitung des Christentums* (4th ed.; Leipzig: Hinrichs, 1924) 2:706; ET based on 2d German ed., *The Mission and Expansion of Christianity in the First Three Centuries* (trans. J. Moffatt; 2 vols.; New York: G. P. Putnam's Sons, 1908). See for this period also G. Méautis, "L'introduction du Christianisme en Egypte," *RThPh* 54 (1921) 169–85; and B. H. Streeter, *The Primitive Church* (London: Macmillan & Co., 1929) 233: "... the early history of the Church of Alexandria is darkness itself."
2. W. Bauer, *Rechtgläubigkeit und Ketzerei im ältesten Christentum* (ed. G. Strecker; 2d ed.; Tübingen: Mohr, 1963) 57; ET, *Orthodoxy and Heresy in Earliest Christianity* (ed. Robert A. Kraft and Gerhard Krodel; trans. P. J. Achtemeier et al. from the Philadelphia Seminar on Christian Origins (Philadelphia: Fortress Press, 1971). See also for this period H. Lietzmann, *Geschichte der Alten Kirche* (Berlin/Leipzig: Walter de Gruyter, 1936) 2:283: "es ist und bleibt eine auffällige Tatsache, dass während der ersten hundert Jahre christlicher Mission, ja noch erheblich darüber hinaus, Ägypten nicht in unserm Gesichtskreis tritt ..."; ET, *A History of the Early Church* (trans. B. L. Woolf; 4 vols. in 2; Cleveland: World Pub. Co.; London: Lutterworth Press, 1961). See also H. I. Bell, "Evidences of Christianity in Egypt during the Roman Period," *HTR* 37 (1944) 185–208; G. Bardy, *La Question des Langues dans l'Eglise Ancienne* (Paris: Beauchesne, 1946) 1:38: "Les origines de l'Église d'Égypte sont enveloppées de l'obscurité la plus complète"; W. Schneemelcher, "Von Markus bis Mohammed," *EvTh* 8 (1948–49) 385–405, esp. 390: "Bezüglich der Anfänge der Kirche am Nil tappen wir noch ziemlich im Dunkeln"; C. H. Roberts, "Early Christianity in Egypt: Three Notes," *JEA* 40 (1954) 92–96; H. E. W.

is represented by Daniélou,[3] Hornschuh,[4] Roberts,[5] and Koester,[6] who suppose that Egyptian Christianity originally showed a Jewish-Christian character.

According to the latest views, therefore, to speak about Jewish Christianity in Egypt is, at the same time, to discuss early Christianity in Egypt in general, and even the origins of Egyptian Christianity. The development of our ideas with regard to early Egyptian Christianity is not accidental. In the first place we notice a shift in attention to relevant sources. Initially, much attention was paid to the presence of gnostic leaders in Egypt at an early date, and to a limited number of Christian writings, such as the *Epistle of Barnabas* and sometimes *2 Clement*. Now emphasis is laid upon the importance of writings such as the *Epistula Apostolorum* and certain gnostic writings in the Nag Hammadi library.

In the second place, however, we notice a shift in our ideas regarding the nature of Jewish Christianity. Initially, one pointed to early Christian heresies like those of the Ebionites and Nazoraeans. Nowadays,

---

Turner, *The Pattern of Christian Truth* (London: A. R. Mowbray & Co., 1954) 57: "Nothing forbids the view that in the early Alexandrian scene the most prominent figures were Gnostic rather than orthodox"; R. Kasser, "Les origines du Christianisme Egyptien," *RThPh* 12 (1962) 11–28; R. M. Grant, "The New Testament Canon," in *The Cambridge History of the Bible* (Cambridge: Cambridge Univ. Press, 1970) 1:284–308, esp. 298: "Christianity in second-century Egypt was 'exclusively "heterodox"'"; and R. Trevijano, "The Early Church of Alexandria," in *StPatr 12* (TU 115; Berlin: Akademie-Verlag, 1975) 471–77.

3. J. Daniélou, *Théologie du Judéo-Christianisme* (Tournai: Desclée, 1958) 29; ET, *The Theology of Jewish Christianity* (trans. J. A. Baker; Philadelphia: Westminster Press; London: Darton, Longman & Todd, 1964), vol. 1 of idem, *A History of Early Christian Doctrine Before the Council of Nicaea*, 3 vols.

4. M. Hornschuh, *Die Anfänge des Christentums in Ägypten* (Inaugural diss., Friedrich-Wilhelms-Universität, Bonn, 1959); idem, *Studien zur Epistula Apostolorum* (PTS 5; Berlin: Walter de Gruyter, 1965). See also C. Detlef G. Müller, "Geschichte der orientalischen Nationalkirchen," in *Die Kirche in ihrer Geschichte* (Göttingen: Vandenhoeck & Ruprecht, 1981) 2:321: "Die Anfänge der ägyptischen Kirche liegen im Dunklen: Das älteste ägyptische Christentum dürfte Judenchristentum gewesen sein . . ."; and G. Quispel, "African Christianity before Minucius Felix and Tertullian," in *Actus: Studies in Honour of H. L. W. Nelson* (ed. J. den Boeft and A. H. M. Kessels; Utrecht: Instituut voor Klassieke Talen, 1982) 257–333, esp. 272–73.

5. C. H. Roberts, "The Christian Book and the Greek Papyri," *JTS* 50 (1949) 155–68: "These considerations prompt some reflections on the history of the Church of Egypt. Christianity must have first reached Egypt from Palestine . . ."; and idem, *Manuscript, Society, and Belief in Early Christian Egypt* (London: Oxford Univ. Press, 1979) 49: ". . . we have found reason to think that Christianity reached Egypt from Palestine in a form strongly influenced by Judaism."

6. H. Koester, "Ägypten," in his *Einführung in das Neue Testament* (Berlin/New York: Walter de Gruyter, 1980) 658–76; ET, "Egypt," in *Introduction to the New Testament* (trans. author; 2 vols.; Philadelphia: Fortress Press; Berlin/New York: Walter de Gruyter, 1982) 2:219–39.

Jewish Christianity is supposed to be a form of Christianity that is closely related to an underlying Judaism in language, ideas, and theology. The character of this language, these ideas, and that theology changes according to the form of Judaism adopted by Christians in a particular area. This form of Christianity is not necessarily "heterodox." The lines between heterodoxy and orthodoxy, on the one hand, and those between Christianity and Judaism, on the other, are vague.[7]

We have already mentioned that a consensus exists with regard, at least, to a considerable influence of Jewish Christianity in Egypt. It is striking that this seems to be corroborated by a number of early traditions about the origin and early development of Egyptian Christianity. The oldest source is Acts 18:24–25 in the New Testament, where it is said that an Alexandrian Jew named Apollos, "an eloquent man and learned in the scriptures," came to Ephesus. He was taught in the way of the Lord and was fervent in the spirit. He taught the things about Jesus accurately, but he only knew the baptism of John. He was taken aside by two other Christians, Prisca and Aquila, who explained to him the way of the Lord more accurately.

It is not the place here to go into this passage extensively, but a few remarks call for our attention. We have to answer the question whether Apollos was a Christian at his arrival in Ephesus; whether he was already a Christian in Alexandria; and why he had to be taught more accurately.

The first question can be answered in a positive way. Somebody who is taught in the way of the Lord and is fervent in the Spirit must have been a Christian, according to Acts. The second question cannot be answered without comment. According to the manuscript D, Apollos "was taught the word of the Lord in his native country."[8] This means that he was already a Christian in Egypt. This is clear, but we do not know whether the additional information is based upon a reliable source or is to be explained as mere guesswork. The latter assumption seems to be correct, but this is certainly not against the meaning of Acts.[9] The last question cannot be answered, since we have no idea

7. See Daniélou, *Théologie*, and A. F. J. Klijn, "The Study of Jewish Christianity," *NTS* 20 (1973–74) 419–31.

8. See E. Haenchen, *Die Apostelgeschichte* (*MeyerK*; 13. Aufl.; Göttingen: Vandenhoeck & Ruprecht, 1961) 485; ET, *The Acts of the Apostles: A Commentary* (trans. B. Noble, G. Shinn et al.; Philadelphia: Westminster Press; Oxford: Basil Blackwell & Mott, 1971). See also F. F. Bruce, *The Acts of the Apostles* (London: Tyndale Press, 1952) 351; and H. Conzelmann, *Die Apostelgeschichte* (HNT 7; Tübingen: Mohr, 1963) 109.

9. See B. M. Metzger, *A Textual Commentary on the Greek New Testament* (New York/London: United Bible Societies, 1971) 466; and H. Conzelmann, *Geschichte des*

what is meant by "the baptism of John".[10] We shall not go into this question, since for our purpose it is sufficient to know that apparently, according to Acts, Christians of Jewish origin were living in Egypt at a very early date.

In the Pseudo-Clementines *Homilies* I.9.1,[11] we read that Clement wished to meet somebody in Alexandria who was acquainted with Jesus personally. He is introduced to a certain Barnabas "who also said that he was one of his [i.e., Jesus'] disciples himself." In *Homilies* II.4.1[12] the reader is referred to this passage when Peter says he has heard how in Alexandria Barnabas explained to Clement "the doctrine about the prophecy entirely." The historical value of this tradition is questionable,[13] but we see that Christianity was supposed to have been introduced from Palestine.

A third tradition we meet in Eusebius *Historia Ecclesiastica* I.16. Here it is said that Mark the Evangelist preached the gospel in Alexandria.[14] The content of this form of Christianity was, according to Eusebius, described by Philo in his work "On the Contemplative Life or on the Suppliants." From this he concluded that Christianity in Egypt "seemingly originated from the Jews and followed for the greater part the ancient Jewish customs" (II.17.2–3). The assumption that Philo wrote about Christians in this work comes from Eusebius,[15] but it remains striking that he also writes about a Jewish origin of Christianity in Egypt.

We want to complete this picture of secondary sources by saying a few words about Clement of Alexandria and Origen. According to Eusebius, Clement wrote a work on the "Ecclesiastical Rule against Judaizers."[16] This proves that "judaizing" was still a great danger to the church in the beginning of the third century. Origen warns against the Jewish practice of circumcision and fasting.[17] He knows of Christians

---

Urchristentums (GNT 5: Göttingen: Vandenhoeck & Ruprecht, 1969) 97: "Apollos stammt von dort; aber leider wissen wir nicht, ob er (*scil.* Apollos) schon dort Christ wurde"; ET, *History of Primitive Christianity* (trans. J. E. Steely; Nashville: Abingdon Press, 1973).

10. See E. Käsemann, "Die Johannesjünger in Ephesus," *ZThK* 49 (1952) 144–54.

11. Bernhard Rehm and Johannes Irmscher, eds., *Die Pseudoklementinen* (ed. Franz Paschke; GCS 42; 2d ed.; Berlin: Akademie-Verlag, 1969) 1:27.

12. Ibid., 37.

13. Cf. Roberts, *Manuscript*, 58 n. 4, about this tradition: "lacks any confirmation."

14. See O. F. A. Meinardis, "An Examination of the Traditions Pertaining to the Relics of St. Mark," *OrChrP* 36 (1970) 348–76; and G. M. Lea, "Eusebius on St. Mark and the Beginnings of Christianity in Egypt," in *StPatr 12* (TU 115; Berlin: Akademie-Verlag, 1975) 422–31.

15. Cf. Koester, *Einführung*, 658, about Eusebius: "diese Auskunft [ist] völlig wertlos."

16. Eusebius *H. E.* 6.13.3.

17. Origen *fr. in Jo.* 114 (Erwin Preuschen, ed., *Origenes Werke* [GCS 10; Leipzig:

who go both to the synagogue and to the church.[18] He obviously knows the Jewish Christians as a separate group, since he is aware that the number of them is not more than the 144,000 mentioned in the *Apocalypse of John*.[19] He also consulted a number of Jewish Christians on certain passages of the Old Testament.[20]

Not less important is both Clement's and Origen's knowledge of a Jewish-Christian gospel called the *Gospel According to the Hebrews*.[21] They do not emphatically reject this gospel as being heretical. This proves that they do not connect this gospel with the Jewish Christian sect called the Ebionites. Elsewhere we concluded that this shows that the *Gospel According to the Hebrews* is still considered to be acceptable and that the Ebionites are representatives of a sect that is known to Origen only by name and tradition.[22]

This is sufficient to show that, according to early Christian traditions, Christianity in Egypt was of a Jewish nature.[23] However, other early traditions speak of some notorious gnostic leaders who were either born in Egypt or who taught in this area for some time. This applies to Valentinus,[24] Basilides,[25] Carpocrates,[26] and Apelles.[27]

Hinrichs, 1899–1919] 4:565), where he speaks of "judaizing" and circumcision; and *hom. in Lev.* 10.2 (ibid., 4:412), about fasting.

18. Origen *hom. in Lev.* 5.8 (Paul Koetschau, ed., *Origenes Werke* [GCS 29; Leipzig: Hinrichs, 1899–1919] 6:349); see also P. Oxy. 6.903 (fourth century), where it speaks of visiting both synagogue and church.

19. Origen *comm. in Jo.* 1.1.7 (Preuschen, ed., *Origenes Werke* 4:4).

20. Origen *hom. in Num.* 12.5 (W. A. Baehrens, ed., *Origenes Werke* [GCS 30; Leipzig: Hinrichs, 1888–1919] 7:114), and *fr. in Jer.* 20(19).2 (Erich Klostermann, ed., *Origenes Werke* [GCS 6; Leipzig: Hinrichs, 1888–1919] 3:178). See for more passages about the relations between Origen and the Jews, G. Bardy, "Les Traditions juives dans l'Oeuvre d'Origène," *RB* 34 (1925) 217–52; idem, "S. Jérôme et les Maîtres hébreux," *RBén* 46 (1934) 145–64; J. Daniélou, "Les Sources juives de la Doctrine des Anges des Nations chez Origène," *RechSR* 38 (1951) 132–37; P. Nautin, "Histoire des Dogmes et des Sacrements chrétiens," *AEPHE.R* (1970–71) 257–60; and N. de Lange, *Origen and the Jews* (COS 25; Cambridge: Cambridge Univ. Press, 1976).

21. See the passages collected in A. F. J. Klijn and G. J. Reinink, *Patristic Evidence for Jewish Christian Sects* (NovTSup 36; Leiden: E. J. Brill, 1973) 124–36.

22. See ibid.

23. Cf. Hieronymus (*vir. illustr.* 8), who writes that up to this time the Alexandrians *adhuc judaizantes*; and Didymus the Blind *Ps.* (M. Gronewald and A. Gesche, eds., *Didymus der Blinde* [PTA 8; Bonn: Habelt, 1969] 184, lines 9–10), who still quotes the *Gospel According to the Hebrews*.

24. See for Valentine, Epiphanius *Pan.* 31.2.2: "born in Egypt"; 31.2.3: "educated in Egypt"; and 31.7.2: "preached in Egypt."

25. See for Basilides, Clement of Alexandria *Strom.* 7.106.4; Hieronymus *de vir. illustr.* 21; and Epiphanius *Pan.* 24.1.1.

26. See for Carpocrates, Clement of Alexandria *Strom.* 3.2.5–10; but cf. H. Kraft, "Gab es einen Gnostiker Kapokrates?" *ThZ* 8 (1952) 434–43.

27. See for Apelles, Tertullian *de praescr.* 30.

This summary provides the basis for the conclusions now drawn about the origin and development of early Christianity in Egypt. Early Egyptian Christianity is characterized by pluriformity, with both Jewish and gnostic influences. In the following we shall try to show that this picture is generally correct but does not present the actual situation. It is still based upon the traditional view of an orthodox church surrounded by heretical sects of a Jewish or gnostic nature. Primary sources will give us a different picture.

No unanimity exists, however, with regard to the writings that can be attributed to Egypt. If we confine ourselves to the points of view defended some time ago, we have to go into the so-called Apostolic Fathers. First of all the *Epistle of Barnabas* was supposed to be a firsthand representative of Egyptian Christianity. This is, however, far from an established fact. Barnabas's allegorizing treatment of the Old Testament is not sufficient to prove an Egyptian origin.[28] The Egyptian origin of 2 *Clement* does not find many defenders anymore.[29] Nevertheless, a certain popularity of both writings in Egypt cannot be denied. The same applies to other writings that were certainly not written in Egypt but were favorably accepted, such as the *Shepherd of Hermas*,[30] *Didache*, and 1 *Clement*.[31] To these can be added other early Christian writings like the *Preaching of Peter*[32] and the *Ascension of Isaiah*.[33]

28. Of those mentioned above who deal with Egyptian Christianity, Streeter (*The Primitive Church*, 238–55) reckons Barnabas and 2 Clement among representatives of Egyptian Christianity. Bauer (*Rechtgläubigkeit*, 52) hesitates. Daniélou (*Théologie*, 45–46) considers Barnabas as a product of Egyptian Christianity. Roberts (*Manuscript*, 36) writes: "no proof with regard to an Egyptian origin." Those who specifically deal with Barnabas, like L. W. Barnard ("The Date of the Epistle of Barnabas—A Document of Early Egyptian Christianity," *JEA* 44 [1958] 101–7), suppose an Egyptian origin; but P. Prigent (*L'Epître de Barnabé I—XVI et ses Sources* [Paris: Libraire Lecoffre, 1961] 219) assumes a Syrian origin, and K. Wengst (*Tradition und Theologie des Barnabasbriefes* [AKG 42; Berlin: Walter de Gruyter, 1971] 114) expresses a "non liquet." The work was quoted for the first time in Egypt; see Harnack, *Geschichte der altchristliche Literatur bis Eusebius* (2d ed.; Leipzig: Hinrichs, 1958) 1/1:58–62.

29. See K. P. Donfried, *The Setting of Second Clement in Early Christianity* (NovTSup 38; Leiden: E. J. Brill, 1974) 2; see, however, Koester, *Einführung*, 670: "Über die Anfänge des nichtgnostischen Christentums in Ägypten . . . könnte uns der 2. Clemensbrief Auskunft geben. . . ."

30. The Pastor of Hermas was part of the New Testament in Egypt; cf. Codex Sinaiticus. See Harnack, *Geschichte* 1/1:53: "Clemens Alex. lebte und webte im Hirten. . . ." In the *Apocalypse of Peter* (Nag Hammadi Codices 7.3, 18, 77) Hermas is mentioned. It apparently applies to the present writing; see K. Koschorke, *Die Polemik der Gnostiker gegen das kirchliche Christentum* (NHS 12; Leiden: E. J. Brill, 1978) 54–56.

31. See J. Kuwet, "Les 'Antilegomena' dans les Oeuvres d'Origène," *Bib.* 23 (1942) 18–42; *Bib.* 24 (1943) 10–58; and *Bib.* 25 (1944) 143–66, 311–34.

32. The work is quoted by Clement and Origen, but about its origin cf. Harnack, *Geschichte* 1/1:25–28.

33. Hornschuh (*Die Anfänge*, 213) considers the *Ascension of Isaiah* as "erstrangige

The traditional group of writings connected with Egypt do not give any basis for a description of early Egyptian Christianity. Their contents are heterogeneous. This again explains the perplexity with which Egyptian Christianity has been approached up to now. We may conclude that many of the writings popular in Egypt show some Jewish-Christian influence, but that does not give us a precise picture of the actual situation.

The character of Egyptian Christianity may be better illustrated by a number of papyri discovered in this area since the beginning of this century. It is striking that many of them show a remarkable love for episodes taken from the "life of Jesus." This holds both for his "words" and his deeds. A famous case is the fragment dated about 120 C.E. with a few verses of the Gospel of John.[34] But apart from this we have a number of fragments with apocryphal stories about Jesus. In some of them conflicts are described between Jesus and the Jewish leaders about Jewish legal practices.[35] If we add to this Clement's and Origen's remarks on a gospel according to the Hebrews and according to the Egyptians[36] and Clement's work on a "Secret Gospel of Mark,"[37] we obtain a good picture of a Christianity centered upon the life of Jesus. It appears that a great number of stories and "words" of Jesus were known in Egypt, both canonical and apocryphal. This already gives us some idea of Egyptian Christianity, but we still do not know in which context this tradition was used.

In order to get some insight into Egyptian Christianity we have deliberately chosen a limited number of writings that were apparently

---

Quelle für die Erforschung des frühesten Christentums in Ägypten." For different opinions see Daniélou, *Théologie*, 23: "Antioche"; A. M. Denis, *Introduction aux Pseudépigraphes Grecs d'Ancien Testament* (SVTP 1; Leiden: E. J. Brill, 1970) 175: "sans doute la Palestine"; G. W. E. Nickelsburg, *Jewish Literature Between the Bible and the Mishnah* (Philadelphia: Fortress Press, 1981) 144: "in the orbit of the Qumran community."

34. Known as P⁵²; see B. M. Metzger, *The Text of the New Testament* (2d ed.; Oxford: Clarendon Press, 1968) 38–39.

35. See P. Oxy. 654.1, and 655, with "Word of Jesus" (*NTApo* 1:61–72 [J. Jeremias]); P. Eger. 2, with some episodes taken from the life of Jesus (*NTApo* 1:58–60 [J. Jeremias]); a fragment discovered in Fayyum, about the betrayal of Peter (*NTApo* 1:74 [W. Schneemelcher]); P. Oxy. 840, about Jesus speaking with "pharisaic highpriests" (*NTApo* 1:57–58 [J. Jeremias]); P. Cair. 10.735, about the birth of Jesus and John the Baptist (*NTApo* 1:73–74 [W. Schneemelcher]); and also P. Oxy. 1224, about Jesus in conflict with Pharisees, scribes, and priests (*NTApo* 1:72–73 [W. Schneemelcher]).

36. See P. Vielhauer, "The Gospel According to the Hebrews," in *NTApo* 1:104–8; and W. Schneemelcher, "The Gospel According to the Egyptians," in *NTApo* 1:109–17.

37. See Morton Smith, *Clement of Alexandria and a Secret Gospel of Mark* (Cambridge: Harvard Univ. Press, 1973).

written in Egypt at an early date and that have already been used earlier in connection with studies about early Egyptian Christianity. These are *Epistula Apostolorum (Epist. Apos.)*,[38] the *Sibylline Oracles (Sib. Or.)*,[39] the *Testimony of Truth (Testim. Truth)*,[40] and the *Apocalypse of Peter (Apoc. Pet.)*.[41] The first two writings have been known for a long time, the second two were discovered among those in the library of Nag Hammadi.

First of all, a few words may be said about the origin of these writings. The first editor of *Epist. Apos.*, C. Schmidt, located it in Syria or Palestine.[42] Hornschuh devoted a study to this writing and assumed an Egyptian origin, which has been accepted by a number of others.[43] The *Sib. Or.* is a composite writing. A Jewish version of this writing was reworked by some Christian editor. Since the Jewish editor is generally located in Egypt we may also assume that the final Christian editor lived in this area. Here we only deal with the Christian interpolations.[44] The *Testim. Truth* is generally accepted as being of Egyptian origin.[45]

38. Edition: H. Duensing, "Epistula Apostolorum nach dem Äthiopischen und Koptischen Texte" (KIT 152; Bonn: Markus und Weber, 1925); see also *NTApo* 1:126–55.

39. Editions: J. Geffcken, *Die Oracula Sibyllina* (GCS 8; Leipzig: Hinrichs, 1902); A. Kurfess, *Sibyllinische Weissagungen* (Munich: Heimeren, 1951); and ET by J. J. Collins in *The Old Testament Pseudepigrapha* (ed. J. H. Charlesworth; vol. 1; Garden City, N.Y.: Doubleday & Co., 1983) 317–472.

40. Editions and translations: G. Giverson and B. A. Pearson, eds., "The Testimony of Truth (IX,3)," in *NHLE*, 406–16; and idem, "NHC IX,3: The Testimony of Truth," in *Nag Hammadi Codices IX and X* (ed. B. A. Pearson; NHS 15; Leiden: E. J. Brill, 1981) 101–203.

41. Editions and translations: "Die Apokalypse des Petrus, eingeleitet und übersetzt von Berliner Arbeitskreis für koptisch-gnostische Schriften," *ThLZ* 99 (1974) 575–84; and J. Brashler, R. A. Bullard and F. Wisse, "Apocalypse of Peter (VII, 3)," in *NHLE*, 339–45.

42. C. Schmidt and T. Wajnberg, *Gespräche Jesu mit seinen Jüngern nach der Auferstehung* (TU 43; Leipzig: Hinrichs, 1919) 364: "Asia Minor"; and 399: "date of origin 180"; but cf. 364: "Jedenfalls steht soviel fest, dass unsere Schrift eine Geschichte innerhalb der Kirche Ägyptens erlebt hat"; but cf. Streeter, *The Primitive Church*, 234: "Egypt"; B. Altaner, *Patrologie* (4th ed.; Freiburg: Herder, 1955) 61: "Asia Minor or Egypt" (ET based on 5th German ed., *Patrology* [trans. H. C. Graef; New York: Herder & Herder, 1961]); J. Quasten, *Patrology* (Utrecht/Brussels: Spectrum, 1950) 1:150: "Asia Minor or Egypt."

43. Hornschuh, *Studien*, 107–9: "Egypt in the first half of the second century"; Roberts, *Manuscript*, 54: "Egypt"; and Koester, *Einführung*, 673–75: "Egypt."

44. See Otto Bardenhewer, *Geschichte der altkirchliche Literatur* (Darmstadt: Wissenschaftlich Buchgesellschaft, 1962) 2:709; J. Geffcken, *Komposition und Entstehungszeit der Oracula Sibyllina* (TU 8/1; Leipzig: Hinrichs, 1902); Daniélou, *Théologie*, 28; J. J. Collins, *The Sibylline Oracles of Egyptian Judaism* (SBLDS 13; Missoula, Mont.: Scholars Press, 1974); J. H. Charlesworth, *The Pseudepigrapha and Modern Research* (SBLSCS 7S; Chico, Calif.: Scholars Press, 1981) 184–88; and Nickelsburg, *Jewish Literature*, 162–65. See for the Christian interpolations *NTApo* 2:498–528 (A. Kurfess). They are 1.324–400; 2.34–56, 150–345; 6.1–29; 7.1–162; and 8.1–500. Of those we shall deal with 1.324–395 (written about 150 C.E.); 6.1–29 (after 150 but before the part of 8); 7.64–95 (end of second century); and 8.217–336, 455–79 (before 180).

45. B. A. Pearson, "Jewish Haggadic Traditions in the Testimony of Truth from Nag

The origin of *Apoc. Pet.*, however, is disputed. Many assume a Syro-Palestinian origin. This, however, is not yet settled. We may only say that even if it is not of Egyptian origin it can only slightly affect our conclusions since its contribution to our study is only minor.[46]

All four of these writings may be called apocalyptic. Each of them has been written to give information hitherto unknown to its readers. The *Epist. Apos.* is a revelation of Jesus to his apostles, the *Sib. Or.* is a revelation supposed to have been given by the Sybilline prophetess, the *Testim. Truth* is a homiletical treatise "to those who know to hear not with the ears of the body but with the ears of the mind."[47] And the *Apoc. Pet.* is an apocalypse of Jesus to Peter during Jesus' supposed suffering and death.

Three of these writings are clearly polemical. *Epist. Apos.* is directed to the threat of Simon and Cerinthus[48] and *Testim. Truth* and *Apoc. Pet.* to "das kirchliche Christentum."[49] If, as we assume, these writings were written in one particular region, we are dealing with a divided church split up in a number of parties.

In spite of their polemical character the writings show a number of common ideas. For our purpose it is important to see that they all share

---

Hammadi (CG IX,3)," in *Ex Orbe Religionum: Studia Geo. Widengren* (ed. J. Bergman et al.; Leiden: E. J. Brill, 1972) 1:457–70; see 470: "Palestine or Syria"; but in his other publications about this work always "Egypt"; cf. Pearson, "NHC IX,3," 117: "There are strong indications in *Testim. Truth* of an Alexandrian milieu"; cf. also idem, "Gnostic Interpretations of the Old Testament in the Testimony of Truth (NHC IX,3)," *HTR* 73 (1980) 311–19; see 312: "doubtless written in Egypt, probably in Alexandria." See also K. Koschorke, "Die Polemik der Gnostiker gegen das kirchliche Christentum: Skizziert am Beispiel des Nag-Hammadi-Traktates Testimonium Veritatis," in *Gnosis and Gnosticism* (ed. M. Krause; NHS 8; Leiden: E. J. Brill, 1977) 43–49; idem, "Der gnostische Traktat 'Testimonium Veritatis' aus dem Nag-Hammadi Codex IX: Eine Übersetzung," *ZNW* 69 (1978) 91–117, esp. 96: date between 180 and 212/3 in Egypt/Alexandria. The same is asserted in idem, *Die Polemik der Gnostiker*, 109.

46. E. Schweizer, "Zur Struktur der hinter dem Matthäusevangelium stehenden Gemeinde," *ZNW* 65 (1974) 139; and idem, "The 'Matthean' Church," *NTS* 20 (1973–74) 216: "an ascetic Judeo-Christian group"; H. M. Schencke, "Bemerkungen zur Apokalypse des Petrus," in *Essays on Nag Hammadi Texts: In Honor of Pahor Labib* (NHS 6; Leiden: E. J. Brill, 1975) 277–85; G. H. Stanton, "5 Ezra and Matthean Christianity in the Second Century," *JTS* 28 (1977) 67–83; see 70: "The *Apocalypse of Peter* confirms that some Judeo-Christian circles were dominated by various forms of gnosticism in the second half of the second century." Cf. Koschorke, *Die Polemik*, 16: "der Ort der Abfassung von ApcPt lässt sich nicht bestimmen"; and 17: date in the middle of the third century; and 16 about character: "eine gewisse juden-christliche Prägung." The Jewish-Christian character is the reason for locating the work in Syria/Palestine.

47. *Testim. Truth* 29.6–9.

48. *Epist. Apos.* 1 (12), and 7 (18).

49. See Koschorke, *Die Polemik*.

the ideas of the so-called Logos Christology.[50] This common background results in a number of identical points of view.

In all four writings Jesus is described as a revealer. He reveals certain knowledge hitherto unknown. He teaches knowledge that takes away ignorance. This knowledge gives life to those who accept Jesus' teaching.[51] The Logos Christology reveals its Jewish background in these passages. Jesus takes the place of the Jewish Wisdom and acts as the intermediary between God and men.

Connected with this Logos Christology is Jesus' fundamental immutability. The Logos remains the same in whatever shape he chooses to appear.[52] This again has a number of consequences with regard to Jesus' incarnation, which can be met in all these four writings. The starting point is the idea that incarnation is only adaptation. It is a way to make himself visible to human eyes that are supposedly not aware of heavenly things.[53]

A few examples can easily make clear that here tradition and doctrine can come into conflict with each other. Tradition spoke of Jesus' virgin birth and his baptism by John. Neither tradition, however, is necessary within the framework of a Logos Christology. It is sufficient to say that the Logos came to earth or took human flesh.[54] If the virgin birth is adopted we meet expressions such as "And I, the word, went into her and became flesh"[55] or "He passed through a virgin's womb."[56] In *Epist. Apos.* it is even said that the archangel Gabriel was himself the Logos who announced his own birth to

50. See F. Loofs, *Theophilus von Antiochien adversus Marcionem* (TU 46; Leipzig: Hinrichs, 1930), and G. Kretschmer, *Studien zur frühchristlichen Trinitätstheologie* (BHTh 21: Tübingen: Mohr, 1956).

51. See *Epist. Apos.* 20 (31) and 28 (39); cf. Hornschuh, *Studien*, 63: "Der Besitz der Offenbarung, die 'Gnosis,' bedeutet für die Jünger das Leben. . . . Ohne Kenntnis der geoffenbarten Lehre befindet man sich im 'Gefängnis' . . . Christus aber führt uns als Offenbarer aus der Finsternis zum Licht . . ."; and Koester, *Einführung*, 674: "Die Epistula Apostolorum übernimmt die literarische Form der gnostischen Offenbarungsrede, in der der Auferstandene den Jüngern himmliche Weisheit und Lehre vermittelt." See *Sib. Or.* 1.333, 379; 6.9–11; 8.367; *Testim. Truth* 29.5–8; 31.38; 36.27–29; 41.4–8; 45.2–6; and *Apoc. Pet.* 70.24; 71.20–26; 72.13; 74.18–19.

52. Cf. *Epist. Apos.* 13 (14): "I have become all in everyone (or: everything)," and 17 (28): "Do you not know that until now I am here as well as there, with Him, who sent me?" Cf. also *Sib. Or.* 6.16–17.

53. Cf. *Epist. Apos.* 13 (24), and *Testim. Truth* 44.14–15: "He makes himself equal to every one."

54. In *Sib. Or.* 6, a separate hymn about Jesus, nothing is said about his birth; the same applies to the passages in 1 and 7.

55. *Epist. Apos.* 14 (25).

56. *Testim. Truth* 45.15; cf. Valentinus according to Irenaeus *Adv. haer.* 1.7.2: "*per Mariam transierit quemadmodum aqua per tubam*"; and *Protev. Jas.* 19.3: "Mary virgin *post partum*"; and also, Clement of Alexandria *Strom.* 7.93.

Mary.[57] In principle the virgin birth is not more than a means to become visible. The Logos itself remains unaffected by the flesh. Even more difficult is the tradition about Jesus' baptism. What has to be given to the Logos at his baptism that he did not already possess? *Epist. Apos.*, which is very much interested in facts taken from the life of Jesus, does not even mention his baptism. The author of *Sib. Or.* knows about Jesus' baptism by John the Baptist, but his ideas remain unclear. He obviously knows about the Jewish-Christian tradition according to which fire appeared in the river Jordan at Jesus' baptism.[58] In one passage it is said that this baptism is meant to abolish the sacrifices,[59] in another there is reference to Jesus' second birth,[60] but all this shows that no real doctrine of Jesus' baptism existed. It belonged to the traditions about Jesus' life, but it could be incorporated in any way one liked. In *Testim. Truth* the passages about Jesus' baptism are of the same tenor. In one it is said that the river Jordan turned back as soon as Jesus appeared, because this river "is the power of the body."[61] This kind of baptism is rejected because it has to do with sexual desire. In other passages, however, it is supposed that Jesus was really baptized.[62] It would be interesting to know whether we are dealing with two different ideas about Jesus' baptism.[63] For our purpose, however, it is important to see that Jesus' baptism is not essential. In a polemical writing one has to be precise and outspoken. Obviously Jesus' baptism is not a particular issue.[64]

Another point of agreement is that all four writings are apparently interested in the life of Jesus. Three of them give a more or less

---

57. *Epist. Apos.* 14 (25). In *Sib. Or.* 8.456–461, we meet a similar passage of which Daniélou (*Théologie*, 181) supposes: "Ici encore c'est le Verbe lui-même qui apparaît à Marie sous l'apparance de l'archange pour lui annoncer son Incarnation avant l'accomplir."

58. *Sib. Or.* 6.6, 7.84; cf. Justin Martyr *Dial.* 88.2; Gospel of the Ebionites, in Epiphanius *Pan.* 30.13.7–8; and Matt. 3:15 in *Codex Vercellensis* and *Sangermanensis*.

59. *Sib. Or.* 7.76–84; see also Pseudo-Clementine's *Recogn.* 1.48.3–6, 1.39.

60. *Sib. Or.* 6.3–4. The influence of Ps. 2.7 may be present. See also D. A. Bertrand, *Le Baptême de Jesus* (BGBE 14; Tübingen: Mohr, 1973) 52–55.

61. *Testim. Truth* 30.20–32.

62. *Testim. Truth* 39.25, 62.11.

63. See Koschorke, *Die Polemik*, 138–42.

64. In *Testim. Truth* 30.18—31.5 it functions in the controversy regarding "carnal procreation"; see Koschorke, *Die Polemik*, 140 n. 54. The "baptism of life" is mentioned in *Epist. Apos.* 27 (38), 42 (55); cf. *Testim. Truth* 69.21–22: "But the baptism of truth is something else; it is by renunciation of [the] world that it is found." See J. Bornemann, *Die Taufe Christi durch Johannes* (Leipzig: Hinrichs, 1896) 49: "... es ist der grossen Kirche klar geworden, dass man im Grunde bei der Logoschristologie die Taufengeschichte christologisch gar nicht mehr zu verwenden weiss."

extensive list of Jesus' deeds on earth. In *Apoc. Pet.* we meet only a number of remarks about Jesus' suffering and death. The other three refer to Jesus' healings, his exorcisms, and especially his walking on the sea and the feeding of the multitude.[65] All this is important to show that the incarnated Logos remained the same. He was able to act as God even in the flesh. Especially his walking on the sea must be seen as a divine act that shows that he is superhuman. In this way the life of Jesus functions in a very particular way.

All four writings accept that Jesus died. We have already said that *Apoc. Pet.* confines itself to Jesus' last days. It is clear, however, that during Jesus' suffering and death he also remained the same. In this connection Jesus' descent to hell is very important. It shows that during his death he was able to continue his work. For *Testim. Truth,* "hades" is the present world.[66] This is not essentially different, however, from the ideas with regard to the realm of death in the other writings. In all circumstances the Logos shows his power and reveals the way back to life.[67]

The above gives a consistent picture of a Logos Christology based upon Jewish ideas about Wisdom. The Logos is God having come upon the earth clothed in the flesh taken from the virgin Mary. He showed his power in his works and revealed life by means of his "words." All this can be circumscribed as "revelation." One has to be aware of the true Logos.

Now we want to go a step further in order to see in which way these ideas took shape in the life of believers.

It appears that none of these four writings was written in a community with official leaders. In *Epist. Apos.* we read that Jesus said to his disciples, "Go and preach, and then you will be laborers, and fathers and servants." But the disciples are amazed and say, "O Lord, did you not say 'Do not call anyone on earth father and master, for One is your father. . . .'"[68] In *Sib. Or.* it is said that in place of prophets, "wise leaders" have appeared.[69] And *Apoc. Pet.* explicitly rejects bishops and deacons, who are called "dry canals."[70]

---

65. *Epist., Apos.* 3 (14); *Sib. Or.* 1.351–69; 6.11–17; and 8.273–86; *Testim. Truth* 32.25—43.1. It is striking that in *Testim. Truth* the feeding of the multitude is not mentioned, which may be due to an ascetic tendency.

66. *Testim. Truth* 32.25.

67. See, for Jesus' descent into hell, *Epist. Apos.* 27 (38), and *Sib. Or.* 1.377–78; 8.313.

68. *Epist. Apos.* 41 (52). We follow the Ethiopic version.

69. *Sib. Or.* 1.385–86: σοφοὶ καθοδηγοί.

70. *Apoc. Pet.* 79.31.

From this we are able to sketch early Egyptian Christianity. We are dealing with a movement more than with a church. This movement took shape in a number of esoteric groups or "schools."[71] These "schools" recruited new members only in so far as they were able to "see with the eyes of their mind." They can be compared to the Philonic *therapeutai*, although the members were not always supposed to live a monastic life. They only serve as an example of how those groups can have come about. They have their roots in Jewish wisdom-schools. Revelations given to their members warranted a constant flow of fresh writings and divergent ideas. We may assume that this kind of Hellenistic-Jewish Christianity was not limited to Egypt but was also present in other regions, particularly in Syria.[72]

In general the various groups must have lived alongside one another without interfering in one another's business. At the time of our writings, however, we see that the groups have become aware of one another. In *Testim. Truth* it is said that some others say, "We are Christians."[73] This means that one group demands the sole right to be called after Christ. We have already pointed to the passage in *Apoc. Pet.* where bishops and deacons are mentioned. This means that some organization exists at least supervised by some of its members. *Apoc. Pet.* provides some information about this organization. It is said:

And still others of them who suffer think that they will perfect the wisdom of the brotherhood which really exists, which is the spiritual fellowship with those united in communion through which the wedding of the incorruptibility shall be revealed. The kindred race of the sisterhood will appear as an imitation. These are the ones who oppress their brothers, saying to them, "Through this our God has pity, since salvation comes to us through this," not knowing the punishment of those who are made glad by those who have done this thing to the little ones, who they saw, [and] whom they took prisoner.[74]

71. Koester (*Einführung*, 668) speaks about "Schulen." Schools, however, are connected with a special tradition. Here we are dealing with groups in which revelations are highly appreciated. See H. Stademann, *Ben Sira als Schriftsteller* (Tübingen: Mohr, 1980). It is striking that a work like *Epist. Apos.* bases itself not upon the tradition but upon a revelation given by Jesus. This means that we have to be very careful about using words like "Frühkatholizismus" or "church" in connection with the four writings we are dealing with. If the *Epistle of Barnabas* was written in Egypt, it is a fine example of Egyptian Christianity with its "gnosis" (1.5) and its "hinter dem Barnabasbrief stehenden Schulbetrieb" (Wengst, *Tradition und Theologie*, 119).

72. For Syria see the inspiring article by Han J. W. Drijvers, "Facts and Problems in Early Syriac-Speaking Christianity," *SCent* 2 (1982) 157–75.

73. *Testim. Truth* 31.24–25.

74. *Apoc. Pet.* 78.31—79.21. See for these passages Koschorke (*Die Polemik*, 60–64), who emphasizes the idea of "Kein Heil ohne die Kirche."

Here we see that one group calls itself a "brotherhood" through which "salvation" is coming, but that it is a brotherhood that, according to others, oppresses its members. A movement consisting of individuals is becoming a communion. Those who believe enter into communion with a group. Those outside this development are afraid that "the little ones" will fall victim to the oppression of the leaders of the communion. It is true that in this way the believer loses part of his individuality, but at the same time "the little ones" become much safer in being part of a new brotherhood.

We certainly believe that all this has something to do with the influence of the apostle Paul. In all four writings we see that Paul is essentially not accepted. It is assumed that in *Apoc. Pet.* a frontal attack is launched against Paul. His teaching about "a dead man" belongs to "the propagation of falsehood."[75] In *Epist. Apos.* a long passage is devoted to the defense of Paul. He is explicitly mentioned as the apostle of the Gentiles who had to come. It appears that originally Paul or Pauline ideas were unknown.[76] In these writings[77] we see that a controversy is starting about him. We assume that Paul is the one who introduced the idea of "brotherhood," of the Christian movement as a "body." He speaks to the individual believers as members of a "church."

All this means that the "schools" have to become a "church." We need not go into the result, viz., that finally the church prevails over the school. Finally "the little ones," the orphan and the widow, were safer in the hands of bishops and deacons than as individuals in a school. In times of persecution the individual member is also much safer within a hierarchy, since the leaders will have to take responsibility. But orthodoxy also meant a reevaluation of "the flesh." The Logos Christology was not able to deal with the "flesh" and creation in

75. By "dead man" the Pauline preaching of the cross is probably meant; see Koschorke, *Die Polemik*, 39–41. See also "Die Apokalypse de Petrus," *ThLZ* 99 (1974) 576: "Möglicherweise liegt p. 74, 16 ff eine Stellungnahme gegen Paulus vor eine ohne Zweifel nicht abwegige Vermutung . . ."; and the careful analysis in A. Lindemann, *Paulus im ältesten Christentum* (BHTh 58; Tübingen: Mohr, 1979) 334.

76. *Epist. Apos.* 31 (42)—33 (44); cf. Hornschuh, *Studien*, 85: "In dem Kreise, dem der Verfasser entstammt und für den er schreibt, muss für das Ansehen des Paulus noch geworben werden." Lindemann (*Paulus*, 371–73) is a little bit more careful, but concludes: "Der Verfasser hat paulinische Briefe [!] gekannt; direkt benutzt hat er sie vermutlich nicht."

77. With regard to *Testim. Truth*, Lindemann (*Paulus*, 339) concludes: "Test Ver ist mithin kein Beleg für eine spezifische Vorliebe der Gnostiker für Paulus und seine Theologie"; and with regard to *Sib. Or.* 376: "In der *Sib* sieht 'Biblia Patristica' an 25 Stellen 'Anspielungen' oder 'Zitate' aus dem Corpus Paulinum. Aber tatsächlich ist ein Zusammenhang lediglich in weinigen Fällen auch nur zu erwägen."

a proper way. The intangible Logos never became flesh. It is this that had to be accepted by a growing number of Egyptian Christians. In *Epist. Apos.* and also in *Sib. Or.* we see a very great emphasis on the significance of the flesh. Christ was connected with creation,[78] and he was raised from the dead in the flesh;[79] the believers will appear before God in the end of time in the flesh.[80] Against these ideas *Testim. Truth* says: "[Do not] expect, therefore, [the] carnal resurrection. . . ."[81] The Gnostics have been drawing the consequences of a Logos Christology. This Christology does not give an answer to the question of the significance of the flesh. This means that also in Egypt Christians shall have to give up their original ideas about Jesus. And with this they shall also cease being Jewish Christians.

If the above can be accepted, Egypt is a fine example of burning questions dealing with orthodoxy and heterodoxy, and with Jewish Christianity and gnosis. Since we are dealing with Jewish Christianity here, we leave it to others to go into these questions, but we also note here that the more deeply we go into these things the more things appear to be connected.

78. See *Epist. Apos.* 3 (14) and *Sib. Or.* 8.264, according to which Jesus was God's Counselor; cf. Hermas *Sim.* 9.12.2; and Theophilus *Ad Autolycum* 2.22.9.
79. Cf. *Epist. Apos.* 2 (13), 3 (14), 10 (21), 11 (22), 12 (23), and other passages, since the whole writing is one long preaching of Jesus' bodily resurrection. Cf. *Sib. Or.* 8.314, 319.
80. *Epist. Apos.* 21 (32), 24 (35), 26 (37); *Sib. Or.* 8.313–314.
81. In 36.29–30, after the remark in *Testim. Truth* 34.26–27: "[And] some say: 'On the last day [we will] certainly arise [in the] resurrection.'"

PART FOUR

THEOLOGICAL
SPECULATION AND DEBATE

Theological Education
at Alexandria

PRE-CHRISTIAN AND
NON-CHRISTIAN DEVELOPMENTS

We need not trace the classical picture of Greek education, beginning with alphabet, moving on to syllables and words, reading simple maxims and excerpts from poetry and prose found in florilegia. These matters were essential but, for our purposes, not very important. We shall consider only some of the more advanced levels of education (and not all of them), beginning with the situation at Alexandria among the more highly educated adherents of various religions. It must be admitted that we know less about actual procedures at Alexandria and elsewhere than many of our modern authors suggest. Unfortunately, the principal ancient authors say little or nothing precise about educational procedures. They take them for granted and make use of the results.

Though two of the greatest representatives of Alexandrian thought, Origen and Plotinus, did much or even most of their teaching elsewhere, it is unlikely that they radically changed their modes of teaching when they left Alexandria. And in any event we do have materials that come down from Philo and Clement (though Clement too left Alexandria in his last years), as well as fragments from a rather large cluster of Jewish authors who wrote in Greek. We also have the writings of the early Origen, notably his treatise *On First Principles*, written before he left Alexandria. And we note the continuing and consistent Alexandrian picture of "philosophy, the handmaiden of theology."[1]

1. This is the title used by A. Henrichs, *GRBS* 9 (1968) 437–50.

We should begin by recalling that there were sharp divisions among ancient educational theorists. Philosophers, beginning with the pre-Socratics, criticized poets severely for their charming presentation of false doctrines about the gods. Plato expelled Homer from his ideal state. Aristotle had no enthusiasm for him either. Only the Stoics, ardently allegorizing everything, could accept the poets because they knew their true Stoic intentions. We shall later see a similar theory emerge in Christian schools. It is also found among the Hellenized Jews or Jewish Hellenists of Alexandria, where Philo often refers to poetry and sometimes makes use of poetic embellishments. We also know of a tragic poet named Ezekiel who put the story of the exodus into hexameters. There were others, whether Jewish or pagan, who sometimes coordinated Greek mythology with the Old Testament.

In his famous *Griechisch-juedischer Schulbetrieb aus Alexandreia und Rom* (1915), W. Bousset tried to go behind Philo's treatises to find samples of school lectures, but few have been fully convinced by Bousset's theory, which has won no more adherents than the more recent theory that homilies lie behind the treatises. Philo does say that he tells the story of Moses as he learned it "both from the sacred books . . . and from some of the elders of the nation,"[2] but this does not prove the existence of "a school of Jewish exegetes" at Alexandria. Indeed, it is not even certain that Philo wrote to be read in the synagogue, though at least one line points that way: "Each seventh day there stand wide open in every city thousands of schools of good sense, temperance, courage, justice and the other virtues in which the scholars sit quietly with ears alert and with full attention . . . while one of special experience rises and sets forth what is the best and sure to be profitable and will make the whole of life grow to something better."[3] Philo is describing his own temperament and abilities and depicting them as valuable not for others but for himself;[4] but what is good for him is obviously good for like-minded pupils.

It is a pity that we know so little about the intended audiences of such writings, like those of many other ancient authors. It is easy enough to see, or at least to imagine, how meaningful a theosophical treatise, or for that matter a cookbook or a treatise on aqueducts or military tactics, might be for a small group. But what of a history? Who would read it? Perhaps a student of rhetoric would search it for useful

2. *Mos.* 1.4.
3. *Spec.* 2.62.
4. *Spec.* 3.1–6.

examples. This is why we often suggest a school setting for documents whose intentions are unclear, and sometimes we must be right.

The best precedent for the Christian schools of Alexandria seems to lie not in Philo but among the Therapeutae by the Mareotic lake, described in Philo's work *On the Contemplative Life*. Certainly their leader is an ideal theological teacher. "He does not make an exhibition of clever rhetoric like the orators or sophists of today but follows careful examination by careful expression of the exact meaning of the thoughts."[5] What this teacher is discussing is "some question arising in the sacred writings," or he may be solving "one proposed by someone else." Another resemblance appears in the exegetical method. "The exegesis of the sacred writings treats the inner meaning conveyed in allegory," for the Bible is like a living creature with the letter for its body and the invisible meaning for its soul.[6] Such Therapeutae would be ready for Alexandrian Christianity.

CHRISTIAN BEGINNINGS AND
ALEXANDRIAN DEVELOPMENTS

In a Jewish setting, whether Alexandrian or not, the first Christians were devoted to learning about the meaning of their Bible or what we call the Old Testament. They were concerned with what Jesus had taught and the interrelations between this teaching and the Bible. And as soon as they possessed the letters of Paul they had to think about what they meant, for as the author of 2 Peter complains, they contain some things hard to understand. The presence of inquiring minds in Christian congregations meant that at least catechetical instruction was needed, and fairly soon something more.

It was probably at Alexandria that "something more" turned up in the Epistle to the Hebrews. Its author was introducing a bold allegorical doctrine about the role of Jesus as the heavenly high priest replacing the priests of the Old Covenant. The author is well aware that his readers need to get on with it. "We have much to say [about this high priesthood] which is hard to explain, since you have become dull of hearing. For though by this time you ought to be teachers, you need someone to teach you again the first principles of God's word." And he urges them to "leave the elementary doctrines of Christ and go

---

5. *Cont*. 31. Cf. 75.
6. *Cont*. 78.

on to maturity, not laying again a foundation of repentance from dead works and of faith toward God, with instruction about ablutions, the laying on of hands, the resurrection of the dead, and eternal judgment" (Heb. 5:11–12; 6:1–2). Here we find a distinction between simpler and more advanced teaching being made by a teacher of Christian higher learning. Presumably those on the way to becoming priests in this community must be able to understand, explain, and defend such doctrine.

Probably we should locate the *Epistle of Barnabas* at Alexandria too. Certainly the writer of this epistle is devoted to a rather intensive use of the allegorical method, with his famous exegesis of Abraham's 318 servants and his insistence that "no one has received a more excellent lesson from me." It cannot be said that his work is notable for cogency of thought, however.

In the following century we see schools developing, for example the one headed by the apologist Justin at Rome and the one presumably in existence at Antioch under the bishop Theophilus, who was also an apologist. Indeed, much second-century apologetic reads like commentary on poetry and philosophy as taught in school. Undoubtedly we must mention Clement of Alexandria, who quoted poetry in vast quantities, usually from anthologies, and as a "pedagogue" wrote lessons in manners and godliness. In many respects Clement reminds me of a little treatise I once picked up for a quarter: *Morals of Manners; or, Hints for Our Young People*. By Miss Sedgwick, author of *Home* and *Poor Rich Man*, it appeared in New York in 1846. It is hard to be fair to Clement. His writings do contain marvelous comments on manners and godliness, on symbolism, on the higher reaches of Platonic theology. But his claim to produce a jumble on purpose is of a piece with his constant use of the medicinal lie. And one always wonders how much truth there was in the claim of Photius that his lost *Hypotyposes* contained a great deal of gnostic speculation.

In the major cities a little earlier gnostic schools had burst forth. Alexandria was the home of both Basilides and Valentinus, famous gnostic teachers whose doctrines were relatively close to the Christian teaching of someone like Clement. Charles Kannengiesser reminds me that an excellent example of a Valentinian teaching document is to be found in the *Epistle to Rheginos On the Resurrection*.[7] And there is also Ptolemaeus's apologetic *Letter to Flora*. At Alexandria it was hard to

7. Cf. *NHLE*, 50–54 (Cod. I,4); M. L. Peel, *The Epistle to Rheginos* (Philadelphia: Westminster Press, 1969) 100–102.

differentiate between gnostic and Christian doctrines, simply because before the advent of the bishop Demetrius about 189 there was no authoritative episcopal teacher comparable to Irenaeus in Lyons. Around that time Origen was a teenage orphan supported by a rich Christian patroness of theology. She paid Origen's expenses but also those of a Valentinian or Marcionite whom she—but not Origen— admired just as much. Presumably during the episcopate of Demetrius she either died (he was bishop for 43 years) or mended her ways. Origen's own patron Ambrose became a convert from the doctrine of either Marcion or Valentinus.

If we turn to a rather higher philosophical level we should like to know more about the teaching of Plato and Platonists at Alexandria, especially in the school of Plotinus. Most of what Porphyry tells us in his *Life of Plotinus* is related to the master's teaching at Rome. We should imagine, however, that his teaching there was not inconsistent with what he taught at Alexandria. Porphyry does tell us that in Plotinus's twenty-eighth year "he felt an impulse to study philosophy and was recommended to the teachers in Alexandria who then had the highest reputation; but he came away from their lectures so depressed and full of sadness that he told his trouble to one of his friends." The friend sent him to Ammonius, and when Plotinus heard him he said, "This is the man I was looking for." He then studied with Ammonius for eleven years. By an interesting coincidence, he began his studies with Ammonius just in the year in which Origen, a former pupil, left Alexandria forever. A comment by Ammonius on his two pupils would be welcome but of course does not exist. All we know is that Porphyry, Plotinus's pupil, regarded Origen as inferior to Ammonius because he abandoned true Greek views.[8]

When Plotinus went to Rome in 244 he "held conferences with people who came to him" and began to give lectures based on the teaching of Ammonius. He wrote nothing and encouraged students to ask questions. In consequence, "the course was lacking in order and there was a great deal of pointless chatter." After ten years, that is, when he was about fifty, he began to write, however, "on the subjects that came up in the meetings of the school."

The method employed was the analysis of texts. "In the meetings of the school he used to have the commentaries read, perhaps of Severus, perhaps of Cronius or Numenius or Gaius or Atticus [all Platonists],

8. Eusebius *H. E.* 6.19.6–7.

and among the Peripatetics of Aspasius, Alexander, Adrastus, and others that were available. But he did not just speak straight out of these books but took a distinctive personal line in his consideration, and brought the mind of Ammonius to bear on the investigations in hand." Two comparisons suggest themselves here. First, the textbooks of the school are essentially the same as those Porphyry claimed the Christian teacher Origen was always reading.[9] This was not unnatural for a fellow disciple of Ammonius. Second, the method of Plotinus was presumably much the same as that of Origen, with one exception. Origen was not trying to repeat what Ammonius taught but was trying to express true interpretations of his own. Perhaps he could do this because he was not burdened by academic philosophical traditions. On the other hand, Rebecca Lyman finds (in a forthcoming essay) some surprising echoes of Numenius in Origen's early works.

Porphyry says that Plotinus's command of Greek was not up to his thought. He made mistakes both in speaking and in writing. He continued to encourage questions and even defended Porphyry for raising them: "If when Porphyry asks questions we do not solve his difficulties we shall not be able to say anything at all to put into the treatise."

Some of the pupils questioned Plotinus's originality. They praised him because "he generally expresses himself in a tone of rapt inspiration, and states what he himself really feels about the matter and not what has been handed down by the tradition."[10] They claimed, however, that "his writings are full of concealed Stoic and Peripatetic doctrines," especially those derived from the *Metaphysics* of Aristotle. This kind of investigation reminds us of the way a Christian like Marcellus of Ancyra could search Origen's writings for echoes of Plato.[11] The purpose was the same: to denigrate one whose philosophy or theology was considered derivative.

On balance, however, Porphyry could and did say of Plotinus what Origen's pupils could have said of him. His opponents did not understand Plotinus, Porphyry said, partly because "he was so completely free from the staginess and windy rant of the professional speechifier: his lectures were like conversations, and he was not quick to make clear to anybody the compelling logical coherence of his discourse." Like Origen, Plotinus had little use for the exuberance of rhetoric.

9. Eusebius *H. E.* 6.19.8.
10. *Vit.* 14, if Armstrong has guessed what the corrupt text means.
11. *Frag.* 88; Klostermann = Eusebius *C. Marcell.* 1.4.24–26.

ORIGEN AT ALEXANDRIA

The earliest writings of Origen undoubtedly reflect school tradition of some sort. Like Clement he wrote *Stromateis* ("Miscellanies"). Clement intended to write *On the Resurrection;*[12] Origen did so. He also wrote commentaries in the Philonic manner, for example on Lamentations. It was only when he tackled a major book of the Old Testament —for him the major book, Genesis—that he turned to the task of collecting what must have been his introductory lectures on theology. The modern problems concerning his exact sources and intentions seem insoluble. Presumably, since as Mme. Harl has shown there are two sets of lectures, or at any rate discussions, in the *First Principles,*[13] he could conceivably have created a third and a fourth, and therefore had not worked out one definitive system. On the other hand, since he did not present further statements of his thought, what there is must be perhaps not a system but at least valid for the time.

Origen obviously knew that he was working toward a Christian philosophical theology. This is clear from his preface to the *First Principles.* Like Irenaeus he insists that one must maintain the "ecclesiastical preaching," transmitted from the apostles by succession and preserved in the churches. And indeed like Irenaeus he also differentiates the basic preaching, given even to those too lazy *(pigriores)* to investigate, from its rationale, to be investigated by the more intelligent and Spirit-inspired.[14] The ecclesiastical preaching turns out to be rather like the rule of faith. The investigations, however, are concerned with the origin and nature of the Holy Spirit; the origin, freedom, and destiny of the soul; the origin and nature of the devil; the origin and destiny of this world in relation to others; questions about allegorical meanings, the word "incorporeal," and finally the origin and nature of angels, the sun, the moon, and the stars. Many of these questions are specifically theological, that is, rooted in Scripture; several are closer to the kinds of topics discussed in the Greek school doxographies.

We sometimes think that such distinctions between faith and

12. *Paed.* 1.47.1; 2.104.1.

13. "Structure et cohérence du *Peri archon,*" in *Origeniana: premier colloque international des études origéniennes, Montserrat, 18–21 septembre 1973* (ed. H. Crouzel et al.; Bari: Istituto di letteratura cristiana antica, 1975) 11–32. Cf. H. Crouzel and M. Simonetti, *Origène: Traité des principes* (SC 252; Paris: Editions du Cerf, 1978) 1:21–22.

14. Writing against the Gnostics, however, Irenaeus sternly discouraged investigation of such questions, as W. R. Schoedel has explained in a forthcoming paper.

theology were confined to people like Origen, but we should note that Irenaeus had raised them too.[15] The bishop of Lyons described various questions that proved the intellectual skill of a Christian teacher. They included the ability to explain parables; to show how God's plan saved mankind and how magnanimous he was before the fall of angels and men; to indicate why the one God made beings both temporal and eternal, celestial and terrestrial; to explain why this God, by nature invisible, appeared to the prophets in various forms; to state why he made several covenants; and so on. Many of the questions raised look like the products of Marcionites, and of course Origen's problems did not arise in a theological vacuum.

CONTINUATION FROM ALEXANDRIA TO CAESAREA

About 232 Origen transferred his teaching from Alexandria to Caesarea in Palestine. In this new school, fully and fulsomely described by Gregory Thaumaturgus, we find Origen's Alexandrian teaching somewhat more fully developed but not essentially changed.

It is worth observing what the curriculum did not include. We have already noted that in the second-century apologists and Clement of Alexandria there was much reference to the ordinary Greek literary curriculum, beginning with Homer and running on through poets and often historians. Though Plato had driven the study of poetry out of his ideal republic, Clement paid no attention to this ban, for he thought that poetry could be impressed into Christian service. Origen disagreed. His systematic and exegetical works contain no references to pagan literature, and in a homily on Psalm 36 he criticized this literature as far inferior to theology, the knowledge of God. He believed there was nothing worthwhile in "the poems of the poets, the fictions of the authors of comedy, the narratives (whether fictitious or horrifying) of the authors of tragedy, and the lengthy and varied volumes of histories." One should not study rhetoric, in which one could find "every artifice of eloquence." (We should note that Origen has to complain about the congregations' inattentiveness to his sermons. John Chrysostom, a brilliant speaker, has to ask his congregation not to applaud so much!)

Origen was not enthusiastic about a literary education. It is clear that he had enjoyed one, for after his father's death he earned his living by

15. *Adv. haer.* 1.10.3.

teaching what we call classical Greek literature. Rather early, however, he turned his back on it, just as Jerome later turned, or tried to turn, away from Latin. Only in his apologetic writing *Contra Celsum* do we find explicit classical quotations and references. That is because he was writing for an audience outside the church, at least ostensibly. The point does not mean that he turned his back on classical culture or civilization. There were aspects of it that he considered permanently valuable, and these turn up not only in his writings but in the curriculum of his school. He insisted on the primacy of logic and the necessity of studying arithmetic, geometry, astronomy, and music—the mathematical sciences approved by Plato (not to mention Philo). Thus we see that he joined Plato both in condemning the seductive charm of Greek poetry and in demanding the study of truly scientific subjects. The school at Caesarea, out of which a good many bishops emerged, was a fairly austere academy.

His teaching methods probably appear in the *Dialogue with Heracleides*,[16] in which he was treating various bishops as if they were candidates for a theological degree. After Heracleides made a declaration of faith ostensibly based on the Scriptures, Origen proceeded to speak, with "the whole church [or assembly, including schools] present and listening," and to quiz the bishop about his statements. He led him to state that both the Father and the Son are God and therefore there are two Gods with one power. He then commented, "But as our brethren take offense at the statement that there are two Gods, we must formulate the statement carefully, and show in what sense they are two and in what sense the two are one God." Obviously this is a dialectical problem of the sort regularly discussed in Origen's school and in other philosophical schools.

Another example out of many that could be given comes when a bishop arrives late and one of his fellows informs him that "Brother Origen teaches that the soul is immortal." Obviously he is suggesting that Origen Hellenizes excessively. Origen gives a typically scholastic reply. "The remark of father Demetrius has given us the starting point for another problem. He asserted that we have said the soul is immortal. To this remark I say that the soul is immortal and the soul is

16. J. Scherer, *Entretien d'Origène avec Héraclide et les évêques ses collègues: Sur le Père, le Fils, et l'âme* (PSFP.T 9; Cairo: L'Institut français d'archéologie orientale du Caire, 1949); idem, *Entretien d'Origène avec Héraclide* (SC 67; Paris: Editions du Cerf, 1960).

not immortal. Let us first define the meaning of the word 'death' and determine all its possible senses."

We should also mention the scholastic discussions that Dionysius of Alexandria undertook, only a few years later, with literalists concerning the authorship of the Apocalypse and Gospel of John. To be sure, he was not introducing novelties. Gaius of Rome had learnedly discussed the problem at the beginning of the third century. What was perhaps more unusual was the way the bishop summoned the presbyters and teachers of Arsinoite villages for three days of public discussion of arguments and counterarguments. As often in Eusebius's excerpts, the account ends[17] with an incomplete conclusion—"Some [hoi men] rejoiced because of the conference"—but we never learn what others (hoi de) thought. In any event, this is school teaching brought to the village level and not watered down.

Origen's school, and presumably that of Dionysius, was not just a graduate school of philosophy or grammatical-rhetorical criticism. Origen laid a great deal of emphasis on ethics and practical morality as well as on the importance of contemplation for himself and his students. And he regarded theology as the queen of the sciences, beyond the philosophy that was merely a crown princess. The mathematical sciences led up to philosophy; philosophy led up to theology. And theology was basically the study and interpretation of Holy Scripture.

Like Origen's ancient critics, we usually recognize that his ideas about interpretation involved not only exegesis, deducing the meaning of scriptural passages, but also eisegesis, reading one's own ideas into them. Origen did not think that this was what he was doing. He recognized the validity of the learning acquired both through the sciences and through the study of Scripture, and as a true Alexandrian he believed that the one God, through his one Logos, was not duping humanity by reason any more than by revelation. Above all, he believed that through contemplation he and his students were coming closer to the one God and perhaps sometimes even to the vision of God. His school thus resembled that of the Therapeutae.

The Alexandrian scheme of theological education set the pattern for much of what followed, at least in the major church centers, roughly until the last two or three centuries. We may recall some of the debates that took place over aspects of it in the medieval church and at the

17. *H. E.* 7.24.

Renaissance and later, especially, for example, in England and North America. Fairly soon after Origen's time, we should note, the study of theology came to include something like what we should call historical theology, with the use of dogmatic florilegia. This field was made necessary and was promoted by the continuing rise of divergent learned theologies and the collection of materials for use by advocates of various sytems. Debate, as is often the case, preceded study.

The study of church history as such was very slow in arising. After all, Eusebius did not even begin his *Church History* until very late in the third century, and apparently not even the emperor Constantine studied it. History in the ancient schools normally meant reading Herodotus and Thucydides and a few other ancients, not any of the more or less contemporary historians. Perhaps church history was ultimately based on antiheretical treatises—reflecting debate once more.

No one in an ancient theological school gave attention to any practical training. The closest they came was in the study of rhetoric, which many early Christian writers denounced. Rhetoric, the art of speaking well and persuasively, has had a very bad press through the ages. When trying to persuade his Corinthian converts, the apostle Paul argued that his speech and his message were not in persuasive words of wisdom but in demonstration of the Spirit and power. He had decided to know nothing when he was with them except Jesus Christ and him crucified. Likewise some of the apologists, not to mention Origen himself, take no pleasure in the showy effects of Asiatic rhetoric but instead rely upon simple, logical—or seemingly logical—statements to produce conviction. This is itself a form of rhetorical argument, one set forth by Aristotle in his *Rhetoric* and elsewhere. It is antirhetorical rhetoric. But Origen evidently could not convince all his students that the plain style was best, for the *Panegyric* produced in his honor by Gregory the Wonderworker is full of rhetorical flourishes.

ALEXANDRIA AFTER ORIGEN: THEOGNOSTUS

We sometimes forget, as Eusebius intended us to forget, that there were important teachers at Alexandria after Origen's time. Eusebius saves for the *Praeparatio Evangelica* his materials about the conflict between Dionysius of Alexandria and Dionysius of Rome. And he never mentions Theognostus, who taught at Alexandria in the third century. For our purpose Theognostus is of special interest because he maintained the old theological curriculum with much of its old content. We know it from Photius, who described it in the ninth century.[18] There were seven books. The first was on the Father and showed that he is the Creator and that matter is not coeternal with him. The second shows that the Father has a Son and the Son can be called a creature, ruling over none but rational creatures. (Photius is much offended by these Origenistic statements.) Third, he tries to prove the existence of the Holy Spirit (Origenism once more, says Photius). The fourth book is on angels and demons, which have "tenuous bodies." The fifth and sixth deal with "the incarnation of the Savior" and state that "we imagine that the Son is circumscribed at various times in various places" but he is not circumscribed in his effective working. Finally he writes "on the creative action of God" in, according to Photius, a more pious manner. We are not concerned with judging Theognostus's theology, which Athanasius did not criticize, but merely with noting how conservative the Alexandrian school became after Origen's departure.

I suppose we might criticize the Alexandrians for their general emphasis on metaphysical theology. Such a criticism would merely affirm a modern lack of enthusiasm for metaphysics. We might also suppose that they tended to fall into two camps, with Philo and Clement, who accepted literature, or with Origen and apparently Theognostus, who concentrate their attention on science and philosophy. But the differences were not as great as the similarities, as Clement's *Stromateis* and Origen's *Contra Celsum* show.

What is significant is that for at least three centuries a tradition of theological learning was maintained in this city. In spite of religious changes the basic philosophical components remained much the same, with a mixture predominantly Platonic but containing borrowings from other schools, and a theological base in biblical ideas or at least terminology. It could be argued that this tradition, like others, gradually deteriorated. Origenism is not Origen, nor is Monophysitism the only heir of Alexandrian thought. The intellectual vigor of the early Alexandrians was related to their historical circumstances. Successors can never be "present at the creation." And this is why it is so important to continue studying the unique contributions of theologians like Philo, Clement, and Origen in their Alexandrian context.

18. *Cod.* 106; *PG* 103, 373–76.

Jewish and Platonic Speculations in Early Alexandrian Theology: Eugnostus, Philo, Valentinus, and Origen

The Nag Hammadi library is most helpful in deepening our understanding of the historical development of early Alexandrian theology as expressed by Jewish, gnostic and early Catholic theologians. We knew that before the arrival of Christianity at Alexandria, Jewish and Platonic speculations already had been merged into a special brand of Judaism that was able to satisfy the religious and intellectual needs of widely Hellenized Jews and was also attractive to interested pagans. But now, we see better than ever how this process of reformulation and assimilation actually took place, and also how much early Christian Alexandrian theology, both in its gnostic and Catholic varieties, was directly based upon these Jewish-Platonic speculations.

In this paper, I aim to demonstrate this important but underestimated aspect of the Nag Hammadi library by a discussion of some ideas of the gnostic writing *Eugnostus the Blessed*—a writing that in my view is able to elucidate some peculiar views of such Alexandrian theologians as Philo, Valentinus, and Origen.

We do not know who the Eugnostus mentioned in the title may have been, nor is there any certainty that the work was actually written by a man called Eugnostus.[1] But from his work we do know that the author,

---

1. The text is preserved in two Nag Hammadi codices, NHC III 70,1—90,13 and V 1,1—17,18, published in *The Facsimile Edition of the Nag Hammadi Codices: Codex V* (Leiden: E. J. Brill, 1975) and *The Facsimile Edition of the Nag Hammadi Codices: Codex III* (Leiden: E. J. Brill, 1976). The text of NHC III was edited by D. Trakatellis, O ΥΠΕΡΒΑΤΙΚΟΣ ΘΕΟΣ ΤΟΥ ΕΥΓΝΩΣΤΟΥ (Athens: private edition, 1977) 170-207 (see my review in *VC* 33 [1979] 405-6; Eng. trans. and introduction are by D. M. Parrott, *NHLE*, 206-28, together with the Christian adaptation of Eugnostus, the *Sophia Jesu Christi*, as found in NHC III 90,14—119,18. The other known version of the *Sophia*, in

whom I shall henceforth call Eugnostus, was a Jewish Gnostic who had some knowledge of Greek philosophy. He opens his work with a short introduction in which he rejects the traditional proofs of God's existence and nature based on the ordering of the cosmos. He does so by making use of the equally traditional counterarguments of the Skeptics.[2] This introduction opens the way to an exposition of the completely transcendent nature of the "God of Truth," which, except for a few positive statements, is described in a negative theology. God is, however, not above thinking: he is unknowable but he knows himself and, therefore, is wholly rational. He is called the Father of the Universe, because he contained the sources of all things in his mind, in his foreknowledge, before they came into existence. Eugnostus's real problem is how the monadic and unchangeable being of the ineffable God can be conceived as becoming an active and multiplying being. His work contains two descriptions of how the way from unity to plurality within the divine can be envisaged. The first of these attempts to grasp the incomprehensible is Greek and, in its main elements, Platonic; the other is Jewish and gnostic. It is clear that, according to Eugnostus, the two views are not contradictory or mutually exclusive, for the divisions of the divine mind made in his first description recur at several levels of the Pleroma developed in the second. I intend to discuss these views elsewhere. Here I confine myself to some peculiar features of Eugnostus's second description of the Pleroma, especially of its first stages.

IMMORTAL MAN, DIVINITY, AND KINGSHIP

Eugnostus begins his description of the coming into being of the second "person" of God, which marks the beginning of the development of the Pleroma, in this way:

---

the Coptic Codex of Berlin (BG), was edited by W. C. Till, *Die gnostischen Schriften des koptischen Papyrus Berolinensis 8502* (ed. H.-M. Schenke; 2d ed.; Berlin: Akademie-Verlag, 1972) 194–295. For the relationship between *Eugnostus the Blessed* and the *Sophia Jesu Christi*, see M. Krause, "Das literarische Verhältnis des Eugnostosbriefes zur Sophia Jesu Christi: Zur Auseinandersetzung der Gnosis mit dem Christentum," in *Mullus: Festschrift Theodor Klauser* (JAC, Ergänzungsband 1; Münster Westfalen: Aschendorff, 1964) 215–23; and now also M. Tardieu, *Ecrits gnostiques: Codex de Berlin* (SGM 1; Paris: Editions du Cerf, 1984). Tardieu's important book contains, among other things, parallel translations of both writings, with an introduction and copious notes, which, however, do not induce me to change the views I expounded at the Claremont conference.

2. See R. van den Broek, "Eugnostus: Via scepsis naar gnosis," *NedThTs* 37 (1983) 104–14.

The First, who appeared in the infinite before everything, is a self-grown, self-created Father, perfect in ineffably shining light. In the beginning he conceived the idea to have his likeness (eine = ὁμοίωμα) come into being as a great power. Immediately the beginning of that Light manifested itself as an immortal, androgynous Man. (NHC III 76,14–24)

Thus, the Second is the *likeness* of the First, which manifests itself in the shape of a *man*. This strongly recalls the vision of the Glory of God in "the *likeness* as the appearance of a *man*" (LXX: ὁμοίωμα ὡς εἶδος ἀνθρώπου) by the prophet Ezekiel, who saw this manifestation of the *kabod* of the Lord in radiant fire and light (Ezek. 1:26–28).[3]

Jewish mystical speculations on the human shape of God or, more exactly, the manifestation of his Glory, were already known at Alexandria before the first century B.C.E. We know this because it is mentioned by Ezekiel the Dramatist in his *Exodus*, 66–89, where he relates a dream or vision by Moses. The leader of the exodus saw a throne on the summit of Mount Sinai on which was seated a man (φώς; cf. φῶς, light) who had a diadem on his head and a scepter in his left hand. Moses was summoned to sit down on that throne or, possibly, on another throne (as *synthronos*), and to accept the *regalia*. After that the Man went away.[4] We need not enter here into a discussion of this vision and the speculations that lay at its base, nor is it necessary to trace its further developments. It is sufficient to say that at an early date speculations about the Anthropos as the hypostasized manifestation of God were known in Jewish circles at Alexandria and from there found their way into gnostic and hermetic writings.

After some remarks on the male and female aspects of the androgynous Immortal Man, which will be discussed below, Eugnostus says, according to the version of NHC V 6,14–22: "From Immortal Man was first revealed the name of the Divinity and the Lordship and Kingship and those which came after them." The reading of NHC III 77,9–13 is somewhat shorter: "Through Immortal Man was revealed a first name: Divinity and Kingship." This statement is repeated a few lines further along, though both manuscripts are lacunar at this point. NHC III

3. This was first pointed out by G. Quispel ("Ezekiel 1:26 in Jewish Mysticism and Gnosis," *VC* 34 [1980] 1–13, esp. 6–7).
4. The importance of Moses' throne vision for the Jewish Merkavah tradition was first seen by I. Gruenwald (*Apocalyptic and Merkavah Mysticism* [AGJU 14; Leiden: E. J. Brill, 1980] 128–29); its relevance for the gnostic Anthropos was seen by G. Quispel ("Gnosis," in *Die orientalischen Religionen im Römerreich* [ed. M. J. Vermaseren; EPRO 93; Leiden: E. J. Brill, 1981] 416–17). See also P. W. van der Horst, "De joodse toneelschrijver Ezechiël," *NedThTs* 36 (1982) 97–112; and idem, "Moses' Throne Vision in Ezekiel the Dramatist," *JJS* 34 (1983) 21–29.

77,23—78,1 reads: "From that Man, then, originated the Divinity [and the Kingship]." The words between brackets are lost but can be safely supplied from the *Sophia Jesu Christi*, BG 96,5–8 and NHC III 102,14–17: "For from this God originated the Divinity and the Kingship."

The peculiar expression "the name of the Divinity and the Lordship and Kingship" should be interpreted as "the divine power that is expressed by the name God and that expressed by the name Lord and King." Eugnostus presupposes here well-known Jewish speculations on the two principal names of God in the Old Testament, Elohim and Yahweh, which in the Septuagint were rendered as θεός and κύριος, "God" and "Lord." According to Philo, the name God represents the creative and beneficent power of God and the name Lord his royal and punishing power. The rabbis of the second and third centuries taught the opposite view, saying that the name Elohim was connected with God's judgment and the name Yahweh with his mercy. They emphasized the equality of these divine attributes lest one would think that God's love and mercy prevailed over his judgment and punishment and that the two names referred in a gnostic manner to different divine beings.[5]

This concern was shared by Philo, who presents the view that the Logos is superior to and mediating between the beneficent and the punitive powers of God. Discussing the symbolism of the ark, the ordinances stored in it, and the two cherubim upon it, he even says that the two powers have their origin in the Logos:

> In the first place there is He who is elder than the One and the Monad and the Beginning. Then comes the Logos of Him who is, the seminal substance of existing things. And from the divine Logos, as from a spring, there divide two Powers. One is the creative, through which the Artificer established and ordered all things; this is named God. And the other is the royal, through which the Creator rules over created things; this is called Lord. And from these two Powers have grown the others. For by the side of the creative there grows the merciful, of which the name is Beneficent, and by the side of the royal there grows the legislative, of which the apt

---

5. For the rabbis, see E. E. Urbach, *The Sages: Their Concepts and Beliefs* (trans. I. Abrahams; 2d ed.; Jerusalem: Magnes Press, 1979) 448–61; for Philo, see H. A. Wolfson, *Philo: Foundations of Religious Philosophy in Judaism, Christianity, and Islam* (Cambridge: Harvard Univ. Press, 1947) 1:218–19; J. Dillon, *The Middle Platonists: A Study of Platonism, 80 B.C. to A.D. 220* (London: Gerald Duckworth & Co., 1977) 161–67; for Philo and the rabbis, see N. A. Dahl and A. F. Segal, "Philo and the Rabbis on the Names of God," *JSJ* 9 (1978) 1–28.

name is Punitive. And below these and beside them is the ark; and the ark is a symbol of the intelligible world.[6] (*Quaest. in Exod.* 2.68)

Philo continues with a threefold enumeration of the seven divine powers that thus can be distinguished: first there is the Speaker, the ineffable God; second, the Logos; third, the creative power; fourth, the royal; fifth, the merciful (of which the creative is "the source"); sixth, the punitive (of which the royal is "the root"); and seventh, the intelligible, incorporeal world of ideas. In this chapter, Philo comes very close to the development of an emanating divine Pleroma. What he means, however, is unequivocally clear: the ineffable God does not directly act himself, but through his first manifestation, the Logos, and it is through the work of this Logos that his creative and ruling powers, expressed in his names God and Lord, become manifest.

Before the discovery of *Eugnostus the Blessed* it could be thought that Philo was the first to reason in this way, by combining the Greek doctrine of the Logos with the Jewish doctrine of the two powers of God that are expressed in his names. But now we have in Eugnostus the same view as in Philo, with the only difference that not the Greek Logos but the heavenly Anthropos, the typically Jewish first manifestation of God, reveals the two principal divine powers. Just like Philo, Eugnostus knew of other powers too, "those that came after them," i.e., after Divinity and Lordship or Kingship, the powers that correspond to the names God and Lord. These two powers, with the Hebrew names, are also found in the *Apocryphon of John*. There it is told that Eve gave birth to two sons, called Elohim and Jave, who are identified with Cain and Abel. Their father, however, is not Adam but Jaldabaoth, the evil Demiurge.[7] The two powers are presented here in a gnostic distortion, but there seems to be little doubt that originally it was *hā-'ādām*, Man, that is to say, the heavenly Anthropos, who was said to be the begetter of these two powers. It is conceivable that in a second development this metaphysical begetting was transposed to the physical realm and applied to Adam and Eve, thus changing the divine powers into anthropological categories. In any case, Eugnostus demonstrates the existence of a Jewish tradition according to which the heavenly Adam

6. The Greek text is in R. Marcus, *Philo Supplement II: Questions and Answers on Exodus* (LCL; Cambridge: Harvard Univ. Press; London: William Heinemann, 1953) 255–56.

7. BG 62,8–15 and NHC III 31,12–16: Jave, who has a bear face, is unrighteous; Elohim, who has a cat face, is righteous. NHC IV 37,27—38,6 presents the opposite view: Jave, with a cat face, is righteous; Elohim, with a bear face, is unrighteous. Cf. NHC II 25,15–20, where there is no specification of who is the righteous one.

reveals God in his creative and royal powers as God and Lord. And this shows that Philo, in attributing this function to the Logos, was not original, but simply Hellenizing a Jewish myth, which, though in itself not gnostic at all, could easily be interpreted in a gnostic sense.

EUGNOSTUS AND VALENTINUS ON THE PLEROMA OF GOD

According to Eugnostus, Immortal Man is an androgynous being whose female side is identified with Wisdom, Sophia, the other hypostasized manifestation of God that played an important part in Judaism and Christianity, especially at Alexandria, as is witnessed by the Wisdom of Solomon, Philo, the Gnostics, and Clement and Origen. Anthropos and Sophia, the two basic entities of gnostic mythology, had become part of Alexandrian theology long before the arrival of Christianity. Here, in Eugnostus, they are the two sides, the male and female aspects, of one androgynous being called the Athanatos Anthropos, or Immortal Man.

The male and female names that in the texts are given to the two sides of Immortal Man show that other, more Greek ideas have been associated with this first manifestation of God. Unfortunately the manuscripts of Eugnostus are lacunar at this point. In NHC III 77,2, the male seems to be called "the perfect Begetting"; in NHC V 6,6–7, it is "the Begetter-*Nous* [who is perfect by] himself." In the *Sophia Jesu Christi*, this passage on the male and female names of Immortal Man has been omitted, but in III 104,8–9, the *Sophia* calls the male "the Begetter, the *Nous* who is perfect by himself." NHC V 6,6 and III 104,8 show with absolute certainty that the Athanatos Anthropos was identified with Nous, "Mind."

In NHC V 6,8–10, the female side of Immortal Man is called by Eugnostus "the Ennoia, she of all the Sophias, the Begettress of the Sophias [who is called] the *Truth*." NHC III 77,3–10 presents a more elaborate phrase: "And his female name is All-wise Begettress Sophia. It is also said of her that she resembles her brother and consort. She is a *Truth* which is uncontested, for here below the truth is contested by the error which exists together with it." Both texts show that Sophia was identified with Truth, Aletheia.

At first sight, it might seem that this identification of Anthropos and Sophia with Nous and Aletheia is simply to be explained as a Valentinian interpretation of Eugnostus's Anthropos-and-Sophia myth, for according to Valentinianism, Nous and Aletheia come forth from the paternal Depth and Silence to form the second pair of the Ogdoad. On second thought, however, this explanation proves to be extremely improbable.

It seems that so far nobody has noticed that the pair Nous and Aletheia was first conceived of not by Valentinus but by Plato. In the sixth book of his *Republic*, Plato argues that the true philosopher is always in pursuit of the truth. Most interesting for our subject is the imagery of procreation used in this connection: with the rational part of his soul the philosopher has sexual intercourse with true being, begets Mind and Truth, Nous and Aletheia, and thus comes to knowledge and true life.[8] Plato alludes here to his view of Nous and Aletheia as noetic entities produced by the Good, which is exposed at the beginning of the seventh book of the *Republic*, in connection with his famous simile of the cave. He explains the prisoners' coming out of the cave as the ascent of the soul to the noetic realm, and concludes that in the visible world the idea of the Good brings forth the light and its lord, the sun, and that in the noetic world, in which she is the Mistress herself, she produces Aletheia and Nous.[9] Plato already placed the Good above being, and accordingly the Middle Platonists identified the Good with the supreme, ineffable God.[10] Read with the eyes of a second-century Platonist, the master himself had taught in the *Republic* that the unknowable, transcendent God puts forth two noetic entities, Nous and Aletheia. There must have been an Alexandrian Jew who identified these first products of the Good with the two preeminent divine hypostases of Judaism, Anthropos and Sophia.

It should be noted that the association of Sophia and Aletheia lay close at hand for every Platonist, since Plato had already brought them together. At the beginning of the sixth book of the *Republic*, he argues that the lover of something also loves that which is related to the object of his love, and so the philosopher, the lover of Wisdom, may also be expected to love what is akin to it. Socrates then asks the rhetorical question, Can you find anything which is more related to Wisdom than the Truth?[11] This phrase became a maxim that found its way into the

8. Plato *Republic* 490b: πλησιάσας καὶ μιγεὶς τῷ ὄντι ὄντως, γεννήσας νοῦν καὶ ἀλήθειαν, γνοίη τε καὶ ἀληθῶς ζώη καὶ τρέφοιτο καὶ οὕτω λήγοι ὠδῖνος, πρὶν δ᾽ οὔ.

9. Plato *Republic* 517b: ἔν τε νοητῷ αὐτὴ κυρία ἀλήθειαν καὶ νοῦν παρασχομένη.

10. Plato *Republic* 509b: ἐπέκεινα τῆς οὐσίας πρεσβείᾳ καὶ δυνάμει. Alcinous *Didaskalikos* 27.1; Numenius, frgs. 16 and 19, des Places (= 25 and 28, Leemans). See for more references J. Whittaker, Ἐπέκεινα νοῦ καὶ οὐσίας, VC 23 (1969) 91–104.

11. Plato *Republic* 485c: Ἦ οὖν οἰκειότερον σοφίᾳ τι ἀληθείας ἂν εὕροις;

gnomic collections known by the names of Clitarchus and Sextus: "Nothing is more related to Wisdom than Truth."[12] This sententious tradition was known at Alexandria in the second century C.E. This may have led a Jew to identify the Jewish Sophia with the Greek Aletheia; from there it was only a small step to the identification of the Jewish Anthropos and Sophia with the Platonic Nous and Aletheia.

The same pair is encountered in the tradition behind the *Apocryphon of John*, as testified by Irenaeus in *Adv. haer.* 1.29.2. There it is said that Ennoia and Logos produce Autogenes and Aletheia. Elsewhere I have shown that this Autogenes is none other than the divine Anthropos, who in the complicated system of the apocryphon had been allotted a place inferior to that which his original dignity required.[13] The author of this system was not aware of this fact, nor did he know that Autogenes and Aletheia originally were Nous and Aletheia, for he placed Nous at a higher level of the Pleroma. This shows that the identification of Nous and Aletheia with Anthropos and Sophia, as found in our texts of *Eugnostus the Blessed* and the *Sophia Jesu Christi*, was not an occasional Valentinian adaptation. The identification must have been made at an early stage of development of the Anthropos-and-Sophia myth. Moreover, it seems probable that Valentinus did not derive his pair of Nous and Aletheia directly from Plato but from a Platonized Jewish-gnostic myth of Anthropos and Sophia of the type found in Eugnostus. In fact, a great deal of the Valentinian Ogdoad finds its explanation in a myth of this kind. This will become apparent from a discussion of the second and third aeonic pairs of Eugnostus's Pleroma.

According to Eugnostus, Immortal Man and his Sophia put forth another androgynous Man, the Son of Man, whose female aspect is also called Sophia. This pair generates a third androgynous Man, the Son of the Son of Man, whose female name is again Sophia. It is clear, as was pointed out by Hans-Martin Schenke long ago, that the addition of these second and third pairs is an amplification of an originally more simple myth that only knew of one Anthropos and Sophia.[14]

12. *Sentences of Clitarchus* 42, and *Sentences of Sextus* 168: οὐδὲν οἰκειότερον σοφίᾳ ἀληθείας (Clit.: ἢ ἀλήθεια).
13. R. van den Broek, "Autogenes and Adamas: The Mythological Structure of the Apocryphon of John," in *Gnosis and Gnosticism: Papers Read at the Eighth International Conference on Patristic Studies (Oxford, September 3rd–8th, 1979)* (ed. M. Krause; NHS 17; Leiden: E. J. Brill, 1981) 16–25.
14. H.-M. Schenke, "Nag Hammadi Studien III: Die Spitze des dem Apocryphon Johannis und der Sophia Jesu Christi zugrundeliegenden gnostischen Systems," *ZRGG* 14 (1962) 355.

In Eugnostos, the male second Anthropos is called "First-Begetter Father" and "Adam, he of the Light" (NHC III 81,10–12). In the *Sophia Jesu Christi*, NHC III 105,12–13 and BG 100,14, the latter phrase is given as "Adam, the eye of the Light," which probably is a Hebraism for "Adam, the source of the Light."[15] In any case, there is no doubt that the second Anthropos, the Son of Man, was called Adam. The female aspect of this divine Adam is called in the *Sophia Jesu Christi*, NHC III 104,17–18 and BG 99,10–12, "First Begettress Sophia, the All-Mother." Most probably, she was also called that in *Eugnostos the Blessed*, for the only preserved but lacunar text of NHC V 9,4–5 begins by calling her Sophia, to which the Greek form of All-Mother ($\pi\alpha\mu\mu\acute{\eta}\tau\omega\rho$) was probably added, and in NHC III 82,21, Eugnostos says: "the second is Panmetōr Sophia." The name All-Mother is reminiscent of Eve, whom Adam called Life, $Z\omega\acute{\eta}$, because she was the mother of all living things (Gen. 3:20: $Z\omega\acute{\eta}$, $\ddot{o}\tau\iota$ $\alpha\ddot{v}\tau\eta$ $\mu\acute{\eta}\tau\eta\rho$ $\pi\acute{\alpha}\nu\tau\omega\nu$ $\tau\tilde{\omega}\nu$ $\zeta\acute{\omega}\nu\tau\omega\nu$). According to Hippolytus, *Ref.* VI.34, the Valentinians called their Sophia by this biblical name of Eve.

If the name All-Mother refers to Eve or Zoe, then the male and female aspects of the second Anthropos were identified with Adam and Zoe, not the Adam and Eve of Paradise but an aeonic pair in the Pleroma of God. In this perspective, we see that the third pair of the Valentinian Ogdoad, Logos and Zoe, are in fact the partly Hellenized counterparts of the Jewish Adam, the Son of Man, and his consort, Eve, the All-Mother Zoe. To interpret Adam, the Son of the Anthropos, as Logos, the son of Nous, lay close at hand: in the *Poimandres* 6, the Logos is also called the son of Nous, and Alcinous *Didaskalikos* 27.2 states that the Good of the *Republic* 517b–c can be attained by *nous* and *logos*.

Valentinus seems to have replaced Adam with the Greek Logos but to have retained the original Jewish Zoe. A similar state of affairs is to be observed in Irenaeus *Adv. haer.* 1.29.3. There it is said that Autogenes (and Aletheia) produce Adamas, also called the perfect Anthropos,[16] and Gnosis ("agnitionem perfectam"/"Gnosin"). In view of the fact that Valentinus combines the Greek Logos and the Jewish

15. The Hebrew word '*ajin* means "eye" and "source"; cf. L. Koehler and W. Baumgartner, *Lexicon in Veteris Testamenti Libros* (Leiden: E. J. Brill, 1953) 699–700. In patristic Greek ὀφθαλμός can also have the meaning of "source"; cf. LPGL 988.

16. That the second Anthropos, Adam/Adamas, is so emphatically said to be the perfect Anthropos may have led the author of the Valentinian *Doctrinal Letter* (Epiphanius *Panarion* 31.5–6), whose description of the Valentinian system was strongly influenced by *Eugnostos the Blessed*, to put the emanation of Anthropos and Ecclesia

Zoe, and the text of Irenaeus the Jewish Adam and the Greek Gnosis, it seems probable that the original Greek interpretation of the Jewish myth presented the following correspondences:

Anthropos and Sophia = Nous and Aletheia

Adam and Zoe   = Logos and Gnosis

In any case, it should be noticed that, just like Nous and Logos, Aletheia and Gnosis are closely related. Here we have to turn again to Plato's discussion of the Good in the sixth book of the *Republic*. In connection with his comparison of the idea of the Good with the visible sun he says that this idea is the cause of knowledge and truth (αἰτίαν δ᾽ ἐπιστήμης οὖσαν καὶ ἀληθείας), but that the idea of the Good is more beautiful than knowledge and truth (γνώσεώς τε καὶ ἀληθείας). In this passage (508e–9a), ἐπιστήμη and γνῶσις are synonyms, just as in another passage of the *Republic* (477a–78c). The connections made by Plato between Nous and Aletheia and between Aletheia and Gnosis may have inspired a Platonizing Gnostic to substitute these concepts for the Jewish Anthropos, Sophia, and Zoe. It is on this *interpretatio platonica* of the Jewish Anthropos-and-Sophia myth that Valentinus and the author of Irenaeus's source must be depending.

The fourth pair of Valentinus's Ogdoad, that of Anthropos and Ecclesia, does not betray any direct Platonic influence, but there is some relationship with the Anthropos-and-Sophia myth as found in *Eugnostus the Blessed*. According to this text, Adam and the All-Mother Sophia produce a third androgynous man, a "great androgynous Light." The male and female epithets of this being are in all the manuscripts: "Savior, Begetter of all things" and "Sophia, All-Begettress" (NHC III 82,2–5 parr.). This third Anthropos, the Son of the Son of Man, possibly hides behind the Anthropos of Valentinus's Ogdoad, but there is nothing to suggest that his Valentinian female counterpart, Ecclesia, could be explained from the third Sophia. The nótion of Ecclesia, however, is not absent from the myth of Eugnostus. There, the name Ecclesia is assigned to the collectivity of the three aeons of Immortal Man, the Son of Man (Adam), and the Son of the Son of Man (the Savior). This aeonic totality, called the Ecclesia of the Ogdoad (NHC III 86,24—87,1 and III 111,2–3), is again androgynous, with a male and a female name. The male aspect is called Ecclesia, the female

---

before that of Logos and Zoe, as was also done by the Valentinians described by Irenaeus *Adv. haer.* 1.12.3; cf. A. H. B. Logan, "The Epistle of Eugnostus and Valentinianism," in *Gnosis and Gnosticism* (ed. Krause) 66–75, esp. 73.

Life (Zoe). It is noteworthy that the male part bears a female name. When this phenomenon occurs it always points to a translation from another language in which the equivalent has the masculine gender.[17] I suggest that in Eugnostus, just as in nearly all the occurrences in the Septuagint, the word "ecclesia" translates the Hebrew word *qāhāl*, "assembly." Therefore, the correct translation of Ecclesia in Eugnostus is not Church but Assembly, as was indeed seen by Douglas M. Parrott. The name of the female aspect, Life, might be the translation of Ḥawwāh, Ζωή, Eve. In any case, it is clear that the author had the explanation of Eve's name in Gen. 3:20 in mind: he explicitly states that the female part of the all-embracing aeon was called Life, "that it might be shown that from a female came life in all the aeons" (III 87,5–8). So it seems plausible that Valentinus borrowed the name of the last aeon of his Ogdoad, Ecclesia, from the collective aeon Assembly of the Anthropos-and-Sophia myth. Most likely, however, in his interpretation, this name received the Christian connotation of Church.

I do not claim that Valentinus was directly inspired by the myth of *Eugnostus the Blessed*. But I hope to have shown that there is strong evidence that the Valentinian Ogdoad depends on a Platonized, amplified Jewish-gnostic myth of Anthropos and Sophia of the type found in Eugnostus. Seen in this perspective, Nous and Aletheia, Logos and Zoe, Anthropos and Ecclesia prove not to have been names chosen at random, but to represent meaningful metaphysical entities that together constitute the predicable essence of the nature of God.

The first pair of the Valentinian Ogdoad, Bythos and Sige, Depth and Silence, cannot be explained from the Jewish myth. In Eugnostus, the supreme, ineffable God is strictly monadic. The principle of androgynous duality is first expressed in Immortal Man and his Sophia. It is to such a concept that Plato's view of the Good as producing Nous and Aletheia could be applied. Valentinus has transferred the principle of duality and fecundity into the deepest ground of being itself, by changing its monadic essence into Bythos and Sige. There must be some connection between the views of Valentinus and those expressed in the *Chaldaean Oracles*, which also speak about the "paternal Depth (Bythos)" (frg. 18, des Places) and the "God-nurtured Silence (Sige)" (frg. 16). It seems possible, however, that Valentinus already found the

---

17. See G. Mussies, "Catalogues of Sins and Virtues Personified (NHC II,5)," in *Studies in Gnosticism and Hellenistic Religions Presented to Gilles Quispel on the Occasion of His 65th Birthday* (ed. R. van den Broek and M. J. Vermaseren; EPRO 91; Leiden: E. J. Brill, 1981) 315–35, esp. 324–35.

name Sige used in connection with Nous and Aletheia but deliberately made it the name of the female aspect of the androgynous ineffable One. In Eugnostus, Sige is said to be another name of Sophia (Aletheia), the consort of Immortal Man (Nous), "because in reflecting without a word she perfected her greatness" (III 88,7–11). The idea is that Silence was broken at the appearance of the Word, Logos, the son of Nous and Aletheia. The same idea is expressed in the *Apocryphon of John*, BG 31,10–11 parr., but there Silence is not a divine hypostasis. The aeons that preceded the appearance of Will and Logos are said to have come into being in silence (σιγή in NHC III 10,15) and thought (ἔννοια). In these texts the introduction of the name or the concept of Silence, just before the appearance of the Word, makes sense. It presupposes the idea of God as a thinking Mind, who comes to external activity by putting forth his Logos. By making Sige a higher aeon than Nous, Valentinus seems to have obscured its original meaning.

It is usually assumed that the Valentinian Ogdoad was primarily inspired by the prologue to the Gospel of John. I do not think it was. Valentinus must have adopted and adapted an already existing mythological scheme, which provided him with the names of most of his first eight aeons. But he certainly put them into a Christian theological framework and most probably found them also mentioned in the Johannine prologue. We know that the Valentinians explained the prologue in this sense. Irenaeus, who gives a short summary of their exegesis on this point, had no difficulty in showing that the author of the prologue had not written with the Valentinian Ogdoad on his mind.[18] Valentinus may have been the first to identify the Grace and Monogenes of John 1:18 with the Sige and Nous of his Ogdoad. He must have taught his pupils to read the prologue as a revelation of essential aspects of the divine nature which, by God's grace, are not completely inaccessible to man, since they have become manifest in Christ. In this respect he was a precursor of Origen.

ORIGEN'S DOCTRINE OF THE SON AND EARLY ALEXANDRIAN THEOLOGY

Finally, I want to point out some interesting parallels between the gnostic speculations on the Pleroma discussed above and Origen's

18. Irenaeus *Adv. haer.* 1.8.5–6, 1.9.1–2.

doctrine of the Son, as expounded in his *De principiis* 1.2.1–4. In his usual manner Origen first speaks speculatively about the problems involved, and then, in the second place, discusses the scriptural evidence. The latter begins at 1.2.5, when he says, "Let us now see how our statements are also supported by the authority of divine Scripture." In the preceding section of 1.2, he deals in a speculative manner with the divine nature of the Son, even though some biblical texts are quoted.

For Origen, the Son is primarily God's Wisdom, his Firstborn (Col. 1:15), not to be conceived of as a divine quality but as a separate hypostasis. "In this very subsistence of Wisdom there was implicit every power and form of the creation that was to be . . . , fashioned and arranged beforehand by the power of the *foreknowledge (virtute prae-scientiae)*" (1.2.2). This is remarkably reminiscent of what Eugnostus says about the powers in the Mind of the Father: "They are the sources of all things, and their whole race, until the end, is in the *foreknowledge* of the Unbegotten" (NHC III 73,13–16). Origen continues by explaining that God's Wisdom is also his Logos, Truth, and Life. It is clear that the Johannine names and epithets of Christ are on his mind here, for he adds that Life also implies Resurrection, which exists in Wisdom, Word, and Truth, and that the Word and Wisdom of God have become a Way that leads to the Father (1.2.4). But there can be no doubt that for Origen the Son is basically Wisdom and Truth, Word and Life.[19] Just as these divine powers are inseparable from God and always produced by him, the Son is eternally generated by the Father: there is an "aeterna et sempiterna generatio" of the Son. In the final chapter of the last book of *De principiis* (4.4.1) Origen returns to these speculations on the Son. He points out that "whoever dares to say that 'There was a time that the Son did not exist' [exactly what afterwards became the Arian slogan], should understand that he also will say that 'Once Wisdom did not exist, and Logos did not exist, and Life did not exist,' whereas we must believe that in all these the substance of God exists in perfection." They are inseparable from his substance: "Although in our mind they are regarded as many, yet in fact and substance they are one, and in them resides the 'fullness of the godhead' (Col. 2:9)."

---

19. Similar ideas were already developed by Irenaeus in his refutation of the Valentinian Pleroma, in *Adv. haer.* 2.13.9: "Appellationi enim Dei coobaudiuntur sensus et verbum et vita et incorruptela et veritas et sapientia et bonitas et omnia talia." Irenaeus, however, is especially concerned with the unity of God and opposed to the idea of emanation within the Deity. He does not speak of the Son in this connection.

Thus, according to Origen, Sophia and Aletheia, and Logos and Zoe are the principal constituents of the divine Pleroma. The last three powers are also part of the first stage of the Pleroma according to the Valentinians, in which, however, Sophia has been assigned the lowest possible position. That alone is enough to show that Origen was not directly dependent on Valentinus. It must be assumed that both were making use of earlier Alexandrian speculations on the nature of God, which most probably had been developed in a Jewish and Platonist milieu. In these speculations God was seen as the absolutely transcendent One, who nevertheless reveals himself through his first manifestation, which forms a separate hypostasis. This hypostasis could be conceived of as Anthropos or Sophia and was thought to be identical with God's Logos, Truth, Life, and other powers, which together form the Pleroma of God. In the Christian view, this Pleroma had become manifest in Christ, the eternal Son. The downgrading of Sophia by Valentinus, and the abundant production of intermediary aeons he assumed, were a typically gnostic development of the original view, meant to make the distance between the ineffable One and the aeon that caused the split in the Deity as large as possible. But it will be clear that his speculations on the basic powers of the Pleroma were not really revolutionary. He was neither the first nor the last to reason about God in this way, as is shown by Eugnostus and Origen. That explains why his teaching was so readily accepted by so many Christians, both in Alexandria and abroad.

Athanasius of Alexandria vs. Arius:
The Alexandrian Crisis

The purpose of this paper is to evaluate the *local* significance of the so-called Arian Crisis in the Alexandrian church during the fourth century. Too many historians from the very time of Athanasius on used to approach the political and ecclesiastical aspects of Arianism, mainly in regard to the global Christian Church as it was entering the Constantinian era, with some uncleared dogmatic issues. From Eusebius of Caesarea to Adolf von Harnack and more recently Timothy D. Barnes,[1] the imposing figure of the emperor Constantine I marked a historical perspective in which the local and properly Alexandrian nature of Arianism remained neglected or misunderstood. It would be worthwhile, for once, to focus on the *birthplace* of Arian traditions, in order to reach a sharper understanding of their original *identity*.

More precisely, as polemics around doctrinal tradition depend essentially on their hostile protagonists, should not one consider the whole problematic and further development of Arianism as illuminated by Arius himself and by his oldest opponents? The facts are well known. The Alexandrian priest Arius, one of the most influential pastoral assistants of the local bishop, was censured by a synod of about a hundred clerics and banished from the cosmopolitan metropolis on the Nile delta. The fateful event occurred in the years before the synod of Nicea was held in May and June 325. Around 318, or let us say between 318 and 323, Alexander, the elderly bishop, found

---

1. Timothy D. Barnes, *Constantine and Eusebius* (Cambridge: Harvard Univ. Press, 1981).

support strong enough among his clergy and laity when he drove Arius out of his presbyterium, and also when he opposed the episcopal front built up in favor of Arius along the oriental border of the Mediterranean Sea. In the winter of 324–325 he succeeded in having the famous Eusebius of Caesarea himself excommunicated at a synod in Antioch among other high-ranking supporters of Arius.[2] He continued to hold the same strong line in the imperial synod of Nicea in the spring of 325. After Nicea, Arius was exiled in Illyricum, a region to the west of the Balkan Peninsula. Alexander died in 328, not before the versatile Constantine had asked him in vain to reintegrate Arius among his clergy. When Athanasius became Alexander's successor, he inherited a shaken and divided community of believers. He had also to face an episcopal administration in disarray because of a schism, lasting already for two full decades, in which a group called Meletians,[3] profiting by their slight majority among the Egyptian bishops and clerics, refused their hierarchical submission to the holder of the Alexandrian see.[4]

The young (perhaps too young) bishop Athanasius[5] continued the policy of his predecessor in the canonically closed affair of Arius. Actually there was no choice for Athanasius. How would he have nullified a solemn condemnation of the local synod that was anything but arbitrary in his eyes, and what was even more unthinkable for him, nullify it under the pressure of the imperial administration or by order of the oriental bishops who had no legal power in his own church? Athanasius's fate was to become the steadfast defender of his canonical right to reinforce the censure of the Arian party promulgated by his predecessor, against any episcopal or political interventions in the Alexandrian state of church affairs. I would only like to stress here one well-known consequence of Athanasius's idealistic rigidity. From 328 on, when he started to apply with a heavy hand the decrees of Nicea in the church under his jurisdiction, he succeeded unwittingly in

---

2. Luise Abramowski, "Die Synode von Antiochien 324/25 und ihr Symbol," ZKG 86 (1975) 336–66. On Alexander, see Charles Kannengiesser, "Alessandro di Alessandria," in DPAC 1:131–32.

3. Annik Martin, "Athanase et les Mélitiens (325–335)," in Politique et Théologie chez Athanase d'Alexandrie, Actes du Colloque de Chantilly, 23–25 septembre 1973 (ed. C. Kannengiesser; Paris: Beauchesne, 1974) 31–61.

4. See the conclusions of Martin, "Athanase."

5. This is according to a Syriac Chronicon opening the collection of Athanasius's Easter letters (PG 26.1352A), which seems better informed than the later Coptic Enkomion whose author accommodated the first stages of Athanasius in the ecclesiastical career to canonical regulations of a later period.

promoting a coalition against himself of the Egyptian Meletians and
the local or foreign followers of Arius. We have quite enough evidence
to know in considerable detail[6] how quickly and to what extent that
fatal alliance became a serious threat against the Alexandrian bishop
during the early thirties, until the imperial synod of Tyre deposed him
in 335, and the aging Constantine sent him into exile to Trier, in Gallia.

I am not piling up biographical data for its own sake but in order to
introduce somehow more concretely the question of what I called the
local significance of the Arian crisis in Alexandria. By local, I mean first
of all the significance it had in Arius's own judgment. Now I must
confess that my question sounds barely adventurous, if not unrealistic,
since we hear from Arius only when he found himself expelled from
Alexandria. His first letter, among the *Urkunden zur Geschichte des
arianischen Streites*, edited by H.-G. Opitz,[7] was most probably written
in Palestine or Syria and was addressed to Eusebius of Nicomedia in
the year 318 (Opitz). But a close analysis shows that this letter, as well
as the few other writings by the exiled Arius handed down to us,
witnesses his pastoral attitude and his intellectual stance in the years
before his condemnation. The same claim to be the original teaching of
the Alexandrian priest is made by the pamphlet entitled *Thalia*, in
which the censured Arius summarized his essential doctrine before he
left Alexandria.[8] From an analysis of the documents it should be
possible to rekindle at least a few sparks of the authentic spirit with
which the elderly priest underwent, at the peak of a rather brilliant
ecclesiastical career, the ordeal of his excommunication by the local
synod of the Alexandrian church.

But there is a further aspect to be considered in insisting upon the
local significance of the Alexandrian crisis. By local I mean also how
the bishops Alexander and Athanasius, Arius's first and very local
opponents, understood it. Alexander contributed actively to the crisis in
acknowledging the accusation of doctrinal misconduct alleged against
Arius by some militant members of the local presbyterium. After a long

6. Eduard Schwartz, "Die Quellen über den melitianischen Streit," in his *Zur
Geschichte des Athanasius* (GS 3; Berlin: Walter de Gruyter, 1959) 87–116.

7. *Athanasius Werke* 3:1–2 (Berlin: Preussen Akademie der Wissenschaften, 1934–35).

8. And not after his banishment from Alexandria when he had secured himself in
Nicomedia under the protection of the influential Eusebius, as is repeated too often
following the Latin version of Nannius reproduced in Migne. See Kannengiesser, "Où et
quand Arius composa-t-il la *Thalie?* in *Kyriakon: Festschrift Johannes Quasten* (ed. P.
Granfield and J. A. Jungman; Münster: Aschendorff, 1970) 1:346–51; and Rudolf Lorenz,
Arius judaizans: Untersuchungen zur dogmengeschichtlichen Einordnung des Arius
(Göttingen: Vandenhoeck & Ruprecht, 1980) 49–52.

period of hesitation he engaged his own authority and that of his successors to condemn Arius as a heretic. He also secured the needed canonical justification for his fateful decision in explaining publicly, through synods and circular letters, the dogmatic urgency of such a solemn procedure. He was himself a man of Arius's generation, namely a Christian leader educated in the light of the philosophical tradition and the theological values characteristic of the Alexandrian church during the third century.

It was the first pastoral priority laid upon Athanasius to explicate at length the significance of the Alexandrian Arianism as perceived immediately in the local context by its hierarchical opponents. Athanasius was over a generation younger than Arius. He had served as a secretary to Alexander, and he accompanied him in that capacity to the Nicean synod in May 325. The devotional and popular *amplificatio* of a short and intentionally biased remark about it in a synodal testimony from the Alexandrian clergy carefully transmitted by Athanasius himself[9] has reached a high level of fantasy with regard to the role played by Athanasius at Nicea.[10] The fact is that the strong defender of Nicea, who held a recognized leadership over the Alexandrian see from 328 to 373, with the exception of during a few dramatic exiles, never mentioned in his many well-documented apologetic writings his own trip to Nicea, far less any sort of personal contribution to the Nicene Creed. Chronology, as well as the very nature of Athanasius's earliest written accomplishments, positions him as a newcomer in the tradition to which Arius and Alexander had paid contrasting tributes—that is, as a young cleric whose capacities matured only *after* Nicea. It is all the more noticeable how the generation gap and a deeply modified theological landscape allowed Athanasius to express in the local church of Alexandria the most striking kind of anti-Arian orthodoxy.

Only if one refers to Arius and to Athanasius, his opponent of a younger generation, in their proper Alexandrian setting, does it become a rewarding task to try to speculate on the local significance of the Arian crisis. Let us then examine the question of that significance for

9. "Athanasius then a deacon . . . [w]hen they [the Arians] became aware of him and of his faith in Christ from the synod convoked in Nicea" *apol. sec.* 6 (*PG* 25.257c.1–4).

10. "Largely through the efforts of St. Athanasius the Council of Nicea met in 325 . . ." (Vincent Zamoyta, *The Theology of Christ: Sources* [Contemporary College Theology Series; Milwaukee: Bruce Pub. Co., 1967] 30). Such nonsense, lacking any sense of the historical perspective and the basic chronology, underlines the need for reevaluations of Athanasius.

itself, first in portraying Arius as a true Alexandrian leader and scholar, and second in analyzing Athanasius's reaction against Arius as witnessed by his writings.

ARIUS IN FOCUS

The Alexandrian

The doctrinal figure of Arius has been blurred by the unfortunate tendency of many historians to underestimate his place in the dynamics typical of the Alexandrian tradition. These have too frequently related his strikingly peculiar interpretation of Scripture to what they thought to be the characteristics of the Antiochene school of exegesis. Many of them speculated about the young Arius, established in Antioch for a couple of years, as a student of the Antiochene exegete Lucian, who died as a martyr on 7 January 312. But such a view rests on the wording of the final salutation of Arius in his letter to Eusebius already mentioned, a letter in which Arius ends in greeting his distinguished addressee as a "true *syllukianista*," a true companion in the Lucianist discipleship. Actually, no convincing support was found to prove that Arius included himself in the same discipleship when he addressed Eusebius as a disciple of Lucian. Hence it became more and more obvious that the theological kinship between Arius and the disciples of Lucian, in particular their accentuated subordination of the Son under the Father in the Christian notion of the godhead, derived from their common allegiance to the Origenian heritage. What brought Arius into the position of a heresiarch was actually ignored, if not rejected, by the Lucianists.

The Alexandrian Leader

Located in Alexandria, even if he was, according to Epiphanius, of Libyan extraction, Arius appears as a man of the big city, from the first mention of his name under the ruling of the bishop and martyr Peter I who died in November 311 to the last records about him at the time of his death in 336. We see him culturally enriched by the Alexandrian setting, pursuing his clerical career in the main Christian community of this city, politically flexible in the ranks of the local hierarchy to which he belonged, and finally promoted to the top of the pastoral administration of the Alexandrian church, next to the Egyptian pope himself.

Also as an ascetic figure, as a spiritual leader of numerous consecrated women and of other disciples, and as an outstanding scholarly commentator of the Holy Scripture in the pulpit, Arius reduplicated, so to say, the classical image of the great Origen in the service of the faithful community. He was about seventy years old when the episcopal synod of the emperor excommunicated him at Nicea in June 325, and we never hear the slightest reference to Arius's leaving the boundaries of the Christian area in the city of Alexandria before he was expelled from there by the bishop Alexander.

The Alexandrian Scholar

This location of Arius in the turbulent and intellectually saturated melting pot of the Hellenistic city "near Egypt" seems remarkably illustrated by the style of his writings and the radical fervor of his thoughts. Not a single line of Arius's meager literary remains is lacking technical clarity or artistic care. Recently, the short preamble to his *Thalia* was qualified by Rudolf Lorenz as a masterfully miniaturized piece of gnostic lyrics. What we know of Arius's letters in the earliest stages of the dogmatic crisis called after him, shows clear evidence of his gifts for carefully adapting his language to the given circumstances. More than anything else, the extracts of his *Thalia* produced by Athanasius witness to the well-educated attitude of a scholar trying to popularize in the age of his retirement some learned theological convictions. So much for Arius at the moment.[11]

Before any attempt to evaluate what it meant for Arius himself to become Arian, if one may speak so, we must briefly sketch the Athanasian anti-Arian reaction. I would point out in Arius's case a rather common intricacy linked with the history of doctrines during the centuries of the classical dogmatic Christianity. On one side, it is obvious that Arius must have singularized himself in a masterly fashion and that he became a public target in the current ideological debate of his local church. The question of Arius's self-understanding makes sense, as a matter of fact, only if one finds a valid access to that debate and to the singular figure that emerged from such a debate. On the other side, the broader dogmatic context of the ancient church imposes severe limitations on our handling of Arian primary sources. At a first glance, we know Arius only through the Athanasian anti-Arian literature. We meet primarily the figure of the heresiarch, thoughtfully carved and publicized by the men in power who con-

11. In my recent "Arius et les Ariens dans les *Contra Arianos,*" in my *Athanase d'Alexandrie évêque et écrivain: Une lecture des traités Contre les Ariens* (Paris: Beauchesne, 1983) 113–254.

demned Arius. Our critical access to the person of Arius as a leader and a teacher in the Alexandrian church of his time includes then a necessary detour through the writings of Athanasius, in which Arius is quoted and qualified in a unique way. The question is whether the "Arian" Arius, as conformed to the Athanasian reaction, obliterates completely for us the image of the pre-Arian and *true* Arius. With R. Gregg and D. Groh,[12] I would firmly answer this question in the negative. I should add that such an inquiry into the highly problematic testimony about Arius by Athanasius imposes a series of painstaking hermeneutical decisions, which makes it quite understandable that so many scholars prefer to profess their suspicion about Athanasius's judgment while at the same time neglecting to become familiar enough with his writings.

At this point I would limit my remarks to a very elementary view of Athanasius, just in order to explicate a little bit more what Arianism meant for him before it was codified in theological textbooks dominated by his orthodoxy. We will see that through the spontaneous position held by the Alexandrian bishop, as well as through Arius's intellectual and religious journey, we are led to identify the Arian crisis as rooted decisively in the vital institutions of Christianity in Egypt—to identify it as *the* Alexandrian crisis.

AN ELEMENTARY PORTRAIT OF ATHANASIUS, ALEXANDRIAN AND COPTIC

Going over to Athanasius, who could have been Arius's grandson, still in his teens when the famous priest and preacher was banished by his bishop, the cultural and ecclesiastical scene changes according to our sources, Greek or Coptic.[13]

A Coptic Kinship?

Athanasius's autobiographical tendency appears more than once in his apologies. It seems the more significant that he shows a complete lack of personal experience when he tries in his very first apology,

---

12. *Early Arianism: A View of Salvation* (Philadelphia: Fortress Press, 1981). I expressed some reservations on the view of the authors, in "Arius and the Arians," *TS* 44 (1983) 456–75, esp. 470–71.

13. See recent presentations of Athanasius by G. C. Stead, *DPAC* 1:413–32; and Martin Tetz, "Athanasius von Alexandrien," in *TRE* 4:333–49.

Contra Gentes,[14] to recall the state of the Alexandrian church in the bloody years of Diocletian's and Maximinus's persecution between 303 and 311. In the preliminary part of his *Life of Anthony*, where he does *not* say that he was living with the venerated hermit in his youth, as is wrongly understood by an old tradition resting on a misreading of the Greek, he nevertheless introduces himself as a devoted admirer of the hermit.[15] It is well known that he spent the best of his time during the first six years of his episcopate among the monastic circles and among the far distant Christian communities spread through the deserts and along the Nile, as well as along the Libyan border. These pastoral visits led him as far as Upper Egypt near the frontier of modern Sudan. Even better known is his dramatic escape to the desert and his hiding among the monks from 356 to 361 during his third exile. It is no surprise if these same monks became his best friends, to whom he dedicated almost all his writings, the dogmatic, the apologetic, as well as the historical ones. It is no surprise, either, if Athanasius chose from among their ranks the bishops he needed for the administration of his immense ecclesiastical territories.[16]

Only to mention it here, the first encounter with Athanasius after a quest for the true Arius leads one to breathe quite a different air. At the Ninth International Patristic Conference at Oxford, England, in September 1983, it was argued by G. H. Bebawi from the Coptic Orthodox Theological Seminary in Cairo that a later Coptic narrative, transmitted in an Arabic fragment, may well be right in locating Athanasius's birthplace in Upper Egypt and in making him a son of a Coptic, partly non-Christian, family. It seems to me hard, I should even say unthinkable, to doubt the Greek descent of Athanasius. But this legend, added to several similar monastic narratives, Pachomian and others, illus-

---

14. In Athanasius's final redaction, including earlier notes collected during the time of his theological training, *Contra Gentes* was coupled with the treatise *On the Incarnation* and published just before or after the exile in Trier (335–337); see Kannengiesser, "Le date de l'apologie d'Athanase *Contre les Païens* and *Sur l'Incarnation du Verbe*," *RechSR* 58 (1970) 383–428.

15. The *Life* was published about a year after Antony's death, that is, in 357. A valuable set of literary and doctrinal observations on the *Vita* has been published by M. Tetz, "Athanasius und die Vita Antonii: Literarische und theologische Relationen," *ZNW* 73 (1982) 1–30.

16. See his *Letter to Dracontius* (PG 25.523–34). The most important figure among the monks who became directly involved in the Athanasian administration was Serapion of Thmuis. Serapion replaced the exiled "pope" from 339 to 346, and Athanasius wrote, on his request, the *Letters on the Divinity of the Spirit* during his third exile, between 356 and 361.

trates the truly Egyptian popular dimension of Athanasius's personality.[17]

The sociological roots of Christianity in Egypt are thus exemplified by Arius and Athanasius in two complementary ways. There are, on the one side, the intellectual tensions of the inner-city life that molded, among many other philosophical "heresies," that which has come to be known as Arianism. On the other side, there is the strategy developed by Athanasius and characterized by his concern for the new monastic horizons of the Coptic hinterland. I already suggested that the political dimension of what is usually called the Arian crisis was, outside Alexandria itself, mainly created by the alliance established between the Arian party, founded in Alexandria, and the schismatic Meletian church, which originated in Upper Egypt. Athanasius, acting as the bishop of Alexandria, reversed this picture. He established the durable authority of his forty-five years in office on the ground of his spontaneous solidarity with Coptic Christianity, and he succeeded, surprisingly enough, in recuperating a majority of supporters among the former schismatic Meletian clerics.[18]

Thus we seem to be introduced into one of the fundamental structures of Christianity in Egypt, namely the constant and vital interplay between Christianity *as emerging from the cosmopolitan religiosity proper to the Hellenistic city of Alexandria* and Christianity *as bound to the spiritual landscape of the Nile valley.*[19]

The Anti-Arian Theologian

In my consideration of the Alexandrian crisis I would by no means exclude the tragic possibility of a complete misunderstanding of Arius by Athanasius. We see Athanasius coming on stage a long time (as much as twenty years, if the "long chronology" of the beginnings of Arianism in Alexandria is correct) after the canonical debate in the local church had ended with the defeat and the synodal rejection of Arius.

17. In particular, useful information is now available thanks to *Pachomian Koinonia: The Lives, Rules, and Other Writings of Saint Pachomius and His Disciples* (trans. Armand Veilleux; 3 vols.; Kalamazoo, Mich.: Cistercian Pubs., 1980–82).

18. According to Martin's statistical and prosopographic conclusions.

19. A comprehensive study of this vital structure of early Christianity in Alexandria and Egypt is still lacking. Penetrating views are shared by Carl Andresen ("Siegreiche Kirche im Aufstieg des Christentums: Untersuchungen zu Eusebius von Caesarea und Dionysios von Alexandrien," in *ANRW* 2.23.1:387–459) and Martin Krause ("Das christliche Alexandrien und seine Beziehungen zum koptischen Ägypten," in *Alexandrien: Kulturbegegnungen dreier Jahrtausende im Schmelztiegel einer mediterranen Grosstadt* [ed. Gunter Grimm; AegT 1; Mainz am Rhein: Von Zabern, 1981] 53–62).

Overwhelmed by the arguments opposed to the Arian view by Arius's earliest opponents among the Alexandrian clergy, and trusting sincerely the decision taken by Alexander against the Arian party, Athanasius could hardly be interested in the metaphysical presuppositions and the more or less esoteric teachings of the condemned and exiled priest, when he became himself a priest and in 328 a bishop.

In fact, all the writings of Athanasius, which he multiplied during his long lasting anti-Arian polemics, betray a complete lack of interest in the genuine theological theory of Arius. Even in his main works, the dogmatic *Treatises against the Arians*, written after ten years in office, it looks as if the spectacular quotations from Arius's *Thalia* had been added in the frame of a well-composed prologue to the treatises already completed. The technical, highly elaborated statements of the philosophical theologian Arius never became the real or immediate target of the pastoral politician and spiritual leader Athanasius, who reinforced the traditional Alexandrian catechesis against the second and third Arian generations of his time.[20]

Here again a constant structure of Egyptian Christianity seems to be exemplified. It looks as if the lack of dialogue and the cultural gap between Arius and Athanasius would illuminate two basic and opposite views of what Christian theology actually meant in this privileged part of the Constantinian empire.

Was Christian theology in Alexandrian terms synonymous with a systematic integration of specific beliefs into the cultural, highly sophisticated, frame of a philosophical attitude favored by the pluralistic abundance of local traditions? Or was Christian theology in fourth-century Alexandria demanding urgently a philosophically warranted but pastorally nontechnical exposition of the basic Christian catechesis?

In the historical dilemma of their opposing views, Arius as well as Athanasius, both as Alexandrian as possible, depended on Philo the Jew and Clement, the first great master of the Christian Didascalion in Alexandria. They are both direct offspring of Origen. They are also

---

20. I discussed at length the features of Athanasius's anti-Arian stance in *Athanase,* 113–254. A problem from an earlier stage of that discussion is treated in my *Holy Scripture and Hellenistic Hermeneutics in Alexandrian Christology: The Arian Crisis* (CHS 41; Berkeley: Graduate Theological Union, 1982), with responses by L. Abramowski, T. A. Kopecek, M. Slusser, and G. C. Stead. A complementary statement by the author about the "Blasphemies of Arius," wrongly attributed by Athanasius to Arius himself, may be found in "The Blasphemies of Arius: Athanasius of Alexandria, *De Synodis* 15," in *Arianism: Historical and Theological Reassessments* (ed. Robert C. Gregg; Papers from the Ninth International Conference on Patristic Studies, Oxford, September 5–10, 1983).

both open to the late classical culture and the more popular mysticism of their own time. Nevertheless, their paths diverged completely.

Arius, as a man trained in the spirit of the third century, conceived theology as a faith-filled scholarly exercise but one that became esoteric under the pressure of the transcendency that was the ultimate pole of his fascination. Arius adapted the teaching of the fifth *Ennead* about one generation after the death of Plotinus and he took the principles of this Plotinian teaching over according to his own Alexandrian Platonic register of metaphysics into the realm of Jewish Christian cosmology. Thus Arius emulated and yet at the same time defied, somehow, Origen and his systematic talk on God in *Peri Archon*. Appearing as the gifted intellectual here of the whole scholarly tradition of the Alexandrian church, Arius claimed knowledge and wisdom, and shared his access to divine revelation with inspired disciples. How could one imagine after the dark decade of the last imperial persecution in Alexandria, and on the threshold of the Constantinian era in the eastern part of the Roman empire, a more characteristic revival of the typical Alexandrian *teaching* hierarchy, going back to the very origins of Christianity in the great city "near Egypt"?

Facing such a remarkable figure, Athanasius, the anti-Arian theologian, appears as a man of the new century and of a new Christian generation, turned towards the official establishment of the church in the public life of the empire. He reminds us of Demetrius vs. Origen, of Dionysius vs. Sabellius, of Peter vs. Meletius, and above all of his immediate predecessor, Alexander—all men invested with the almost impossible pastoral duty of keeping Upper and Lower Egypt, the deserts and the Delta, the Cyrenaica and the Pentapolis, together in peace and unity.

Paradoxical as it may sound, the anti-Arian theologian in the episcopal office of Alexandria from 328 to 373 never became involved in a single and immediate showdown with Arius or with any of his first companions. He is not to be identified as only, and maybe he was not at all, the intellectual zealot eager to convert noble ladies in the salons of Alexandrian upper-class sympathizers—those sympathizers who outraged the imperial theologian Julian in 362, according to Julian's letter to the Alexandrian church, in sending the bishop into his fourth exile. Nor was Athanasius a member of the theological intelligentsia in the local Christian community, as Arius had been, and his intellectual capacities were not focused by the passion of metaphysical dialectics in the way fashionable among Alexandrian intellectuals of his time.

Athanasius had the common touch. Fighting against what was denounced to him as Arian propaganda and speaking from the background of a solid academic education, he addressed both the elite and the poor, the philosophers and the illiterate, among the highly diversified groups in his church. Being anti-Arian meant for him becoming the educator of a new generation of Christian believers, something quite beyond the theoretical speculations urgently needing clarification in the thought of Arius.

The thesis argued in this paper is that during the first three decades of the fourth century the tragic antagonism between Arius and Athanasius focused the decisive issues in the intricate and long-lasting process of reevaluating the Alexandrian-Christian self-definition. This process led to the last creative invention of new theological structures in Alexandria, the initiative by the audacious Arius, which may be compared to the task fulfilled in Rome and on a larger philosophical scale by Plotinus. After his move from Alexandria to Rome, not so long before Arius's time, Plotinus had built up a magisterial body of doctrines that was to become the last innovative system nurtured by the Platonic tradition. Athanasius opposed the Arian teaching, not at all in order to denounce its recognized protagonist, or in order to have him condemned. For he came more than a generation later, out of the popular Alexandrian hinterland, kin to Coptic and monastic mysticism, and pleading in favor of the basic catechesis traditional in the Alexandrian church. His ambition was, it seems to me, much more to give a voice to the silent majority in the local church he was responsible for than to engage in any speculative combat with the esoteric minority representing the Alexandrian followers of the exiled heresiarch. In his reaction, which was probably based on a deep misunderstanding of Arius's original project, Athanasius fixed for later generations the historical shape of the Arian crisis. He certainly did not intend to solve it so far as Arius's metaphysical teaching was concerned. The lack of real communication between those two powerful men, each of them devoted to the local church in his own passionate way, exemplifies the fourth-century crisis of the most genuine structure of Egyptian and Alexandrian Christianity.

13
DAVID W. JOHNSON, S.J.

Anti-Chalcedonian Polemics
in Coptic Texts,
451–641

INTRODUCTION

It has been thirty years since Maria Cramer and Heinrich Bacht published "Der antichalkedonische Aspekt im historisch-biographischen Schrifttum der koptischen Monophysiten (6.–7. Jahrhundert): Ein Beitrag zur Geschichte der Entstehung der monophysitischen Kirche Ägyptens."[1] The purpose of this paper is to augment their *Beitrag* by setting forth in summary what scholars have accomplished in this area since 1953. Suggestions for the direction further research might take, largely in the form of unanswered questions, and some observations based on my own research will be offered for consideration and criticism. Except for some references to inscriptions, archaeological data will not be treated, although Cramer and Bacht included a short section on this topic in their article. In that article, the authors point out that their treatment is not an exhaustive survey of Coptic sources, and as you will see presently, neither is this one. This is due to two factors: first, I make no claim to having uncovered every published Coptic source relating to Monophysite anti-Chalcedonian polemic; second, there no doubt remains a large amount of material in unpublished manuscripts that will further illuminate this important aspect of Coptic church history.

A great deal has been accomplished since 1953. Works Cramer and Bacht knew only from the inspection of unpublished manuscripts have since been edited or are being prepared for publication. A number of works, either unknown to them or simply passed over, have come to

---

1. *Das Konzil von Chalkedon: Geschichte und Gegenwart* (ed. Alois Grillmeier and Heinrich Bacht; 3 vols.; Würzburg: Echter, 1951–54) 2:315–38.

light and again have either been published or are forthcoming. Examples of the first sort are A. Alcock's edition of the Sahidic text of the *Life of Samuel of Kalamūn*[2] and the forthcoming edition of the life of Abraham of Pboou being prepared by James Goehring.[3] Examples of the second sort are more numerous. Tito Orlandi has edited the life of Apa Longinus, one of the preeminent Monophysite heroes.[4] His edition of the second *Encomium on Athanasius* contains a short polemical passage of great interest.[5] And finally, there is his extensive work on the Coptic sources for the Arabic *History of the Patriarchs of Alexandria*, with both edited texts and a commentary that, among other things, relates the latter part of the Coptic *History of the Church* to other important anti-Chalcedonian works.[6] An expanded and revised edition of these texts has been announced by Orlandi. Another text with an important and fairly lengthy anti-Chalcedonian polemic embedded within it is the *Panegyric on Apollo* by Stephen of Hnēs.[7] My edition of the *Panegyric on Macarius of Tkōw*[8] by Ps.-Dioscorus adds two Sahidic recensions of an almost totally polemical work, the incomplete Bohairic version of which was published by Amélineau.[9] I am also in the final stages of collecting the unedited fragments of the life of Apa Zenobius, the alleged successor to Apa Besa as abbot of the White Monastery. This work has some interesting remarks on the actual writing of polemical literature in a segment already published by Walter Till without any commentary. Most of these works will be referred to again in the latter part of the paper.

An indispensable tool for anyone pursuing the kind of research being discussed here is the second part of Tito Orlandi's *Elementi di lingua e letteratura copta* (Milan: La Goliardica, 1970). It is the closest thing we possess to a work like Ortiz de Urbina's *Patrologia Syriaca*,

2. *Life of Samuel of Kalamūn* (ed. A. Alcock; Warminster: Aris & Phillips, 1983).
3. See Antonella Campagnano, "Monaci egiziani fra V e VI secolo," *VetChr* 15 (1978) 223–46, which lists the extant texts and gives a summary of their contents. See also the reference to these texts in T. Orlandi, "Coptic Biblical and Ecclesiastical Literature," in *The Future of Coptic Studies* (ed. R. McL. Wilson; Leiden: E. J. Brill, 1978) 157–58.
4. *Vita dei monaci Phif e Longino* (ed. T. Orlandi; TDSA 51; Milan: Cisalpino, 1975).
5. Constantini episcopi urbis Siout, *Encomia in Athanasium duo* (CSCO 349/350, 1974).
6. *Storia della chiesa di Alessandria* (2 vols.; TDSA 17, 21; Milan: Cisalpino, 1967–70, and *Studi copti* (TDSA 22; Milan: Cisalpino, 1968).
7. Stephen, bishop of Heracleopolis Magna, *A Panegyric on Apollo, Archimandrite of the Monastery of Isaac* (ed. K. H. Kuhn; CSCO 394/395, 1978).
8. Ps.-Dioscorus, *Panegyric on Macarius of Tkōw* (ed. D. W. Johnson; CSCO 415/416, 1980).
9. E. Amélineau, "Panégyrique de Macaire de Tkoou," in *Monuments pour servir à l'histoire de l'Egypte chrétienne aux IVe et Ve siècles* (Memoires: Mission arachéologique française au Caire 4.1; Paris: Leroux, 1888) 92–164.

and its importance is highlighted by the extensive citations found in Martin Krause's article on Coptic literature in the *Lexicon der Ägyptologie* (2:694–728).

In light of all this recent scholarly activity, it is also possible and desirable to return to earlier publications and scrutinize them anew. One area that calls for systematic attention is the collection of works and fragments relating to Dioscorus of Alexandria. Bentley Layton has informed me that there is additional material relating to Dioscorus among the British Library fragments he has catalogued. A continuing study of the relationships between the Coptic texts and the extant Syriac material should throw more light on the relationship between these two branches of the Monophysite movement. Since several unpublished Arabic translations of the *Panegyric on Macarius of Tkōw* are extant, and lost Coptic works are known to be preserved in the *History of the Patriarchs*, one suspects the area of Christian Arabic literature will prove to be a rich source from which to fill the gaps in our knowledge of the situation in Egypt during the two centuries following Chalcedon. Its only partially tapped resources are currently the focus of research for a number of scholars.

TERMINOLOGY

The most important terminological difficulty involves the use of the word "Monophysite." Cramer and Bacht use the expressions "writings of the Coptic Monophysites" and "origins of the Monophysite church in Egypt" in the title of their article. Few people today are satisfied with the word, not least among whom are those Eastern Christians to whom it has been customarily applied. W. H. C. Frend addresses the problem and concludes that, although the word is a later coinage (it is not in G. W. H. Lampe's *Patristic Greek Lexicon*) and does little justice to the concrete historical situation of the fifth to seventh centuries, it should be retained in order to avoid cumbrous circumlocutions.[10] An alternative is "anti-Chalcedonian," but this too has the disadvantage of including more points of view than intended. In the polemics with which we are dealing, the adversaries include not only the leftists or adherents of Chalcedon and their Nestorian allies, but also the extreme right, or extreme Monophysites as they are sometimes called, namely

---

10. W. H. C. Frend, *The Rise of the Monophysite Movement* (2d rev. ed.; Cambridge: Cambridge Univ. Press, 1979) xiii.

the Julianists, Gainites, and Eutychians. These latter were also anti-Chalcedonian but were rejected by the party that followed Archbishop Timothy II Aelurus and his successors. Our topic is the polemical literature of this last group. Merely for the sake of convenience, then, the term "Monophysite" will be retained to designate the Egyptian Christian majority who rejected the Council of Chalcedon and gave allegiance to the non-Melkite succession of patriarchs of Alexandria whose legitimacy is attested by the *History of the Patriarchs* and who are referred to in our Coptic texts simply as "the orthodox." A more accurate term is a desideratum.[11]

Besides the doctrinal division within Egypt, other divisions are at least hinted at in the Coptic texts or have some grounding in the Greek sources.[12] Some of these other possible divisions are urban (i.e., Alexandrian) versus rural (i.e., Egyptian proper),[13] Lower versus Upper Egypt, Greek-speaking versus Coptic-speaking,[14] landowners versus the rural peasantry,[15] secular clergy versus monks (which may be reducible to clergy versus laity),[16] and Greens versus Blues.[17] This list is probably not exhaustive, and I have not tested fully the validity of all the divisions mentioned and how they correlate with one another and with the religious controversies of the period in question. Perhaps such a study will add intelligibility to some of our texts. While it is certainly

11. Perhaps "Egyptian Orthodox" would suffice since it uses the designation "orthodox" defined by an adjective that encompasses both Greek- and Coptic-speaking Egyptians and reflects the situation during the period before the Arab conquest.

12. See the suggestions of Michael Brett ("The Arab Conquest of Egypt and the Rise of Islam in North Africa," in *The Cambridge History of Africa* [8 vols.; Cambridge: Cambridge Univ. Press, 1978] 2:497).

13. Discussed in numerous articles by H. I. Bell; cf. Bell, "Alexandria," *JEA* 13 (1927) 171–84; and idem, *Egypt from Alexander the Great to the Arab Conquest* (Oxford: Clarendon Press, 1948). The designation "Alexandria ad Aegyptum" typifies the Roman attitude. In reference to the consecration of Timothy II Aelurus, Zacharias Scholasticus (*Chronicle of Zachariah Scholasticus* [trans. F. J. Hamilton and E. W. Brooks; London: Methuen & Co., 1899] 64) says, "For at that time, Dionysius the general was not there [i.e., in Alexandria], but was on a visit to Egypt."

14. The distinction is highlighted in the *Panegyric on Macarius of Tkōw* (ed. Johnson) 2–4, 11.

15. For works covering this question in our period, see Bell, *Egypt*, 162. The earlier period is now covered by Naphtali Lewis, *Life in Egypt Under Roman Rule* (Oxford: Clarendon Press, 1983), which goes up to 285 C.E.

16. Frend, *Monophysite Movement*, 143–44; and Besa, *Life of Shenoute* (trans. D. Bell; Kalamazoo, Mich.: Cistercian Pubs., 1983) 62–63 and 78, where Nestorius says to Shenoute, "What business do you have in this synod? You yourself are certainly not a bishop, nor are you an archimandrite or a superior, but only a monk!"

17. Alan Cameron, *Circus Factions: Blues and Greens at Rome and Byzantium* (Oxford: Clarendon Press, 1976) esp. chap. 6 ("Religious Sympathies of the Factions"), where the author concludes that there was no correlation between a given faction and a set of religious beliefs.

a mistake to reduce religious controversies to social or political struggles, it is equally naive to ignore these other factors and pretend that doctrine develops or decays in some sort of ideal vacuum.

LITERARY TYPES AND RECURRENT THEMES

For the purpose of this paper, "polemic" refers to the type of literature that seeks to justify a position by presenting it in the best possible light, and more especially by presenting the adversaries' positions in the worst possible light, even to the point of outright distortion. If not totally adequate, this is at least an approximate characterization of the kinds of defensive writings produced by the Monophysite party that survive in Coptic. In their polemics, the Monophysites are no different from other religious groups throughout history who have had to engage in controversy.

The polemics appear in various literary guises. I know of no preconquest polemic that bears a title like "The Treatise of Our Holy Father So-and-So Against the Council of Chalcedon." Instead the polemics are either the dominant component or are embedded in histories, the lives of holy men, and hagiographical or topical sermons. Of the histories we have only one surviving Coptic example, *The History of the Church in Twelve Books*. It may be the only example unless the sections of the *History of the Patriarchs* attributed to George the Syncellus and those following him were composed in Coptic and not Greek and were originally histories rather than biographies. The Coptic *History of the Church* is certainly a polemical work in its later chapters, so much so that it is virtually useless as an objective historical source. Real events are distorted, though perhaps through ignorance rather than by design, while other reported events are total fabrications. That the bulk of the *History of the Church* covers events prior to the Council of Chalcedon, beginning with the foundation of the Egyptian church by Saint Mark, and only devotes the last few chapters (down to the restoration of Timothy II in 475) to the post-Chalcedonian period, is no reason to restrict our examination to only the last few chapters. To the contrary, much of the earlier material is crucial to the polemic against Chalcedon, especially the prestige and authority implied by the Markan foundation of the church, the struggle between Athanasius and the Arians at the Council of Nicea and afterwards, and the conflict between Cyril and Nestorius. These form the backdrop against which the polemics must be viewed. Chalcedon, especially as represented by the *Tome* of Pope Leo, is consistently characterized as a rejection of the faith of Nicea as expounded by Athanasius and a capitulation to the Nestorianism condemned by Cyril, albeit a Nestorianism that would probably have been rejected by Nestorius.

The overall theme is expounded at great length in one of the major surviving hagiographic polemics, the *Panegyric on Macarius of Tkōw* by Ps.-Dioscorus. This popular work is exceptional among the polemical hagiographical sermons produced after Chalcedon in that it involves the violent death of the main character precisely because he rejects the Council and the *Tome*. Its tone is highly dramatic, and its numerous episodes leave the reader with little doubt about the Coptic stance on Chalcedon. Macarius is clearly meant to speak for the Copts in a way that the Greek-speaking Dioscorus cannot do. Other hagiographic works survive that to a lesser extent make use of anti-Chalcedonian polemic, and they span the whole period we are dealing with. One with a lengthy polemical section is the *Panegyric on Apollo* by Stephen of Hnēs. The section is too long to summarize here.[18] It is written in reaction to the new offensive launched by the emperor Justinian to force a Chalcedonian settlement throughout the empire. Unlike other polemical pieces, it is not woven into some dramatic scene but stands separately, as though it were lifted from a theological discourse.

Other works record shorter episodes. The *Life of Apa Longinus* recounts what is probably the archetypal confrontation between an Egyptian and imperial authorities over the acceptance of the *Tome* of Leo.[19] It is also one of the most dramatic, featuring an interrogation of the bones of the departed fathers. Their voiced rejection of the *Tome* is decisive. Similar confrontation stories involving the *Tome* are found in the lives of Daniel of Scetis, Abraham of Phbow, Apa Moses, and Samuel of Kalamūn. Of a slightly different type is the second *Encomium on Athanasius* by Constantine of Siout, where the polemic is broadened to include the Phantasiasts who were pressing the Monophysites on their other flank. The author addresses Athanasius:

> It is not only the Arians whose mouths you have shut through your discourses, but others as well who have become traitors to the Faith; I mean those who assembled at the Synod of Chalcedon, those who

18. See *A Panegyric on Apollo* (ed. Kuhn; CSCO 394) xiv, for a summary of this section; 13–19, for the Coptic text (trans., CSCO 395:10–14). On p. 12 of the translation is a good example of the standardized confession of Monophysite christological belief, one or several of which confessions appear in almost all our texts.

19. *Phif e Longino* (ed. Orlandi), 78–89; also found in *Macarius of Tkōw* (ed. Johnson; CSCO 415) 70–78 (trans., CSCO 416:54–59).

dissolved the unity of the entire world daring to divide into two natures after the union this Indivisible One, God the Word, who took flesh for our salvation; and these who have gone mad with the madness of Mani, Valentinus, Marcion, Apollinaris, and Eutyches, unto Julian the wretched elder, that is, the Manichaean Phantasiasts.[20]

Finally, mention must be made of the important *Synodicon* of Archbishop Damianus of Alexandria, which, in its Coptic form, constitutes what amounts to a theological sermon in defense of Monophysite Christology.[21] It will be discussed later in a different context.

Besides these Coptic texts, there is a group of texts that seem to have existed in Coptic in some form, because fragments of them have survived in that language. One, the *Life of Dioscorus* by Ps.-Theopistus, survives in a complete Syriac version translated from the Greek.[22] The Coptic fragments probably come not from a complete version but from one that extracted material that pertained to Egypt.[23] Or it may simply represent a different recension. The same may be true of the minuscule fragments of the *Plerophoriai* of John of Maiuma.[24] Another fragment, which Evelyn White thinks is from a life of Timothy II, borrows heavily from, if it is not an outright translation of, the *Life of Peter the Iberian*.[25] These texts are valuable not only for the added light they throw on the kind of polemical literature available to Coptic readers but also because they are part of the pool of material from which subsequent Egyptian polemics took their form and sometimes their content. From the viewpoint of Coptic polemics all roads seem to lead back to the *Plerophoriai* and probably beyond that to the recollections of Timothy II. Peter the Iberian, whose reminiscences contributed substantially to the *Plerophoriai*, was in Alexandria in 455 and again from 457 to 474. He knew Timothy II, helped consecrate him in fact, and had almost three years to consult with Timothy personally before the latter's exile in 460. It is difficult to imagine that he was not privy to letters that Timothy sent from his place of exile. From the *Plerophoriai*, then, there emerges the basic stance and structure, the tradition

20. My translation of *Encomia in Athanasium duo* (CSCO 349) 36.21–37.2.

21. H. E. Winlock and W. E. Crum, *The Monastery of Epiphanius* (2 vols.; New York: Metropolitan Museum, 1926) 2:148–52 (trans., 2:331–37).

22. F. Nau, ed., *JA* 1 (1903) 1–108 and 241–311.

23. This is the conclusion of W. E. Crum ("Coptic Texts Relating to Dioscorus of Alexandria," *PSBA* 25 [1903] 267–76).

24. W. E. Crum, *Theological Texts from Coptic Papyri* (Oxford: Clarendon Press, 1913) 62–63. Some Coptic book lists attribute this work to Peter the Iberian.

25. H. G. Evelyn White, *The Monasteries of Wadi 'n Natrun* (3 vols.; New York: Metropolitan Museum, 1932) 1:164–67.

Egyptian Monophysite polemics were to follow down to the Arab conquest and beyond: a firm adherence to the teachings of Cyril of Alexandria as interpreted by Dioscorus and Timothy over against the Nestorian Chalcedonian doctrine, and a rejection of Eutychianism and similar beliefs. Onto this basic structure the Egyptian writers grafted characters and stories indigenous to Egypt. These stories were no doubt meant to enhance the role of Egypt, especially the role of the Copts, in the unfolding of the struggle against the Chalcedonians. Thus, formidable characters and newsworthy events appear that either found no place in Greek histories of the time or are related in a quite different form from that found in the Greek sources. An example of the former is the story of the confrontation between Shenoute and Nestorius at the Council of Ephesus,[26] and of the latter, the divergent accounts of the exile of Nestorius in Evagrius Scholasticus and the Coptic *History of the Church*.[27]

The polemics seem to fall into three major periods: those composed in the first quarter of the sixth century, when the main focus is the Council of Chalcedon and its immediate aftermath; those from the mid- to late sixth century written in reaction to Justinian's religious policies; and finally, those written in reaction to the religious policies of Heraclius, especially the persecution launched by his vicar in Egypt, Cyrus al-Mukaukas, the repercussions of which are discernible in works written after the Arab conquest. Dating any given work is problematic, and we must usually resign ourselves to identifying *termini ante quem* or decades and quarters of centuries at best. The time during which the first polemical pieces congealed, as it were, into the written form we now possess seems to be the first half of the fifth century. Perhaps this marks the initial reaction to the incipient neo-Chalcedonian offensive begun by Justin I and Justinian after the death of the tolerant Anastasius in 518. It also marked the beginning of Severus of Antioch's exile in Egypt. Might not these texts, woven from separate stories drawn from various locales inside and outside Egypt, mark the beginnings of a sense of real separation and alienation from the imperial church, a decision to gather one's traditions into historical-

26. Besa, *Life of Shenoute* (trans. David N. Bell; Kalamazoo, Mich.: Cistercian Pubs., 1983) 78–79.
27. Evagrius Scholasticus, *Ecclesiastical History* (ed. J. Bidez and L. Parmentier; London: Methuen & Co., 1898) 12–16; also D. W. Johnson, "Further Fragments of a Coptic History of the Church: Cambridge Or. 1699R," *Enchoria* 6 (1976) 15.

doctrinal syntheses based on the *isnad* that goes back from John of Maiuma through Peter the Iberian to Timothy II? In the process, typically Coptic figures were introduced into the stories, either as main characters or as figures mentioned in passing. Other stories circulating at that time inside Egypt found their way into the biographies, sermons, and the *History of the Church.* Examples include the confrontation between the exiled Nestorius and Shenoute at Shmin,[28] and the consultation between Longinus and the bones of the fathers.[29] A stock cast of villains appeared in the earlier stages: Marcian and Pulcheria, Pope Leo, Proterius, Juvenal of Jerusalem, and later on they are joined by Justinian, Julian of Halicarnassus, and Cyrus al-Mukaukas. Of the earlier villains, Marcian and Leo continue to appear in later works. Opposition to Pope Leo in the guise of his *Tome* is one of the most persistent negative constants in the polemical literature. Dioscorus, Macarius of Tkōw, Longinus, Daniel of Scetis, Samuel of Kalamūn are all commanded to subscribe to the *Tome* of Leo. Many scholars have noted how Egyptian opposition focused not so much on the conciliar decrees but on this hated document. All of the Monophysite confessors refuse to submit, while giving short speeches that set forth the error of Leo's position and defend the orthodoxy of Monophysite Christology. The consequences are variously exile, physical abuse, and in one case, death. The most conspicuous positive constant throughout the polemics is the appeal to the Council of Nicea. Even the opposition is aware of the esteem in which the teachings of this council are held by Egyptians, especially the monks. When the imperial courier confronts Macarius of Tkōw with the decrees of Chalcedon, he tries to convince the bishop that they conform to Nicea. But Macarius rejects this out of hand and is killed.[30] In this context of dramatic confrontations, we find the short rudimentary confessions of faith that are another constant found in the polemics. These formulas persist throughout the post-Chalcedonian period, and their consistency is witness to the constancy of the Coptic Monophysites in the face of what they perceived to be blatantly erroneous doctrinal innovations perpetrated without justification.[31]

28. Johnson, "Further Fragments," 15; also *Macarius of Tkōw* (ed. Johnson; CSCO 415) 102–4; (CSCO 416) 79–80.

29. *Phif e Longino* (ed. Orlandi) 79–89; also *Macarius of Tkōw* (CSCO 415) 70–78; (CSCO 416) 54–59.

30. *Macarius of Tkōw* (CSCO 415) 122–23; (CSCO 416) 95–96.

31. For some examples of the formulas, see W. E. Crum, "A Coptic Palimpsest," *PSBA* 19 (1897) 219–20; and idem, "Dioscorus," *PSBA* 25 (1903) 272. See also William H. P.

The variable elements found in the polemics give us clues, however tenuous, about the provenience of the various strands of the traditions as well as the approximate dating for some of the works. Stories about someone like Shenoute almost certainly indicate the White Monastery as a source, although the composition into which they are finally incorporated might originate elsewhere. Works that make no mention of Justinian should probably be dated prior to his reign or at least before a firm opinion of him had been established. Mention of him or some other later figure of course indicates a late sixth- or early seventh-century composition, as was pointed out above. One must also consider the use of certain Greek and Latin technical terminology, either ecclesiastical or civil, that might help to date a work. Such, for example, is the use of the word "Theopascite" that seems to be attested no earlier than 519. This is not to say that much or even most of the traditions embodied in a work may not be much earlier than the date suggested for the final redaction.

Besides what can be called obvious polemical texts, there are other less obvious examples of polemic and its influence in Coptic literature. These might be termed subliminal blips that go unnoticed save for a careful scrutiny of the text. One example is brought out in the work of James Goehring on the *Life of Pachomius*,[32] where he detects an attitude toward the notions of heresy and orthodoxy that reflects a post-Chalcedonian *Sitz im Leben*. Another is set forth in Harold Drake's examination of the Eudoxia legend, where he detects the possibility of the appropriation or modification of the legend to bolster the prestige of Egyptian Monophysitism in the period of Heraclius.[33] Both these examples point to the necessity of looking beyond overtly polemical material for clues about the nature and development of Monophysite self-consciousness. What, for example, might be tucked away in the Coptic translation of a sermon attributed to one of the fathers that says something about a question from the post-Chalcedonian point of view? A choice of words, perhaps, or an interpolation? This is an area for further investigation.

Hatch, "A Fragment of a Lost Work on Dioscorus," *HTR* 19 (1926) 378, for a fragment that the author thinks might have Monothelite overtones; also see the formulas preserved in John of Nikiu, *Chronicle* (trans. R. H. Charles; London and Oxford: Williams & Norgate, 1916) 126–29, 146–47, 148–49.

32. James Goehring, "Pachomius' Vision of Heresy: The Development of a Pachomian Tradition," *Muséon* 95 (1982) 241–62.

33. H. Drake, B. A. Pearson, and T. Orlandi, *Eudoxia and the Holy Sepulchre* (TDSA 48; Milan: Cisalpino, 1980) 85–179.

THE ROLE OF THE COPTIC LANGUAGE

The question of the original language of the polemics is a particular instance of the question whether a given work was composed in Coptic or translated from the Greek. The older question of whether any original Coptic literature existed at all has been settled. But there is an abundance of translation literature, and it still remains necessary in each instance, especially for earlier works, to attempt to decide whether a given text with no known Greek *Vorlage* was composed in Coptic or simply translated from a Greek source that was subsequently lost when Egypt de-Hellenized. No sure test has been devised for making such a determination with anything approaching certitude, but some criteria have been suggested. Reymond and Barns[34] suggest that if a text is not intended to have any circulation or interest outside Egypt, it may well have been composed in Coptic. Otherwise it was probably composed in Greek. One might add that a biography of a holy man or a work, especially if it is from Upper Egypt, may have been originally Coptic. But there is a cautionary note. Crum points out that the Coptic text of the *Synodicon* of Damianus, which is extant in Syriac, seems to have been shorn of non-Egyptian references, and even the original purpose of the piece seems to have been changed so that it resembles a homiletic work rather than a letter.[35] Was this technique widespread among Coptic translators? If so it would tend to detract from the value of the Reymond-Barns rule of thumb. Kuhn applies this rule to the *Panegyric on Apollo* with interesting implications for our present topic.[36] If the text is meant primarily to be a life of Apollo, then he thinks that it could have been composed in Coptic. If, however, it is meant to be a polemic against Chalcedon, then it was probably meant for a wider public and was composed in Greek. That Kuhn ties polemic to Greek composition is significant. As we have already proposed, the anti-Chalcedonian works or polemical interludes found in Coptic texts seem to be derived from prototypes composed in Greek and to have passed pretty much intact into later compositions, even where one might expect original Coptic composition. Other indications of a Greek original might be a play on words that makes sense only in Greek (the converse would of course suggest Coptic), constructions that are

---

34. E. A. E. Reymond and J. W. B. Barns, *Four Martyrdoms from the Pierpont Morgan Coptic Codices* (Oxford: Clarendon Press, 1973) 18–19.
35. Winlock and Crum, *Epiphanius* 2:331.
36. *A Panegyric on Apollo* (ed. Kuhn; CSCO 394) xi.

awkward in Coptic but explainable by an assumed Greek *Vorlage*, and apparent breakdowns in the Coptic translation that result in varying degrees of unintelligibility. Birger Pearson has suggested the possibility of a Coptic original for *Eudoxia and the Holy Sepulchre*, based on an analysis of Greek and Latin loanwords and "the total absence of any linguistic hint of translation Coptic—such as frozen oblique forms or prepositional phrases." But in a footnote at the end of the introduction, the text's editor, Tito Orlandi, gives a contrary opinion: "Actually the non-Chalcedonian literature in Egypt seems to have been produced mainly in Greek at the beginning. I would rather place the Eudoxia legend in that category, and consider our text a translation from the Greek."[37] Since the text is dated to the seventh century, I assume that "at the beginning" includes the period 451–641. Neither scholar is suggesting that his case is airtight. Each has simply stated what slim evidence there is in this case and drawn different tentative conclusions from it. A further remark of Kuhn's with reference to the *Panegyric on Apollo* might sum up the situation. After giving reasons why this text might be either a Greek or Coptic original, he says:

> More subjectively, long and close study of the work has left me with the impression that the author's thought and language show strong Greek influence. How then are these opposing views to be reconciled? Is it possible to suggest that the author was bi-lingual, that he was imbued with the Greek language and thought, but that he composed the work for a Coptic-speaking audience in Coptic? This hypothesis, although at first sight somewhat artificial, is by no means unthinkable in the context of a strongly bi-lingual Byzantine Egypt.[38]

The historian will no doubt like to know how bilingual Egypt was in terms of even rough percentages, classes of people, and regions. Evidence again is slight. There were bishops in 451 who did not know Greek. Kalosirius of Arsinoe and Macarius of Tkōw are two examples.[39] In the eighth century, Bishop Abraham wrote only Coptic, but some of his monks still knew Greek.[40] No doubt the agrarian workers who were the majority spoke only Coptic. But what about the skilled artisans and the monks? It is often suggested that Coptic held more sway in Upper Egypt than in the Delta, but can this be substantiated? Even Shenoute,

---

37. Drake, Pearson, and Orlandi, *Eudoxia*, 17–19.
38. *A Panegyric on Apollo* (CSCO 394) xi–xii.
39. For Kalosarius, see Mansi 6.856, 923.
40. *Greek Papyri in the British Museum* (ed. F. G. Kenyon; 5 vols.; London: British Museum, 1893) 231–36.

everyone's archetypal Copt, was possessed of a Greek education of some sort.

Assuming, as I do, that the Coptic Monophysite polemics we possess were composed in Greek, the question arises, Were these translations produced at the behest of the Greek-speaking establishment to indoctrinate the Coptic-speaking population? Or did some bilingual Copts translate the material on their own initiative to demonstrate their loyalty to the Alexandrian patriarchate and to instruct their brethren? I can offer no evidence for the actual process of transmission from the Greek. But my investigations of the *Panegyric on Macarius of Tkōw* have led me to conclude that, at least in this case, there is evidence that a Greek writer composed a work instructing his readers on the doctrinal stance that they should take, and that this instruction was then translated into Coptic. In commenting on the *Synodicon* of Damianus, Crum makes the following relevant observation: "We have no evidence to show whether patriarchal documents such as these were sent from Alexandria already translated, or whether the Coptic version was made at Thebes."[41] I think that the same must be said about the polemical texts that originated in circles centered on the patriarchate and the monasteries in or around Alexandria.

We have already mentioned that group of Coptic fragments that seem to be adapted translations of works otherwise attested only in Syriac. The fact that they exist either as fragments of codices or as entries in Coptic book lists indicates that they were available to Coptic readers. They should therefore be included in the broader data pool of works to be examined by anyone who is interested in studying the origins and development of Egyptian Monophysitism. The wealth of still-unedited Syriac manuscripts makes the possibility of further such finds a reasonable expectation. Even already-published Syriac material might yield a heretofore unnoticed matchup with one of the numerous Coptic fragments already published or with those that await study.

A final group of texts that must be considered and that indeed has been examined are those texts which are thought to have had Coptic antecedents but that survive only in Arabic and Ethiopic. The obvious examples, already alluded to above, are those parts of the Arabic *History of the Patriarchs of Alexandria* that predate the translation project initiated by Severus of Ashmunein, and at least portions of the *Chronicle* of John of Nikiu. One must also add the Arabic synaxaries to

---

41. Winlock and Crum, *Epiphanius* 2:332.

this list, as well as those that survive in Ethiopic. Other possible Ethiopic sources are the *Anathemas* and the treatise *On the Orthodox Faith* by John of al-Burullus that are preserved in several manuscripts of the *Hāimānōta 'Abaw*.[42]

This wider casting of the net takes us beyond Coptology strictly defined, but for the benefit of the historian intent on gathering all possible information on the Coptic Monophysite movement, it is clearly a necessary step.

HISTORICAL VALUE AND THEOLOGICAL SOPHISTICATION

Historians have not always been kind to Coptic Christianity in general and the theological endeavors of the Copts in particular. Preeminent in this regard is Jean Maspero. In his *Histoire de patriarches d'Alexandrie*, which covers the period 518-616, he saves some of his harshest criticism for Coptic anti-Chalcedonian polemics.[43] He says, and I am paraphrasing, that the very extensive theological literature of the Copts does not possess a single work of value or even of simple mediocrity; that the *Panegyric on Macarius of Tkōw* contains an abundance of dogmatic discussions whose childishness is only equaled by their pomposity; that the *History of the Patriarchs*, when it dares to dogmatize, demonstrates mean intelligence—its account of the response of Patriarch Damianus to Peter of Antioch being characterized as inconceivable balderdash. In another place, Maspero states that the indigenous literature consists of crudely composed apocrypha and lives of saints. The bishops were for the most part rough-hewn, ignorant peasants with little talent for training their flocks by their example. Historians who accept Maspero's views will hardly be tempted to devote much time to the study of the texts that we are discussing. Maspero's remarks force us to focus on the last topic, namely the question about the historical worth and the theological sophistication of these texts. It should be pointed out that we have a good deal more material at our disposal than Maspero did in 1915. But if he were able to inspect the texts that have appeared since his time, I suspect that his conclusions would be pretty much the same. The

---

42. W. Wright, *Catalogue of Ethiopic MSS in the British Museum* (London: British Museum, 1877) 234-35.

43. Completed in 1915, revised and published posthumously by A. Fortescue and G. Wiet (Paris: Champion, 1923); see esp. 17-18, 51.

Coptic texts that we are discussing are not at all sophisticated or subtle.[44] Nor are they of great historical value in the older, more traditional sense. The dialogues among the various adversaries are often crude and throw little objective light on anything but the bare essentials of the controversies of the day. The theological positions of opponents are often badly distorted, sometimes entirely erroneous. What we have is not enlightened dialogue or sophisticated controversy but crude propaganda couched in highly affect-laden language. Dogmatic formulas are embedded in stories of exile, persecution, and even racism. One might easily conclude then that such literature has no historical value, but only if one's view of historical value is limited to studying the antics of the upper-class establishment, ecclesiastical and civil, as told by its own members. The historical value of a piece must be determined in part by determining the audience for which it is intended. Simply ignoring such material after comparing it with the best available works constricts the scope of history. Fortunately today, due to the work of people like Arthur Darby Nock and, more recently, Peter Brown, attention has been focused on the religion of the uneducated masses in whatever part of the empire they dwelt. That Coptic-speaking Christians, with few exceptions, belonged to this underclass is generally accepted and has been pointed out as early as A. J. Butler in his *Arab Conquest of Egypt*, where he defends the Copts as a group against accusations that they betrayed Egypt to the Muslims by demonstrating that they were in no position, socially or economically, to influence Byzantine government policy one way or the other.[45] Certainly under the Romans and Byzantines there seem to have been sharp curbs on any kind of upward mobility. This, coupled with the declining economy of Egypt and the concentration of property in a few hands, kept the Coptic-speaking majority in a kind of agrarian servitude not unfamiliar in our own day in many parts of the world. Added to this are indications of racial prejudice in various forms: disparagement of the Coptic language, of the Coptic character, and of the Coptic ability to think abstractly, or even to think at all, as illustrated by the remark of one Anastasius the Sinaite who talks about "intelligences of

44. This is not to say that sophisticated material was not available to Coptic readers. There were translations of authentic patristic texts; see, for example, R. G. Coquin and E. Lucchesi, "Une version copte du *de anima et resurrectione* ("Macrina") de Grégoire de Nysse," *OLP* 12 (1981) 161–201.

45. A. J. Butler, *Arab Conquest of Egypt* (ed. P. M. Fraser; 2d rev. ed.; Oxford: Clarendon Press, 1978).

the Egyptian type, that neither know nor comprehend things."[46] We do have examples of anti-intellectualism among the monks as is shown, for example, by the works of Shenoute, even though he seems to have had some form of Greek education. Crum points out that in western Thebes there is very little evidence that the Coptic monks were interested in theological questions except for some theological texts that were copied on the walls of a tomb. Rather, the Coptic clergy and laity seemed to be content with religious practice without much concern for theorizing, drawing appropriate material from the Bible. An almost fundamentalist biblicism was the touchstone of their daily lives. What was not in the Bible was suspect, as had been dramatized during the dispute between Theophilus and the monks over anthropomorphism and between Cyril and the monks over the term *Theotokos*.[47] In both instances the patriarchs defused monastic opposition in ways that might be viewed variously as cynical, deceptive, brilliant, or pastorally sensitive, depending on the viewpoint of the observer. However inadequate their replies might seem to us or to contemporary writers who recorded them, the tactic worked and most probably set a precedent for the way in which the controversies after Chalcedon were handled by the Monophysite patriarchate when dealing with the monks and the common people.

If one is willing to accept the picture of the Coptic-speaking majority sketched out above, there still remains the question—perhaps unanswerable—whether the quality of Coptic theological literature in general and anti-Chalcedonian polemics in particular is such because that is what the Copts consciously chose to produce or were willing to accept, going back to their alleged anti-intellectualism, or whether it is because this was what was filtered down from the establishment to conform with the educational level of the intended recipients. Were those Copts who were bilingual any less inclined to rely on the kind of polemics that have survived in Coptic? Shenoute comes to mind again. W. H. C. Frend says this about Shenoute:

With him one can detect the growth of a self-conscious Coptic spirit

---

46. Quotation from Alexander Badawy, *Coptic Art and Archaeology: The Art of the Christian Egyptians from Late Antiquity to the Middle Ages* (Cambridge: M.I.T. Press, 1978) 13.

47. For the former, see White, *Wadi 'n Natrun*, 125–44. For the latter, see Frend, *Monophysite Movement*, 139; and Cyril of Alexandria's epistle to the monks (ep. 1) in *Acta conciliorum oecumenicorum* (ed. E. Schwartz; Strassburg/Berlin/Leipzig: Walter de Gruyter, 1914–40) 1/1:10–23.

growing away even linguistically from the previously dominant Greek, and which combined Monophysitism and prophecy as formidable weapons against outsiders. Shenute's work, too, of gathering in the traditional riff-raff of Egyptian society and giving its members the standing of monks and an assurance of personal salvation, as well as his passionate eloquence in their native tongue, provided the Monophysite movement in Egypt with a popular basis that it never lost.[48]

What we do not have is any direct evidence of Shenoute's reaction to Chalcedon except where he is quoted in later polemical texts. If these texts can be relied upon as accurate portrayals of his attitudes, then Shenoute must be placed among the unsophisticated. The same must be said of his successor Besa. When, however, we come to the alleged successor of Besa, Apa Zenobius, a different picture emerges. Among the fragments of his *Life* that have survived is the following:

> His collected works bear witness for us, these that he wrote in the time of Nestorius the heretic that oppose his error and uphold the orthodox faith. For he was educated in the Greek language as we have previously mentioned. [He wrote books] lest anyone say, "If he is such a wise man, where are the oblations that he has slain through his wisdom? Or where is the wine he has mixed for the thirsty through his piety? Why has he not written a multitude of works and commentaries? Or why has he not left behind useful discourses that many people might be nourished? Perhaps he is a sluggard, or perhaps too he is being silent out of envy like someone who would close off a spring. . . . [the fragment breaks off][49]

This text may well indicate a situation at variance with the one presented above. Unfortunately, none of the works of Apa Zenobius have been identified, so that there is no way of testing the accuracy of his biographer's remarks. Nevertheless, the attitude of the author himself seems clear. This piece could be interpreted as an attack on monastic anti-intellectualism and indifference to the controversies of the day. But is this work a Coptic original or itself an attempt by some Greek-speaking author to influence the monks of the Shenoutian monasteries? We do not know. What we do know is that a *Life of Apa Zenobius* is mentioned in an inscription on the walls of the library of the White Monastery and thus must have been available to the monks.[50]

48. Frend, *Monophysite Movement*, 72–73.
49. My translation of the text found in W. Till, *Koptische Heiligen- und Martyrerlegenden: Texte, Übersetzungen, und Indices* (OCA 102; Rome: Pontifical Institute of Oriental Studies, 1935).
50. W. E. Crum, "Inscriptions from Shenoute's Monastery," *JTS* 5 (1904) 565–66.

From the Greek-speaking side there is one text that may throw light on the subsequent development of polemical literature as it evolved among the Copts. In his letter to Faustinus the Deacon, which is extant in Syriac, Timothy II says:

> If, therefore, an ordinary, simple person comes to you, confessing the holy faith of the consubstantial Trinity, and desirous of being in communion with you who acknowledge our Lord's fleshly consubstantiality with us—I entreat you, not to constrain those who hold such views as these at all with other words, nor require from them additional verbal subtleties, but leave such people to praise God and bless the Lord in simplicity and innocence of their hearts.[51]

This letter is specifically concerned with Eutychianism, one of the concerns found in some of our polemics as well. It certainly can be interpreted as a normative statement. If, as seems to be the case, the bulk of the Coptic-speaking population were simple, ordinary people, then we have at least one explanation for the type of polemical literature that has come down to us in Coptic. And it comes from a very significant source, as our previous remarks on the origins of anti-Chalcedonian polemics have indicated. The intent of the letter is not without precedent, as we have seen above in the situations involving Theophilus and Cyril with the monks. Unlike their reported statements, the words of Timothy are hardly open to accusations of insincerity or political skulduggery. They are the words of a man renowned for his own asceticism, a man who emerges as a gentle and compassionate pastor, and one who knew his audience. The last-mentioned item is, when all is said and done, the crux of the matter. To assess the Coptic Monophysite polemics, one must appreciate the socioeconomic and educational level of those for whom they were composed and translated. Because of economic circumstances and Byzantine state policy, that level was low, and it was kept low for the great majority of Egyptians. For Coptic speakers there existed nothing like the cultural centers of Edessa, Nisibis, and Seleucia-Ctesiphon with their great schools. But however unsophisticated this polemical material, it provided the Coptic Monophysite community with a written tradition that extolled as exemplars of orthodoxy the Christ-like holy men who stayed loyal to the Monophysite succession of patriarchs of Alexandria. This written tradition, coupled with the common liturgy

---

51. R. Y. Ebied and L. R. Wickham, "A Collection of Unpublished Letters of Timothy Aelurus," *JTS* 21 (1970) 131, 165.

shared by all classes, Greek- and Coptic-speakers alike, sustained the Egyptian church well beyond the Middle Ages. The self-images and self-perceptions that these texts reveal are precious contributions to the total picture of early Egyptian Christianity.

PART FIVE

MONASTICISM

14

JAMES E. GOEHRING

New Frontiers in
Pachomian Studies

From its origins in the first quarter of the fourth century until its demise in the Chalcedonian controversies of the sixth century,[1] Pachomian monasticism played a significant role in Egyptian Christianity. Though its influence certainly spread beyond Egypt and has long outlived the movement's own existence, it is the evidence of its rise, its success, and its decline that concerns us here. Its significance beyond its own temporal and geographical boundaries is important only insofar as these periods and places external to the movement impressed their own concerns on the Pachomian sources.[2]

The presentation of the Pachomian movement preserved in the traditional sources suggests a division of the movement's history into three periods. The first period covers the lifetime of Pachomius and ends with his death in 346 C.E. A brief transitional period follows and leads into the second period of the movement under Theodore and Horsiesios.[3] It is from this period that the majority of the sources

1. The end of the movement is unclear. Justinian's efforts to force the Chalcedonian position on the Pachomians resulted in the departure of many from the monasteries. While he did have Chalcedonian abbots installed, the total lack of sources after this date suggests the movement's rapid demise. See *A Panegyric on Apollo Archimandrite of the Monastery of Isaac by Stephen Bishop of Heracleopolis Magna* (ed. K. H. Kuhn; CSCO 394, 1978) xiii–xvi; P. van Cauwenbergh, *Etude sur les moines d'Egypte depuis le Concile de Chalcédoine (451) jusquà l'invasion arabe (640)* (Paris: Imprimerie Nationale, 1914) 153–59; J. Goehring, "Pachomius' Vision of Heresy: The Development of a Pachomian Tradition," *Muséon* 95 (1982) 243.
2. The abridgment of the Pachomian rule for Italian monasteries is a good example. L. T. Lefort, "Un texte original de la règle de saint Pachôme," in *CRAIBL* (Paris: Picard, 1919) 341–48.
3. The transitional period belongs neither to the first period under Pachomius nor to the second period that begins with the leadership of Theodore. It represents the first

derive. The final period follows Horsiesios's death and continues through the breakup of the movement during the reign of Justinian I (527–565 C.E.).[4] It must be cautioned that while the division between the first and second periods is clear, the transition between the second and third is less certain. The former represents a historical and sociological division recognized by the movement and preserved in its writings. The latter is at least in part the result of the nature and quantity of the sources preserved.[5]

The vast majority of the written sources date from the middle period under Theodore and Horsiesios. These include the original form or forms of the *Vita Pachomii*, the *Paralipomena*, the *Letter of Ammon*, the Pachomian *Rule*, the letters and instructions of Theodore, the letters and instructions of Horsiesios, the regulations of Horsiesios, and the *Liber Horsiesii*.[6] The only sources that claim to derive from the lifetime of Pachomius, on the other hand, are the letters of Pachomius and two instructions attributed to him.[7] The authenticity of the letters is beyond repute, while that of the instructions is debated.[8] As for the last period, the written sources are sparse and more legendary in nature. An

---

unsuccessful attempt to continue the authority of a central abbot after Pachomius's death.

4. Even the date of Horsiesios's death remains unclear. See H. Bacht, *Das Vermächtnis des Ursprungs: Studien zur Theologie des geistlichen Lebens* (Würzburg: Echter, 1972) 27.

5. The death of Horsiesios would certainly have marked a transition for the movement. But the sources do not preserve the history of that transition as they do for that marked by the death of Pachomius. It is the lack of sources for the period after Horsiesios that requires this division.

6. L. T. Lefort, *S. Pachomii vitae bohairice scripta* (CSCO 89, 1925; reprint ed., 1965); idem, *S. Pachomii vitae sahidice scriptae* (CSCO 99/100, 1933–34; reprint ed., 1965); idem, *Les Vies coptes de S. Pachôme et de ses premiers successeurs* (BMus 16; Louvain: Bureaux du Muséon, 1943; reprint ed., 1966); idem, *Oeuvres de S. Pachôme et de ses disciples* (CSCO 159 [text] and 160 [translation], 1956); F. Halkin, *Sancti Pachomii Vitae Graecae* (SHG 19; Brussels: Société des Bollandistes, 1932); idem, *Le corpus athénien de saint Pachôme* (CO 2; Geneva: Cramer, 1982); idem, "Une Vie inédite de saint Pachôme. BHG 1401a," *AnBoll* 97 (1979) 5–55, 241–87; J. Goehring, "The Letter of Ammon and Pachomian Monasticism" (Diss., Claremont Graduate School, 1981; Berlin: de Gruyter, 1985); A. Boon, *Pachomiana latina* (BRHE 7; Louvain: Bureaux de la Revue, 1932); H. van Cranenburgh, *La Vie latine de S. Pachôme traduite du grec par Denys le Petit* (SHG 46; Brussels: Société des Bollandistes, 1969); E. Amélineau, *Monuments pour servir à l'histoire de l'Egypte chrétienne au IVe siècle: Histoire de S. Pakhôme et de ses communautés* (AMG 17; Paris: Leroux, 1889); A. Veilleux, *Pachomian Koinonia* (3 vols.; Kalamazoo, Mich.: Cistercian Pubs., 1980–82). See Veilleux's bibliographies.

7. H. Quecke, *Der Briefe Pachoms: Griechischer Text der Handschrift W.145 der Chester Beatty Library eingeleitet und herausgegeben von Hans Quecke. Anhang: Die koptischen Fragmente und Zitate der pachombriefe* (TPL 11; Regensburg: Pustet, 1975); E. A. W. Budge, *Coptic Apocrypha in :he Dialect of Upper Egypt* (London: British Museum, 1913) 146–76, 352–82; Veilleux, *Pachomian Koinonia* 3:13–89.

8. Veilleux, *Pachomian Koinonia* 3:2–3; T. Orlandi, "Coptic Literature," in this volume.

account of the dedication of the great fifth-century basilica at Phbow, the central Pachomian monastery, contains some useful information.[9] A few *vitae* and panegyrics deal with later abbots and record events that led to the dissolution of the community in the sixth and seventh centuries.[10]

PERIOD 1	The lifetime of Pachomius (ca. 323–346)	Letters of Pachomius Instruction of Pachomius
PERIOD 2	The movement under Theodore and Horsiesios (ca. 346–400)	*Vitae* *Paralipomena* *Letter of Ammon* Pachomian *Rule* Letters of Theodore Instructions of Theodore Letters of Horsiesios Instructions of Horsiesios Regulations of Horsiesios *Liber Horsiesii*
PERIOD 3	From the death of Horsiesios through the reign of Justinian I (ca. 400–565)	Speech of Timothy of Alexandria Life of Abraham Life of Manasseh Panegyric on Apollo

Given this division of the sources and their nature, it is clear that the history of the first and third periods is the most difficult to reconstruct accurately. The problem in the final period is straightforward. The sources are few and legendary. They supply no continuous history. Rather the reader catches sight of a few moments in history as these moments reflect off a particular saint. While more work needs to be done with these sources, we cannot expect major new revelations about later Pachomian history from them.[11]

9. A. van Lantschoot, "Allocution de Timothée d'Alexandrie prononcée à l'occasion de la dédicace de l'église de Pachôme à Pboou," *Muséon* 47 (1934) 13–56.

10. Cauwenbergh, *Etude*, 153–59; Kuhn, *Panegyric*, passim; A. Campagnano, "Monaci egiziani fra V e VI secolo," *VetChr* 15 (1978) 223–46.

11. The Corpus dei Manoscritti Copti Letterari, directed by T. Orlandi, is preparing microfiche copies of certain of these texts. The published microfiche will include photographs of the original manuscript, transcriptions, and translations.

It is with the first period that the most acute problems arise. The difficulty has nothing to do with a lack of sources or the failure of these sources to offer a relatively continuous history of the movement in this period. Rather, the problem centers on the question of the accuracy of the depiction of the first period in sources that date from the second period. No one would deny that the *vitae* accurately record the growth of the movement, the acquisition and foundation of new monasteries, the devastation by plagues, and the change of abbots through time. There is basic agreement about these events. However, the sources are also in basic agreement about the practices and beliefs of the movement throughout its development. The practices and beliefs are presented in the sources as relatively static. The impression given is that these elements, endowed with authority through their institution by Pachomius, remained constant throughout the movement's history.[12] While one expects this in the sources, one must question whether it represents a concern for historical accuracy or for an authority that has its basis in a continuity with the past.

The fact that the *vitae* preserve an accurate account of the movement's external historical events does not guarantee that they represent with equal accuracy the developments and changes in the more internal matters of practice and belief. Insofar as modern presentations of Pachomian history do not take this distinction into account, they perpetuate the hagiographic thrust of their sources.

This problem is particularly acute in matters of belief and its boundaries. In the eyes of the believer, belief is related to ultimate truth. Since the latter cannot change, neither should the former. While the writing of hagiography cannot change the fact that abbots die and are replaced, it can alter earlier belief patterns that no longer fit a current situation.[13] In fact, not only can it change them, it is compelled to change them. If the purpose of writing a *vita* lies in the notion of *imitatio patrum*, it follows that the fathers to be imitated must meet the theological requirements of those who composed the *vita*.[14]

---

12. The rule attributed in toto to Pachomius is a prime example. The notion of its angelic origin entered very early. See Palladius *Historia Lausiaca* 32.1–3.

13. The anti-Origenist sentiments attributed to Pachomius (d. 346) are a good example. J. Dechow, "Dogma and Mysticism in Early Christianity: Epiphanius of Cyprus and the Legacy of Origen" (Ph.D. diss., Univ. of Pennsylvania, 1975) 172–95.

14. This is not the process of a single author. It is part of the changing self-understanding of the movement after the death of its founder. The raison d'être of the composition demands it, whether the author realizes it or not. *Sancti Pachomii Vita prima* 17, 98–99 (this earliest Greek life shall henceforth be labelled *G1*); Bohairic Life of Pachomius *(Bo)* 194.

The one source that assuredly comes from Pachomius's lifetime, namely his own letters, underscores the problem. The mystical alphabet contained in these texts is in this form significantly absent in the later sources.[15] The possibility of a Pachomian origin for the Nag Hammadi Codices with their many heterodox texts is another case in point. Pachomian ownership can no longer be discounted simply because of the "orthodoxy" of the Pachomian sources. It is becoming clear that the sources composed in the period under Theodore and Horsiesios tell us as much about the period of their composition as about the earlier period they purport to describe, if they do not tell us more about the period of their composition.[16]

Given the recognition of this fact, it is little wonder that the desire to unravel the stemmatous relationship of the various *vitae* is now a thing of the past.[17] While these efforts offered many valuable insights into Pachomian history, it is now clear that the earliest form of the *vita*, even if it were recoverable, would still not supply an unbiased version of the period under Pachomius. New methods are needed.[18]

THE MOVEMENT IN THE LIFETIME OF ITS FOUNDER: A SOCIAL-HISTORICAL APPROACH

The death of a movement's founder marks a major turning point in its history. A crisis is averted and the movement survives only if the authority vested in him has a clearly defined new resting place. If the founder was able to share or surrender his authority before his death, the movement's continuity is maintained. Thus Elijah passed his

15. Compare the description of such letters in Palladius *Historia Lausiaca* 32.4; *G1* 99; Veilleux, *Pachomian Koinonia* 3:3–5; Quecke, *Der Briefe*, 18–40; F. Wisse, "Language Mysticism in the Nag Hammadi Texts and in Early Coptic Monasticism I: Cryptography," *Enchoria* 9 (1979) 101–20; idem, "Gnosticism and Early Monasticism in Egypt," in *Gnosis: Festschrift für Hans Jonas* (ed. B. Aland; Göttingen: Vandenhoeck & Ruprecht, 1978) 438.

16. P. Rousseau, *Ascetics, Authority, and the Church in the Age of Jerome and Cassian* (London: Oxford Univ. Press, 1978) 68; Goehring, "Pachomius' Vision of Heresy," 241–62.

17. Various accounts of the history of this debate exist. Rousseau, *Ascetics*, 243–47; J. Timbie, "Dualism and the Concept of Orthodoxy in the Thought of the Monks of Upper Egypt" (Ph.D. diss., Univ. of Pennsylvania, 1979) 23–58; Goehring, "The Epistle of Ammon," 4–45; J. Vergote, "La valeur des Vies grecques et coptes de S. Pakhome," *OLP* 8 (1977) 175–86.

18. It needs to be stated that these "new" approaches are well under way. The point to underscore is that Pachomian scholarship has moved beyond its desire to rank the *vitae* in value and instead has begun to ask new critical questions about the movement.

authority on to Elisha before his own departure. Alternatively, if the founder appointed a clear successor or established the path through which the authority was to flow after his death, continuity is maintained. This path may be hereditary, by appointment, or by election. The important point is that it was established by the authority of the founder in his own lifetime.[19] When the founder fails in this matter, a crisis of continuity inevitably follows. The difficulty is heightened when the founder dies unexpectedly.[20]

Social theorists have long recognized this process. Its earliest and clearest spokesperson was Max Weber.[21] He understood the process as an evolution to more stable forms of the charismatic authority of the process of originating. He termed this evolution "the routinization of charisma."[22]

Weber defined charisma as

a certain quality of an individual personality by virtue of which he is set apart from ordinary men and treated as endowed with supernatural, superhuman, or at least specifically exceptional powers or qualities. These are such that they are not accessible to the ordinary person, but are regarded as of divine origin or as exemplary, and on the basis of them the individual is treated as a leader.[23]

The desire to continue the community founded by such an individual after his death demands that his followers give radical attention to this charisma and the authority based upon it. The continuity of the movement depends upon the successful transferral of this authority to a more stable basis. While the kinds of forms vary, the nature of this stability over against the charismatic moment is the same.[24]

---

19. Objections or alternatives to the founder's choice are possible. This is particularly true when the founder alters a developing pattern shortly before his death. Such was the case in the Pachomian movement.

20. The case of Jesus is notable. In the early Christian movement the transfer of authority followed various patterns, including hereditary (James), apostolic (Peter), and revelatory (Paul).

21. M. Weber, *The Theory of Social and Economic Organization* (trans. A. M. Henderson and Talcott Parsons; New York/London: Oxford Univ. Press, 1947) 358–92; idem, "The Social Psychology of the World Religions," in *From Max Weber: Essays in Sociology* (ed. H. H. Gerth and C. W. Mills; New York/London: Oxford Univ. Press, 1946) 295–301; Talcott Parsons, *The Structure of Social Action* (New York: McGraw-Hill, 1937) 658–72; T. F. O'Dea, *The Sociology of Religion* (Englewood Cliffs, N.J.: Prentice-Hall, 1966) 22–24, 36–39.

22. Weber, *The Theory*, 363–73.

23. Ibid., 358–59.

24. Ibid., 363–66. It is not simply a matter of finding a new charismatic leader. While such a person may solve the immediate problem, he does not offer the more stable basis of authority that will ensure the community's existence after *his* death.

When one looks at the events that surround Pachomius's death and the eventual continuity of the community under Theodore, it is remarkable how well the facts fit this abstract theory.[25] Pachomius died unexpectedly in a plague that ravaged his community in 346.[26] A serious crisis of continuity followed, a crisis that had its origins not only in his death but in a series of events that had taken place approximately two years before it. At that time too a serious illness threatened Pachomius's life. On that occasion the community's leaders made premature plans for his replacement. They clearly recognized the problem of continuity. They compelled Theodore, who had entered the community circa 328 and had since become a confidant and the heir apparent to Pachomius, to agree to succeed Pachomius if he should die.[27] But Pachomius did not die. He recovered and took offense at Theodore's acceptance of the elders' recognition of him as his successor. As a result he removed all authority from him. Theodore spent two years in penance.[28]

While there is some indication that Pachomius's reaction against Theodore softened in the following two years,[29] it is certainly no accident that on his deathbed in 346 he appointed Petronios as his successor. Petronios was a wealthy landowner and a relatively recent addition to the community.[30] The older brothers who represented support for Theodore were bypassed.[31] Petronios led the community for only two and one half months. He died in the same plague that killed Pachomius. Before he died he appointed a certain Horsiesios from the monastery of Sheneset (Chenoboskeia) to succeed him.[32] Horsiesios too was a relative newcomer to the community.[33]

25. Rousseau, *Ascetics*, chaps. 1–5. Rousseau describes the changing concept of authority in the relationship between early monasticism and the church. He does not, however, link this account to the abstract theory of the social scientists. One should also note K. Holl, *Enthusiasmus und Bussgewalt beim griechischen Mönchtum* (Leipzig: Hinrichs, 1898; Hildesheim: Olms, 1969).

26. *G1* 114–17; *Bo* is missing at this point. The material is supplied from various Sahidic versions (*S7, S3, S5*). A number of the community's leaders perished in this plague.

27. *G1* 106; *Bo* 94.

28. *G1* 106–7; *Bo* 94–95.

29. *Bo* 97; *G1* 109; Veilleux, *Pachomian Koinonia* 1:282, *SBo* 97 n. 3 (*SBo* = Veilleux's Sahidic-Bohairic compilation).

30. *G1* 80; *Bo* 56.

31. D. J. Chitty, "A Note on the Chronology of the Pachomian Foundations," *StPatr II* (TU 64; 1957) 384–85; Veilleux, *Pachomian Koinonia* 1:420, *G1* 129 n. 1.

32. *G1* 117–18; *S5* 130–31.

33. In *G1*, Horsiesios is first mentioned in section 114, shortly before Pachomius's

Horsiesios appears to have maintained control for little more than a year.[34] His own weakness and the desire among many of the brothers to be led by Theodore worked against him.[35] Before long a major revolt broke out in the monasteries. Led by Apollonios, the abbot of the monastery of Thmousons, the breakdown of authority threatened the very existence of the movement. Apollonios's monastery seceded and others allied themselves with him.[36] Cries such as "We no longer belong to the community of the brothers" and "We will have nothing to do with Horsiesios nor will we have anything to do with the rules which he lays down" were heard.[37] It is clear that a stable form of authority had not yet evolved to replace the charismatic authority enjoyed by Pachomius.

Horsiesios recognized the serious nature of the problem and his own inability to deal with it. He summoned Theodore and turned the authority of the community over to him.[38] It is at this juncture that the routinization of Pachomius's charismatic authority occurs. The brief reigns of Petronios and Horsiesios represent an interruption in this process, an interruption caused by an event that occurred two years before Pachomius's death and set aside the path of authority that had been evolving prior to it. Theodore represented the established power base of the older brothers. Petronios and Horsiesios were newcomers imposed upon them by Pachomius because of their earlier indiscretion in championing Theodore.[39] While the choice of Petronios had Pachomius's authority behind it, it represented an aberration from his longer sharing of authority with Theodore prior to the latter's indiscretion. Theodore's acceptance of the leadership role from Horsiesios signals a return of authority to the natural course that had evolved during Pachomius's lifetime.

Theodore quelled the revolt and restored unity to the system with relative ease.[40] In the eyes of the brethren he was the repository of

---

death in 116 and Horsiesios's appointment as general abbot in 117. The earliest reference in the Coptic sources (*Bo* 91) is a reference to his latter period as general abbot. Apart from this reference, he first appears in the account of Pachomius's appointment of Petronios (*S5* 121).

34. *G1* 118–30; *S5* 125–32 (*SBo* 131–38).

35. Theodore's succession had been short-circuited only two years before. *G1* 106–7; *Bo* 94–95.

36. *S6* (*SBo* 139); *G1* 127–28; *Bo* 204; Theodore *Instruction* 3.46.

37. *S6* (*SBo* 139); *G1* 127. I have used Veilleux's translations.

38. *G1* 129–30; *S6* (*SBo* 139–40).

39. See above, n. 33.

40. *G1* 131; *S6*; *S5*; *Bo* (*SBo* 141–44).

Pachomius's authority. The recent events underscored, however, the need to stabilize this authority in institutions and not individuals if the movement were to survive. Thus to avoid a similar revolt in the future, a revolt dependent upon a single abbot's power base within his own monastery, Theodore instituted the practice of shuffling the various abbots among the various monasteries twice each year.[41] But Theodore did not institute a system for selecting his own successor. He apparently expected, as Pachomius had before him, to appoint his successor prior to his death.[42]

While Theodore did not solve the problem of continuity through an institutionalized basis of succession,[43] he did further stabilize the authority recognized in the community by more fully joining it with the ecclesiastical authority centered in Alexandria. Pachomius's charismatic authority was institutionalized not only in the internal regulations of the community but also through the community's closer identification of its own internal authority with the ecclesiastical authority and institutions representing the Athanasian party.[44]

It is no accident that Theodore moved in this direction. Throughout the *vitae* it is clear that he is more closely tied to the Alexandrian hierarchy and Athanasius than was Pachomius. His closer association may well be the result of his social status. He was born into a wealthy

41. S6 (*SBo* 144). This practice is not recorded in the Greek *Vita prima*. A subsequent letter of Horsiesios's suggests that it was not easily accepted and caused discord after Theodore's death. The letter, unpublished in the original, has been translated by Veilleux (*Pachomian Koinonia* 3:161–65). This author has discussed this particular letter at length in an unpublished paper entitled "A New Letter of Horsiesios and the Situation in the Pachomian Community Following the Death of Theodore." The paper will be published in the volume containing the critical edition of the text in preparation by T. Orlandi.

42. *Bo* 204–9; *G1* 145–49. One should note the juristic method of designating the abbot's replacement during his absence recorded in P. Lond 1913. Pageus, the abbot of the Meletian monastery at Hathor, had been summoned by Constantine to attend the Synod of Caesarea. The document records an agreement between himself and the priors of the monastery that his brother Gerantius shall take his place and discharge his function during his absence. H. Idris Bell, *Jews and Christians in Egypt* (London: Oxford Univ. Press, 1924; Westport, Conn.: Greenwood Press, 1972) 45–53. It must be pointed out that this was an interim agreement and not a matter of succession. Nothing similar is known from the Pachomian milieu.

43. The lack of sources after Theodore's death makes the question of succession and the means of deciding upon it unclear. It seems that Horsiesios faced renewed difficulties when he succeeded Theodore upon the latter's death. See above, n. 41; Bacht 24.

44. Rousseau, *Ascetics*, chaps. 1–5; F. Ruppert, *Das pachomianische Mönchtum und die Anfänge klösterlichen Gehorsams* (Münsterschwarzach: Vier Türme, 1971) 428–43; Goehring, "Pachomius' Vision of Heresy," passim.

Christian family that had ready access to the bishop.[45] Pachomius was a pagan. It is no accident that whereas Pachomius hid from Athanasius to avoid ordination when the latter journeyed upriver, Theodore on a similar occasion after Pachomius's death marched out with the leaders of the community to greet him.[46] It is no accident that Pachomius controlled his community from his own base of authority. He did not venture out to meet Antony or to visit Alexandria. Theodore did.[47] It is no accident that the source that most clearly strives to link the Pachomian movement with Athanasian orthodoxy, the *Letter of Ammon*, was authored by an individual who knew the movement only as it existed under Theodore and who held Theodore as his hero.[48] In this context it should also be noted that there is an apparent shift away from the authority and power of vision, as one moves from Pachomius to Theodore. Although both Pachomius and Theodore were visionaries, the evidence of Pachomius's ecstatic trances and the charges against him at Latopolis are in stark contrast to Theodore's milder approach to the subject.[49]

Now in this same period when the community was redefining its concept of authority, it was also emphasizing the need to emulate the idealized period under Pachomius. While the community's authority structure was routinized in a combination of monastic and ecclesiastical institutions, support for this new structure of authority was sought in the concept of *imitatio patrum*. This means that the community's writings during the era under Theodore and Horsiesios were under the

45. *G1* 33, 37; *Bo* 31, 37. Theodore's Greek Christian name is noteworthy. On the increasing use of Christian names in Egypt, see R. S. Bagnall, "Religious Conversion and Onomastic Change in Early Byzantine Egypt," *BASP* 19 (1982) 105–24.

46. *G1* 30, 143–44; *Bo* 28, 200–203. It is significant that in the two accounts of Pachomius's hiding from Athanasius, the Bohairic has Athanasius marvel at Pachomius while *G1* would have its readers believe that Pachomius was in awe of the archbishop from his place of concealment.

47. *G1* 109, 113, 120; *Bo* 96–97; *S5* (*SBo* 126–29); *Letter of Ammon* 28–29; H. Chadwick, "Pachomius and the Idea of Sanctity," in *The Byzantine Saint: University of Birmingham Fourteenth Spring Symposium of Byzantine Studies* (ed. S. Hackel; London: Fellowship of St. Alban and St. Sergius, 1981) 17–19.

48. Goehring, "The Letter of Ammon," 158–84.

49. *Bo* 33–34, 66, 87–88, 103; *S2*; *G1* 71, 96, 135; *Letter of Ammon* 12. Pachomius is made to play down the importance of visions in *G1* 48–49. Neither these sections nor *G1* 135 have a clear parallel in the Coptic material. This, coupled with the fact that *G1* alone records the Council of Latopolis, where Pachomius was charged with being a clairvoyant, makes one wonder about the intent of the *Vita prima*. Veilleux (*Pachomian Koinonia* 1:412; *G1* 48 n. 1) suggests that *G1* 48–50 stem from a lost collection of Pachomius's instructions. I would argue that it represents a later position on vision important to the circle behind *G1*, a position that was written back into the lifetime of Pachomius. See Ruppert, *Das pachomianische Mönchtum*, 431–34.

influence of this newly developed structure of authority. In fact, the writings functioned to support this new authority.[50] While this development insured the survival of the movement, it renders questionable the reliability of the writings in presenting the nature of the movement prior to the institution of this newer structure of authority. Since the movement at the time of composition had institutionalized its authority in part by closely associating itself with the Athanasian party, and since support of this new authority was sought through the principle of *imitatio*, it was necessary that the writings describe a movement in the early ideal period that is in close accord with the new institutionalized authority. Evidence that exists within these sources to the contrary represents survivals of earlier material. It is of particular importance for reconstructing the earlier period before the composition of the sources.[51] Evidence that aligns the early period with the new institutionally based authority must remain suspect.[52]

This does not mean that the movement under Pachomius was heretical nor that Pachomius opposed Athanasius. Rather, in the early period the movement simply did not understand authority in these terms. Our understanding of church history depends in large part on the writings of the great theologians (Greek and Latin!) for whom doctrinal issues and definitions were of vital significance. It is doubtful that the Copt Pachomius felt the same need for systematic theology. Henry Chadwick has observed that "it is not inherently probable that Pachomius was interested in the niceties of orthodox doctrine or a theological system . . . ; it is reasonable to think the early Pachomian tradition largely indifferent where dogma is concerned, content to make use of a diversity of gifts so long as they all encouraged renunciation of the world."[53]

50. Rousseau, *Ascetics*, 68. It may well be that the sources showed an even stronger movement in this direction under Horsiesios. Horsiesios completed what Theodore had begun.

51. The problem confronted by Pachomius at the Council of Latopolis, preserved in *G1* 112 alone, is a good example. So too the recording of Pachomius's first failure when he attempted to organize a monastic community, recorded in *S1*. Likewise the call for the removal of apocryphal books would suggest that they were used in the community at an earlier date (*Bo* 189; *S3b*; Lefort, *Les vies coptes*, 371).

52. On the matter of Pachomius's opposition to Origen, see above, n. 13. The reference to the bishops in communion with the heretics that has found its way into Pachomius's vision of heresy in *Bo* 103 suggests a period after Chalcedon (cf. *G1* 102; *Letter of Ammon* 12; Goehring, "Pachomius' Vision of Heresy," 252–53). Sometimes it is the stylized form that suggests a late date, as with the styled liturgical prayer attributed to Pachomius in *S1.16*.

53. Chadwick, "Pachomius," 18; idem, "The Domestication of Gnosis," in *The Rediscovery of Gnosticism: Proceedings of the Conference at Yale, March 1978* (ed. Bentley

The recognition of the process that routinized Pachomius's charismatic authority after his death makes the movement's acquisition and use of the documents discovered near Nag Hammadi more understandable. The "orthodoxy" of the movement portrayed in the sources can no longer be accepted as an accurate representation of the facts. Again, the alternative to this "orthodox" movement is not a heretical movement but a movement that did not yet define its being in these either/or terms. As difficult as it may be for us to fathom in this modern age of reason, it was not impossible for one to support Athanasius and read the Nag Hammadi texts.

The prevalence of this either-orthodoxy-or-heresy attitude among many historians accounts for the early denial of a Pachomian origin of the Nag Hammadi Codices. Doresse simply stated that "already the contents of these Gnostic collections had led us to suppose that whoever may have possessed them, they cannot have been monks."[54] Others have followed him in this conclusion.[55] The number of scholars who argue for a Pachomian origin of the texts, however, is growing. While the evidence currently in hand cannot firmly establish the Pachomian origin of the Nag Hammadi texts, the circumstantial evidence is mounting for such a relationship. References in the Pachomian sources to the removal of apocryphal works and against the

---

Layton; 2 vols.; Leiden: E. J. Brill, 1980) 1:3–16. The dating of the cartonnage suggests that at least some of the Nag Hammadi Codices were copied during the leadership period of Theodore. I do not consider this a problem for the theory of Theodore's routinization of Pachomius's charismatic authority. Routinization is not a rapid process. Theodore certainly emphasized closer ties with the Alexandrian hierarchy. Witness his reading of Athanasius's festal letter concerning apocryphal books in 367 (*Bo* 189). This does not mean, however, that he succeeded in converting the entire movement to his position overnight. Indeed, in his later years he bemoaned the growing wealth of the brethren (*Bo* 197–98; *G1* 146). Theodore, in a sense, functions as an intermediate stage. He shares in Pachomius's charisma (*Bo* 34; *Letter of Ammon* 14). Hence he rules with charismatic authority while at the same time institutionalizing that authority. The charismatic factor fades much further into the background with Horsiesios, who composed his own series of regulations. He undoubtedly carried the ecclesiastically based authority to its conclusion; the removal of the Nag Hammadi Codices ensued.

54. J. Doresse, *The Secret Books of the Egyptian Gnostics: An Introduction to the Gnostic Coptic Manuscripts Discovered at Chenoboskeia; with an English Translation and Critical Evaluation of the Gospel According to Thomas* (trans. P. Mairet; New York: Viking Press, 1960) 135.

55. M. Krause, "Der Erlassbrief Theodors," in *Studies Presented to Hans Jacob Polotsky* (ed. D. W. Young; East Gloucester, Mass.: Pirtle & Polson, 1981) 230; J. Shelton, "Introduction," in J. W. B. Barns, G. M. Browne, and J. C. Shelton, *Nag Hammadi Codices; Greek and Coptic Papyri from the Cartonnage of the Covers* (NHS 16; Leiden: E. J. Brill, 1981) 1–11; A. de Vogüé, "Foreword" in Veilleux, *Pachomian Koinonia* 1:xix; P. Rousseau, *Pachomius: The Making of a Community in Fourth-Century Egypt* (Berkeley: Univ. of Calif. Press, 1985) 26–28. Timbie ("Dualism," 230–33) is very cautious.

idea that Cain was conceived by the devil, which were earlier taken as evidence of the system's opposition to the Nag Hammadi texts, are now seen to support the existence of such texts in the movement during its initial stages.[56] Wisse has supplied data on the diversity of monasticism in Upper Egypt and the congruity of ideas shared between the Nag Hammadi texts and monasticism.[57] Hedrick, who worked with the *Vita prima* alone, has suggested the existence in the movement's early stage of a vision-oriented group. He argues that this group, which was played down in the later periods, offers the most obvious link to the Nag Hammadi texts.[58] Parrott has suggested that concern with heresy in Pachomius's day centered on the Meletians and the Arians. In this scenario, the gnostic controversies were a thing of the past and hence their literature was once again usable.[59] This author has elsewhere noted a tendency in the sources to generalize the movement's opposition to heresy and to write this more general opposition back into the lifetime of Pachomius.[60] Finally, Dechow has argued that the texts were removed from the monastery as a result of the fourth- and fifth-century Origenist controversy that raged in Egypt.[61]

The most intriguing but uncertain bit of evidence that has come to bear on this question is that preserved in the cartonnage of the Nag Hammadi Codices. In his preliminary report on this material, Barns noted a significant correspondence between the proper names preserved in the cartonnage and those found in the Pachomian sources.[62] One letter in particular seemed almost to offer the "smoking gun" that

56. See above, n. 51; Doresse, *Secret Books*, 135; J. M. Robinson, ed., *NHLE*, 19.

57. Wisse, "Language Mysticism," 101–20; idem, "Gnosticism and Early Monasticism in Egypt," 431–40; idem, "The Nag Hammadi Library and the Heresiologists," *VC* 25 (1971) 205–23; Chadwick, "Pachomius," 17–19.

58. C. Hedrick, "Gnostic Proclivities in the Greek Life of Pachomius and the *Sitz im Leben* of the Nag Hammadi Library," *NovT* 22 (1980) 78–94.

59. D. Parrott, "The Nag Hammadi Library and the Pachomian Monasteries," unpublished paper presented at the International Conference on Gnosticism at Yale, New Haven, Connecticut, March 28–31, 1978.

60. Goehring, "Pachomius' Vision of Heresy," 241–62.

61. Dechow, "Dogma and Mysticism," 172–95. This later date for the removal of the codices from the monastery is acceptable. I do not think that the institutionalization process under Theodore was completed during his lifetime (see above, n. 53). Various others have supported a Pachomian origin for the Nag Hammadi texts (see Chadwick, "Pachomius," 17–19; idem, "The Domestication of Gnosis," 14–16; R. van den Broek, "The Present State of Gnostic Studies," *VC* 37 [1983] 47–48).

62. J. W. B. Barns, "Greek and Coptic Papyri from the Covers of the Nag Hammadi Codices," in *Essays on the Nag Hammadi Texts* (ed. M. Krause; NHS 6; Leiden: E. J. Brill, 1975) 9–18.

would link the texts to the movement. It was from a certain Papnoute to Pachom. While the precise identity of the two is not given in the letter, Barns pointed out that the chief economic officer for the community during Pachomius's lifetime was a certain Papnoute.

It is now clear that Barns overstated the case. A significant number of proper names are shared in the two sets of sources. But this in and of itself proves nothing. Shelton, who studied the cartonnage in depth for his production of the critical edition, concluded that "there are no certain traces of classical Pachomian monasticism in the cartonnage."[63] The cartonnage sources include, after all, accounts that mention large amounts of wine, wheat, and barley, and they include tax lists, imperial ordinances, contracts for shipping goods, contracts for weavers' goods, private letters, monastic letters, and bits of Scripture. Shelton argued that "it is hard to think of a satisfactory single source for such a variety of documents except a town rubbish heap."[64]

Shelton's conclusions are acceptable in the sense (contra Barns) that the cartonnage offers no indisputable evidence òf the codices' manufacture by the Pachomian monks. However, it is wrong to move beyond that position and to suggest that the cartonnage and hence the codices could not, therefore, have come from a Pachomian monastery. Shelton himself has suggested that the monks may have gathered materials from the town rubbish heap for use in the manufacturing of their books.[65] Dechow has argued more recently that the economic life of the Pachomian community could indeed account for many of the documents preserved in the cartonnage.[66]

While the connection of certain texts in the cartonnage to the Pachomians is difficult to understand,[67] Dechow's position is well taken. The fact that the various documents do not mention specific Pachomian connections is not proof that they did not belong to the Pachomians. Certainly the monastic letters and bits of Scripture could come from the Pachomian monastery. In fact, a monastery might seem the more likely place of origin. The other private letters could equally

63. Shelton, "Introduction," 11.
64. Ibid.
65. Ibid. A similar unprovable suggestion was offered by Robinson in *NHLE*, 16–17. He suggested that uninscribed codices might have been produced and sold by the Pachomians.
66. J. Dechow, "The Nag Hammadi Milieu: An Assessment in the Light of the Origenist Controversies," paper presented at the annual meeting of the Western Region of the American Academy of Religion, March 1982.
67. This is particularly true for the agreement of the oil-workers guild in Codex I (Barns, Brown, and Shelton, *Nag Hammadi Codices*, 15–17).

be found in a monastic setting. Letters from outside the community undoubtedly came in to the monks.[68] There is no reason that these would always use monastic titles. Indeed, an outsider may well have been unfamiliar with them.[69]

When one turns to tax lists, contracts, shipping papers, etc., many of which were certainly drawn up in government offices, we must not be too quick to assume that they have no connection with the Pachomian system. One should not automatically extend the division between the spiritual and secular world in Pachomian monasticism into the economic realm as well. While the movement divided itself from the world by a wall, it must be remembered that it built its monasteries in the greenbelt of the Nile. The monks practiced various crafts, gathered their own materials for weaving and building, retained their own boats for travel up and down the Nile, conducted business outside the monastery, and farmed.[70] It is certainly improbable that the Byzantine government in Egypt granted the movement a tax-exempt status. Indeed, another document has come to light that reports on tax paid by a Tabennesiote monk.[71] Likewise, imperial ordinances and guild contracts, while more difficult to explain, do not exclude a Pachomian origin. If the movement had grown large and influential in Upper Egypt and had begun to play a significant role in the economy of the region, it is not improbable that local government offices would send copies of such matters to the monastery.[72]

While these observations do not prove the Pachomian origin of the Nag Hammadi Codices, they show that the cartonnage documents

---

68. Theodore's mother had letters from the bishop sent in to Pachomius (Bo 37; G1 37). Rule, Praecepta 51–54 reports on the role of the gatekeeper to insure the separation from the world. Yet food from relatives, while not allowed for the individual, was received for the monastery. General communication concerning farming, business, and governmental requirements should be expected as well.

69. The earliest preserved reference to a monachos dates to 324. E. A. Judge, "The Earliest Use of Monachos for 'Monk' (P. Coll. Youtie 77) and the Origins of Monasticism," JAC 20 (1977) 72–89; idem, "Fourth Century Monasticism in the Papyri," in Proceedings of the XVI International Congress of Papyrology (Chico, Calif.: Scholars Press, 1981) 613–20.

70. Palladius Lausiac History 32.9–10; Regulations of Horsiesios 55–58, 62; Dechow, "The Nag Hammadi Milieu," 6–11. The sources seem to indicate that farming and self-sufficiency were not practiced during Pachomius's lifetime but developed after his death, particularly under Horsiesios's influence. E. Wipszycka, "Les terres de la congregation pachomienne dans une liste de payments pour les apora," in Le monde grec—Pensée, litterature, histoire, documents: Hommages à Claire Préaux (ed. J. Bingen, G. Cambier, et G. Nachtergael; Brussels: L'Université Bruxelles, 1975) 625–36.

71. Wipszycka, "Les terres," 625–36; S. Schiwietz, Das morganländische Mönchtum (Mainz: Kirchheim, 1904) 1:347. The document dates to 367–368 C.E.

72. Paralipomena 21 records the purchase of wheat from the city of Hermonthis.

themselves do not clearly refute it. In this connection it is interesting to consider the type of documents found at the late monastic settlement of Deir el-Bala'izah.[73] The 1914 excavation of this site, some twelve miles south of Assiut, produced fragments of some 3,000 texts. A large number of these are nonliterary documents, and most fall into the Arabic period (675–775 C.E.). Although this is admittedly late, it is important to note that these documents include tax receipts, letters from Arab governors, accounts relating to taxation, deeds of sale, repayments of debts, private letters, various article lists, lists of names, and even a marriage contract.[74] The site is non-Pachomian, but the makeup of this collection stemming from the Bala'izah monastery would suggest that the various documents preserved in the cartonnage of the Nag Hammadi Codices could indeed have come from a monastery.

An additional point of parallel needs to be drawn from the Bala'izah case. Among the Bala'izah texts were a large number of biblical fragments, lives of the saints, homilies, and other literary pieces. This is to be expected in the remains of the monastery.[75] The vast majority of these texts fit the standard depiction of Coptic orthodoxy. They include a story about Athanasius and Antony, and a sermon by Athanasius. Now one might suspect that such an interest in Athanasius would keep such a monastery from dabbling with more heterodox materials. Such is often the assumption about the Pachomian movement. However, the Bala'izah literary documents also contain magical texts, a possible amulet and horoscope, and what is most interesting, a gnostic treatise. The treatise dates from the fourth century and is very fragmentary. The text is a revelation to John. Even though it does not correspond to any other known gnostic text to date, it is replete with the usual gnostic terminology. It belongs to the type of document represented by the *Apocryphon of John*, which offers a gnostic reinterpretation of the events recorded in Genesis.[76]

What I want to underscore is not the precise nature of the text but the mere fact of its existence in a monastic library that also contained

---

73. P. E. Kahle, *Bala'izah: Coptic Texts from Deir el-Bala'izah in Upper Egypt* (2 vols.; London: Oxford Univ. Press, 1954).

74. Ibid., 1:xi–xvii, the table of contents, lists the variety.

75. Such documents, apart from some biblical fragments, were not in the cartonnage from Nag Hammadi because of the early date of the codices. The hagiographic material was coming into existence at this time and hence would not yet be worn enough for the scrap heap.

76. Kahle, *Bala'izah*, 1:473–477; W. E. Crum, "Coptic Anecdota," *JTS* 44 (1943) 176–79.

works connected with Athanasius. The fact that it was preserved to such a late date is also striking. While we do not know the nature of the monasticism practiced at Bala'izah, this evidence at least allows the possibility of the use of gnostic and Athanasian literature in the same movement![77]

In conclusion, the Pachomian sources, when viewed in light of the social theory of authority and its routinization, betray their own participation in this routinization process. They support adherence to authority in its new routinized form by demanding monks to imitate the heroes of the past. These two facts can work together only if the heroes of the past are portrayed as supportive of the new institutionalized form of authority. This being the case, the historicity of the sources in such matters is highly questionable.

This brief analysis has also demonstrated that certain presuppositions about Pachomian monasticism do not warrant support on closer examination. The notion that monastic withdrawal includes a strict division between the spiritual matters of the monastery and the economic concerns of the state is not always correct. The Pachomian sources themselves do not support it, nor does it gain support from other monastic sites where our documentation is more complete.[78]

The same problem has been shown to exist with the idea that one could not read works of Athanasius and express support of him, and yet read a gnostic text. Rationalism has taught us to appreciate a systematic theology. But to write these expectations back into the early stages of Pachomian monasticism is simply to continue the hagiographic process already begun in the *vitae* in the time of Theodore.

THE MOVEMENT AFTER HORSIESIOS: ARCHAEOLOGICAL EVIDENCE

The other period of Pachomian monasticism of which we know very little is that from the death of Horsiesios (ca. 400) through the movement's disintegration in the Chalcedonian controversy of the sixth and seventh centuries. The problem in this case arises not so much from a

---

77. One should note the monk Annarichus in Gaza as another example. See E. A. W. Budge, *Miscellaneous Coptic Texts in the Dialect of Upper Egypt* (London: British Museum, 1915) 58–60, 636–38; van den Broek, "Present State," 47–48.

78. Shenoute spoke to secular leaders and dealt harshly with the pagan elements in his area. See J. Leipoldt, *Schenute von Atripe und die Entstehung des National ägyptischen Christentums* (Leipzig: Hinrichs, 1903) 162–66, 175–82.

distortion in the sources that deal with the movement of this period as from the simple lack of sources themselves.

The creative period of the movement occurred in the lifetime of Pachomius. The second period under Theodore and Horsiesios represents a period of institutionalization and written preservation. The final period after Horsiesios's death represents a stage of literary stagnation. While the movement did apparently grow and did build the great fifth-century basilica at Phbow,[79] its own identity was tied to the past. The past was now available in written documents that bore their own authority.

Though we have a highly imaginative account of the dedication of the great basilica, and a few later lives and panegyrics, they preserve relatively little historical information on the period. It is true that more work needs to be done with this later material, including the production of critical texts and translations.[80]

A second source of data on the later period of the Pachomian movement has received only minor attention, namely, the archaeological evidence. Lefort did conduct a surface survey in 1939 in an attempt to identify the sites of the various Pachomian establishments,[81] but the only site that has been clearly identified by archaeological evidence is that of the central monastery of Phbow.[82] This site has never been lost, because of the pillars of the large fifth-century basilica that strew the surface.

The site was visited in the early twentieth century[83] but received its first actual excavation in 1968 under the direction of Fernand Debono of L'Institut français d'archéologie orientale.[84] Debono's analysis of the surface remains suggested to him evidence for two basilicas. The large fifth-century structure that was recognized by all was built with brick walls and used rose granite columns in its interior. A number of

---

79. Lantschoot, "Allocution," passim; A. Salih, *The Churches and Monasteries of Egypt and Some Neighboring Countries* (trans. B. T. A. Evetts; Oxford: Clarendon Press, 1895).

80. See above, n. 11.

81. L. T. Lefort, "Les premiers monastères pachômiens: Exploration topographique," *Muséon* 52 (1939) 379–407.

82. Ibid., 387–93.

83. M. Jullien, "Quelques anciens couvents de l'Egypt," *MissCath* 35 (1903) 283–84; M. L. Massignon, "Seconde note sur l'état d'avancement des études archéologiques arabes en Egypte, hors du Caire," *BIFAO* 9 (1911) 88–90; Lefort, "Les premiers monastères," 387–93.

84. F. Debono, "La basilique et le monastère de St. Pacôme (Fouilles de l'Institut pontifical d'archéologie chretienne, à Faou-el-qibli, Haute-Egypte—janvier 1968)," *BIFAO* 70 (1971) 191–220.

architectural blocks gathered at the southeast edge of the site were, however, identified by Debono as remnants of a second church, in view of their different proportions and materials. He tentatively suggested that this second church was the modest chapel described in the sources, a chapel that was demolished to make way for the later basilica.[85] It was apparently this identification that led Debono to excavate beside these remains of the second church.

Debono's excavation uncovered the ruins of several brick buildings and a rather sophisticated channel for running water. The objects unearthed included a large amount of pottery (mostly shards), a few pieces of metal, several coins, and animal bones. The coins identified by Debono date from Constantius II (337–361) through Theodosius (379–395).[86]

Debono's efforts represent but a start. His report is unfortunately preliminary, and we can no longer expect a final report on his work. While the structures he unearthed cannot be clearly identified, his efforts did establish the existence of the monastery to the west of the basilica.[87] Debono did not return to the field.

Between 1975 and 1980, the Institute for Antiquity and Christianity conducted four excavation seasons and one survey in the Nag Hammadi area.[88] The caves of the Jabal al-Tarif, the site of the discovery of the Nag Hammadi Codices, were thoroughly explored. Evidence of the use of the sixth-dynasty tombs in this cliff by Byzantine monks is plentiful. Red painted crosses and a Coptic psalm inscription are to be noted.[89] Excavations also unearthed pottery from this period and

85. Ibid., 205–7.
86. Ibid., 218.
87. Efforts by the Institute for Antiquity and Christianity to locate accurately Debono's squares failed, though their approximate position is clear.
88. J. M. Robinson and B. Van Elderen, "The First Season of the Nag Hammadi Excavation, 27 November–19 December 1975," ARCE *Newsletter* 96 (1976) 18–24, and *GöMisz* 22 (1976) 71–79; idem, "The Second Season of the Nag Hammadi Excavation, 22 November–29 December 1976," ARCE *Newsletter* 99/100 (1977) 36–54, and *GöMisz* 24 (1977) 57–73; B. Van Elderen, "The Nag Hammadi Excavation," *BA* 42 (1979) 225–31; Peter Grossmann, "The Basilica of St. Pachomius," *BA* 42 (1979) 232–36; G. Lease, "The Fourth Season of the Nag Hammadi Excavation, 21 December 1979–15 January 1980," *GöMisz* 41 (1980) 75–85; M. Meyer, "Wadi Sheikh Ali Survey," ARCE *Newsletter* 117 (1982) 22–24, and *GöMisz* 64 (1983) 77–82; M. Meyer and K. Beebe, "Literary and Archeological Survey of Al-Qasr," ARCE *Newsletter* 121 (1983) 25–29.
89. M. P. Bucher, "Les commencements des psaumes LI à XCIII: Inscription d'une tombe de Kaṣr eṣ Ṣaijād," *Kemi* 4 (1931) 157–60. Graffiti to Sarapis are also present. J. M. Robinson ("The Discovery of the Nag Hammadi Codices," *BA* 42 (1979) 213, pp. 202 and 228 of the same issue) offers photographs of the psalms inscription. See B. Van Elderen, "The Nag Hammadi Excavation," 226.

Byzantine coins from the reign of Anastasius I (491–518) through Heraclius (610–641).[90]

Excavations at the monastery of Phbow began in the second season (22 November–29 December 1976). Two further seasons have been undertaken, and we are hopeful of future work. The excavations centered on the basilica itself and have been successful in delineating the architectural structure of this great fifth-century church. The basilica was indeed massive, measuring approximately 36 meters in width by 72 in length. It retained the usual architectural features of a Coptic basilica. The five aisles of the interior were separated by rose granite columns and the floor was paved with limestone slabs of uneven size.[91] The outside walls were brick. That they were large is evidenced by the massive foundation walls that remain.[92] The apse has not been excavated. It lies below an existing house.

Excavations below this fifth-century basilica have also revealed a fourth-century basilica of similarly large dimensions. Its width is 30 meters and its length at least 35 meters. The excavations have not yet located the western wall. The size of this lower basilica underscores the early success of the movement. It is doubtful, however, whether this building should be identified with the small chapel in the Pachomian sources, built by Pachomius.[93]

Other structures have been located below this fourth-century basilica, though their precise dimensions and function are unclear. One at least contained a series of large storage jars sheared off to level the site for the fourth-century basilica.[94]

To date, these excavations have identified two basilicas (the largest and the oldest in Egypt). It is possible though doubtful that they correspond to Debono's two basilicas.[95] It would be my view that the

90. J. Goehring, "Byzantine Coins from the Jabal al-Tarif," *BSAC* 26 (1984) 31–41; idem, "Two New Examples of the Byzantine 'Eagle' Countermark," *NumC*, series 7, 23 (1983) 218–20; idem, "A Byzantine Hoard from Upper Egypt," *NFAQJ* 26 (1983) 9–10. It is interesting to note that the coins identified by Debono were late Roman. The earliest from the cave hoard is Byzantine.

91. B. Van Elderen, "The Nag Hammadi Excavation," 229; Lease, "Fourth Season," 79.

92. Grossmann, "Basilica," 233–34. Many of the foundation walls have been plundered for the stone.

93. Ibid., 234–35; Lease, "Fourth Season," 80; *G1* 54; *Bo* 49; *Paralipomena* 32. The size of the lower basilica is too large to fit the *vita* description. The dating of the lower basilica is not precise. Pottery analysis has pointed only to the fourth century. Pachomius died in 346. Thus it could well date after this point. The *vita* accounts are all situated early in Pachomius's career.

94. B. Van Elderen, "The Nag Hammadi Excavations," 229, photograph on 232.

95. Debono, "La basilique," 201–7; Grossmann, "Basilica," 233–35; Lease, "Fourth Season," 80.

earlier basilica dates to the very last years of Pachomius's life or even more probably to the years under Theodore and Horsiesios. Its size is to be interpreted not in terms of the number of monks at Phbow itself but in terms of the two annual gatherings of the entire community at Phbow held each Easter and in August.[96]

In addition to the work at the basilica and Jabal al-Tarif, the Institute's team has also learned of other sites in the area that are of importance for our understanding of the milieu of Pachomian monasticism. A government project to dig a large canal some 750 meters to the north of the basilica site unexpectedly turned up large quantities of early Roman pottery.[97] An inspection of the trenching operation further revealed large limestone blocks at one point in the newly dug canal. The heavy machinery had clearly cut through a sizable early Roman wall. While this discovery was accidental and no scientific effort has yet been undertaken on it, it raises some interesting questions about the nature of the "deserted village" that Pachomius chose for his central monastery.[98]

A second intriguing site was learned of through James Robinson's inquiries about manuscript discoveries in the area. It lies in a desert wadi that proceeds in a northeasterly direction from the northeast corner of the Dishnā plain. It is called the Wadi Sheikh Ali.[99] Several kilometers back into the wadi there exists a pilgrimage site. Large rock overhangs at the site allowed respite from the sun. The site was used very early. It preserves numerous incised graffiti of animals and ships and a crude cartouche of Menkaure of the Old Kingdom. More significant for our period are the large number of monastic inscriptions. They are mostly painted on the rock overhang in the typical red paint or occasionally scratched into the surface of the rock. The inscriptions ask for the usual remembrance in prayer or love and frequently include a statement identifying the writer as a sinner. Thus, for example, "+ I am Chael the sinner. Please pray for me." A piece of rock found at the site and used in the fashion of an ostracon preserved the words "+ I am Archeleos. Remember me please." One particular monk, John, even drew his likeness on the wall in the orant position.[100] Roman bricks and

96. See above, n. 90; G1 83; Bo 71; Bacht 23 n. 74; Veilleux, *Pachomian Koinonia* 1:278, SBo 71 nn. 2, 3.
97. B. Van Elderen, "The Nag Hammadi Excavations," 230–31.
98. Bo 49; G1 54.
99. Meyer, "Wadi Sheikh Ali Survey," 22–24.
100. Ibid., 24.

potsherds from the early Roman through the Byzantine periods were also found. Further work needs to be done to record this site. While the Pachomian use of the site cannot be established, it is further evidence of the widespread monastic presence in this area.

Finally, brief mention must be made of a survey of the town of al-Qasr carried out by the Institute for Antiquity and Christianity in December, 1980.[101] The village, ancient Chenoboskeia, was a fairly significant Roman station in Pachomian times. Nearby stands the existing monastery of Apa Palamon, the possible site of the Pachomian monastery of Sheneset. The village also borders the inner desert.[102] The survey produced considerable evidence of the Roman presence. Excavation would, however, be difficult because of the modern village situated over the site.

Further field work awaits. While another season can surely complete the effort to delineate the dimensions of the lower basilica and possibly excavate the apse, much more work awaits in the monastery itself.[103] It is here that one might hope to gather significant information that can be related to the description of the monastery complex in the *Lives*. It is indeed unfortunate that the effort has not received greater support. Phbow is the only authentically Pachomian site so far identified and offers a chance to uncover the remains of this center of cenobitic origins. Though the significance may be magnified for the Pachomian scholar, the importance of the movement for monastic origins in general should broaden the site's appeal.

101. Meyer and Beebe, "Survey," 25–29.
102. Lefort, "Les premiers monastères," 6. A NASA satellite photograph of this area that I obtained recently offers a vivid view of the inner desert.
103. The Institute for Antiquity and Christianity is hopeful of returning to the field in the near future.

15

JANET TIMBIE

The State of Research on the
Career of Shenoute of Atripe

Writing in 1903, Johannes Leipoldt gave certain reasons for undertaking to study the life and works of Shenoute. These reasons (which he gave in *Schenute von Atripe*) had mainly to do with Shenoute's role as more than a religious leader of the Coptic population and with his importance as a Coptic writer.[1] Can we add to these reasons? Have eighty years of research shown Shenoute to be more or less significant, or significant in a different way?

The longstanding, dominant view has been that Christianity, beginning sometime in the third century, was the main vehicle for the expression of Coptic national feeling. Monophysitism became linked to Coptic Christianity for a variety of reasons and then served to set Christian Egypt apart from the Christian Empire. Monophysitism was understood to be another outlet for national feeling. But several developments seem to indicate that this view must be modified. Walter Bauer, in *Orthodoxy and Heresy in Earliest Christianity*, gave early (1934) forceful expression to the view that Christianity in Egypt, at least through the third century, was theologically diverse.[2] Of course, Bauer mainly dealt with Greek sources and drew a picture of the Hellenized element in Egypt. Colin Roberts, in *Manuscript, Society, and Belief in Early Christian Egypt*, examined the evidence of the early papyri and the use of *nomina sacra* and concluded that Gnosticism was influential in second-century Egypt, beside forms of Christianity that were under

---

1. Johannes Leipoldt, *Schenute von Atripe* (Leipzig: Hinrichs, 1903).
2. Walter Bauer, *Orthodoxy and Heresy in Earliest Christianity* (ed. and trans. Robert Kraft and Gerhard Krodel; Philadelphia: Fortress Press, 1971).

Jewish and Stoic influence.[3] Roberts disputes Bauer's contention that heresy was "primary" and orthodoxy was "secondary" in Egypt. Roberts states:[4]

> We may surmise that for much of the second century it was a church with no strong central authority and little organization; one of the directions in which it developed was certainly Gnosticism, but a Gnosticism not initially separated from the rest of the Church.

The Nag Hammadi documents should lead us to examine the possibility of some diversity of belief among Coptic-speaking Christians in the fourth century.[5] For, at the very least, the Nag Hammadi texts show that there was interest in Gnosticism, Hermeticism, and popular philosophy among some Coptic speakers. And these documents put Shenoute's role in a different light. In his own time, Shenoute was an important spokesman for the interests of certain Coptic Christians in their struggle against the Hellenized, pagan element in the local area. He became one of the founders, without realizing it, of the independent, monophysite church of Egypt. To the twentieth-century scholar, Shenoute may seem to be the most important leader of Coptic Christians in his day, simply because he left the largest collection of writings (which express a theology consistent with that which has endured in Egypt). But we should not be misled by these facts into overestimating or misinterpreting his importance.

If there was greater diversity of belief in Coptic-based Christian thought than had previously been suspected (referring to the fourth century and later only), then Shenoute is important for a reason different from those given by Leipoldt. His writings give glimpses of the various viewpoints that competed in the region around the White Monastery: Hellenized Egyptian religion, nominal Christianity dominated by popular philosophy, Manichaeism, Meletian doctrine, and other unorthodox forms of Christianity. Nothing is described in all the detail we would like, but there are bits of information that no other source gives us.

All of the above reveals a historian's bias in this paper. I am primarily interested in "Shenoute as a historical source," to quote the title of an article by John Barns. Others may see Shenoute as a source

3. Colin Roberts, *Manuscript, Society, and Belief in Early Christian Egypt* (London: Oxford Univ. Press, 1979) 53.
4. Ibid., 71.
5. Roberts doubts that gnostic interests among the Copts can be antedated (see ibid., 69).

of linguistic data that, if carefully examined, can greatly improve our understanding of the Coptic language. I will review recent work on the text of Shenoute's writings and studies of his language with an eye toward identifying any outstanding problems in those areas. But then I will turn to historical questions.

It may be helpful to take a closer look at Leipoldt's work before turning to recent research, for his work has been the starting point for much that has been done later. I will review the chronology of the life of Shenoute, Leipoldt's analysis of Shenoute's writings (including questions of text, grammar, and style), and his views on Shenoute's activities in the monastery and the local community. The chronology has few fixed points.[6] Shenoute entered the monastery around 370 and took control after the death of Pgol in 388. He accompanied Cyril to Ephesus in 431. The construction of the White Monastery is dated to 440. Finally, Leipoldt places the death of Shenoute in 451. This chronology is derived in part from Leipoldt's reading of the *Life of Shenoute*, which he takes to be an early work.[7] Of the surviving versions (S, Bo, Ar, Syr), the Bohairic is judged to be the closest to the original composition in Sahidic.[8]

Leipoldt assembled the corpus of Shenoute's writings from the manuscript collections of Naples, Bologna, Leiden, Cairo, Paris, and London.[9] The Paris collection was the most important. He does not attempt a grammatical commentary on Shenoute but sketches the main characteristics of his writing style, stressing its forcefulness and singularity.[10]

For Leipoldt, Shenoute's importance as a monastic leader lay in the strict discipline he imposed on the monastery.[11] Eventually he required an oath of obedience from the monks. But Shenoute does not seem to be an isolated case to Leipoldt, but seems to be merely one element in a larger trend toward ascetic severity in Egyptian Christianity.

The White Monastery also became the focal point of activity for Christian laymen.[12] They attended services in the monastery and listened to the sermons of Shenoute. He became the champion of the native population against the abuses of the upper classes and

6. Chronology in Leipoldt, *Schenute*, 42–47.
7. Ostensibly by Besa (Leipoldt, *Schenute*, 13).
8. Ibid., 14.
9. Ibid., 3.
10. Ibid., 58–62.
11. Ibid., 92–158.
12. Ibid., 159–75.

government officials. Leipoldt also describes how he provided refuge in the monastery at a time of barbarian invasions. His work as advocate of the poor became entwined with the struggle against paganism, since the Hellenized upper class was the main supporter of the old religion at this period.[13]

For Leipoldt, Shenoute achieved lasting significance mainly through his activities outside the monastery, as one who shaped Coptic Christianity. Thus, he can sum up Shenoute's career with the statement that Shenoute means nothing in world history but means everything in the history of the Copts.[14]

Next I would like to review developments since Leipoldt's work was published. As for the chronology, most of the dates in Shenoute's life are unchallenged. K. H. Kuhn corrected the date of his death to 466[15] (from 451), following the lead of J. F. Bethune-Baker.[16] The latter argued that since Nestorius died after the Council of Chalcedon, and Nestorius is mentioned as someone long dead in Shenoute's writings, Shenoute himself must have lived past 451. The only other date that fits, as Leipoldt stated, is 466.

The standard edition of the *Life of Shenoute* continues to be the Bohairic text edited by Leipoldt.[17] A. F. Shore has published a fragment of a Sahidic text: "Extract of Besa's *Life of Shenoute* in Sahidic," *JEA* 65 (1979) 134–43. This fragment is equivalent to Leipoldt's *Vita* 54–58, plus sections referring to Shenoute's illness and death and to the bishop of Ashmunein. It omits large sections of the Bohairic *Life*, and those it contains are treated more concisely. In this, the Sahidic fragment published by Shore differs from the Sahidic material from the *Life* that Leipoldt knew. Recently, David Bell has published a translation of Besa's *Life of Shenoute*, with an introduction and notes, that is based on Leipoldt's text.[18]

Leipoldt's editions of the *Life of Shenoute* and of the writings of Shenoute have not been superseded. For years scholars have recognized the need for a new edition, but no one has undertaken the task. The difficulty in producing a complete edition arises from the fact

13. Ibid., 175–82.
14. Ibid., 191.
15. K. H. Kuhn, *Letters and Sermons of Besa* (CSCO 157, 1956) i.
16. J. F. Bethune-Baker, "The Date of the Death of Nestorius: Schenute, Zacharias, Evagrius," *JTS* 9 (1908) 601–2.
17. *Sinuthii Vita Bohairice* (ed. J. Leipoldt; CSCO 41, 1906).
18. Besa, *Life of Shenoute* (trans. David N. Bell; Kalamazoo, Mich.: Cistercian Pubs., 1983).

that the manuscripts containing Shenoute's writings are scattered among various libraries. Pages of a single text were separated and housed in different collections. Thus all the early editions of Shenoute's writings—those by Amélineau, Leipoldt, Wessely, and Chassinat—contain fragmentary works.[19] More recently, scholars have reassembled single texts (letters, sermons, etc.) by piecing together published and unpublished material by Shenoute. For example, Pierre du Bourguet, in "Entretiens de Chenoute sur les devoirs des juges,"[20] has combined material published by Amélineau (vol. 1, pp. 410–14) with some published by Chassinat (pp. 84–94) to complete the text. Du Bourguet has published several more articles of this type, as have Lefort, Koschorke, Shisha-Halevy, E. Lucchesi, and others.[21] Tito Orlandi has recently shown that an anonymous text dealing with Gnosticism is, in fact, the work of Shenoute.[22] A new, complete edition of the works of Shenoute has long been desirable; it now seems possible as well. Orlandi's work in cataloguing all collections of Coptic manuscripts and tracing the location of manuscripts from the White Monastery has made the project feasible. His article "The Future of Studies in Coptic Biblical and Ecclesiastical Literature" stressed the need for scholars willing to edit or reedit Coptic texts.[23] Until then, we depend on Amélineau (who has more texts) or Leipoldt (who is more accurate) for the works of Shenoute. They did not attempt to reconstruct codices, but this could now be done and an edition published that assembled many partial texts.

Considerable work has been done on Shenoute's language. But the

19. Emile Amélineau, *Oeuvres de Schenoudi* (2 vols.; Paris: Leroux, 1907–14); J. Leipoldt, *Sinuthii Archimandritae Vita et Opera Omnia* (CSCO 43, 73, 1906–13); E. Chassinat, *Le quatrième livre des entretiens et epîtres de Shenouti* (Cairo: L'Institut français d'archéologie orientale, 1911); C. Wessely, *Griechische und koptische Texte theologischen Inhalts* (SPP 9 and 18; Leipzig: Avenarius, 1909–17).

20. Pierre du Bourguet, "Entretiens de Chenoute sur les devoirs des juges," *BIFAO* 55 (1956) 85–109.

21. L. T. Lefort, "Catechèse christologique de Chenoute," *ZÄS* 80 (1955) 40–45; Pierre du Bourguet, "Diatribe de Chenoute contre le démon," *BSAC* 16 (1961–62) 17–72; idem, "Entretiens de Chenoute sur des problèmes de discipline ecclésiastique et de cosmologie," *BIFAO* 57 (1958) 99–142; Klaus Koschorke et al., "Schenute: De certamine contra diabolum," *OrChr* 59 (1975) 60–77; Ariel Shisha-Halevy, "Unpublished Shenoutiana in the British Library," *Enchoria* 5 (1975) 53–108; E. Lucchesi, "Deux feuillets coptes inédits de Shenoute," *Muséon* 91 (1978) 171–78; idem, "Localisation d'une pièce manuscrite isolée dans la litterature chenoutienne," *ZÄS* 104 (1979) 80–81.

22. Tito Orlandi, "A Catechesis Against Apocryphal Texts by Shenute and the Gnostic Texts of Nag Hammadi," *HTR* 75 (1982) 85–95.

23. T. Orlandi, "The Future of Studies in Coptic Biblical and Ecclesiastical Literature," in *The Future of Coptic Studies* (ed. R. M. Wilson; Leiden: E. J. Brill, 1978) 143–63. See 157 n. 64 for comments on the available editions of Shenoute.

focus has been on the grammar rather than the style in a broader sense. Ariel Shisha-Halevy is the primary researcher. After writing a dissertation on the circumstantial sentence in Shenoutian Coptic, he published various articles and announced a larger work, *Studies in Shenoutian Syntax*. Meanwhile, other scholars have published grammatical studies: D. W. Young wrote on the use of first-present and conditional sentences; L. Rudnitzky examined є with a following infinitive.[24] A Shenoute lexicon would be helpful and this could be produced with the aid of a computer if one wanted to base it on Leipoldt's edition. The works of Shenoute could be stored in the computer, which could then list all instances of a particular word. The technology is now available for this project, but perhaps it should wait for the definitive edition of Shenoute's writings. Meanwhile, in the absence of such a lexicon, the researcher often relies on overall familiarity with Shenoute's writings to determine the meaning of words in any single passage.

There is less to say about research on the style of Shenoute's writing. Little has been written on Coptic style in general and less on Shenoute. In his introduction to the works of Shenoute, Amélineau noted that his style is marked by lack of agreement in number, difficult allusions, references to himself in the third person, and convolutions. We turn to Amélineau's remarks because so little has been written about this. C. D. G. Müller has written on Coptic style. His article "Koptische Redekunst und griechische Rhetorik" includes comments on Shenoute.[25] A graduate student at the Catholic University of America, in Washington, D.C., is at present working on a study of rhetorical forms in selected works of Shenoute.

Literary genres have received somewhat more attention. Coptic hagiography has been studied, building on studies of Greek hagiography, and this is discussed in the Orlandi article mentioned above.[26] The results of this research could be applied to Besa's *Life of Shenoute*. Several scholars have examined Shenoute's use or citation of

24. D. W. Young, "On Shenoute's use of Present I," *JNES* 20 (1961) 115–19; idem, "Ešope and the Conditional Conjugation," *JNES* 21 (1962) 175–85; idem, "Unfulfilled Conditions in Shenoute's Dialect," *JAOS* 89 (1969) 399–407; L. Rudnitzky, "Zum Sprachgebrauch Schenutes I–III," *ZÄS* 81 (1956) 48–53, 129–39, and *ZÄS* 82 (1957) 143–45; A. Shisha-Halevy, "ⲧⲱⲉⲧⲱ: A Shenoutian-Coptic Idiom and A Suggestion for its Analysis," *WZKM* 69 (1977) 33–39; idem, "Akhmimoid Features in Shenoute's Idiolect," *Muséon* 89 (1976) 353–66.

25. C. D. G. Müller, "Koptische Redekunst und griechische Rhetorik," *Muséon* 69 (1956) 53–72.

26. Orlandi, "The Future of Studies," 154–55. See also his article in this volume.

other works. Lefort noted borrowing from the works of Athanasius,[27] Garitte discussed Shenoute's use of the *Life of Antony*,[28] and Shisha-Halevy examined Platonic references.[29] I would like to see a study of biblical allusions and citations in the works of Shenoute. My doctoral dissertation touched on this question briefly and I argued that Shenoute's use of the Bible and style of exegesis derived from a preference for discourse that was immediately relevant to Christian life, either inside or outside the monastery.[30] But other questions can be raised. For example, is Shenoute's exegesis the same as, or different from, that of other non-Greek (e.g., Syriac) monastic writers?

Next we turn to research on the activities and influence of Shenoute in the monastery, among local Christians, in opposition to paganism, and in support of the bishop of Alexandria.

From the beginning, scholars who have commented on Shenoute's monastic activities have compared him unfavorably with Pachomius. Ladeuze, in 1898, noted the strictness and violence in Shenoute's monastery, compared with the Pachomian system.[31] Armand Veilleux, in his 1983 introduction to Bell's translation of the *Life of Shenoute*, essentially shares Ladeuze's opinion and goes on to argue that Pachomius and Shenoute stand near the beginning of two separate monastic pathways that can be followed to the present day.[32] But the strictness is also shown in the oath that was sworn by those entering the monastery. The monk is not to defile his body, steal, or lie. "If I do not do that which I have sworn, I will see the kingdom of heaven and not enter it . . ." (CSCO 42:20). This oath can be seen as a precursor of monastic vows. But the picture is not entirely clear. This oath and Shenoute's other measures of control must be explained in a way that accounts for the preceding text in Leipoldt's edition, "On Monastic Vows" (CSCO 42:16). In this text, Shenoute is arguing with someone (probably an older monk) about the efficacy of oaths in producing good behavior in the monastery.

But now I say to you after thinking this over . . . not only if you have them

27. L. Lefort, "Athanase, Ambrose, et Chenoute," *Muséon* 48 (1935) 55–73.

28. Gérard Garitte, "A propos des lettres de S. Antoine l'ermite," *Muséon* 52 (1939) 11–31.

29. A. Shisha-Halevy, "Shenoute and Plato," *Muséon* 91 (1978).

30. Janet Timbie, "Dualism and the Concept of Orthodoxy in the Thought of the Monks of Upper Egypt" (Ph.D. diss., Univ. of Pennsylvania, 1979) 208–9.

31. Paulinus Ladeuze, *Etude sur le cénobitisme pakhomien pendant le IVe siècle et la première moitié du Ve* (Louvain: Linthout, 1898) 326.

32. A. Veilleux, "Preface," in Besa, *Life of Shenoute*, v–xv.

swear by the name of God whom they do not see, but even if God Jesus were to appear in the place where you had them swear and they swore while looking at him, even then, those who want to sin will do so in his community, regardless. Which is greater, the lord of the oath or the oath? If the thought of God cannot stop a person from sinning, there is no oath that can stop him.

Shenoute may have tried many different methods of control, including restricting entry into the monastery, requiring an oath, and expelling wrongdoers. Those judging the character of Shenoute's rule need to consider all the texts and perhaps look for the evolution of his thought as he tries one measure after another to control the uneducated, undisciplined group that entered the monastery.[33] In addition, no one has examined Shenoute's relationship with communities of nuns in the area. Approximately 1800 nuns were part of the White Monastery complex and thus under the direct control of Shenoute. But other women's communities seem to be independent in some ways. Shenoute can advise them—sometimes very vehemently—but he seems to lack formal authority. He writes to Tachom, the leader of a convent: "If you are not a wise mother, truly all those who call you 'Mother', what will they do to become wise without you?" (CSCO 42:21–22). He continues in this vein of criticism, particularly because she seems to have ignored someone Shenoute sent to the convent.

Another type of monastic activity is the building of monasteries. Badawy dated the construction of the White Monastery to 440 in an article dealing with many of the early church foundations in Egypt.[34]

Shenoute was involved in the lives of local non-monastic Christians in several different ways. We have the texts that mention these activities, but there have been few comments on them. We know that Shenoute sheltered the local population in the monastery during barbarian invasions (CSCO 42:67–77). He also tried to defend them from economic exploitation, mainly by threatening the wealthy pagan landowners (CSCO 42:79). We would like to know how this compares with the activities of other heads of monasteries at this period, in Syria and elsewhere.

Shenoute also tried to shape the religious beliefs and practices of the local Christians. The evidence for this is found, in part, in texts criticizing unorthodox belief and practice. Guérin published a very

33. Leipoldt, *Schenute*, 140–45.
34. A. Badawy, "Les premières églises d'Egypte," in *Kyrilliana* (Cairo: Editions du scribe égyptien, 1947) 319–80.

interesting text in which Shenoute criticizes local Christians—labeled Meletians—who celebrate the Eucharist in their homes several times a day.[35] They believe that the elements are an antidote to sin: "If you sin many times today, you take from the Eucharist many times, your sins will be forgiven."[36] As I said, Shenoute labels them "Meletians," but we know little about the nature of the Meletian movement at this time (ca. 400). Theodoret states that the Meletians split with their former allies the Arians but would not unite with the catholic party. The Meletians had developed special practices, including ritual bathing and enthusiastic singing and clapping during worship.[37] In the text edited by Guérin, Shenoute accuses another group of avoiding the Eucharist altogether.[38] Guérin tried to explain the avoidance by citing the Synod of Alexandria (362), which condemned "Judaizers" who kept the Sabbath, not Sunday. But other explanations suggest themselves. Those avoiding the Eucharist could be excessively "spiritual" Christians—perhaps Gnostics—who saw no value in the material elements of the sacrament. Another group is mixing the Eucharist with an ordinary, profane meal.[39] Guérin suggests an Arian connection, but there is no other evidence for such practices by Arians, as du Bourguet pointed out in his article "Diatribe de Chenoute contre le demon."[40] It would be difficult to connect the practices condemned by Shenoute with known heresies. Nonstandard eucharistic practices were widespread at this time. The Council of Carthage (ca. 390) condemned private masses, which were somehow related to rites conducted in cemeteries.[41]

We know that Shenoute played several different roles in relation to the local Christian population: source of refuge, spokesman for their economic rights, and spiritual adviser. To my knowledge, no one has tried to make a theoretical connection between the roles. Peter Brown's analysis of the role of the holy man in Syria may be helpful. In his article "Town, Village, and Holy Man: The Case of Syria," Brown describes the way the holy man functions as the patron of the local population.[42] Services performed by the holy man, especially as a

35. H. Guérin, Sermons inédits de Senouti (Paris: Leroux, 1903).
36. Ibid., 17–18.
37. Theodoret Compendium 4.7.
38. Guérin, Sermons inédits, 18.
39. Ibid., 10.
40. P. du Bourguet, "Diatribe de Chenoute contre le démon," BSAC 16 (1961–62) 57.
41. Jean Gaudemet, L'église dans l'empire romain (Paris: Sirey, 1958) 663.
42. Peter Brown, "Town, Village, and Holy Man: The Case of Syria," in his Society

mediator with various authorities, increased his personal power and influence. He could use this power to guide religious belief and practice. Shenoute, as the head of a large monastic community, must have acted in ways that were different from those of the Syrian holy man, in his classical form. But Brown's theory indicates a direction that research might profitably follow. We may eventually be able to understand the relationship between the archbishop of Alexandria, monastic leaders such as Shenoute, and the Egyptian monks—hitherto a puzzling example of intense loyalties and few obvious benefits—as an organized hierarchy of patronage.

There are a few other references to heresy (specifically Manichaeism) in Shenoute's writings. In these it is not clear whether he is addressing a threat inside or outside the monastery. And how serious is the threat? He condemns "Manes, the Manichaean atheist, who rejects the law and the prophets . . ."[43] Elsewhere, Shenoute argues that the Lord remains God while becoming man but that those drowned in the "bad faith of Manes" do not believe it.[44] As Leipoldt noted, others asked for Shenoute's advice about the Manichees.[45] The evidence from Shenoute's writings needs to be combined with other evidence for Manichaean activity. Eventually we may have a clearer picture of Manichaean activity in this part of Egypt in the fifth century.

More has been written about Shenoute's anti-pagan activities. His attacks on paganism were combined with criticism of the way the wealthy landowners and public officials treated the peasants. Barns's article "Shenoute as a Historical Source" deals with both topics.[46] Judging by Shenoute's writings, paganism seems to have survived among upper-class Egyptians. Johannes Geffcken, in his very thorough examination of the subject, noted, "Reactionary paganism at this time in Egypt regularly combined Egyptian belief with Greek cultural habits and ideas."[47] Greek culture would be largely the property of the educated classes. Thus it is easy to see the dual function of Shenoute's violent attacks on local pagans. Raids on temples and private homes to confiscate idols, books, and other equipment of pagan religion also

---

and the Holy in Late Antiquity (Berkeley and Los Angeles: Univ. of California Press, 1982) 153–65.

43. Amélineau, Oeuvres 1:194.

44. Ibid. 1:133.

45. Leipoldt, Schenute, 160.

46. John Barns, "Shenoute as a Historical Source," IKP (1964) 156–59.

47. Johannes Geffcken, The Last Days of Greco-Roman Paganism (trans. Sabine MacCormack; Amsterdam: North Holland, 1978) 154.

allowed Shenoute's followers to express their anger over economic oppression. In one text, which is Shenoute's response to the pagan priests of Pneueit who tried to have him prosecuted for the destruction of their property, these economic and religious factors are linked.[48] We know that the destruction of temples was a widespread phenomenon at this time, and monks often took the lead in attacks on rural temples, according to Libanius.[49] Frend, in *The Rise of the Monophysite Movement*, describes how monks came to Alexandria in 391 to witness the destruction of the Serapeum.[50] Du Bourguet has also studied these texts dealing with anti-pagan attitudes and actions. He argues that anti-paganism is simply one manifestation of the enduring Egyptian concern for demons. He further states that the gods of the underworld were the dominant figures in Egyptian religion of late antiquity.[51] Shenoute's references to the god Cronus (to be identified with the Egyptian deity Petbe, according to Amélineau[52]) imply that he is a demon and thus an adversary. This fear of demons is pervasive in late antiquity. Some sort of demonology is part of all the religions of the Empire; it is not just an Egyptian phenomenon.

Another point that needs clarification is Shenoute's use of the term "pagan." In several texts there is a loose pairing of heretics and ΝⲌⲈⲀⲀHN (pagans).[53] Both classes are sometimes found *inside* the churches, according to Shenoute. Some of these "pagans" may have been Christians. Or, perhaps, they considered themselves Christians while Shenoute considered them pagans. I suspect, though I have not yet tried to prove, that ⲌⲈⲀⲀHN is sometimes a code word in Shenoute for a Hellenized Egyptian of the upper classes. If so, a "pagan" could practice either Egyptian religion or Christianity. Religious and economic hostility are thoroughly intertwined at this time and place, and Shenoute's writings reflect this.

Finally, we can turn to Shenoute's activities in support of the bishops of Alexandria. A few researchers have looked into this area. Everyone is familiar with the picture of Cyril, and later Dioscorus, accompanied to the church councils by a gang of fanatical monks.[54] Shenoute's

48. CSCO 42:86. See also 42:79–80 and 42:90, referring to activities in Atripe.
49. Libanius *Pro templis* 8.
50. W. H. C. Frend, *The Rise of the Monophysite Movement* (Cambridge: Cambridge Univ. Press, 1972) 6.
51. Du Bourguet, "Diatribe," 20.
52. Amélineau, *Oeuvres* 1:383.
53. CSCO 42:45, 48, 51, 85.
54. Frend, *Rise*, 82.

writings imply, and Besa's *Life of Shenoute* specifically states, that Shenoute attended the first Council of Ephesus.[55] He physically attacked Nestorius, according to Besa. But the references to the council in Shenoute's works are vague. He mentions "decisions" that "we" made at the synod of Ephesus but does not spell them out (CSCO 42:95). In the same text he states: "In the place of the chest in which Moses was put, behold the holy manger and the tomb which is honored, Christ was put in it . . . the covering of linen, the son of God was swathed in them." As E. R. Hardy stated in *Christian Egypt*:

> This is as close as Shenoute comes to grasping the Alexandrian theology. He certainly accepted the essentials of Alexandrian theology, but the primary source of his religion was his own meditation on the Coptic Bible.[56]

This may be "as close as Shenoute comes," but it shows no great familiarity with the issues of the council. H. F. Weiss, in one of the few recent attempts to study the thought of Shenoute, looked at the same texts and reached essentially the same conclusion.[57] One expects to find more allusions to christological problems than there are. Hardy implied that Shenoute attended the council but was uninterested in Alexandrian theology and never tried to understand it. But perhaps Shenoute never attended a church council and the incident in his *Life* was invented by his admirers.[58] This would account for the vagueness of the few references to the christological controversy in Shenoute's writings. And in that case, there would not necessarily have been any personal contact between Cyril and Shenoute. We have one purported letter from Dioscorus to Shenoute. No personal relationship is suggested in it. The letter has two sections—one addressed to Shenoute and another to three bishops, with some form of public reading implied.[59] Dioscorus states that a certain Helias, a former priest, is to be expelled from Panopolis, from any other city in the Thebaid, or from a monastery or cave. He is an Origenist and must not be allowed to contaminate others with heresy. In the section addressed to the bishops, Dioscorus further states, "But since I have heard moreover that there are books and numerous treatises of the pest named Origen and

55. Besa, *Life of Shenoute*, 128; CSCO 42:34, 95, 219.
56. E. R. Hardy, *Christian Egypt* (New York/London: Oxford Univ. Press, 1952) 103.
57. H. F. Weiss, "Zur Christologie des Schenute von Atripe," *BSAC* 20 (1970) 177–210.
58. A suggestion made by D. W. Johnson.
59. Herbert Thompson, "Dioscorus and Shenoute," *BEHE* 234 (1922) 367–76. The letter is found in a seventh-century manuscript, Cairo 9285.

other heretics in that convent and in the former temple of Shmin and elsewhere, let your Reverences inquire after them carefully ... and send them to us. ..." This text may be an example of the *kind* of contact that Shenoute had with the archbishops of Alexandria. Shenoute's own letters give the other side of the relationship.[60] If Shenoute did not attend the Council of Ephesus at Cyril's invitation, our picture of Shenoute must be slightly redrawn. He would still be a very important leader in the Thebaid, but he may not have been highly regarded in Alexandria.

Dioscorus's letter to Shenoute gives rise to other theories as well. It suggests one set of circumstances for the concealment of the Nag Hammadi texts. Perhaps a similar letter prompted the owners of the texts to hide them before they were confiscated by the ecclesiastical authorities. This is one of the many problems connected with the life and works of Shenoute that need further study.

After Leipoldt's basic work in the early years of this century, little work was done on Shenoute for many years. Meanwhile, important studies of the Coptic language and Pachomian monasticism appeared. These can help us in a new effort to study the life and works of Shenoute. The discovery of the Nag Hammadi texts stimulated all Coptic studies and we find a new interest in Shenoute beginning in the 1960s. But so far no one has attempted the necessary textual work: a new critical edition of the works of Shenoute. If anything is clear from this review of research, it is the need for a new, complete text. Until this appears, historical studies of limited scope are possible and could yield valuable results.

60. CSCO 42:13–14.

Monasticism and Gnosis
in Egypt

It was near the site of the first Pachomian foundations, in an abandoned cemetery, near Kasr es-Sayyad,[1] that the Coptic manuscripts, most of them gnostic,[2] known as the Nag Hammadi library, were discovered. That proximity, as well as the dates discovered on the fragments of papyri used to strengthen the leather covers of the codices,[3] seemed to confirm that the decline of Gnosticism in Egypt coincided with the growth of Christian monasticism.[4] The question of the relationship between Gnosticism and Christian monasticism, especially Pachomian cenobitism, was then raised.[5]

1. James M. Robinson has treated all the questions concerning the place and the date of the discoveries of the Nag Hammadi manuscripts in several publications. His most detailed presentation is probably "From the Cliff to Cairo; The Story of the Discoverers and the Middlemen of the Nag Hammadi Codices," in *Colloque international sur les textes de Nag Hammadi (Québec, 22-25 août 1978)* (ed. Bernard Barc; BCNH 1; Quebec: L'Université Laval, 1981) 21-58.

2. Several of the texts from the Nag Hammadi library are not gnostic. See the list given by G. Quispel, "The *Gospel of Thomas* Revisited," in *Colloque international* (ed. Barc) 254-55.

3. See John C. Shelton, *Nag Hammadi Codices: Greek and Coptic Papyri from the Cartonnage of the Covers* (ed. J. W. B. Barns, G. M. Browne, J. C. Shelton; NHS 16; Leiden: E. J. Brill, 1981) 1-11; and J. M. Robinson, "The Construction of the Nag Hammadi Codices," in *Essays on the Nag Hammadi Texts: In Honor of Pahor Labib* (ed. M. Krause; NHS 6; Leiden: E. J. Brill, 1975) 170-90.

4. See F. Wisse, "Gnosticism and Early Monasticism in Egypt," in *Gnosis: Festschrift für Hans Jonas* (ed. B. Aland; Göttingen: Vandenhoeck & Ruprecht, 1978) 433. The connection had already been mentioned by J. Doresse (*Les livres secrets des gnostiques d'Egypte* [Paris: Plon, 1958] 135-38) and R. McL. Wilson (*Gnosis and the New Testament* [Philadelphia: Fortress Press, 1968] 87).

5. According to Epiphanius's testimony, some gnostic sects were still active in Egypt in the middle of the fourth century. See Kurt Rudolph, *Die Gnosis: Wesen und Geschichte einer spätantiken Religion* (Leipzig: Koehler & Amelang, 1977) 23.

The question acquired a greater importance when John Barns claimed he could demonstrate that at least some of those codices had been made in a Pachomian monastery or, in any case, by Pachomian monks.[6] Although it was soon proved that Barns had stated more than the paleographical data permitted,[7] the close relationship between the Nag Hammadi library and Pachomian cenobitism has been taken for granted ever since.[8] On that fragile basis many hypotheses were put forward concerning the reasons for which the monks would have assembled those documents in the first place and later got rid of them. It seems that the time has come to analyze and evaluate each of these theories.

Three series of questions can be distinguished, each requiring the elaboration of a good methodology:[9]

1. Historical contacts that may or may not have existed between Pachomian monks and the manuscripts discovered near Nag Hammadi at the end of 1945
2. Literary contacts that can or cannot be demonstrated between documents known through the Nag Hammadi library and the early monastic literature in general
3. Points of contact of a historical and doctrinal character between monasticism and Gnosticism.

THE NAG HAMMADI LIBRARY AND PACHOMIAN CENOBITISM

Before analyzing the various hypotheses concerning the possible

6. J. Barns, "Greek and Coptic Papyri from the Covers of the Nag Hammadi Codices," in *Essays on the Nag Hammadi Texts* (ed. M. Krause; NHS 6; Leiden: E. J. Brill, 1975). His findings had already been presented in 1972 in "The International Committee for the Nag Hammadi Codices: A Progress Report," *NTS* 18 (1972) 240. See also J. M. Robinson, "Introduction," in *The Facsimile Edition of the Nag Hammadi Codices: Codex VII* (Leiden: E. J. Brill, 1972) ix.
7. See E. G. Turner's commentary, in the appendix to Barns's posthumous article "Greek and Coptic Papyri," 17–18; and Shelton, *Nag Hammadi Codices*, 1–11.
8. Törgny Säve-Söderbergh ("The Pagan Elements in Early Christianity and Gnosticism," in *Colloque international sur les textes de Nag Hammadi* [ed. Barc] 74) speaks of "the established connection between the library and the Pachomians"; and still more recently R. van den Broek ("The Present State of Gnostic Studies," *VC* 37 [1983] 47) affirms: "The books were bound in a Pachomian monastery in the middle of the fourth century."
9. The only general study of the whole question is that of G. G. Stroumsa, "Ascèse et gnose: Aux origines de la spiritualité monastique," *RevThom* 89 (1981) 557–73. A. Guillaumont also gives a good methodological orientation in "Gnose et Monachisme," in *Gnosticisme et monde hellénistique: les objectifs du colloque de Louvain-la-Neuve (11–14 mars 1980)* (Louvain-la-Neuve: Institut Orientaliste, 1980) 97–100; ET: 101–4.

relationship between Pachomian monasticism and the Nag Hammadi documents, it might be useful to make a quick survey of the origin and first development of Pachomian cenobitism.[10]

Origin of Pachomian Cenobitism

Pachomius was born in Egypt in the diocese of Sne[11] (a little to the south of Sheneset, in the diocese of Diospolis Parva) in 292. After becoming a Christian in 312–313, he settled down at Tabennesi about ten years later in order to live a monastic life there. Before coming to that place he had been initiated into monastic life by the old man Palamon near Sheneset, where he had lived for three years after his baptism.[12]

It was in 324 that Pachomius began to receive disciples, and their number increased so rapidly that he had to make a foundation in Phbow as early as 329. That was the beginning of a long series of foundations. Some of them were, as in the case of Phbow, simply an offshoot of a too-populated monastery. But in other cases, for example in Shmin, the foundation was a response to a request made by a bishop who wanted a monastery in his diocese. And there were cases, as in Thmoushons and Thbew, where existing communities asked to be incorporated into the Pachomian *Koinonia* so as to live according to Pachomius's rules and under his authority.[13]

We can divide the foundations into two groups, geographically and probably also chronologically—although the chronological data of the

---

10. For an easy access to all the Pachomian sources I refer to my English translation of the whole corpus, *Pachomian Koinonia: The Lives, Rules and Other Writings of Saint Pachomius and His Disciples* (3 vols.; CistSS 45, 46, 47; Kalamazoo, Mich.: Cistercian Pubs., 1980–82). In the introduction to each of the volumes the reader will find the technical information concerning each document and mention of all the existing editions. I had already presented the whole Pachomian corpus in *La liturgie dans le cénobitisme pachômien au quatrième siècle* (StAns 57; Rome: Herder, 1968) 1–158. The first volume of my French translation of the corpus has just appeared in *La Vie de saint Pachôme selon la tradition copte* (Spiritualité orientale 38; Bégrolles-en-Mauges, France: Abbaye de Bellefontaine, 1984). I use the sigla that are now generally accepted: Bo = the Bohairic *Life* of Pachomius; *S1, S2*, etc. = the first Sahidic *Life*, the second Sahidic *Life*, etc.; *SBo* = the standard Coptic *Life* known through the various Sahidic fragments (*S4, S5*, etc.), the Bohairic translation (*Bo*), and the Arabic translation of the Vatican (*Av*); *G1, G2*, etc. = the first Greek *Life*, the second Greek *Life*, etc.; *Paral.* = the *Paralipomena*; *EpAm* = the *Letter of Bishop Ammon*.

11. *SBo* 3; and not in Sheneset, as T. Säve-Söderbergh says in "Holy Scriptures or Apostolic Documentations? The 'Sitz im Leben' of the Nag Hammadi Library," in *Les Textes de Nag-Hammadi* (ed. J. E. Ménard; NHS 7; Leiden: E. J. Brill, 1975) 6.

12. *S1* 1–9; *SBo* 3–22; *G1* 3–23.

13. *SBo* 23–58; *G1* 24–54 and 80–83.

Lives are not absolutely consistent.[14] The first four foundations, established in 329 and in the following years, were very close to one another in time and space, and Pachomius seems to have kept an immediate personal authority over all of them during the first years. It was, after Tabennesi and Phbow, Sheneset (a little to the west of Phbow) and Thmoushons (a little farther, on the other shore of the Nile, but in the same diocese). With Thbew a second series of foundations was initiated, probably toward the end of Pachomius's life, between 340 and 345. The first three of that group were near one another in the region of Shmin, and a fourth and last one was in a completely different direction, rather far south of the first group, at Phnoum. At a rather early date Pachomius gave to Petronios (who had founded and administered the monastery of Thbew before it was integrated into the Pachomian *Koinonia*) a general responsibility over all the monasteries of the region of Shmin.[15]

Petronios succeeded Pachomius as the head of the *Koinonia* in 346, but for only a few months. He was replaced by Horsiesios who, after a serious crisis of authority, was obliged to hand the government over to Theodore five years later. At Theodore's death, in 368, Horsiesios again assumed the direction of the *Koinonia* until his own death around 380.[16]

I mention that crisis in order to stress the fact that according to what the sources say very clearly, it was a crisis of authority and not, as was claimed at times, a crisis of orthodoxy.[17] The "ancients" *(oi archaioi)* of the community were the initiators of that crisis. Who were they? The study of the various contexts where the expression is used reveals that it is a question here of "ancients" in the obvious meaning of the word, that is, those who were the first to come to the *Koinonia*. There is no justification for assimilating them to a group of "perfect ones" in the community.[18] To the contrary, the *Lives* seem to enjoy depicting them as not so perfect! They tended to murmur, and they did not like too much to be governed by someone younger than themselves.[19]

---

14. See D. J. Chitty, "A Note on the Chronology of Pachomian Foundations," in *St Patr II* (TU 64; Berlin: Akademie-Verlag, 1957) 379–85.

15. *SBo* 56–57; *G1* 80.

16. *SBo* 123–end; *G1* 116–end.

17. That crisis was studied at length, although from the limited point of view of the concept of poverty, by B. Büchler (*Die Armut der Armen: Ueber den ursprünglichen Sinn der mönchischen Armut* [Munich: Kosel, 1980] 138–45).

18. As does Jon F. Dechow in "The Nag Hammadi Milieu: An Assessment in the Light of the Origenist Controversies" (AAR Western Region, annual meeting, Stanford University, 26 March 1982) 13–14.

19. See, e.g., *SBo* 69 and *G1* 77 (cf. *Paral.* 1); *SBo* 92 and *G1* 100.

At the time of Pachomius's death, the *Koinonia* was composed of nine monasteries of men and two of women. The number of the monks may have reached a few thousand.[20] But it would be an exaggeration to say that the Pachomians dominated the whole monastic world of the region. As a matter of fact, the growth of Pachomian monasticism slowed down precisely at that time. No foundation was made during Horsiesios's first superiorship, from 346 to 350, and only two foundations of monks and one of nuns during the eighteen years of Theodore's mandate, from 350 to 368.[21] The period that followed is less well known but we have no indication of foundations made during the twelve years or so of Horsiesios's second mandate.

At the very time when the development of Pachomian cenobitism was considerably slowed, after the founder's death, monasticism developed rapidly in some other places in Egypt. Amoun retired to Nitria in 325, and by the end of the century, his disciples had reached the figure of five thousand monks. In 330, Macarius the Egyptian withdrew to Scetis, followed by several disciples. The Kellia were founded in 338, and Paladius spoke of six hundred monks there in 390.[22]

Even in Upper Egypt there were not only Pachomian monasteries. Palamon, Pachomius's master, had several disciples, and there is no reason to think that they followed Pachomius.[23] The latter's first disciples were Coptic peasants without any previous monastic background.[24] There were probably several monastic groups in the region similar to that of Palamon; an example would be the community where Theodore lived before he came to Tabennesi.[25] While a few of those groups joined Pachomius's *Koinonia*,[26] most did not. The *Lives of Pachomius* often show him and his monks in contact with non-Pachomian monastic groups—some orthodox, some not.[27] We also know of the existence of communities of Meletian monks in Upper

20. Jerome, in the preface to his translation of the Rule of Pachomius, speaks of 50,000 monks. That obviously is an exaggeration. Palladius, who certainly does not tend to use small figures, speaks in his *H. Laus.* of 1300 monks (according to chap. 32.8) or of 1400 (according to chap. 18.13) living in Phbow during his time, the other monasteries having between 200 and 300 monks each.
21. *SBo* 134.
22. See A. Guillaumont, "Histoire des moines aux Kellia," *OLP* 8 (1977) 187–203.
23. *SBo* 10, 16, 18.
24. *S1* 10–14; *SBo* 23; and *G1* 24.
25. *SBo* 31; *G1* 33.
26. *SBo* 50, 51, 56; *G1* 54, 80, 83.
27. See for example *SBo* 28 and *G1* 30 (the bishop of Nitentori wants to have Pachomius ordained by Athanasius so as to be able to establish him over all the monks

Egypt as early as 334, and they continued in existence for a long time.[28] And Epiphanius affirms that he met gnostic groups there in the middle of the fourth century, therefore at the same time.

One should not forget, either, that some monasteries followed the regulations of Pachomius (or of the Tabennesiotes)—often modifying them—without, for all that, belonging to the Pachomian *Koinonia* or Congregation. That was the case of the monastery of Canopos near Alexandria[29] and also of the great White Monastery of Atripe, near Shmin, where Pjol, the great Shenoute's uncle, had introduced a Pachomian rule.[30] That the White Monastery did not belong to the

---

of his diocese, but Pachomius runs away); *SBo* 29–30 and *G1* 33–35 (monastery of the region of Sne where Theodore lived before coming to Tabennesi); *SBo* 40 and *G1* 40 (on the reception of visiting monks—cf. *Praecepta* 51–52 of the Rule of Pachomius); *SBo* 42 and *G1* 42 (a non-Pachomian monastery only three km away from Tabennesi); *SBo* 68 and *G1* 76 (a bishop sends a monk of his diocese to Pachomius to be judged by him); etc. In his book *Die Armut der Armen*, Büchler has a section on the question of the encounter of Pachomius with heterodox currents: "Pachomius und heterodoxe Strömungen," 138–45; he says, e.g.: "Uebereinstimmend geben die Texte Zeugnis davon, dass im unmittelbaren Umkreis des *Pachomius* heterodoxe Strömungen hervortraten und heterodoxe Mönche lebten" (p. 138); and: "Als gesichert will uns darum mindestens folgende Auffassung scheinen: es gab schon zur Zeit des *Pachomius* 'fremde Mönche', mit denen *Pachomius* und die mit *Pachomius* keine Gemeinschaft hatte(n)" (p. 141).

28. In *SBo* 129 Antony's disciples express their displeasure at being asked whether they are Meletians when they visit the monasteries of the Pachomian *Koinonia*. *EpAm* 12 tells us that Pachomius was bothered by them, as well as by the Marcionites, during his first few years as a Christian. These Meletians were the followers of Meletios, bishop of Lycopolis in Egypt, not to be confused with the other Meletians, followers of Meletios of Antioch, a half century later. This early Meletian schism seems to have originated with Meletios's disagreement with Peter, archbishop of Alexandria (d. 311), over the treatment of the *lapsi* during the Decian persecution. Later they went into the camp of the Arians and were bitter enemies of Athanasius. In fact it is mostly with them and *their* apocryphal books that Athanasius is preoccupied in his famous festal letter of 367, of which we shall speak below. The papyri published by H. I. Bell (*Jews and Christians in Egypt* [London: British Museum, 1924]) inform us about Meletian monks who lived in the vicinity of Antony around 330. There were still Meletian monks in Egypt in the sixth century, as is witnessed by two contracts signed in 512 and 513 by a certain Eulogios, son of Joseph, who introduces himself as "a former Meletian monk, now orthodox"; see A. H. Sayce, "Deux contrats grecs du Fayoum," *REG* 3 (1890) 131–44.

29. Around 390, the patriarch Theophilos, Cyril's uncle and great anti-Origenist, destroyed the temple of Sarapis in Canopos, about 20 miles to the northeast of Alexandria, and established there a monastery to which he invited Pachomian monks. See P. Ladeuze, *Etude sur le cénobitisme pakhômien pendant le IV siècle et la première moitié du V* (2d ed.; Frankfurt am Main: Minerva, 1961) 202; and A. Favale, *Teofilo d'Alessandria (345–412): Scritti, Vita, e Dottrina* (Biblioteca del Salesianum 41; Turin: Società editrice internazionale, 1958) 61–71. See also H. Bacht, *Das Vermächtnis des Ursprungs* (Studien zum frühen Mönchtum 1; Würzburg: Echter, 1972) 9–10.

30. Shenoute became a monk at the White Monastery in 370 or 371 (see J. Leipoldt, *Schenute von Atripe und die Entstehung des national-ägyptischen Christentums* [Leipzig: Hinrichs, 1903] 42–44). That monastery must therefore have been founded by Pjol around the middle of the century, certainly before the time when the *Life* of Pachomius and Theodore (d. 368) received its definitive form in Coptic and in Greek.

Pachomian *Koinonia* is proved by the fact that it is never numbered among the Pachomian foundations in the *Lives*, which were written at a time when the White Monastery was certainly already in existence.

At that time the name of Tabennesiote is attributed not only to all the Pachomian monks, but also to all those who lived according to Pachomius's rules. And therefore, when a chronicler tells us that he has visited Tabennesiote monks, one should not necessarily conclude that he went as far south as Tabennesi. Cassian probably never saw a monastery of the Pachomian *Koinonia*;[31] and Palladius did not go further than Shmin in Upper Egypt.[32] There is therefore no conclusion to be drawn from the fact that the Origenist Palladius was well received by Tabennesiote monks![33]

This may be the occasion to mention that Palladius, in his Pachomian chronicle, in chapters 32 and 33 of the *Lausiac History*, used a written source originating from a non-Pachomian milieu, as René Draguet has demonstrated.[34] The famous *Regula Angeli*, which was to become so popular during all the Middle Ages, is in clear contradiction with the *Life* and the authentic *Rules* of Pachomius on so many points that it can absolutely not come from a Pachomian milieu.[35] It must be used with extreme caution. And one should not forget that it is in the Palladian chronicle and not in any authentic Pachomian document that we find a list of crafts exercised in the Pachomian monasteries, in which tanners are mentioned.

It has been said during the last few years that the discovery of the Nag Hammadi library will oblige us to do a new evaluation of what we know of Pachomian origins.[36] If by this, one means that it is now more necessary than before to bring as much light as possible on the various problems of textual, literary, and historical criticism of the Pachomian sources, everyone will agree. But it would be wrong to think that such light can come—barring an exception or two—from documents of the Nag Hammadi library. One cannot elucidate what is clearer by what is more obscure. Now, it is a fact that a good many of the critical

---

31. See A. Veilleux, *La liturgie*, 146–54.

32. Ibid., 138–46.

33. As does Säve-Söderbergh, "Holy Scriptures or Apostolic Documentations?" 11.

34. See R. Draguet, "Le chapitre de HL sur les Tabennésiotes dérive-t-il d'une source copte?" *Muséon* 57 (1944) 53–145, and 58 (1945) 15–95.

35. On the evolution of modern criticism about Palladius, esp. concerning the *Regula Angeli*, see Veilleux, *La liturgie*, 138–46.

36. E.g., recently, C. Kannengiesser, in his review of the Acts of the *Colloque international sur les textes de Nag Hammadi* held at Quebec in August 1978, in *RechSR* 70 (1982) 619.

problems concerning the Pachomian sources have been solved—although much still remains to be done[37]—while the question of the origin of the Nag Hammadi library and of the circumstances in which those documents were buried is still surrounded by a deep mystery.[38]

The cartonnage of some of the codices may help to solve part of the mystery.

The Cartonnage of the Codices from the
Nag Hammadi Library

The codices of the Nag Hammadi library were found in 1945 on the side of the Jabal al-Tarif cliff, near Kasr es-Sayyad, a few kilometers from the site of the first three Pachomian foundations (Tabennesi, Phbow, and Sheneset). The question has been raised of possible contacts between these documents and Pachomian monasticism.[39] The geographical proximity, however, does not prove anything, for we know that other monastic groups—orthodox as well as heterodox—existed in the area, to say nothing of monks leading an eremitical form of life, a fact to which the *Life of Pachomius* bears witness.

But there is something more to it. The leather bindings of eight of these codices were strengthened with pieces of used papyri, and their examination has revealed very interesting information. First of all, the fact that some of these fragments bear dates ranging from 333 to 348 gives us a date *post quam* for the fabrication of the books. It must have taken place shortly after Pachomius's death.[40]

After a study of these fragments, most of which are very small and extremely difficult to interpret, John Barns came to some rapid conclusions—not without some degree of enthusiasm—concerning the Pachomian origin of the codices.[41] Since the publication of Barns's first provisional report, most scholars seem to have taken that conclusion as

37. For a good, succinct, and up-to-date presentation of the scientific criticism of the Pachomian sources, see Büchler, *Die Armut der Armen*, 14–19: "Ueberblick über den Forschungsstand." Concerning the *Lives*, see J. Vergote, "La valeur des Vies grecques et coptes de S. Pakhôme," *OLP* 8 (1977) 175–86.

38. On the present state of the research on this question, see R. van den Broek, "The Present State."

39. According to the figures given by W. C. Unnik (*Evangelien aus dem Nilsand* [Frankfurt: Scheffler, 1960] 13) the site of the discovery is 12 km from Tabennesi, 8 km from Phbow, and 9 km from Sheneset. The distances given by J. M. Robinson ("Introduction," in *NHLE*, 21ff.) are slightly different (Phbow: 5.3 km and Sheneset 8.7 km), but that slight difference is without importance.

40. Photographic edition of all those fragments in *The Facsimile Edition of the Nag Hammadi Codices: Cartonnage* (Leiden: E. J. Brill, 1979); ET in *Nag Hammadi Codices*.

41. Cf. above, n. 6.

definitively demonstrated, although J. C. Shelton and others, reevaluating Barns's own arguments, have clearly shown that things were not that evident.[42]

Without going over all the aspects of that problem that other scholars have studied in more detail, let us review rapidly the main aspects of the question.[43] From the point of view of possible Pachomian contacts, the only documents that are clearly relevant are those found in the cartonnage of Codex VII. The documents found in the cartonnage of other codices (I, IV, V, VI, VIII, IX, and XI) are mostly fragments of accounts of taxation, contracts, etc. Nothing there has any specifically monastic flavor, certainly not, for example, that contract from the cartonnage of Codex I, signed between a guild of oil workers and the city of Diospolis Parva. Barns, it is true, saw a monastic background precisely in that fragment; but it was because he read the Greek word *monē* where we must read *kōmē*, and because he took for a monastic superior the *proestōs* mentioned there who was actually the chairman of the guild of oil workers.

While Barns tended to see too easily a monastic background in these texts, it is possible that Shelton rejected that possibility too categorically, as Dechow has shown.[44] For example, one cannot exclude the possibility of some accounts coming from a monastery simply because the figures are so high that they invite us to think of the accounts of a civilian or military administration.[45] For, if the Pachomian monasteries were as populated as they are said to have been, to supply them must have required a considerable quantity of some products. But, when all is said, it remains that some of those documents clearly come from a civilian adminstration, as, for example, the taxation accounts, and one wonders how they came into the hands of the monks. The hypothesis of the Pachomian origin of those documents is not ruled out, but it is not confirmed by anything really positive.

There remains the cartonnage of Codex VII. It is the most important of all, for it is there that Barns found the largest number of indications of a Pachomian origin. In any case, we find in it some documents of an unquestionably religious character and a few explicit mentions of monks.

---

42. Cf. above, nn. 7 and 8.
43. For a succinct presentation of the various theories, see G. G. Stroumsa, "Ascèse et gnose," 558; and van den Broek, "The Present State," 47–49.
44. J. Dechow, "The Nag Hammadi Milieu."
45. That hypothesis should not, however, be excluded, as we shall see below.

The religious documents in question are a few fragments of the Book of Genesis[46] and an exhortation to virtue that may come either from a homily or from a letter. Barns made the suggestion that its author could have been Pachomius. That is not impossible, but there is no positive reason whatsoever to attribute the exhortation to Pachomius rather than to anybody else. Would it not be surprising, however, that Pachomian monks (if they made the cartonnage) would have used papyri containing writings of their father Abba Pachomius to strengthen the leather cover of a book, barely a few years after the founder's death? Along the same line, I think that Shelton is right when he writes: "I do not know whether a fourth-century monastery would be more or less likely than other groups or individuals to use bits of Holy Scripture to strengthen a book cover."[47]

The same cartonnage of Codex VII also contains some fragments of contracts from which not much can be learned, except that they can be dated between 336 and 348. Finally, we find there also an important collection of private letters, most of them in Greek, in which, for the first time, one can read clear references to monks. Every time the religious orientation of the writers can be discerned, they appear to be Christians, and one cannot perceive any suggestion either of orthodoxy or heterodoxy.

In reality, there are only two letters in the cover of Codex VII that unquestionably were written either to or by monks: nos. 72 and C8. The first is a letter written by a woman to two monks named Sansnos and Psatos. She asks them to try to find some chaff for her asses and let her know how much it costs per wagonload. All these details, according to Shelton, would suppose a context quite different from the Pachomian one. Jon Dechow reacted rather forcefully to that position, which he considers based upon a preconceived and too narrow idea of the practice of separation from the world in the Pachomian monasteries. I agree with Dechow in saying that Shelton refuses too easily to see the possibility that the monks in question were Pachomian. But on the other hand, I would insist on saying that nothing indicates, even indirectly, that they were. Moreover, I can but find it a little difficult to reconcile that kind of request made by a woman to two monks with the image of a Pachomian monastery that we can gather from the Pachomian sources. Of course, I am ready to admit that the sources

---

46. These fragments were published by R. Kasser, "Fragments du livre biblique de la Genèse cachés dans la reliure d'un codex gnostique," *Muséon* 85 (1972) 65–89.

47. Shelton, *Nag Hammadi Codices*, 4.

may be giving us an edited image of reality, but here again, this would have to be proved. And in any case, nothing allows us to know what the unedited image would have been! The situation of free association between individuals looking after their own needs, to which J. Dechow makes a reference, is clearly presented in the *Life of Pachomius* as a situation of transition that came to an end very soon after the beginnings, around 328.[48] The cartonnage documents that can be dated are from 336–48, well after that date.

The possibility of a monastic context is present in many other letters, although no monk is mentioned by name. Many of the letters concern a certain Sansnos, who is said at times to be a priest and who is probably not always the same person. No detail constitutes a positive Pachomian indication. One should not give too much attention to the mention of very common names of persons, like that of Sourous.

There is a Coptic fragment, however, that must retain our attention, since it is a letter written by a certain Paphnoute to a certain Pachomius. Is there a question here of Paphnoute who was the brother of Theodore and for many years the great steward of the *Koinonia* residing in Phbow, and of the great Pachomius himself?[49] That is not impossible. But one must not forget that Paphnoute and Pachomius were among the most common Coptic names. The *Life of Pachomius* mentions two Pachomiuses and at least two Paphnoutes if not three.[50] In the above-mentioned letter, our Paphnoute speaks to his Pachomius and addresses him by the title: "my prophet and father Pachomius." The title "prophet" is never used in the whole Pachomian literature in an address to Pachomius or to anybody else. Such a title, however, will often be given to Shenoute, a little later. Since Pachomius and Paphnoute lived in the same monastery of Phbow, and since Pacho-

48. Cf. *S1*, Coptic text: L. T. Lefort, *S. Pachomii Vitae sahidice scriptae*, 4 (*S3*, ibid., 112–13); ET in Veilleux, *Pachomian Koinonia* 1:430–31; French translation in Lefort, *Les Vies coptes de Saint Pachôme et de ses premiers successeurs* (BMus 16; Louvain: Bureaux du Muséon, 1943) 3 and 65.

49. Paphnoute, Theodore's brother, came to join him at Tabennesi shortly after Theodore's arrival (*SBo* 119; *G1* 114).

50. Pachomius's junior belonged to the second group of disciples that came to Pachomius at Tabennesi at the beginning of the foundation (*SBo* 24; *G1* 26). He was still alive in 368, at the time of Theodore's death (*SBo* 208). On the name "Pachome" there is an interesting note by Von Lemm, in his *Kleine Koptische Studien I–LVIII* (2d ed.; Leipzig: Zentralantiquariat der DDR, 1972) 44–45. Besides Theodore's brother, mentioned in the last note, the Coptic *Life* speaks of another Paphnoute who died during the plague of 366–367, at the end of Theodore's superiorship (*SBo* 181). The monk called Paphnoute who was for a while superior of Phbow according to the Greek *Life* (*G1* 124) is distinct from the two we just mentioned, unless it is simply a question here of a confusion of the last redactor of *G1* (see Veilleux, *Pachomian Koinonia* 1:291 n. 1).

mius's absences to visit the other monasteries were short and rapid, although frequent, it is rather improbable that they would have communicated with each other by letters. But, evidently, that is not impossible.

What can be concluded from all this? From all the cartonnage in which fragments of papyri can be found, there is only one where some of these fragments have an undeniable relationship with monks: it is the cartonnage of Codex VII. Were these monks Pachomian? It is not impossible, but no positive evidence permits us to affirm it. The presence of some letters written either by or to monks in the cartonnage of one codex does not permit us to affirm that such a cartonnage has been made by monks. All the suppositions are possible concerning the manner in which the person who made the cover has been able to get hold of these papyri. Shelton's remark concerning Codex VII seems to me valid for all the cartonnage: "It is hard to think of a satisfactory single source for such a variety of documents except a town rubbish heap—which may indeed have been the direct source of all the papyri the bookbinders used."[51]

A hypothesis proposed by J. Barns for the fragments' having an administrative character should have received more attention than it has so far. It is the suggestion that the origin of these materials could be sought in the direction of a public administration, civilian or more probably military.[52] The important number of documents having a clearly administrative character, such as accounts of taxes and copies of imperial ordinances, invite us to look in that direction. And the extracts of accounts bearing extremely large figures would find an explanation in that hypothesis at least as well as in that of a monastic origin.[53]

If, as Guillaumont recently noted, gnostic speculations were not of a nature to interest beyond measure the monks of Egypt, most of whom were illiterate,[54] they could easily interest an officer of the civilian or military administration who came from the educated circles of Alexandria or of Shmin and who had been relegated for a time to the Thebaid.

A text from Shenoute used by Young in a quite different context is very interesting in this regard.[55] Shenoute relates that he has met in

51. Shelton, *Nag Hammadi Codices*, 11.
52. Cf. ibid., 26.
53. Cf. ibid., 6.
54. Guillaumont, "Gnose et monachisme," 97.
55. D. W. Young, "The Milieu of Nag Hammadi," 130.

town the son of a *stratēlatēs* who expressed erroneous opinions, in particular that the body does not rise:

> Some began manifesting their error in that town, and when I discussed with them what is right, they ceased from their verbosity, knowing that it was the truth I was telling them from the Scriptures. Then the son of the *stratēlatēs* who was in the town in those days ventured these confusing opinions, as he had argued against another just man, saying, "This body will rise."[56]

Of course one cannot deduce anything definite from such a text, but the fact that in Shenoute's time the son of a *stratēlatēs* expressed in public, doctrines that were similar to those of certain Gnostics must be added to the evidence we are studying. Perhaps we must also add to the evidence a curious Greek fragment that speaks of the presence of a detachment of Roman soldiers in the monastery of Phbow, although that must have been in the sixth century.[57] After all, it is not impossible that our manuscripts were buried at a much later date than we have believed up to now, since all the indications that we have inform us only of a date *post quam*.

When we study the various hypotheses concerning the circumstances in which the codices were gathered and buried, we must not forget that most of those hypotheses were elaborated from the postulate that the "Pachomian connection" of these documents had been solidly established, while, in fact, it is only one possibility to be considered among many others.

Why Was the Nag Hammadi Library Gathered?

The various theories concerning the gathering and the burying of the manuscripts of the Nag Hammadi library have already been described in detail, in particular by T. Säve-Söderbergh and by G. G. Stroumsa.[58] We mention them here only insofar as they have something to do with our topic. First of all, it is important to mention the very great variety of the documents contained in the thirteen codices of Nag Hammadi as

---

56. Leipoldt, *Schenute von Atripe*, 3:32.23–33.5. ET from Young, "Milieu."
57. "Paid by the church of Apollonopolis on account of supplies for the most noble Scythians quartered in the monastery of Bau . . ." Cf. A. S. Hunt and C. C. Edgar, *Select Papyri II: Non Literary Papyri* (LCL 282; Cambridge: Harvard Univ. Press; London: William Heinemann, 1966). This text was kindly communicated to me by James M. Robinson.
58. Säve-Söderbergh, "Holy Scriptures or Apostolic Documentations?" 3–5; idem, "The Pagan Elements," 71–72. See also above, n. 45.

this variety was described in particular by M. Krause. This makes some authors hesitate to speak of a "library."[59] Moreover, since some of the documents mentioned do not show any gnostic character—as, obviously, for example, the fragment of the *Republic* of Plato—other authors refuse to speak of a "gnostic" library.[60]

The content of the documents cannot tell us much concerning the motives for their gathering, since they were originally written in Greek and since they came from other places, probably Syria in many cases.

J. Doresse has suggested that our texts came from a gnostic community of the region.[61] Since the "discovery" by J. Barns of their Pachomian origin, that hypothesis seems to have been put aside. Maybe it should not be totally discarded, since according to Epiphanius's testimony, gnostic communities still existed in Egypt at the time that our documents were bound, that is, toward the middle of the fourth century.[62]

Nobody so far has expressed the hypothesis that our documents belonged to a community of Meletian monks. Such communities are known to have existed in Upper Egypt at the time that interests us.[63] And that hypothesis, as gratuitous as it is, is as worth considering as the other ones that were proposed. What we know about the Meletians makes this quite plausible.

Two reasons have been proposed to support the hypothesis that our manuscripts have been assembled by orthodox Christian monks, Pachomians or others: the first one is that these texts were assembled to serve as matter for pious reading, their heterodox character not being perceived or not creating problems; the second is that they were assembled for heresiological purposes.[64]

59. See M. Krause, "Zur Bedeutung des gnostisch-hermetischen Handschriftenfundes von Nag Hammadi," in *Essays on the Nag Hammadi Texts: In Honor of Pahor Labib* (ed. Krause) 65–89; idem, "Die Texte von Nag Hammadi," in *Gnosis: Festschrift für Hans Jonas* (ed. Aland) 216–43, esp. 242–43. See also George W. MacRae, "Nag Hammadi and the New Testament," in *Gnosis: Festschrift für Hans Jonas*, 151–52.
60. See Wisse, "Gnosticism," 432.
61. Doresse, *Les livres secrets*, 155.
62. Cf. above, n. 5.
63. Cf. above, n. 30.
64. The first of these two hypotheses is defended with different nuances by Wisse ("Gnosticism"), J. M. Robinson (in *NHLE*, 14–21), C. Hedrick ("Gnostic Proclivities in the Greek *Life of Pachomius* and the *Sitz im Leben* of the Nag Hammadi Library," *NovT* 22 [1980] 78–94), and H. Chadwick ("The Domestical of Gnosis," in *Proceedings of the International Conference on Gnosticism at Yale, New Haven, Connecticut, March 28–31, 1978* [ed. Bentley Layton; 2 vols.; NovTSup 41; Leiden: E. J. Brill, 1980] 1:14–16). The second hypothesis was put forward by T. Säve-Söderbergh, first at the Congress of

F. Wisse, who aligns himself more with the first explanation, thinks that the Gnostics who still existed in Egypt at the time of early monasticism withdrew to the monastic communities, into which they were gradually assimilated.[65] This hypothesis is not lacking in attractiveness, but so far has not been confirmed in any way. Wisse also claims that Pachomian monasticism was not, in its origin, as orthodox as it is generally believed to have been.[66] This is possible but also remains to be proved. The examples of heterodoxy that he gives—the use by Pachomius of a mystical alphabet, the visions, the angelology, and the demonology—are not very convincing.[67] Angelology, demonology, and visions were quite common in the literature of the time, throughout the whole Christian world, even in circles totally protected from gnostic influences.[68] The explanation of that phenomenon should rather be sought in the direction of influences of early Judaism on primitive Christianity. As for the mystical alphabet, its use by Pachomius is very different from the use found in the writings of Nag Hammadi. The liking of Egyptians for cryptograms would be enough to explain the use of cryptograms by orthodox Christians as well as by

Messina, in "Gnostic and Canonical Gospel Traditions," and then in a more elaborate form in "Holy Scriptures or Apostolic Documentations?" F. Wisse has questioned that position in "Language Mysticism in the Nag Hammadi Texts and in Early Coptic Monasticism," *Enchoria* 9 (1979) 101–19. Säve-Söderbergh in "The Pagan Elements in Early Christianity and Gnosticism" seems to come closer to the first hypothesis, although with some hesitation.

65. See Wisse, "Gnosticism," 440.

66. "There is good reason to believe that concern about heresy was much less deeply and concretely felt by the Pachomian monks than by the church hierarchy in Alexandria. It is very questionable whether Pachomius and Theodore knew what they were talking about when they anathematized the writings of Origin [*sic*]" (ibid., 437).

67. "One clear example of unorthodox views sponsored by Pachomius himself did survive. I am referring to the famous alphabet mysticism and enigmatic speech in the letters of the founder of monasticism" (ibid., 437–38). "Furthermore, these texts have much material that is relevant to angelology and demonology, subjects of prime interest to Coptic monks" (ibid., 438).

68. To angelology is connected the very important theme of the *bios angelikos* that we find in all the sectors of the great monastic tradition. Among the abundant literature on the subject, see S. Frank, *Angelikos Bios: Begriffsanalytische und begriffsgeschichtliche Untersuchung zum "Engelgleichen Leben" im frühen Mönchtum* (Münster: Aschendorffsche Verlagsbuchhandlung, 1964). On demonology, see the article of A. Guillaumont, "Le démon dans la plus ancienne littérature monastique," in *DSp* 3:col. 190–91; there is a very good study by L. Bouyer also, in *La vie de saint Antoine: essai sur la spiritualité du monachisme primitif* (Paris: Editions de Fontenelle, 1950) 99–112. K. Heussi had already studied that theme in *Der Ursprung des Mönchtums* (Tübingen: Mohr, 1936) 108–15. Concerning visions, see A. Guillaumont, "Les visions mystiques dans le monachisme oriental chrétien," in *Les visions mystiques* (colloque organisé par le Secrétariat d'Etat à la Culture, Paris, 17–18 mars 1976) [*Nouvelles de l'Institut Catholique de Paris*, February 1977, 147].

Gnostics in Egypt, without necessitating any contact between the two groups.[69]

The efforts of C. Hedrick to find gnostic proclivities in the Pachomian writings did not have convincing results.[70] What he succeeded in finding were tendencies vaguely identical to what can be found not only in gnostic documents but also in most of the authors of the same period. What makes an author or a book gnostic is the presence of a certain system of thought as well as a certain explanation of the universe and of human destiny. Many elements of that system, taken individually, can be found in authors and milieus that are not gnostic in that way.

Against the first explanation (i.e., that the texts are a collection of works used by the monks themselves), T. Säve-Söderbergh put forth arguments that are not without some weight. Even granting that the orthodoxy of our monks may have been less strict than we used to suppose, there are certain books of the Nag Hammadi library that do not have any religious character and others that contain explicitly pagan elements one does not expect to find in the bedside books of Pachomian monks. Even disregarding these clearly pagan elements, there are gnostic doctrines in the books that are so clearly in opposition to Christian monastic ascesis that it is difficult to imagine Christian monks using them for their spiritual reading.[71]

Säve-Söderbergh's hypothesis is that our documents may have been assembled for heresiological purposes, somewhat like Epiphanius's assembly of his *Panarion*. That is certainly not impossible. But the Pachomian texts do not show in Pachomius and his disciples an

---

69. Hans Quecke has studied at length the use of a coded language by Pachomius in some of his letters, in *Die Briefe Pachoms: Griechischer Text der Handschrift W. 145 der Chester Beatty library eingeleitet und herausgegeben von Hans Quecke* (Regensburg: Pustet, 1975) 18–40. Nothing in that long and careful analysis indicates any connection with the gnostic writings. A certain connection with ancient Egyptian traditions is more probable: "Die altägyptische Hieroglyphenschrift lud geradezu zu Schriftspielereien ein, und die alten Aegypter haben immer und in vielfaltiger Weise von solchen Möglichkeiten Gebrauch gemacht. Das gilt bis in die Spätzeit der altägyptischen Kultur. . . . Nun ist natürlich mit dem Uebergang zur griechischen Schrift in koptischer Zeit eine Kryptographie der alten Art nicht mehr möglich. Aber die Mentalität ändert sich nicht schlagartig. . . ." (pp. 34–35). G. G. Stroumsa, for his part, notes that "Les vertus mystiques ou théurgiques de l'alphabet se retrouvent dans des milieux aussi variés que chez les pythagoriciens ou dans des spéculations juives qui n'ont rien de gnostique" ("Ascèse et gnose," 559); and he refers to F. Dornseiff, *Das Alphabet in Mystik und Magie* (Stoicheia 7; Leipzig: Teubner, 1922).

70. Hedrick, "Gnostic Proclivities"; see the remark of G. G. Stroumsa: "Hedrick ne réussit à glaner qu'une bien maigre récolte qui n'emporte pas vraiment la conviction" ("Ascèse et gnose," 559).

71. Säve-Söderbergh, "The Pagan Elements," 75–78.

eagerness to hunt heresies and to exterminate heresiarchs so great as to justify such a collection of writings. Pachomius was certainly concerned with preserving the orthodoxy of his monks and he knew how to refute heretics when they came to bother him, but we never see him going out on a crusade after the manner of an Epiphanius or a Shenoute.[72] Furthermore, the heretics mentioned in the *Lives of Pachomius* are generally the Arians and the Meletians who joined the Arians in the time of Athanasius and who were the explicit target of his festal letter of 367.[73]

Some anti-Origenist texts found in the Pachomian documents have been mentioned more than once as signs of the anti-heretical militancy of the Pachomian monks at least at a certain period.[74] It will be interesting to study that question a little more, since it is one of the points where the progress already achieved by the critique of the Pachomian sources may bring some useful light.

Two texts deserve our attention. They are section 31 of the first Greek *Life* and section 7 (chap. 4) of the *Paralipomena*. The anti-Origenist passage can be read in both *G1* and *SBo*. It is now admitted by all that neither *G1* nor *SBo* can be considered the translation of the other. They are two parallel witnesses. But their relationship is such that their respective authors must have had a common written source. In the several cases where the Coptic *Life* has stories absent from *G1*, it is possible to find their source in other Coptic documents, in particular in the tradition *S10*, *S20*, etc. (documents that had been used by the common source of *SBo* and *G1*); but when *G1* has narratives that are absent from *SBo*, with the exception of the case of the famous Council of Latopolis, the particularities of *G1* are always manifestly later additions. The particular vocabulary of these additions demonstrates that they are additions made to the primitive Greek text by a copyist who was not conversant with the terminology and the customs of the Pachomian monks and who, therefore, was not a Pachomian monk

---

72. It is well known that the zeal of Shenoute against paganism was as great as his hatred of Nestorius. For a succinct and well-documented presentation of the person and the work of Shenoute, see David Bell in the introduction to his English translation of the *Life* of Shenoute, *Besa: The Life of Shenoute* (Cistercian Pubs. 73; Kalamazoo, Mich.: Cistercian Pubs., 1983). D. W. Young has shown that some of Shenoute's teachings could have been in reaction to positions found in some gnostic texts of Nag Hammadi, particularly the *Gospel of Thomas*; see his "The Milieu of Nag Hammadi."

73. On the Arians, see *SBo* 96 and *G1* 113; *SBo* 185 and *G1* 137; *EpAm* 6, 11, 18, 31. On the Meletians see above, n. 28. Note that in *EpAm* 12 the Marcionites are mentioned with the Meletians.

74. On that question see Büchler, *Die Armut der Armen*, 139–40.

himself. That copyist to whom we owe the late form in which we know
G1 wrote at a date posterior to Athanasius's death.[75] All this is
important, because G1 31, as well as the last sentence of G1 30, is one of
these additions made at a later date by a copyist. That text shows an
anti-heretical preoccupation posterior to the period in which the
original *Life of Pachomius* was written, and probably a preoccupation
coming from a non-Pachomian milieu.[76]

What about the text of the *Paralipomena?* Here we have two reasons
for being cautious. The first comes from the very nature of the
Paralipomena. Although these stories belong to the authentic Pachomian sources, the redactor of the version that we have of them is
probably not a Pachomian monk. His terminology is different from
that of either the Greek or the Coptic *Lives of Pachomius,* and he seems
not to know many of the Pachomian customs.[77] The text of the
Paralipomena is extant in two Greek manuscripts (and fragments of a
third) and in a Syriac translation.[78] It is in chapter 4, section 7, of these
Paralipomena that we find a story in which Pachomius receives foreign
monks who give off a strong stench. It is only after their departure that
an angel reveals to him that they were heretics who read Origen's
books.

But here we must be cautious. As I said before, there are two
complete manuscripts of the *Paralipomena* in Greek, the *Florentinus* (=
F) and the *Atheniensis* (= B), as well as a fragmentary one, the
Ambrosianus (= A), that fortunately has the story we are studying at
present. The two manuscripts A and B have simply a mention of
"heretics," not that of Origen. Usually the text of F is safer, the one of B

75. I have studied that question in *Pachomian Koinonia* 1:4–6.
76. F. Halkin (*Sancti Pachomii Vitae Graecae* [SHG 19; Brussels: Société des Bollandistes, 1932] 103*) had already expressed the opinion that this anti-Origenist passage
was not in the *Life of Pachomius* at the time when Palladius wrote his *Historia Lausiaca*
at the end of the century. A.-J. Festugière (*Les moines d'Orient, IV/2: La première Vie
grecque de saint Pachôme* [Paris: Editions du Cerf, 1965] 22) writes: "Ce couplet sur la
haine de Pachôme à l'égard d'Origène, ayant été amené par les derniers mots relatifs à
la foi d'Athanase . . . pourrait sembler n'être qu'un développement propre à l'auteur de
G1, mais en fait il paraît dans l'arabe (Am. 599s.)." Unfortunately, Festugière did not
realize that the Arabic text is here a translation of G3, and therefore an indirect witness
of G1. On this point, see Veilleux, "Le problème des Vies de Saint Pachôme," *RAM* 42
(1966) 287–305.
77. See Veilleux, *Pachomian Koinonia* 2:1–2.
78. In his *Sancti Pachomii Vitae Graecae,* Halkin has published the *Paralipomena*
according to ms. F and the few short fragments of ms. A, since he did not have access
to ms. B. It is only recently that he produced a superb edition of the Athenian ms. (=
B), along with a French translation by Festugière, *Le corpus athénien de saint Pachôme*
(CO 2; Geneva: Cramer, 1982) 73–93 (text), 123–45 (translation).

being a stylistic reworking of it. But there are cases where B gives us the primitive version while the text of F is corrupt. And usually the editing of B is purely of a stylistic character. The various late Greek *Lives* that have incorporated the *Paralipomena* have an inconsistent tradition as far as the present story is concerned. We would have to study in detail all the various versions in order to arrive at a more certain conclusion. But it seems to me more probable that the anti-Origenist note is a late addition to the primitive text of the *Paralipomena*. If it had been in the original version, it would be difficult to imagine why it would have been suppressed later on, at the time of a virulent anti-Origenism. Here again, as in *G1* 31, the anti-Origenist note seems to respond to a preoccupation posterior to the first redaction of the Pachomian texts.

There is another Coptic text where one may legitimately think that there is a question of Origen, although his name is not explicitly mentioned. But the Pachomian character of that text is altogether hypothetical. It is a Coptic fragment from the Berlin Museum, first published by G. Hoehne and then reproduced by L. T. Lefort in his *Sancti Pachomii Vitae sahidice scriptae* only because that folio seemed to him to come from the same scriptorium, if not the same hand from which came other fragments that he had related to the third Sahidic *Life*.[79]

The Pachomian sources as a whole are anterior to the Origenist controversies of the end of the century, and the only traces of anti-Origenism that can be found in them are later additions, made quite probably by non-Pachomian scribes.[80]

Why Was the Nag Hammadi Library Buried?

Influenced by the studies on Qumran and almost obsessed by the conviction that the codices of Nag Hammadi had been buried by Pachomian monks, scholars have easily taken for granted that those codices had been hidden.[81] But were they really? A hypothesis put

79. Coptic text by G. Hoehne, *ZÄS* 52:124–26, and L. T. Lefort, *S. Pachomii Vitae sahidice scriptae*, 309–10. French translation in Lefort, "Les Vies coptes de Saint Pachôme et de ses premiers successeurs" (Bibliothèque du Muséon 16; Louvain, 1943) 352–53.

80. It is therefore exaggerated to say that "several anecdotes in the Vitae show the great monk to be most vigilant at least in keeping out the forbidden works of Origin [*sic*]" (Wisse, "Gnosticism," 437).

81. "It seems to be a common assumption that growing pressure exerted by orthodox monastic figures led to the internment around 400 C.E. of these writings" (Young, "The Milieu of Nag Hammadi," 127).

forward by M. Krause certainly deserves consideration. According to him, it would not have been uncommon even for Christians, in the period under study, to bury such documents beside their owners at their deaths. The fact that they were found in a cemetery (which was almost certainly other than the cemetery of the Pachomian monks) makes that hypothesis all the more plausible.[82] More study on the spot could give more light on the question.

The most commonly proposed hypothesis is that—whether the manuscripts had been the property of gnostic monks (inside or outside Pachomian monasteries) or the property of Pachomian monks (at a time when their heterodoxy was not perceived or did not create a problem)—they were buried on the occasion of an antiheretical purge.

The problem with this is that although we have testimonies about an anti-Origenist purge at the end of the century among the monks of Egypt, especially after Evagrius's death in 399,[83] we do not have witnesses permitting us to speak of an anti-gnostic purge among them.

Athanasius's festal letter for 367, received in the Pachomian monasteries like those of every year[84]—since this was how the monks knew when to start the fast of the forty days and the fast of the Pascha, and therefore when to gather together at Phbow for the great assembly of all the monks of the *Koinonia*—has often been mentioned as a possible occasion for such a purge. In fact it is said in one passage of the *Life of Pachomius* that Theodore had that letter translated and placed in the monastery.[85] I would agree with Jon Dechow that the connection between that letter and the burying of the Nag Hammadi library is one

---

82. "Das Auffinden der Bibliothek in einem Grabe spricht für eine, und zwar wohl reiche, Einzelperson als Besitzer. ... Es ist ein auch in christlicher Zeit noch nachweisbarer altägyptischer Brauch, dem Toten heilige Bücher ins Grab beizugeben" (Krause, "Die Texte von Nag Hammadi," 243). On the presence of two distinct cemeteries, see Doresse, *Les livres secrets*, 155. See also Säve-Söderbergh, "The Pagan Elements," 78.

83. The year 399 is the year when, shortly after Evagrius's deaths, Theophilos of Alexandria, who had been an admirer of Origen, became—for reasons that were not at all metaphysical—an implacable adversary of the Alexandrian master and unleashed a persecution of the Origenist monks of Nitria. For a brief presentation of the Origenist controversies of the fourth century, see A. Guillaumont, *Les "Kephalaia gnostica" d'Evagre le Pontique et l'histoire de l'origénisme chez les Grecs et chez les Syriens* (PatSor 5; Paris: Editions du Seuil, 1962); for bibliographical notes see 63 n. 67.

84. For good bibliographical indications on the various versions of Athanasius's festal letters, see L. T. Lefort's "Introduction" to his *S. Athanase: Lettres Festales et Pastorales en copte* (CSCO 150, 1955) i–xviii. Athanasius obviously wrote his letters in Greek. Their translation into Coptic for the Egyptian peasants seems to have been left to private initiatives. We have an example of this in the translation of the letter of 367 procured by Theodore for the monks of Phbow.

85. *SBo* 189.

of those scientific hypotheses that are put forward without any real proof, and then are repeated by everyone as if they had been demonstrated.[86] But my own explanation would differ from his. It seems to me that to state that all that Athanasius does here is to warn the "simple," *akaraoi*, against books that the perfect one could (seemingly) continue to read, is to venture on very unsafe ground, especially if one claims to establish an equation between the "ancients" of the Pachomian monasteries and the "perfect ones" of the Palladian chronicle, which in fact is not a reliable Pachomian source.[87] Moreover, all through his letter Athanasius is clearly preoccupied by heretics, and very specifically by the Meletians.

It is time to conclude that long inquiry. Were there any historical links between Pachomian monasticism, on the one hand, and the Nag Hammadi library (the gathering of the documents, their binding, their burying), on the other? It is possible, but nothing permits us to affirm it with any degree of certitude. Other explanations are just as legitimate.

LITERARY AND DOCTRINAL CONTACTS BETWEEN MONASTICISM AND GNOSIS

One would be on a firmer basis to elaborate theories about the relations between Egyptian monasticism and Gnosticism if real literary contacts between the two could be found, that is, if quotations of Nag Hammadi texts were found in monastic sources or vice versa. In fact, as we will see, the harvest is rather meager. No text of Nag Hammadi uses a source that is monastic in the strict sense, Egyptian or not, and no monastic source quotes a Coptic document from Nag Hammadi.

We have the impression of being in the presence of two universes of thought that have evolved on parallel courses. There are certainly points of contact, and probably mutual influences, but they did not leave traces in the known literary sources.

One of the major differences between these two worlds is certainly the manner in which the Scripture is used in each of them. It would be worth making a detailed and exhaustive study of that point. For

86. "A purge of apocrypha throughout Egypt, or even in Pachomianism, about 367–370 seems to me to be one of those scholarly myths that someone starts, others pick it up, some with notable names, and finally it becomes widely quoted and is taken as the 'informed consensus' or the 'assured results' of modern scholarship. Unfortunately, there is no historical evidence for it" (Dechow, "The Nag Hammadi Milieu," 12).

87. See above the observations concerning "the ancients" in the Pachomian monasteries.

example, there is nothing in the gnostic documents that is comparable to the extremely frequent and altogether orthodox use of all the documents of the Scripture in the Pachomian sources.[88] One may, of course, speak of a late correction of these monastic writings in a more orthodox direction; but, apart from the fact that until further proof is given, such a work of correction is purely hypothetical, it seems very unlikely that at a period without concordances or computers, an editor could have succeeded so well in expurgating the whole of Pachomian literature of any trace of a heterodox or gnosticizing use of the Scripture.

There are, however, a few documents of which a translation is found in the Nag Hammadi library and with which the monastic literature has some contacts. There are the *Sentences of Sextus*, the *Teachings of Silvanus*, and the *Gospel of Thomas*. Each one of the three deserves a special treatment.

The Sentences of Sextus and Monasticism

The *Sentences of Sextus*, of which fragments of a Coptic translation are found in Nag Hammadi Codex XII, can certainly not be considered a typically gnostic document. It is, in fact, a very ancient gnomic collection, quite probably of a non-Christian origin but Christianized at a very early stage, and largely used in the East as well as in the West. Witnesses to this are the numerous translations in Latin, Syriac, Armenian, Georgian, and Ethiopian, as well as our Coptic version in the Nag Hammadi library and, of course, the Greek text that was already known to Origen. Quotations of these *Sentences* in monastic and nonmonastic sources are listed in Chadwick's edition.[89] One must add a quotation in the Rule of Saint Columban, pointed out by Adalbert de Vogüé.[90]

88. One has a good idea of the place of Scripture in the life of the Pachomian monks when one realizes that the table of biblical quotations, at the end of the 3d vol. of *Pachomian Koinonia* covers 60 pp. and includes more than 2500 entries. Practically all the books of the Old and New Testaments are quoted. A very interesting study of the use of Scripture by the Pachomian monks could be done.

89. An indispensable work about the *Sentences of Sextus* is obviously H. Chadwick, *The Sentences of Sextus: A Contribution to the History of Early Christian Ethics* (TextS 5; Cambridge: Cambridge Univ. Press, 1959). Concerning the Coptic version see Paul-Hubert Poirier, *Le texte de la version copte des Sentences de Sextus*. Poirier has recently given a critical edition of that Coptic version, *Les Sentences de Sextus (NH XII.1). Fragments (NH XII.3)* (BCNH 11; Quebec: L'Université Laval, 1983). F. Wisse gave an English translation in *NHLE*, 454–59.

90. A. de Vogüé, "'Ne juger de rien par soi-même': Deux emprunts de la Règle colombanienne aux Sentences de Sextus et à saint Jérôme." Before it was mentioned by

According to A. Guillaumont, one should study "quels rapports l'éthique qui s'y exprime a . . . avec l'éthique gnostique, d'une part, avec l'éthique monastique d'autre part."[91] F. Wisse made a study concerning the links to Gnosticism,[92] but nobody has made any as yet concerning monasticism. Guillaumont adds: "L'utilisation de ce même manuel par les moines et par les gnostiques conduit naturellement à se poser la question des rapports entre gnose et monachisme sur le plan doctrinal."[93] But can we speak of "utilization" of the *Sentences of Sextus* by Gnostics on the sole basis that we find a Coptic translation of them in the manuscripts of Nag Hammadi? Certainly not as long as we do not know more about the reasons for the assembling of these various writings.

Furthermore, the fact that some monastic authors have quoted these *Sentences* does not necessarily mean that they were their daily reading—not even that they ever knew the collection itself. Such a gnomic genre easily lends itself to partial quotations. When Columban, for example, quotes one of the *Sentences of Sextus* in his Rule, one must not conclude that the collection was his bedside reading. It is highly probable that he did not know the collection itself but quoted that particular sentence from one of those florilegia that were so popular in his time.

The Teachings of Silvanus and Monasticism

The second text of Nag Hammadi that has some contact with monastic literature is the document known under the name of *Teachings of Silvanus*, found in Codex VII. And here we have a textual contact in a stricter sense, since one passage of the *Teachings of Silvanus* is substantially identical with a text attributed to Antony. But that point of contact has to be interpreted. And in order to interpret it, one must first of all take into consideration the exact nature of the *Teachings of Silvanus*, on the one hand, and that of the text attributed to Antony on the other.

---

de Vogüé, that quotation from the *Sentences of Sextus* by Saint Columban was unknown to the modern editors of the *Sentences* (O. Seebass and G. S. W. Walker, and even H. Chadwick) although it had been pointed out as early as 1638 by Dom Hugues Ménard in his *Concordia Regularum*.

91. See Guillaumont, "Gnose et monachisme," 98.

92. F. Wisse, "Die Sextus-Spruche und das Problem der gnostischen Ethik," in *Zum Hellenismus in den Schriften von Nag Hammadi* (ed. A. Böhlig and F. Wisse; GOF 6/6; Wiesbaden: Harrassowitz, 1975) 55–86.

93. See Guillaumont, "Gnose et monachisme," 98.

The *Teachings of Silvanus* is a text that belongs to the sapiential genre, often used at a very early date and quite favored by monastic authors. As for the format, it has great affinities with the biblical book of Proverbs, particularly with Proverbs 1–9. The Silvanus to whom the document is attributed is probably the one mentioned as a companion of Paul in the Pauline letters (2 Cor. 1:19; 1 Thess. 1:1; 2 Thess. 1:1) and then as a companion of Peter in 1 Pet. 5:12, and whom we find again in chapter 15 of the Acts of the Apostles as a prophet of Jerusalem with the name of Silas, having exercised his apostolic mission in the region of Antioch. That attribution to a biblical figure seems artificial, all the more since it is found only in the title and nothing in the text itself corroborates it. The only purpose of such an attribution was probably to give some authority to the book.[94]

Here again, as in the case of the *Sentences of Sextus*, we are not in the presence of a typically gnostic document. Besides elements of Judaic origin, other elements coming from Hellenism, especially from Stoicism, are present. At most we can find a few gnostic elements in its anthropology, which bases its distinction of the three states of man (pneumatic, psychic, and carnal) on a gnosticizing interpretation of the two narratives of creation in Genesis.

The origin of the document is not known for certain, but it is quite probably posterior to the first century. A possible Egyptian origin, near Alexandria, at the end of the second or beginning of the third century, has been mentioned, but that theory is based on the point of contact with Antony, which still needs clarification.

On the other hand, the problem of the various writings attributed to Antony is far from being solved.[95] According to Athanasius, Antony was illiterate, but that is not certain, and in any case, nothing prevents an illiterate person from dictating letters or other types of writings. As a matter of fact, seven letters are attributed to him. These have the characteristic of manifesting decisive signs of a form of Origenism before its time.

These letters of Antony are perhaps, among all the writings of Egyptian monasticism of the first centuries, the texts where some clear doctrinal contacts of a general nature with Gnosticism can be found! But no study has been made in this area.

First of all, a more accurate study of the various versions of these

---

94. See A. Guillaumont, "Le dépaysement comme forme d'ascèse dans le mona-chisme ancien," *AEPHE.R* 84 (1976–77) 327–30.
95. See *Vit. Ant.* 1.

letters is still needed.[96] Saint Jerome knew of seven letters of Antony written in Coptic, similar to those of Paul in content and style, and addressed to various monasteries. He knew them in a Greek translation that existed in his time. After that, they seemed not to have left any trace in written sources either in the East or in the West. But they continued to be copied and translated. In the West they reappear in the sixteenth century in a Latin translation made by Valerius of Sarasio from the Greek text that is now lost, and in the seventeenth century in another Latin version made by Abraham Echellensis from an Arabic text also lost.[97]

Although not entirely unknown to a few erudites[98] who, however, did not perceive their importance, it was only in 1938 that they were rehabilitated by A. Klejna.[99] Since the beginning of this century partial remnants in Coptic and Syriac have been published.[100] Finally the edition of the Georgian version with a Latin translation by Garitte in 1955 made the whole dossier more accessible,[101] and an English translation by D. J. Chitty was published after his death by Kallistos Ware.[102] More recently a French translation was also published, based essentially on Garitte's Latin version of the Georgian text.[103]

The various ancient versions are not simply translations. The austere spirituality of Antony's text and some startling doctrinal expressions were probably the reasons for the little popularity these writings enjoyed throughout the centuries.[104] The same reasons probably pre-

96. See G. Garitte, "A propos des lettres de S. Antoine l'Ermite," *Muséon* 52 (1939) 11–31. See also the study of G. Couilleau in *Commandements du Seigneur et Libération évangélique* (StAns 70; Rome: Herder, 1977).

97. Valerius de Sarasio's translation was published in Paris in 1516. The text is published in *PG* 40:977–1000. That of Abraham Echellensis, published in Paris in 1641, is found in *PG* 40:999–1019. On the late Arabic compilation used by Abraham Echellensis, see G. Graf, *Geschichte der christlichen arabischen Literatur* (StT 118; Vatican City: Biblioteca apostolica vaticana, 1944) 1:456–59.

98. See, e.g., A. Baumstark, *Geschichte der syrischen Literatur* (Bonn: Marcus und Weber, 1922) 84; and O. Bardenhewer, *Geschichte der altkirchliche Literatur* (Fribourg: Herder, 1923) 3:80–82.

99. A. Klejna, "Antonius und Ammonas: Eine Untersuchung über Herkunft und Eigenart der ältesten Mönchsbriefe," *ZKTh* 72 (1938) 309–48.

100. O. Winstedt, "The Original Text of One of St. Anthony's Letters," *JTS* 7 (1906) 540–45 (Coptic text of the seventh letter); F. Nau, "La version syriaque de la première lettre de saint Antoine," *ROC* 14 (1909) 282–97 (the only letter existing in Syriac).

101. G. Garitte, *Lettres de saint Antoine: Version géorgienne et fragments coptes* (CSCO 148/149, 1955). Original text and Latin translation.

102. *The Letters of St. Antony the Great* (trans. D. J. Chitty; Fairacres Publication 50; Oxford: SLG, 1975).

103. *Saint Antoine: Lettres* (Traduction par les Moines du Mont des Cats; Spiritualité orientale 19; Bégrolles-en-Mauges, France: Abbey of Bellefontaine, 1976).

104. See the review by Guerric Couilleau of the book quoted in the last note, in the *Bulletin monastique of Collectanea Cisterciensia* (1977) 189–91.

vailed in the pruning and correction of the original text by the various translators. It is not by chance that the Syriac translation has preserved only one letter, the first one, and this not without doctrinal modifications. The Latin version of Sarasio and the Georgian version are rather obscure, but that obscurity itself should inspire more confidence.

The Latin version of Abraham Echellensis, translated from an Arabic manuscript of the eighth or ninth century, not only offers a Latin text more difficult and often impossible to understand, but offers an amplified collection where, besides the seven letters already known by Jerome and attested by the Georgian corpus, thirteen other letters are introduced, the origin of which was then unknown. It was discovered later that at least some of them are from Ammonas.[105] Moreover, they are followed, in that collection, by a brief text having a rather exact parallel in the *Teachings of Silvanus* and bearing the name of *Spiritualia documenta regulis adjuncta*.[106]

The very presence of that text in the collection of Abraham Echellensis, after Antony's letters and among Ammonas's letters falsely attributed to Antony, should not be a very strong guarantee of their Antonian authenticity. But it happens that on the recto of a parchment in the British Library bearing the number *Or 6003* (BL 979 according to Crum's numbering) we find a short text explicitly attributed to Apa Andònios where that brief passage translated by Abraham Echellensis is found.[107] That parchment, a palimpsest, seems to be from the tenth or the eleventh century. It seems to be an isolated folio on which a reader has written down a text that interested him.

W.-P. Funk was the first to draw attention to that doublet and to make an extensive study of it.[108] From the comparison between the two Coptic texts (the one of the BL and that of the *Teachings of Silvanus*),

---

105. See *The Letters of Ammonas, Successor of Saint Antony* (trans. Derwas Chitty; Oxford: SLG, 1979). See also an older French translation by F. Nau in PO 11 (1915) fasc. 4.

106. Latin text of Abraham Echellensis in *PG* 40:1073C–1080A. The passage that interests us here is found in col. 1077A–B. On this point see Graf, *Geschichte*, 457; and J.-M. Sauget, "La double recension arabe des 'Préceptes aux novices' de l'abbé Isaïe de Scété," in *Mélanges Eugène Tisserant* (StT 233; Vatican City: Biblioteca apostolica vaticana, 1964) 3:304–7.

107. W. E. Crum, *Catalogue of the Coptic Manuscripts in the British Museum* (London: British Museum, 1905) 407.

108. That parallel was first mentioned in the German translation of the *Teachings of Silvanus* by the team of Berlin: see W.-P. Funk, "*Die Lehren des Silvanos*: Die vierte Schrift aus Nag-Hammadi-Codex VII eingeleitet und übersetzt vom Berliner Arbeitskreis für koptisch-gnostische Schriften," *ThLZ* 100 (1975) 7–23. Funk later gave a more elaborate study in "Ein doppelt überliefertes Stück spätägyptischer Weisheit."

we must conclude that although they have practically the same content, the several variants at the level of the syntax and most of all of the vocabulary, along with an almost complete semantic identity, lead to but one explanation: these are two independent translations of the same text, which was probably in Greek. If one of the two versions was a Coptic original, the other would have been an independent retroversion from a translation of it. It is also to be noted that in the case where the two Coptic versions offer different nuances, the Arabic version (i.e., that of the *Spiritualia*) always follows Antony as against the *Teachings of Silvanus*. That makes one think that the Coptic text of the manuscript of the BL depends directly on the Coptic original of the Arabic text translated by Abraham Echellensis, both witnessing to the same tradition.[109]

According to W.-P. Funk, the *Teachings of Silvanus* do not have any trace of a monastic ideal and must therefore be anterior to the beginnings of Egyptian monasticism. If that hypothesis is confirmed, Antony may have known the *Teachings of Silvanus* and may have taken his inspiration from them. The text of the *Teachings of Silvanus* has an introduction and two passages that manifest a more marked pessimism than the rest of the piece, and those parts do not appear in Antony's text. According to Funk, those lines could have been added in the Coptic version of the *Teachings of Silvanus* preserved in Codex VII of Nag Hammadi. The text of the *Teachings of Silvanus* and that of the palimpsest would both go back to an anonymous wisdom writing that he dates from around the second century, taking into account the link with the tradition of Antony. Between that anonymous writing and Antony, some editing would have taken place. The *Spiritualia* would go back to that reworked version, and that would explain the divergences touching the substance of the text.[110]

According to Guillaumont's analysis, however, an attentive study of the contexts—that of the *Teachings of Silvanus* and that of Antony—leads to the conclusion that the passage in question appears as an interpolation in the Latin text and that it finds a more natural place in the context of the text of the *Teachings of Silvanus*.[111]

---

109. See a good summary of Funk's position in Y. Janssens, "Les *Leçons de Silvanos* et le monachisme," in *Colloque international sur les textes de Nag Hammadi (Québec, 22–25 août 1978)* (ed. Barc) 352–53.

110. The passages of *Silvanus* showing a more accentuated pessimism are 97.3–8, 97.21–30 and 97.35–98.2.

111. Guillaumont, "Le dépaysement."

Things are certainly not clear. On the one hand we have a text connected with Antony's letters in an Arabic compilation of the eighth or ninth century, where writings belonging to Ammonas are also attributed to Antony. In the tenth or eleventh century that same document is copied in Coptic as an isolated text on a piece of parchment, where it is attributed to Antony. Those two texts have enough points of contact to allow us to speak of two absolutely distinct witnesses of the same source. The second is probably a translation, either of the first one or, more probably, of the same source. The rather late date of the Arabic version, the value of which is very poor, makes the attribution of that text to Antony very hypothetical. Fictitious attributions were very frequent in that period.

Three explanations are possible: (a) Antony may have known the *Teachings of Silvanus* and may have quoted that passage in one of his writings. This explanation admits the Antonian authenticity of that writing. (b) Again, if one admits the Antonian authenticity of that document, one may suppose that a quotation from that text was introduced at a later period in the text of the *Teachings of Silvanus*, where it did not belong originally. (c) Finally—and this is the hypothesis that seems to me most plausible—the author or the translator of late writings attributed to Antony, falsely in most of the cases, knew the *Teachings of Silvanus* and introduced a quotation from them into the text that he attributed to Antony. The Coptic text of the British Library would depend directly—or more probably indirectly—on that pseudo-Antonian document.

Yvonne Janssens tried to bring more light to the question by a comparison between the Coptic terminology of the *Teachings of Silvanus* and that of the Coptic translation of the *Life of Antony*.[112] This seems to me hardly acceptable from a methodological point of view. A comparison with Antony's letters of which we have the Coptic text or at least fragments of it would have made more sense. It is true that Janssens selected chapters of the *Life* in which Athanasius claims to relate a long ascetical discourse that sums up Antony's thought. But even if Athanasius may have had direct access to Antony's thought, it is clear that the discourse as we find it in the *Life* is Athanasius's own composition. As for the Coptic translation of that *Life*, it reveals not the Coptic terminology of Antony but that of the person who made the translation at an uncertain date.

112. Janssens, "Les *Leçons*."

Janssens also establishes a comparison with a catechesis attributed to Pachomius. This choice is as problematic as the first one, since the Pachomian authenticity of that catechesis is extremely dubious. Even if one recognizes in it a Pachomian character in the broad sense of the word, it is very unlikely that it is from Pachomius himself. It integrates a long section taken from a Coptic text of Athanasius.[113] In any case, the few conclusions to which Janssens arrives are rather meager and are expressed with much prudence. She finds it probable that Antony and Pachomius knew and perhaps used, if not the *Teachings of Silvanus* as we know them, at least a rather similar collection. Even that seems to me a dubious conclusion if one takes into account the very vague character of the similarities that she found between the texts.

As one can see, the harvest is not in any way richer with the *Teachings of Silvanus* than it was with the *Sentences of Sextus*.

The Gospel of Thomas and the Monastic Tradition

Of all the writings of the Nag Hammadi library, the *Gospel of Thomas* is certainly the one that has more contacts, at least indirect ones, with the ascetic—if not the monastic—tradition.

The thesis, generally admitted some decades ago, that saw Egypt as the cradle of Christian monasticism has now been abandoned.[114] We now know that the monastic phenomenon appeared more or less at the same time in Mesopotamia, Syria, Egypt, and Cappadocia, and also in the West. It appeared not as a mushroom unexpectedly sprouting overnight, but in continuity with the various ascetic currents that marked the life of the church during the first few centuries, particularly in areas under Judeo-Christian influence.[115]

---

113. That catechesis (or instruction) is probably Pachomian in a broad sense, that is, coming from a Pachomian milieu. But its attribution to Pachomius himself is much less certain. (About this see my *Pachomian Koinonia* 3:2–3.) The Coptic text, already published by E. A. Budge in 1913, was published again by L. T. Lefort, *Oeuvres de s. Pachôme et de ses disciples* (CSCO 159, 1956) 159 [text], 1–24 and 160 [French trans.], 1–26. Various Arabic manuscripts are also extant; see K. Samir, "Témoins arabes de la catéchèse de Pachôme 'A propos d'un moine rancunier,'" *OrChrP* 42 (1976) 494–508.

114. For example, J. Vergote, "Egypte als bakermat van het christelijke monnikendom," *NThS* 24 (1941; French trans.: "L'Egypte, berceau du monachisme chrétien," *CEg* 34 [1942] 329–45).

115. There are several studies on the origin of monasticism, esp. in Syria. The studies of A. Vööbus remain a priceless source of information, although they should be read in the context of later studies that have somewhat qualified Vööbus's findings. The essential elements of Vööbus's studies are found in his two big volumes *History of Asceticism in the Syrian Orient: A Contribution to the History of Culture in the Near East* (CSCO 184/14 and 197/17, 1958 and 1960). See also G. Kretschmar, "Ein Beitrag zur Frage nach dem Ursprung frühchristlicher Askese," *ZThK* 61 (1964) 27–67; Nagel, *Die*

The origins and early developments of Christian asceticism in Egypt are still obscure, as is the history of the origins of Egyptian Christianity.[116] But several indications lead us to think that the development of ascesis in Egypt is not without relationship with that of asceticism in Syria and in Mesopotamia. During the last few decades a good deal of new light has been shed on that aspect.[117] So much so that if one wants to study the problem of the origins of monasticism in Egypt and its relationship with gnosis, it is not possible to do so without taking into account the general context of the evolution of Christian asceticism during the first four centuries of the church, particularly in Syria.

The *Gospel of Thomas*, originating in Mesopotamia, perhaps in Edessa, around 140,[118] has close links with Syrian Christian asceticism.[119] Passages borrowed from the *Gospel of Thomas*, or at least having some kinship with it, have been found in several Syriac authors. The *Liber Graduum* and *Pseudo-Macarius*, as well as the *Acts of Thomas*, borrowed elements from the gnostic *Gospel of Thomas*, although they do not show traces of Gnosticism.[120] But, on the other hand, other important authors of Syria—for example, Ephrem and

Motivierung der Askese in der alten Kirche und der Ursprung des Mönchtums (TU 95; Berlin: Akademie-Verlag, 1966). A good synthesis of the present scholarship on this subject can be found in A. Guillaumont, "Perspectives actuelles sur les origines du monachisme," in *The Frontiers of Human Knowledge: Lectures Held at the Quincentenary Celebration of Uppsala University 1977* (ed. T. T. Segerstedt; Atlantic Highlands, N.J.: Humanities Press, 1978) 111–23, and idem, "Esquisse d'une phénoménologie du monachisme." As an example of the older criticism, one may still read H. Koch, *Quellen zur Geschichte der Askese und des Mönchtums in der alten Kirche* (Tübingen: Mohr, 1933).

116. See A. Veilleux, "The Origins of Egyptian Monasticism," in *The Continuing Quest for God: Monastic Spirituality in Tradition and Transition* (ed. William Skudlarek; Collegeville, Minn.: Liturgical Press, 1982) 44–50. In spite of several scientific studies on various sources of Egyptian monasticism (*Life of Antony, Apophtegmata, Lives of Pachomius,* etc.), little has been done concerning the *origins* of Egyptian monasticism.

117. To the studies mentioned above in n. 115, we can add for Syria the excellent study of Gabriele Winkler, "The Origins and Idiosyncrasies of the Earliest Form of Asceticism," in *The Continuing Quest* (ed. Skudlarek).

118. No text of Nag Hammadi has occasioned as many studies and commentaries as the *Gospel of Thomas*. The time seems right for an evaluation of all the theories and a synthesis of the findings.

119. See G. Quispel, "L'Evangile selon Thomas et les origines de l'ascèse chrétienne," *VC* 12 (1958) 181–96.

120. See H.-C. Puech, "Une collection de paroles de Jésus récemment retrouvée, L'Evangile selon Thomas," *CRAIBL* (1958) 155 (on the utilization of the *Gospel of Thomas* by the *Acts of Thomas*); A. Baker, "Pseudo-Macarius and the Gospel of Thomas," *VC* 18 (1964) 215–25; idem, "The Gospel of Thomas and the Diatessaron," *JTS* 16 (1965) 449–54; idem, "The 'Gospel of Thomas' and the Syriac 'Liber Graduum,'" *NTS* 12 (1965–66) 49–55. Young ("The Milieu of Nag Hammadi," 131) suggests that Shenoute, in some of his exhortations, may have reacted against positions of the *Gospel of Thomas*. The argumentation does not seem convincing, the positions mentioned being in no way exclusive to the *Gospel of Thomas*.

Aphraat—seem not to have used at all the *Gospel of Thomas*, which must have been well known in their times.[121]

The study of these facts led Quispel to distinguish in Syria, already around 140, two ascetic currents. One came from the type of Judaism developed in the Diaspora, in particular by Philo, that is from the Alexandrian tradition.[122] Aelred Baker also showed that the *Gospel of Thomas* was submitted to Alexandrian influences. The other current was influenced by Judeo-Christianity and Judaism in Syria. Without any doubt, it was the second of these two traditions that more influenced Christian monasticism, including the Egyptian one.

In any case, according to Quispel, the first of these two traditions was at the origin of Messalianism (either in its mitigated form as in Pseudo-Macarius, or in its radical form).[123] The second tradition, found in Ephrem, Aphraat, and the *Didascalia*, which finds its expression in the Sons and Daughters of the Covenant as well as in various ascetic groups living either within the local Christian communities or in solitude, remained impermeable to the type of radical Encratism we find in the *Gospel of Thomas*. Here we are already at the point where the distinction between premonasticism and monasticism has become almost imperceptible. The passage from one to the other was quite natural. And nothing in the texts that we know allows us to suppose a foreign element as a catalyst for that passage.[124]

ORIGIN OF CHRISTIAN ASCETICISM AND GNOSIS

Although the history of the origin of Christianity in Egypt is still obscure,[125] it seems clear that there were innumerable points of contact between Egyptian asceticism and Judeo-Christian asceticism. Before making too many general statements on the orientation of Egyptian asceticism and Egyptian monasticism, it would be important to study

121. See G. Quispel, "The Syrian Thomas and the Syrian Macarius," *VC* 18 (1964) 234.
122. See Quispel, "L'Evangile selon Thomas," 109.
123. On the relationship of Pseudo-Macarius with Messalianism, see A. Kemmer, "Messalianismus bei Gregor von Nyssa und Pseudo-Makarius," *RBén* 72 (1962) 278–306; J. Meyendorff, "Messalianism or Anti-messalianism? A Fresh Look at the Macarian Problem," in *Kyriakon, Festschrift J. Quasten* (ed. P. Granfield and J. A. Jungmann; Münster: Aschendorff, 1971) 2:585–90. For an excellent bibliography on Messalianism, see the article by A. Guillaumont, "*Messaliens,*" in *DSp*, col. 1074–83.
124. As does G. G. Stroumsa, "Monachisme et Marranisme chez les Manichéens d'Egypte," *Numen* 29 (1983) 184–201. See also his contribution to this volume.
125. See J. Helderman, "Anachorese zum Heil: Das Bedeutungsfeld der Anachorese bei Philo und in einigen gnostischen Traktaten von Nag Hammadi," in *Essays on the Nag Hammadi Texts* (ed. Martin Krause) 42.

more systematically each one of the sources in order to see their connection with the various currents of primitive Syrian asceticism, now better known than a few decades ago. Although literary contacts are not to be excluded a priori, what will be found in most of the cases will probably be parallel evolutions, due to the simple fact of their being rooted in the same spiritual soil.

The presence in Egypt of Hieracas, mentioned by Epiphanius of Salamis, witnesses to the fact that the most radical branch of Encratism manifested itself in that area. Of course, one cannot simply reject Epiphanius's testimony, claiming that many monks followed Hieracas. Since, however, Hieracas and his disciples are very rarely mentioned in the contemporary sources, it is certainly exaggerated to say, as did Wisse, that Hieracas was one of the most important figures of Egyptian monasticism.[126] D. J. Chitty, one of the best authorities on that period of monasticism, is clearly right to consider Hieracas as marginal and not representing in any way the common position of Egyptian monasticism.[127]

The tradition of lay anachoresis in Egypt was also mentioned as one of the sources of Christian anachoresis.[128] But I think that a historical link between the two still needs to be proved. If—as it seems clear to me—Egyptian Christianity was in its origins strongly Judeo-Christian, it seems more plausible to see in the Syrian tradition of *xeniteia* the model imitated by Egyptian monks.[129] In any case, the Egyptian monks always refer explicitly to that model and to the example of the apostles, and never to the pagan model.[130]

---

126. See Wisse, "Gnosticism," 439–49. His efforts to establish a connection between the *Testimony of Truth* and Hieracas are certainly very suggestive, but the evidence is meager.

127. See D. Chitty, *The Desert a City* (Oxford: Basil Blackwell, 1966) 4: "A dualism which regards matter as evil has been typical of most ascetic religions, and has been a besetting temptation also to the Christian. Hints of it will be constantly turning up in our path. About this very time, at Leontopolis in the Delta, Hierax was treating marriage as an Old Testament condition, and denying the resurrection of the body. But the central teaching of the monks is free from this, even in the extremes of ascetic practice."

128. On this phenomenon, see H. Braunert, *Die Binnen-wanderung: Studien zur Sozialgeschichte Aegyptens in der Ptolemäer- und Kaiserzeit* (Bonn: Röhrscheid, 1964) 165–67, 328–33. But see also A. Guillaumont ("La conception du désert chez les moines d'Egypte"), who shows how the theme of the desert is rooted in biblical tradition.

129. See Guillaumont, "Le dépaysement."

130. In the West the practice of *peregrinatio* remained alive through the Middle Ages, even when the Rule of Benedict—with its ideal of *stabilitas loci*—had imposed itself. See the two studies of Jean Leclercq, "Mönchtum und Peregrinatio im Frühmittelalter," *RQ* 55 (1960) 212–25; and idem, "Monachisme et pérégrination du IXth au XIIth siecle," *StMon* 3 (1961) 33–52. These studies were published again in J. Leclercq, "Monachisme

The literary sources of Egyptian monasticism, the *Life of Antony* and the *Life of Pachomius* in particular, reveal the presence in Upper and Lower Egypt—before Antony and Pachomius—of monks living a life of asceticism either in their local communities or in the nearby desert, near their villages. Urban monastic communities, including clerical ones, are also found. Antony entrusted his sister to a community of virgins;[131] and the *Lives of Pachomius* often mention non-Pachomian communities near the Pachomian monasteries. It would be interesting, for example, to examine how some Pachomian documents in Coptic usually reserve the word "monastery" to those non-Pachomian communities, using the Coptic words *soouhs* and *heneete* for the communities or monasteries of Pachomius. In the same manner, the most ancient Pachomian documents in Coptic speak of "brothers" rather than "monks" when they refer to members of the Pachomian *Koinonia*, the name "monks" being given to all the others, including the members of the clerical community living around the patriarch of Alexandria.[132]

Recently G. G. Stroumsa claimed to find in Manichaeism the catalyst that produced the passage from premonasticism to monasticism in Egypt.[133] This thesis, it is true, was presented with much prudence and subtle nuances. In fact all that can be said is that Manichaeans were present in Egypt before the spectacular development of Christian monasticism. Since they did live in communities elsewhere, one is entitled to suppose that such Manichaean communities existed in Egypt at the time of the origins of Christian monasticism. It is also possible to suppose that those Manichaeans continued to exist in Egypt under a *marran*, i.e., a hidden form. All of this is possible, but all remains unproved for lack of sufficient documentation. Moreover, we must not forget that Manichaeism owes much to Judeo-Christian tendencies, and these were present in Egypt. The similarity is therefore in no way surprising.

---

et pérégrination," in his *Aux Sources de la spiritualité occidentale* (Paris: Editions du Cerf, 1964) 35–90.

131. *Vit. Ant.* 3. Whether one adopts the reading *eis parthenona* or the reading *eis parthenian*, the meaning is not fundamentally different, since the second reading, which seems better attested, implies the existence of groups of virgins. See G. Garitte, "Un couvent de femmes au IIIème siècle? Note sur un passage de la Vie Grecque de S. Antoine," in *Mélanges historiques Etienne Van Cauwenbergh* (Louvain: Publications Universitaires, 1961) 150–59.

132. For a study of Pachomian terminology, see F. Ruppert, *Das pachomianische Mönchtum und die Anfänge klösterlichen Gehorsams* (Münsterschwarzach: Vier-Türme, 1971) 60–84.

133. See the article mentioned above, n. 124.

Once the origins and the development of Christian asceticism in general and Egyptian Christian asceticism in particular are better known,[134] it will be possible to compare each one of the aspects of that ascesis with the gnostic ascesis.[135]

In elaborating such a comparison, many pitfalls will have to be avoided. The first one would be to stick to a purely phenomenological description of ascetical practices. Such practices can be understood only if they are seen in their immediate and their general contexts, and if their motivations are perceived.[136]

Right from the start it should be remembered that in the whole of primitive Christian spirituality, ascesis occupies a central place, while in Gnosticism it occupies only a peripheral one, and even this only in a few of the gnostic systems. Moreover, one must remember that asceticism is but one aspect of monastic spirituality. It is a means used in order to arrive at something else considered superior to it. The doctrine attributed by Cassian to Abba Moses, in his first *Conference*, expresses rather well the whole Eastern monastic tradition of that time: the ultimate end of monastic life is the Kingdom of God, that is, contemplative union with God in prayer. The immediate goal—and the means to arrive at that ultimate end—is the conversion of the heart that is realized under the action of the Holy Spirit and through ascesis.[137]

Once this is clearly perceived, one may study each of the aspects of monastic asceticism, as, for example, continence, fasting, night watches, silence, continuous prayer, *xeniteia*, etc., trying to discern what their motivations were.[138] Of course, each author and each

---

134. See the methodological notes of Guillaumont, "Gnose et monachisme," 98–99. The only comparative study of some importance is the excellent article of Stroumsa, "Ascèse et gnose." On the basis of our present knowledge, he recognizes the existence of fundamental differences between gnostic ascesis and Christian monastic ascesis, at the level of motivations as well as at the level of the spirit in which asceticism is practiced.

135. Several aspects of monastic asceticism have been studied in depth during the last half-century. But very little has been done concerning gnostic asceticism. See, however, concerning the ascetical character of the Nag Hammadi library, the article of Wisse, "Die Sextus-Sprüche."

136. It is this pitfall that A.-J. Festugière did not avoid in the tendentious introduction to his otherwise excellent edition of ancient monastic texts, *Les moines d'Orient. I: Culture ou sainteté. Introduction au monachisme oriental* (Paris: Editions du Cerf, 1961). See the pertinent critique of A. de Vogüé in "Le procès des moines d'autrefois," *Christus* 45 (1965) 113–28.

137. Edition by E. Pichery (SC 42; Jean Cassien: Conferences I–VII; Paris: Editions du Cerf, 1955) 78–108.

138. One only has to look through the *Monastic Bulletin* published every year since

writing will have to be studied individually, since monastic tradition, even within a limited geographical area, was far from monolithic. It is only after having done all that preparation that it will be possible to make a serious comparison between monastic ascesis and gnostic ascesis, and this on the condition that as serious a study be done analyzing the ascetical tendencies that can and cannot be found in each one of the gnostic texts known to us. No comparison done at a lower price will bring any valuable light to the subject.

Two Universal Human Archetypes

Finally, to set such a study in a much larger context, an analysis should be made of the points of contact between monasticism and Gnosticism, considered as two great archetypes of human existence, both transcending their cultural boundaries.[139]

Monasticism is not a purely Christian phenomenon, indeed, and is not reserved to religious groups having contacts with Christianity. It is rather a transcultural and universal human phenomenon found in most of the great cultures and great religions of the world since the most ancient of times. It is legitimate therefore to speak of a universal monastic archetype, to use an expression of Raimundo Panikkar.[140]

No more than monasticism is Gnosticism a phenomenon easy to circumscribe in time and space. Not only do we know several gnostic sects, especially through the writings of Christian heresiologists, but we know that the rather structured form of Gnosticism of the second century C.E. had a prehistory. The efforts made at the Congress of Messina and after to clarify the concepts of gnosis and Gnosticism have occasioned several discussions, and the question is still open.[141] But one

---

1959 in *CCist* (with an English translation in CistS) in order to realize how many of these questions have been studied scientifically and in depth. It is unfortunate that these studies are often unknown to those who elaborate theories on the origins of monasticism and its relationship with Gnosticism.

139. I have treated that aspect more at length in a French version of the present study, "Monachisme et Gnose," in *LTP* 40 (1984) 275–94, 41 (1985) 3–24.

140. See Raimundo Panikkar, *Blessed Simplicity: The Monk as Universal Archetype* (New York: Seabury Press, 1982), in dialogue with Ewert Cousins, Cornelius Tholens, Myriam Dardenne, Armand Veilleux, M. Basil Pennington, and Paolo Soleri. See also J. Leclercq, "Le monachisme comme phénomène mondial," *Le Supplément* 107 (1973) 461–78; and idem, 108 (1974) 93–119. As a basic work on this question, although not explicitly dedicated to the monastic phenomenon, see Julian Ries et al., *Homo Religiosus. 1. L'expression du sacré dans les grandes religions. I. Proche-Orient ancien et Traditions bibliques* (Louvain-la-Neuve: Centre d'Histoire des Religions, 1978).

141. See the Acts of the Congress of Messina, *Le Origini dello Gnosticismo*, 552–62. See also Rudolph, *Die Gnosis*, 291–312.

thing is certain: All the various gnostic schools known to us tried to respond to an innate searching of the human heart, of which we find echoes in all the periods of history—in the cultures of Asia thousands of years before Christ as well as in the modern world. We can say that there is a universal gnostic archetype that assumes various forms and expressions in various times and places.[142]

A very interesting study would consist in comparing the basic aspects of these two archetypes in order to see what they have in common and what distinguishes them from each other.

After such a comparison is done, I think we will discover that when a large number of Coptic Christians chose the ascetical life and went to the desert, they conformed to an archetype, an aspiration firmly rooted in the human soul and in the collective psyche of mankind. External influences may have played a role, of course; but these influences did nothing else than put them in touch with that archetype or—to use a language closer to theirs—with their *heart*. What were their explicit motivations? All the motivations that they themselves revealed to us in their writings came from the Scripture. Do we have any right to pretend that we know their secret motivations better than they did?

If someday it could be proved that the Nag Hammadi library was assembled by Pachomian monks, I would like to think that we shall find that they assembled it not out of ignorance or because they did not care for orthodoxy but because, beyond all that separated them from the gnostic *Weltanschauung*, they perceived in those writings the same spiritual thirst and the same search for the primordial Unity that animated their whole life.

---

142. Cf. the very suggestive title of the work of vulgarization by H. Cornelis and A. Leonard, *La gnose éternelle* (Paris: Librairie Arthème Fayard, 1961). There are several good studies about gnosis as a universal phenomenon. See, e.g., H. Jonas, *The Gnostic Religion* (Boston: Beacon Press, 1963), and G. Quispel, *Gnosis als Weltreligion* (Zurich: Origo, 1951). Quispel has also studied the presence of a gnostic current in contemporary literature, under the influence of Jung; see his "Herman Hesse and Gnosis," in *Gnosis: Festschrift für Hans Jonas* (ed. Aland) 492–507. On the contemporary gnostic currents, see R. Abellio, *Approches de la nouvelle gnose* (Paris: Gallimard, 1981).

The Manichaean Challenge
to Egyptian Christianity*

The times are long past when a scholar such as W. E. Crum could write that the presence of Manichaeans in Egypt was not well attested.[1] In fact, the major discoveries of Manichaean texts in this century, apart from that of Turfan, were made in Egypt. Their publication, and the fresh studies of Egyptian Manichaeism to which they have led, have shown the Egyptian chapter in the history of Manichaeism to be less poorly documented than others—although here too, darkness still prevails over light. Indeed, it can be said with confidence that in the fourth century, Manichaeism had become part of the Egyptian scene, just as it had become part of the Syrian one.[2]

This fact alone should be enough to justify a renewed analysis of various aspects of Egyptian Manichaeism, from its implantation to its dimming survival. The results of such an analysis may clarify by inference our picture of the fate of Manichaeism in other areas, both inside and outside the Roman Empire. There are other reasons, however, which render such a study even more promising. First, the fact that in Egypt, Manichaeism seems to develop when the gnostic impetus fades might indicate that the Manichaeans "took over" the same dualistic and encratistic tendencies that had been previously

*George W. MacRae, S.J., in memoriam.
1. W. E. Crum, "A 'Manichaean' Fragment from Egypt," *JRAS* 73 (1919) 208. Unfortunately, the importance of Egyptian Manichaeism does not seem to be recognized yet by all scholars. A. Martin's survey ("Aux origines de l'église copte: l'implantation et le développement du Christianisme en Egypte (1-4)," *REA* 83 [1981] 35–56) refers to Jews and Gnostics, but makes no mention of Manichaeans.
2. See P. Brown, "The Diffusion of Manichaeism in the Roman Empire," *JRS* 59 (1969) 92–103 [= *Religion and Society in the Age of St. Augustine* (London, 1972) 94–118].

crystallized in gnostic communities of the Nile valley.[3] One of the main riddles raised by the Nag Hammadi discovery is the nature of the relationship of the codices' readers with Pachomian monasticism.[4] If anything could be said about the situation of the Manichaean elects vis-à-vis the monks, it might help toward the solution of that riddle.

Second, and even more important, is the question of the impact of Manichaeism on Egyptian Christianity. In historical terms, one cannot see the conflict between Manichaeism and Christianity as a conflict between two independent religions.[5] There is much evidence to show that in the Roman Empire, at least, the Manichaeans considered themselves to be Christians, nay, the true Christians, while they condemned the Catholics for "judaizing," and hence for being unfaithful to the true doctrine of Christ.[6] It would be surprising had not such a radical challenge left its imprint on the minds of those who successfully confronted it.

In a paper read at the Cairo meeting of the Société d'Archéologie Copte in 1982, I referred to the evidence showing Adda and other early Manichaean missionaries in the 270s to have established "houses" (mānistān, the Middle Persian term, is translated "Kloster" by W. B. Henning) in Egypt.[7] From various sources, we know that the life of the communities of elect was tantamount to monastic life. The area of Lycopolis/Assiut, from which all Manichaean texts found in Egypt, both in Coptic and Greek, originally come, was one of the main propaganda centers for the sect. It is thus unlikely, I argued, that the Manichaean ascetical movement, which preceded the emergence of Christian cenobitic monasticism by about half a century, did not influence the latter in some way. As a religious phenomenon, early Manichaean monasticism probably owed its existence to a combination of Elchasaite communal life, itself influenced by Qumran, as L. Koenen

3. See W. H. C. Frend, "The Gnostic-Manichaean Tradition in Roman North Africa," *JEH* 4 (1953) 15.

4. For a new attempt at a solution, see F. Wisse, "Gnosticism and Early Monasticism in Egypt," in *Gnosis: Festschrift für Hans Jonas* (ed. B. Aland; Göttingen: Vandenhoeck & Ruprecht, 1978) 431–40. See also Goehring and Veilleux in this volume.

5. For a different opinion, see R. Grant, "Manichees and Christians in the Third and Early Fourth Centuries," in *Ex Orbe Religionum: Studia G. Widengren ... oblata* I (Supplements to Numen 21; Leiden: E. J. Brill, 1972) 438.

6. See G. Stroumsa, "The Words and the Works: Religious Knowledge and Salvation in Augustine and Faustus of Milevis," in *Cultural Traditions and Worlds of Knowledge,* ed. S. W. Eisenstadt and I. F. Silber (Philadelphia: ISHI, forthcoming).

7. G. Stroumsa, "Monachisme et Marranisme chez les Manichéens d'Egypte," *Numen* 2 (1982) 184–201; esp. see 197 n. 8.

has convincingly argued,[8] and Buddhist monasticism, which Mani himself had encountered in India. It stands to reason, I argued, that Manichaean monasticism acted in Egypt as a ferment, a catalyst that helped the early Christian expressions of ascesis crystallize into Pachomian monasticism.[9] My second claim in that article was that the Manichaeans, who had been outlawed and savagely repressed already by Diocletian at the turn of the fourth century, survived probably longer than is usually thought, since they were able to go underground in the most effective of ways: by keeping their faith secret and appearing to be, for all practical purposes, plain Christians. This phenomenon of crypto-Manichaeism I proposed to call Marranism, by analogy with the outward conversion of so many Jews who did not want to leave Spain after the Expulsion Edict of 1492. The continuous official repression of Manichaeism in the empire—of which we see the clear traces in *Codex Theodosianus* XVI.5: *de haeresis*[10]—consistently sought to exclude the Manichaeans "from the whole world," or, in a less radical but more feasible way, from the cities (which might have meant, more often than not, mainly from Alexandria—in a province not always well controlled by imperial power).[11] At least some Manichaean elect, who had most to fear from delation to the authorities, must have looked for a hiding-place in the ascetical communities in the desert, i.e., in the Pachomian monasteries. This may be assumed as one of the paradoxical channels through which the *Fortleben* of Manichaeism—and hence of dualistic trends—was ensured in the early Byzantine Empire.[12]

8. See L. Koenen, "Manichäische Mission und Klöster in Ägypten," in *Das römisch-byzantinische Ägypten* (AegT; Mainz am Rhein: Von Zabern, 1983) 93–108.

9. This was Karl Heussi's opinion. See his *Der Ursprung des Mönchtums* (Tübingen: Mohr, 1936) 290. For him the Manichaeans *at least* contributed to the atmosphere in which early monasticism developed, and may well have been a source of inspiration for Christian monks. On the social conditions in which asceticism became institutionalized in Christian Egypt in the late third or early fourth century, see E. A. Judge, "The Earliest Use of *monachos* for 'Monk' (P. Coll. Youtie 77) and the Origins of Monasticism," *JAC* 20 (1977) 72–89.

10. The texts edited by Mommsen are conveniently reprinted and translated by J. Rougé, "La législation de Théodose contre les hérétiques: Traduction de *C.Th.* XVI, 5, 6–24," in *Epektasis: Mélanges . . . Jean Daniélou* (ed. J. Fontaine and C. Kannengiesser; Paris: Beauchesne, 1972) 635–49.

11. On the various revolts and razzias by Saracens and Blemmyes which at times prevented actual control of Upper Egypt by imperial administration, see, e.g., G. Rouillard, *L'administration civile de l'Egypte byzantine* (Paris: P.U.F., 1923) 169; and W. Seston, "Achilleus et la révolte de l'Egypte sous Dioclétien," *MAH* 55 (1938) 184–200. On the repression of Manichaeism in the empire, see E. H. Kaden, "Die Edikte gegen die Manichäer von Diokletian bis Justinian," in *Festschrift Hans Lewald* (Basel: Helbing & Lichtenhahn, 1953) 55–68.

12. It should be emphasized here that even in later periods, dualist heretics in

Since the main problem in such a presentation—which I readily grant remains hypothetical—is the scarcity and the limited trustworthiness of our sources, I would want here to analyze some additional pieces of evidence, which could not be treated in my aforementioned study. Although we know that Adda and Patteg, the Manichaean missionaries, reached Egypt much before the end of the third century, we cannot be quite specific about dates and ways. Did the first Manichaean missionaries reach Egypt, as Syriac-speaking merchants, via the ports of the Red Sea and Thebaid (Hypsele, 7 km south of Lycopolis, is mentioned by Epiphanius as the birthplace of Egyptian Manichaeism) or rather from the north? Michel Tardieu has recently argued that Adda and Patteg reached Egypt together with Zenobia's army in 270.[13] Indeed, Oedenat's widow, whose sister Nafsha we know to have been a Manichaean convert, launched an abortive conquest of Egypt when she sat on Palmyra's throne. To be sure, the rich Palmyra/Tadmor, at a major crossroads on the Syrian *limes*, was renowned for its commerce and seems to have been one of the first targets of the Manichaean mission.[14] No evidence has yet been found, however, that would corroborate Tardieu's guess. What is probable, in any case, is that the Manichaean missionaries—who were certainly no Persian "fifth column," despite the insinuation of Diocletian's rescript—were of Aramaic culture. Some Syriac documents have been found among the Coptic Manichaeica discovered in the Fayyum. The *Cologne Mani Codex* was translated from Aramaic, a language in which the Coptic texts themselves appear to have been originally written. A major question connected with early Egyptian Manichaeism is that of language, or rather of languages: Can we assume that early Manichaean teachers were bi- (or indeed tri-) lingual, that they spoke Coptic as well as Greek, like the "encratite" ascetic Hieracas? It should be noted that the mention of a Hierax in the Byzantine Formula of Abjuration has led some scholars to speculate on Hieracas's possible relationship with the Manichaeans.[15] Indeed, the *Codex Theodosianus* (XVI.5.7) mentions

Byzantium appear to be very closely related to monastic circles; see M. Loos, *Dualist Heresy in the Middle Ages* (Prague: Academia, 1974) chap. 5, esp. p. 71.

13. M. Tardieu, "Les Manichéens en Egypte," *BSFE* 94 (1982) 5–19, esp. 8–10.

14. On Palmyra's place in the early diffusion of Manichaeism, see S. N. C. Lieu, *The Diffusion and Persecution of Manichaeism in Rome and China* (Diss., Oxford Univ., 1981) 24 ff. [= *Manichaeism in the Later Roman Empire and Medieval China* (Manchester Univ. Press, 1985)].

15. On Hieracas, see Epiphanius *Panarion* 67.3.7 (II, 136 Holl). On Hieracas's possible connections with early Christian monasticism, see Wisse, "Gnosticism." F. Cumont

"Encratites" as one of the pseudonyms used by Manichees in hiding. In other words, were the Manichaean texts that survive in Coptic translated into that language in the first generation of Egyptian Manichaeism, or rather later on at a time when prospective readers did not understand Greek anymore? I am unable to answer this question and can only point out that both Aramaic and Egyptian names occur in the Coptic *Psalm-Book*, of which one group, the *Psalmoi Sarakōtōn* ("Psalms of the Wanderers," as P. Nagel has convincingly shown[16]) clearly have their original *Sitz im Leben* in groups of wandering ascetics—a phenomenon paralleled in early Syriac monasticism.

To be sure, the fact that vagrancy might have been one of the original life-forms of Manichaean elects does not mean that their asceticism could not find more sedentary expressions. After all, we have very clear evidence of highly organized forms of cenobitic monasticism in Eastern Manichaeism, both in Turkestan and in China itself (where our single archaeological site of a monastery is found). In the West, literary evidence testifies to the phenomenon. Although he never uses *monachus* or *monasterium*, Augustine mentions the Manichaean *sanctimoniales* (= *electae*), speaks of a *domus*, and refers to the short-lived attempt of some Manichaeans to establish a religious community of strict observance in Rome. Many of the members, who originally intended to live according to Mani's rule, soon left, since they could not stand its strictness, while those who remained quarreled until the community finally disbanded.[17] This testimony on Manichaeans' trying to develop collective forms of ascetical life is corroborated by a law enacted by Theodosius in 382, which sentenced to death any elects found living in common (*Cod. Theod.* XVI.5.9).

Manichaean monasticism, obviously, could not flourish under such a drastic legislation, and the elect were soon driven to hide—under the robe of Christian monks. Such an attitude was not new. According to the *Chronicle of Séert*, the Manichaeans had masqueraded as Christians

---

already suggested that the figure might have been related to the early development of Manichaeism in Egypt. See S. Lieu, "An Early Byzantine Formula for the Renunciation of Manichaeism: the *Capita VII Contra Manichaeos* of (Zacharias of Mitylene)," *JAC* 26 (1983) 152–218, esp. 197.

16. See P. Nagel, "Die *Psalmoi Sarakoton* des manichäischen Psalmbuches," *OLZ* 62 (1967) 123–30.

17. Augustine *Mor. Man.* 20.74 (*PL* 32:1376–77). See also *Haer.* 49. chap. 36; *c. Faust.* V.5 (277 Zycha). Cf. J. K. Coyle, *Augustine's 'De Moribus Ecclesiae Catholicae'* (Par 25; Friburg: U.P., 1978) 217 nn. 833–34. Jerome witnesses to the readiness of the Roman populace to identify an ascetic woman with a Manichaean nun (Letter 22.13; cf. ibid., 38).

already under persecution by Vahran II (who had executed Mani in 276). As a consequence, the king, who had originally been favorable to the Christians, turned to persecuting them too.[18] Various testimonies reflect the same phenomenon in the Roman Empire. Both Popes Gregory I and Gregory II felt obliged to issue warnings against accepting African priests entering Italy without investigation, since they might actually be Manichees.[19] Indeed, the phenomenon seems to have been particularly widespread in North Africa. Augustine mentions the case of a Catholic *sanctimonialis* in his own diocese confessing to be a Manichaean catechumen.[20] Elsewhere, he reports that a certain Victorinus, an old man and one of his subdeacons, was recognized as having been a Manichaean *auditor* for years and having taught Manichaean doctrine throughout his career in the church.[21]

In Egypt itself, Serapion of Thmuis, the friend of Athanasius and Antony and the first Egyptian Christian to write a full-fledged refutation of Manichaean doctrine, states at length at the outset of his work that the Manichaeans hide their evil nature by claiming to be Christians: they call Jesus in their prayers while actually fighting him, using the name of Christ while staging war against him.[22]

The main document, however, about Manichaean infiltration into the Egyptian church (both among priests and monks), is a passage in the *Annales* of Sa'ad ibn Batriq, usually called Eutychius, Melkite patriarch of Alexandria from 933 to 940.[23] The historical value of this work is not beyond question. Eutychius uses suspect sources, poor Byzantine chronicles and popular legends. Yet, through these very weaknesses he seems to preserve many details of ecclesiastical history that are not found in earlier writers.[24] There is no disputing the fact that

18. *Chronicle of Séert*, sec. 9 (PO 4:238), referred to by S. Brock in "A Martyr at the Sasanid Court under Vahran II: Candida," *AnBoll* 96 (1978) 167 ff.

19. Gregory *Ep.* 2.37; and Gregory II *Ep.* 4.

20. Augustine *Contra litteras Petiliani* 3.17 and 20.

21. Augustine *Epistle* 236. These texts are cited by W. H. C. Frend, "Manichaeism in the Struggle between Saint Augustine and Petilian of Constantine," in *Augustinus Magister* (Paris: Etudes Augustiniennes, 1955) 2:865.

22. R. P. Casey, ed., *Serapion of Thmuis, 'Against the Manichees'* (HTS 15; Cambridge: Harvard Univ. Press, 1931) chap. 3, p. 30.

23. The text is edited by L. Cheikho in the CSCO. The relevant passage is in vol. 1, pp. 146–48. I wish to thank Dr. Sarah Stroumsa for having prepared a translation of that passage for me.

24. This is the opinion of such a good specialist as F. Nau; see his article "Eutychius," in *DThC* 5:1609–11. On the importance of Eutychius's *Annales* as a historical source, see S. H. Griffith, "Eutychius of Alexandria on the Emperor Theophilus and Iconoclasm in Byzantium: A Tenth Century Moment in Christian Apologetic in Arabic," *Byzantion* 52 (1982) 154–90.

Eutychius's testimony is not only very late but obviously exaggerated, and needs critical reading. Yet, by rejecting it outright—as do, for instance, H. H. Schaeder explicitly[25] and M. Tardieu implicitly[26]—one is deprived of a source of major importance on Egyptian monasticism.

What Eutychius has to tell us occurred under the patriarchate of Timotheus I (d. 377), that is, a short time before the reign of Theodosius, who issued such severe laws against the Manichaeans.[27]

Indeed, the emperor had renewed in 381 previous laws forbidding Manichaeans from holding meetings in towns, and expelling them from large cities, adding: "nor shall they defend themselves with malignous fraud under the pretense of those misleading names by which many, as we have learned, wish to be called and signified as of approved faith and chaste character; especially since some of the aforesaid persons wish to be called the Encratites, the Apoctites, the Hydroparastae or the Saccophori, and by a variety of diverse names...."[28] Another law, published in 382, mentions the Manichaeans' "false pretense of the solitary life."[29]

Eutychius reports that in Timotheus's time the two classes of Manichaeans, the *electi* (*ṣaddiqūn*) and the *auditores* (*samma'ūn*) were very numerous among Egyptian priests and monks. His remark that "most of the metropolitans and bishops of Egypt were Manichaeans," though, should not be taken *au pied de la lettre*. Knowing the manichaeans' aversion to animal flesh, Timotheus had ordered the eating of meat on festive days in order to discover heretics among clergy and

25. In his review of C. Schmidt and H. J. Polotsky, *Ein Mani Fund in Ägypten*, H. H. Schaeder (*Gn* 9 [1934] 342) argues that Eutychius describes events that would have happened in the time of Mani, not of Patriarch Timotheus (1, 146, 1.17 Cheikho), and concludes, "Dadurch sind seine Angabe freilich nur noch unglaubwürdigen." Now, Schaeder obviously misreads the sentence, which refers quite obviously to the flourishing of Mani's heresy, not of Mani himself. In literal translation, the passage reads thus: "[All] this happened at the time of Mani, the contradictor, the heretic. When Mani and his sect perished, the orthodox patriarchs, their bishops and their monks returned to their first practice...."

26. Tardieu, "Les Manichéens," 15: "Tous les textes antimanichéens, allant du V au X s., cités ici et là, ne sont en effet que des poncifs hérésiologiques. En consequence, le dernier témoignage connu, faisant état d'un contact précis entre Églises chrétienne et manichéenne, reste l'*Historia monachorum*." This obiter dictum, rejecting a priori all later evidence as untrustworthy, may appear rather supercilious.

27. Severus of Ashmunein notes in his *History of the Patriarchs of the Coptic Church of Alexandria* (ed. and trans. B. Evetts; PO 1:424–25) that the Council of Constantinople was held during Timotheus's patriarchate. See also Brown, "Diffusion of Manichaeism," 110–11. (He mistakenly refers to the patriarch as Theophilus.) Cf. his "Religious Coercion in the Later Roman Empire: The Case of North Africa," *History* 48 (1963) 301.

28. *Cod. Theod.* 16.5.6.

29. Ibid., 16.5.9.

monks. The measure was later recalled, adds Eutychius, after the Manichaean danger had passed. One might mention here that similar meat-tests were applied to Manichaeans under Islamic rule, and also to Cathars in medieval Provence.[30] In order to avoid eating meat without being discovered, the heretics would fast on these festive days (an odd way to remain unnoticed!) or else would eat fish rather than the meat of a slaughtered animal.[31] According to Eutychius, fish-eating was tolerated under duress, in particular for *auditores*—hence Eutychius's confusion, when he calls them *sammakūn*, fish-eaters, rather than *samma'ūn* (the mistake is easily made in Arabic script).[32]

Eutychius's report thus testifies to the presence in late fourth century Egypt of numerous crypto-Manichaeans inside both secular clergy and monasteries. If these heretics stood out in any way among ascetics, it was by their even more strongly ascetical behavior.

Each source has to be evaluated on its own merits. One should remember that in the early Byzantine Empire "Manichaean" soon became a term of opprobrium, commonly hurled at political or theological opponents of all sides. When Justinian, in his letters to the monks of Alexandria, cites some passages allegedly from epistles of Mani to his disciples according to which Christ had only one nature, he merely uses anachronistic language. Mani certainly did not express himself as a Monophysite.[33] But when Severus of Ashmunein accuses

30. See G. Vajda, "Les Zindiqs en pays d'Islam au début de la période abbasside," *RSQ* 17 (1938) 185 and n. 3. Cf. "Monachisme et Marranisme," 201 n. 53.

31. As Prof. Koenen reminds me, Mani himself had behaved in a similar way in order to avoid eating with the community when he was still living with the Elchasaites. See *CMC* 142; and L. Koenen, "Manichäische Mission und Klöster," 105 ff. It would seem, however, that abstinence from meat was not limited to crypto-Manichaeans in early Egyptian monasticism; see the text edited by F. Nau, "Histoire des solitaires égyptiens," *RDC* 13 (1908) 47 ff., 53 *(peri egkrateias)*, where the monks, guests of Patriarch Theophilus, object to eating meat. There is nothing in the text to suggest Manichaeism or anything except supererogatory behavior. My thanks to Prof. Peter Brown for calling my attention to this text.

32. This was already noted by Schaeder, "Review," 342. J. Jarry ("Le Manichéisme en Egypte Byzantine," *BIFAO* 66 [1968] 121–37) ignores this point, and goes into a rather far-fetched attempt to show that *sadiqūn* and *sammakūn* were in fact Marcionites, not Manichaeans. See esp. pp. 128–31. I was unaware of this article when I wrote "Monachisme et Marranisme." Jarry knows the story of the Manichaean woman's conversion, which I analyzed there, but attributes it to Cyril of Alexandria, ignoring the judgment of its editor, who dates this spurious work from the ninth or tenth century. (See "Monachisme et Marranisme," 200 n. 42.) On the laxer rules about meat-eating for *auditores*, see Augustine *Epist.* 236.2 (*PL* 33:1033).

33. Justinian, *c. Monophys.* 89/92, cited by Lieu, "Early Byzantine Formula," 167 n. 121. In his writings, Athanasius twice accuses the *dux* Sebastianus of being a Manichaean—a fact not mentioned by Ammianus. H.-G. Optiz (*Athanasiuswerke* [Berlin: Walter de Gruyter, 1940] 2/1:216) points out that by calling his enemy a Manichaean,

Julian, a Chalcedonian bishop, of agreeing with the unbelievers Eutyches, Apollinarius, Manes, and Eudoxius, "because he divided the Lord Christ," his slander carries no echo of historical truth.[34]

In any case, the indisputable presence of Manichaeans among Christian clerics raises the important question of their possible influence not only on ascetical practice but also on patterns of theological thinking.

We know of various *Auseinandersetzungen* between the Manichaeans and their opponents on Egyptian soil. The piece of polemical writing most important for our knowledge of Manichaean theology, written at the turn of the fourth century, is Alexander of Lycopolis's *Against the Manichaeans*. A pagan philosopher, Alexander probably met the early Manichaean missionaries in his native city.[35] From approximately the same period, we have the anonymous *Epistle against the Manichees* (= Papyrus J. Rylands 469), which its editor, C. H. Roberts, assigns to the reign of Diocletian and possibly to the chancery of Theonas, bishop of Alexandria from 282 to 300.[36] The *Epistle's* author polemizes against Manichaean Encratism, arguing, on the basis of 1 Cor. 7:1, that marriage is honored by God; he accuses the Manichaeans of worshiping creation (alluding, like so many other pamphleteers, to the part played by the sun and moon in their cult) and of abominable practices involving the *electae's* menstrual blood, and he refers to their ἀπολογία πρὸς τὸν ἄρτον, a formula rendering bread-consumption by the elect licit.

Coptic literature keeps a few traces of Manichaeans in later periods. Shenoute boasts of once having burned two Manichaean priests[37]—the man was no doubt capable of such a deed—and develops against them

---

Athanasius styles him an enemy of the state. On Sebastianus, see A. H. M. Jones et al., *The Prosopography of the Later Roman Empire* (Cambridge: Cambridge Univ. Press, 1971) 1:812.

34. Severus, *History of the Patriarchs of the Coptic Church of Alexandria*, in PO 1:454.

35. This text is extant only in one ms. from a Byzantine corpus of anti-Manichaean writings in the Laurentiana; ed. A. Brinkmann, *Alexander Lycopolitanus, "Contra Manichaei opiniones disputatio"* (Leipzig: Teubner, 1895), trans. and annot. P. W. van der Horst and J. Mansfeld, *An Alexandrian Platonist Against Dualism* (Leiden: E. J. Brill, 1974). See new Fr. trans. and commentary: A. Villey, *Alexandre de Lycopolis: Contra la Doctrine de Mani* (Paris: Cerf, 1985). Cf. G. Stroumsa, "Titus of Bostra and Alexander Lycopolis: A Christian and a Platonic Refutation of Manichaean Dualism," in *Neoplatonism and Gnosticism* (ed. R. T. Wallis; SN.AM 4; Albany: State Univ. of N. Y. Press, forthcoming).

36. C. H. Roberts, *Catalogue of the Greek and Latin Papyri in the John Rylands Library* (Manchester: Manchester Univ. Press, 1938) 3:38–39.

37. H. de Vries, *Homélies coptes de la Vaticane* (Houniae: Gyldendal, 1922) 1:80–88. Cf. Stroumsa, "Monachisme et Marranisme," 201 n. 54.

an exegesis in which he identifies the Shunamit's two breasts in *Canticle* as the Old and the New Testaments.[38] According to J. Leipoldt, Shenoute shows more concern with Manichaeans than with Meletians, Arians, or "Hellenes" (i.e., pagans).[39] The latest Coptic testimony would seem to be a spurious sermon of Cyril of Alexandria. The text, which I have analyzed in "Monachisme et Marranisme," testifies to the existence of crypto-Manichaeans up to the ninth or tenth century, the presumed date of its writing.[40]

Yet, it is to the fourth century that most of our information, which stems from ecclesiastical literature in Greek, refers. In his *Church History*, Philostorgius reports how Aetius, the well-known Arian theologian, came from Antioch to Alexandria in order to confront Aphthonios, a Manichaean theologian.[41] According to Bidez, the trip took place around 340. Philostorgius adds that Aetius completely silenced his opponent thanks to his superior argumentation, the opponent thus falling "from great fame into great shame."

The *Historia Monachorum in Aegypto* corroborates the existence of public *disputationes* between Christians and Manichaeans. We are told that Abba Copres, having gone once to town, had met there a Manichaean teacher preaching with some success. Copres's oratorical gifts were not enough to convince the heretic, and thus our Abba left dialectics for the more forceful argument of ordeal. While he himself went away unhurt from the stake he had kindled, the Manichaean was burned all over his body and then expelled from the city.[42] According to the *Historia Monachorum*, which reports on a trip to Egypt made about 395, Copres was then almost 90 years old. Since he was already able to accomplish a miracle and to argue in public with a successful preacher at the time of our story, one may assume that it took place in the second half of the fourth century. It is worth noting that the Manichaean, who could preach more or less freely in the city until Copres arrived, was able to enter into an open discussion and was, at

38. See the texts cited by J. Leipoldt, *Schenute von Atripe und die Entstehung des national ägyptischer Christentums* (TU 25; Leipzig: Hinrichs, 1903) 87.
39. Ibid.
40. M. Chaine, S.J., "Sermon sur la Pénitence attribué à Cyrille d'Alexandrie," *MUSJ* 6 (1913) 493–519.
41. J. Bidez, ed., *Philostorgius, Kirchengeschichte* (GCS; Leipzig: Hinrichs, 1913) chap. 3/15, pp. 46–48. Tardieu points out that Aphthonios is the only Egyptian Manichee whose name is preserved ("Les Manichéens," 14).
42. A. J. Festugière, ed., *Historia Monachorum in Aegypto* (SHG 53; Brussels: Société des Bollandistes, 1971) 87–88. For a translation, see idem, *Les Moines d'Orient* (Paris: Editions du Cerf, 1964) 4/1:75–76.

its predictable outcome, simply expelled, not lynched or denounced to the authorities.

Finally, the only two extant full-fledged refutations of Manichaeism written by Egyptian Christian theologians also stem from the fourth century. Serapion of Thmuis's tractate *Against the Manichees* has already been mentioned. Although it has been remarkably edited, it has not elicited much attention until recently.[43] As R. P. Casey points out in his introduction to the text, it shows very little knowledge of Manichaean mythology. The discussion, he goes on to say, seems to be rather abstract and singularly deprived of passion. Confronted with the Manichaean conception, which, like those of Paul and Augustine, sees the universe as "primarily . . . a reflection on a grand scale of the inner moral struggle," Serapion's argumentation looks rather pale.[44] This by no means implies, however, that Serapion did not have real Mani-chaeans before him—as Jacques Jarry seems to believe.[45] It merely reflects the topics that were likely to appear as most threatening from the bishop's point of view. These were of an ethical rather than a mythological nature. It stands to reason that inside Christian society the Manichaeans probably tended to emphasize their moral strictness rather than the more ludicrous details of their cosmological myths.

One of the highlights of those *disputationes* thus seems to have been about the nature of the body. "Is the body good or evil?": this is the topic of the one such discussion with a Manichaean in the *Apoph-tegmata Patrum*.[46] It echoes the argument developed by Serapion in his pamphlet: were the body essentially evil, it could not be the instrument of virtue, let alone the temple of the Spirit and the dwelling place of the Logos.[47] Against Manichaean pessimism about the nature of the body, and resulting Encratism, Serapion insists, in the footsteps of both Greek philosophical tradition and Christian apologetics, that man is by nature good and that evil is behavior dictated by an unhealthy will—similarly to the Alexandrian bishop who had felt the need to defend the legitimacy of marriage against Manichaean Encratism.

Didymus the Blind, the great Alexandrian exegete, also wrote a

---

43. A. Villey is preparing a French annotated translation of this text; cf. Tardieu, "Les Manichéens," 18 n. 27.

44. *Serapion of Thmuis* (ed. Casey) 19–21.

45. Jarry, "Le Manichéisme," 123.

46. *Apophthegmata Patrum*, PG 65:202D–204A, on Amma Theodora. For another encounter between Egyptian Manichees and monks, see Rufinus *Verba Seniorum: De vitis Patrum Liber* 5.13.2 (PL 73:945 C–D).

47. This is the argument of chap. 5.

tractate *Against the Manichaeans*.[48] There is no doubt that Didymus was much preoccupied by the Manichaeans. His works abound in references to them, both specific and indirect. He argues with them about the nature of angels—and in particular the devil, whom he claims to have been created and to have become evil of his own will. Against them, he defends Providence, God's creative activity, human freedom. Indeed, as Gustave Bardy has noted, a proselytizing Manichaeism seems to have been a constant danger for orthodox Christianity in Didymus's milieu.[49]

Similarly to Serapion's tractate, that of Didymus seems to remain at a rather abstract level, using *koinē* philosophical argumentation. In his case, however, we have actual proof that his pamphlet reflects a *Sitz im Leben* of actual discussions with Manichaeans. In his *Commentary on Ecclesiastes*, found among the Tura papyri, he reports in detail about a conversation he held with a Manichaean, namely on the legitimacy or illegitimacy of marriage.[50] He deals with the same question in the eighth chapter of his *Contra Manichaeos* in a remarkable way.[51]

Didymus points out that all marriages had been sinful before Christ. Indeed, because of his sin, Adam had received a material body which was then inherited by all men. It was only with the Savior's coming and his sacrifice, which delivered the world from sin, that marriage became licit, or rather, sinless—at least for those living according to the gospel.

Altogether, therefore, Didymus's view of marriage and of the body is rather positive. Against the Manichaeans he insists, together with most other Christian authors, that the body is not naturally evil. Yet, it remains possible that he is slightly influenced by his opponents when he recognizes as sinless only Christian marriage. In this context, it has been noted that his anti-Manichaean polemics force upon him a much more precise wording on original sin—a doctrine then in the making—

48. *PG* 39:1085–1110. The text is edited from a *codex unicus*, in the same corpus of anti-Manichaean tractates that includes Alexander of Lycopolis's work. The first three chaps. of the work are lost, those printed in the *PG* being parts of other texts. See M. Geerard, *Clavis Patrum Graecorum* (Turnhout: Brepols, 1974) 2:104, sect. 2545.

49. G. Bardy, *Didyme l'Aveugle* (ETH 11; Paris: Beauchesne, 1910) 34; cf. 33–35. Much of Bardy's information on Didymus and Manichaeism is taken from J. Leipoldt, *Didymus der Blinde von Alexandria* (TU 29; Leipzig: Hinrichs, 1905) 14–16.

50. M. Gronewald, *Didymos der Blinde: Kommentar zum Ecclesiastes* (PTA; Bonn: Habelt, 1979) 5:8–11. Cf. ibid. (1977) 2:114–15 for a refutation of the Manichaean conception of the devil. For a similar discussion, in which Paphnutius, a Thebaidan bishop, defends the legitimacy of marriage, see Socrates *H. E.* 1.11 (*PG* 67:101–4).

51. *PG* 39:1096 B–D. My thanks to Prof. Ludwig Koenen for helping me to understand this text correctly.

than that of earlier theologians, including Athanasius.[52] Such evaluations should be checked in the light of the newly published papyri of Didymus's writings.

In particular, further research should assess whether Manichaeism acted as a catalyst, permitting old theologoumena to crystallize into a new dogma, which was to become one of the cornerstones of later Christian thought. It is probably no mere chance that the main theologian of original sin in the West, Augustine, was a repented Manichee, whom Julian of Eclanum accused of having borrowed his thinking on original sin from his former heresy.[53]

52. See for instance "Péché Originel," *DThC* 12:275 ff. Cf. J. Turmel, *Histoire des Dogmes* (Paris: Rieder, 1931) 1:60; and J. Gross, *Entstehungsgeschichte des Erbsundendogmas* (Munich/Basel: Reinhardt, 1960) 135–40. See also Bardy, *Didyme l'Aveugle*, 133–34. On Titus of Bostra's reference to original sin in his *Adversus Manichaeos*, see J. Sickenberger, *Titus von Bostra: Studien zu dessen Lukashomilien* (TU 26, n.f. 6; Leipzig: Hinrichs, 1901) 14 n. 3. On the doctrine of original sin, see L. Scheffczyk, *Urstand, Fall und Erbsunde, von der Schrift bis Augustinus* (HDG; Friburg/Basel/Vienna: Herder, 1981).

53. See references in A. von Harnack, *History of Dogma* (Boston: Little, Brown & Co., 1899) 5:211 n. 5. Cf. P. Brown, *Augustine of Hippo* (Berkeley: Univ. of Calif. Press, 1967) 386, 393, and nn. 11–12. I wish to thank the Trustees of Harvard Univ. for a fellowship at Dumbarton Oaks in 1983–84, during the tenure of which I did research on various aspects of the survival of Manichaeism in the early Byzantine Empire.